Cyber Insecurity

Cyber Insecurity

Navigating the Perils of the Next Information Age

Edited by
Richard M. Harrison and Trey Herr

PUBLISHED IN ASSOCIATION WITH
THE AMERICAN FOREIGN POLICY COUNCIL

ROWMAN & LITTLEFIELD
Lanham • Boulder • New York • London

Published in association with The American Foreign Policy Council

Published by Rowman & Littlefield
A wholly owned subsidiary of The Rowman & Littlefield Publishing Group, Inc.
4501 Forbes Boulevard, Suite 200, Lanham, Maryland 20706
www.rowman.com

Unit A, Whitacre Mews, 26-34 Stannary Street, London SE11 4AB

British Library Cataloguing in Publication Information Available

Library of Congress Cataloging-in-Publication Data Available
ISBN: 978-1-4422-7284-2 (cloth : alk. paper)
ISBN: 978-1-4422-7285-9 (electronic)

♾™ The paper used in this publication meets the minimum requirements of American National Standard for Information Sciences—Permanence of Paper for Printed Library Materials, ANSI/NISO Z39.48-1992.

Printed in the United States of America

Contents

Acknowledgments

This book has taken several years to materialize. Back in 2013, with the help of Eric Ormes, we began planning a briefing series for professional staffers on Capitol Hill to address what they saw as a glaring lack of understanding about cybersecurity in official Washington. That program got underway in 2015, when—in collaboration with the American Foreign Policy Council's Defense Technology Program and a rotating group of experts—we held five events for Congressional staff. The briefings received an overwhelmingly positive reception, and were attended by staff from more than half of the Senate and nearly a hundred House offices. The success of this series, as well as the numerous requests for additional information that followed, made it clear that a larger and more comprehensive treatment of the subject matter was necessary. Hence this book.

We could not have done this alone. A number of individuals and organizations played a critical role in the development of this book, and deserve mention.

First, American Foreign Policy Council (AFPC) president Herman Pirchner Jr. has our thanks for his support of the inaugural briefing series and, thereafter, of this book project. His unwavering confidence in our abilities throughout was crucial to our success. We were also fortunate to have the support of a generous friend and donor, who—while anonymous—was instrumental in helping shape the direction of this project.

Nor could either the briefing series or the book have happened without the generosity of the Donner Foundation, which deserves our deep gratitude for understanding the importance of cyber threats to U.S. national security and economic vitality. So, too, do the contributors to this volume, who are the real talent behind a work that draws together a broad range of complex and arcane concepts.

Several others deserve credit as well. The New America Foundation, including Rob Morgus and Ian Wallace, played an integral role in connecting us with many of the experts who ultimately became the contributors for the book. AFPC vice-president Ilan Berman provided guidance with proposal writing and the publication process. Elizabeth Wood, AFPC's Special Programs Coordinator, gave first-rate copy editing assistance. We also benefited from the efforts of several dedicated researchers, who helped fact check the manuscript, format the citations, and lent a hand in graphic design: Amanda Azinheira, Christine Beauchemin, Ivanna Kuz, Georgina O'Shea, Paige Rotunda, Hannah Tyrrell, Alex Werman, and Simone Worthy. Additional thanks go to our outside reviewers, and to those who provided feedback, including Dr. Allan Friedman, Michael Specter, Richard Barnes, Dr. Peter Singer, and Eric Ormes.

On a personal note, Richard would like to thank his loving wife Allyson, his sons James and Nathan, and his extended family for their invaluable support and understanding during the production of this book. Trey would like to thank his Dad and brothers for their patience during this process—and to his advisors, Drs. Lance Hoffman, Allan Friedman, Susan Sell, Robert Adcock, and Steve Balla, for support on this and related projects.

Foreword

The challenges and discontinuities introduced by digital information systems are so diverse that no single analogy can properly capture them. However, one apt description may be contained in the observation that, in some important respects, the leaders of American government respond to the problems of cyber technology the same way Americans and their leaders responded to our Western frontier two hundred years ago.

We are excited by what we already have experienced, and believe that future discoveries and exploitations will have immense and transformative effects. At the same time, we are uncertain and conflicted. What is the shape of this new territory? How should it be governed? Must it be insecure for decades to come? How do we reconcile old values, interests, power relationships, and practices with the frontier's unfamiliar risks, demands, and ways of doing things?

Like our forbearers, we can only partially comprehend and map the unknown. We do so by relying on reports filtering back from scattered settlements and from explorers who tell us, sometimes inaccurately, where some trails lead. With haphazard information, we try to regulate areas that are at least somewhat settled, attempt occasional forays to maintain a modicum of order in some critical areas, and more or less acquiesce to anarchy in the remainder. Barely able to comprehend what will come, we project our hopes and fears onto our mental maps of the future.

American leaders concerned with national security have a particularly strong imperative to develop these maps, but have a deep difficulty in doing so. For all of our professional lives, we have built our security on a foundation of technological innovation that consistently, sometimes exclusively and usually disproportionately, came from initiatives largely directed by the national security establishment. Furthermore, these developments came (again, with some exceptions) at a pace that we could assimilate and control. Now, though the internet famously evolved from DARPA and the semiconductor industry significantly in response to military and NASA needs, we have all become sorcerers' apprentices: we have little, and sometimes no, control over technology innovation generally, and information technology in particular.

At this frontier, there is a sense that no claims are exclusive, that the pace and direction of development cannot be bounded or well-predicted, that the settlers recognize no special allegiance to us, and that the bounty they produce may make us more, rather than less, vulnerable. Moreover, developments come with a speed that exceeds the ability of many decision-makers to gain familiarity with new developments, the capabilities of bureaucracies to adapt to them, and legislative efforts to respond to them.

To cope with this, we depend even more than our predecessors on explorers—in this realm, we call them "experts." The following pages are a select group's reports from the field. They give us slices of perception about a world we only partly comprehend. But those slices begin to map paths and suggest policies.

Of course, these contributors explore only with their minds, while their nineteenth-century predecessors were exposed to great physical risks and discomforts. But since cyber space is not, by and large, physically accessible, what more could we ask? In fact, it takes immense energy, imaginative planning, and meticulous care to build the kit required for this mental expedition. And it requires no small amount of moral courage to put yourself out there, recommending policy paths based on information that is necessarily incomplete and flawed.

I don't know if what is in these pages will stand the test of time. I do know, though, that however tentative, the maps provided here are among the best we have and provide a basis for building a better future. For that, we are indebted to these authors and privileged to read these pages.

The Honorable Richard J. Danzig
71st Secretary of the Navy, November 1998–January 2001

Introduction

Trey Herr and Richard M. Harrison

Computing is built on an architecture of trust. All of us who use computers trust that we will be able to distinguish data from instructions, and content which is malicious from that which is benign. That foundation also supported the creation of the internet itself; the earliest users of the world wide web were members of an academic network who trusted one another because they were also part of many of the same extended social networks.[1] Accordingly, the architecture of cybersecurity is built around technical and policy mechanisms that are designed to create trust in people's identity, access and the integrity of our systems, and the secrecy of our data.

But while trust is key, it is only equal in importance to what we know. How we understand cybersecurity, categorize it, debate it, and learn about it influences our awareness of shared challenges and practical opportunities. For the policy community, what we know may actually be more important than trust because that information shapes the formation of our laws, rules, and regulations.

In recent years, computer systems at the U.S. Department of Defense (DoD) have been hacked by foreign powers, China has carried out extensive efforts to steal digital information from U.S. companies in what has been called "the greatest transfer of wealth in history," and the number of commercial enterprises victimized by data breaches has increased exponentially. The array of states and criminal organizations that are working daily to target government agencies, companies, and individuals is a growing challenge to existing policies.

A steady drumbeat of computer attacks and infiltrations has laid low organizations across the public and private sectors. Embarrassed adulterers had their personal lives exposed (the Ashley Madison hack), an online password manager firm was penetrated (the Last Pass hack), 22 million federal government officials and contractors with security clearances were compromised (the Office of Personal Management hack), and a portion of a sovereign country's critical infrastructure was successfully taken offline (power plant disruption in Ukraine). These are just a small sampling of how people, corporations, and governments can be affected by malicious actors in cyberspace.

As the scale of these threats has grown, so too has the interest of the policy community. Beginning in earnest in the mid-1990s, successive congresses and presidential administrations have sought to provide regulatory frameworks for information assurance and to stake out coherent positions on internet security governance and cyber crime issues, often with middling success and occasionally causing overt harm. Efforts to regulate cryptographic software through the use of export controls, for example, created a burden for researchers and vulnerabilities whose effects we still suffer today.

These export rules also provoked questions about whether the laws of nation-states could be applied to the social fabric of a network of geographically separated computers. These efforts have further clashed with industry groups, researchers, and the cultural milieu of security innovation. "Cyberspace consists of transactions, relationships, and thought itself, arrayed like a standing wave in the web of our communications," wrote John Perry Barlow in 1996, "Ours is a world that is both everywhere and nowhere."[2] This world and the security culture it engendered have come into conflict—at times direct, at others implicit—with public policy and political institutions.

The internet and computing technology has embedded itself in the way we work, live, and play throughout the world. The presence of these technologies has diminished certain human instincts, and transformed the labor necessary to collect and collate information. At the same time, it has magnified other trends, unleashing a powerful creative instinct seen in everything from parody videos on YouTube to cutting-edge data science. Individual's ability to connect to one another, to gather information about themselves, and to process it has expanded in nonlinear fashion with rapidity that is without historical parallel.

However, this spreading computational capability and connectivity pose a challenge for public policy. How should we address the key security challenges that these technologies engender while preserving the economic and social benefits that they provide? In the next decade, these challenges will be magnified as the Internet of Things (IoT) begins to spread connectivity to devices that were never designed for secure use online, thereby exponentially expanding the number of possible targets for new attacks. Growing, too, are the capabilities of potential adversary states, against whose activities the U.S. government must prioritize the defense of cyberspace—and whose intentions necessitate the formulation of a comprehensive strategy to protect critical national infrastructure and adapt to information as both means and medium of conflict.

Crafting Understanding

The security of the internet and computer systems sits at the intersection of technology and policy. The ability of law enforcement to pursue malicious hackers across borders is predicated upon complex international legal agreements, while the technical failures to protect vulnerable entities (from a Hollywood movie studio to financial institutions on Wall Street) can reverberate across both domestic and international politics. Some of the most important issues confronting policymakers in this arena still lie ahead. It is impossible to reduce interconnectivity or society's reliance on computing, so it is imperative that we work to better understand this next set of challenges.

Unfortunately, the policymaking community has struggled to keep pace with the depth and diversity of issues, both technical and political, which span the field of cybersecurity. According to a recent Congressional Research Service report, "despite many recommendations made over the past decade, most major legislative provisions relating to cybersecurity had been enacted prior to 2002."[3] Over the course of 2014 and 2015, there were six separate bills related to cybersecurity that were signed into law by the president, but none were transformative in nature or took major steps to address security issues relating to individual users, internet security, military operations, or crime. For example, the debate over information sharing in Congress, which finally ended with a tenuous embrace of liability reforms for private companies that share information with the government, has taken more than eight years and a tremendous expenditure of energy to materialize.

The reasons for the lack of progress, from a public policy perspective, are myriad. Not even the basic nomenclature has been agreed upon. Cybersecurity is an often abused and much misused term that was originally intended to cover security-related issues associated with "cyberspace," a phrase coined by author William Gibson in the short story "Burning Chrome."[4] It has become the buzzword for a staggeringly diverse array of topics, frustrating for practitioners and interested citizens alike.[5] It encompasses a complicated set of policy issues, most of which are motivated not by fantastic technology but by the uncertain integration of internet-enabled activities and actors into existing laws and policies.

Structure of the Book

The complexity of cybersecurity, in other words, comes less from the devices we use than from the people behind them. This book aims to provide a deep understanding of these issues by identifying four interrelated topic clusters, each organized into a separate section, which together address the complexity of cybersecurity policy.

The chapters that follow are intended to play three roles. For those new to these topics, they are intended as a guide to a complex space. In these pages, the authors attempt to explain the critical features of cyberspace and to simplify its essential components, in a sort of primer on many of the key policy issues covered under the expansive umbrella of cybersecurity. For the initiated generalist, sections I to IV provide relevant details, both technical and policy related, as well as references for further reading. For the policymaker and harried staffer, meanwhile, this book should serve as a resource for informed work in crafting public policy. Each of its sixteen different chapters articulates specific policy recommendations—from securing cars and trucks against remote attack to improving the laws that enable the United States to carry out influence operations against the Islamic State and other terrorist groups. Taken together, they constitute an agenda for the first 100 days of the 45th Presidency, and for the 115th Congress.

This book also seeks to highlight new voices with valuable ideas. The authors presented here constitute an intellectual cross-section of cybersecurity. They are lawyers, veterans, members of industry, and academics. They represent universities from across the country, including Stanford, Harvard, and the U.S. Military Academy. They come from policy centers such as the Atlantic Council, the RAND Corporation, the Berkman Center, and New America. They serve in policy positions in both state and federal governments, and have served in the U.S. Army, Air Force, and Navy. Each contributor has been asked to tackle a topic on the frontier of the cybersecurity policy debate. In each chapter, they explain a pressing challenge and highlight potential policy recommendations. Some of these are fresh takes on long debated proposals, such as liability for software vendors and the problem of cyber insurance. Many others address issues on the cutting edge of policy, such as government's purchase of software vulnerabilities and the question of how best to secure automobiles. The four sections of this book include:

Section I—Securing Data, Devices, and Networks

How do you secure the software and hardware that make up a network, be it an enterprise e-mail system or a power plant? This is the principal question addressed in this section, and a major focus of most cybersecurity professionals in the technical community. The work can be tedious and uncertain; for example, reverse engineering the latest strain of malware. Or it can be simple and repetitive, like making sure users in a system change their passwords every three months. Information assurance includes writing secure software, deploying it safely, and managing it to minimize the risk of compromise. The key principles are Confidentiality (that the information on a computer remains secret), Integrity (that data or a computer system remain accurate and complete), and Availability (that the computer system is ready and able to function when needed).[6]

When the computer systems of retail giant Target were breached in 2013, malware was able to enter the company's point of sale systems not because of some "Mission Impossible"-style covert operation but because someone clicked on the wrong attachment. A third-party company which supplied heating and ventilation-control services to Target inadvertently disclosed login credentials to a billing website that sat on Target's corporate network.[7] Using this server as a launch pad, attackers were able to move their code onto point of sale systems around the country. Securing the third-party vendor's systems, as well as Target's corporate network, against these sorts of attackers is an information assurance challenge for which there are a broad array of standards and practices. Add to this the problem of building secure software, locating vulnerabilities to fix them in existing software, and managing information technology infrastructure, such as cloud e-mail services, as well as critical infrastructure protection (CIP) and you have a broad spectrum of topics. Chapters in this section discuss the internet-related vulnerabilities of cars and trucks, explore cybersecurity and information sharing at the state and local level, detail the liability of software developers in cyber-attacks, and address the problem of how best to secure industrial control systems.

Section II—Combating Cyber Crime

The Target and Home Depot data breaches were spectacular examples of a long-running effort by criminal groups to steal customer payment information. This game of cat and mouse between retailers and payment processors, on the one hand, and criminal groups on the other has been ongoing since the birth of the retail industry on the internet. The defensive efforts of firms to secure their systems is an information assurance challenge, the sort of issue dealt with in section I, but the incentives for using secure systems and disrupting the activities of their attackers are topics for this section. Importantly, this section does not deal with attacks that cause damage or harm people (a very small fraction of the total). In terms of the total cost of attacks to governments and individuals alike, cyber crime represents a far greater portion of the total than those addressed in section IV.

Cyber crime deals with actors interested in anything short of destructive attacks, including financial fraud and credit card theft or disrupting services for ideological goals ("hacktivism"). From a policy perspective, this section includes the legal basis for law enforcement's efforts to track and prosecute criminals who operate over the internet, including the *Computer Fraud and Abuse Act (CFAA).*[9] Cyber crime also covers both regulatory and legal action to drive good security practices as well as law enforcement activity to interdict the trade in stolen goods and malicious tools. The chapters in this section explain the importance and potential of data breach notification laws, describe the emerging role of cyber insurance, and evaluate new ways to disrupt the malicious software markets.

Section III—Governing the Security of the Internet

The internet crosses national and jurisdictional boundaries, so to take legal action outside U.S. borders or implement new protocols can require the involvement of other state and nonstate actors.[8] This section addresses technical and legal security issues that affect or require the involvement of more than a single country. The topic is distinct from *Internet Governance*, which deals with managing the internet's underlying architecture and broader administrative challenges like routing and content control, which are not security issues per se.

The ability to pass information over the internet in a secure manner underpins the modern economy, from online retail to personal banking. Transport Layer Security (TLS) is a protocol that allows computers to create encrypted links over the internet and communicate securely. When a computer connects to an internet service, such as an online bank, the website responds with a certificate containing a cryptographic key, establishing it is indeed the intended bank and not a fraudulent site waiting to steal user's data. These certificates are issued and verified by a small number of firms, certificate authorities, which have proven vulnerable to compromise. In addition to these certificate authorities, this section deals with the resulting cybersecurity challenges, including lawful hacking and cryptography, designing a more secure system of identity verification for the web, using multistakeholder models for security governance, and countering the proliferation of malicious software.

Section IV—Military Cyber Operations

Military Cyber Operations (MCO) encompass the acquisition and use of cyber capabilities for the strategic, operational, and tactical levels of conflict. This involves operations to find and develop exploits for vulnerabilities in software and the establishment of long-term access to systems in use by potential targets. At the strategic level, this could involve attacks against critical infrastructure such as nuclear weapons refining or heavy industrial facilities,[10] while at the operational and tactical levels, military organizations may use cyber capabilities to target enemy logistics networks or air defense systems.[11]

A well-recognized set of policy issues deals with the development and use of cyber capabilities by states and nonstate actors to injure or kill individuals and destroy data or equipment. This section discusses not only the organizational and budgetary issues involved in U.S. military operations in cyberspace, but also the legal and normative constraints on all states and nonstate actors. An emerging challenge is the question of how governments acquire and use software vulnerabilities. The Stuxnet attack on Iran's centrifuge facility may be the most prominent example of a cyber weapon in use to date, but the potential for physically destructive attacks has so far remained small, largely because of the complexity involved in crafting the tools required.[12]

This section encompasses the organizations, policy, and law related to deploying destructive digital or physical effects on target computer systems or defending against such. The chapters found here address the government's purchase and use of zero-day software vulnerabilities, discuss how to organize and equip the military for both defensive and offensive cyber operations, highlight the negative impacts of overclassification, and detail a new way to think about the use of information in creating influence around the world.

Why This Book Now?

The purpose of this book is to provide an understanding of the foundations of cybersecurity policy, as well as the frontier issues that are now or will soon be at the center of national policy debate. The book taps into the minds of experts across the different fields embedded in cybersecurity to deliver a roadmap for policymakers in the coming decade. It also serves as a primer and potential reference work for corporate leaders, academics, students, and the general public. In an era of systemic cyber*insecurity* the challenge is not only to understand the bits and bytes of modern computing and connected devices, but also to grasp the larger political and policy framework within which technological changes are occurring.

NOTES

1. Miles Townes, "The Spread of TCP/IP: How the Internet Became the Internet," *Millennium-Journal of International Studies* 41, no. 1, (September 2012): 43–64, http://mil.sagepub.com/content/41/1/43.short.

2. John Perry Barlow, "A Declaration of the Independence of Cyberspace," 1996.

3. Rita Tehran, "Cybersecurity: Legislation, Hearings, and Executive Branch Documents," Congressional Research Service Report, R43317, March 30, 2016.

4. William Gibson, "Burning Chrome," in *Burning Chrome* (Harper Voyager, 2003).

5. Mike Masnick, "The Cyberpolitics of Cyberbellicosity Cyberpushing Cybersecurity to Cyberprevent Cyberwar," *TechDirt*, June 14, 2012, https://www.techdirt.com/articles/20120614/01590919314/cyberpolitics-cyberbellicosity-cyberpushing-cybersecurity-to-cyberprevent-cyberwar.shtml.

6. "What is Security Analysis?" Imperial College London, http://www.doc.ic.ac.uk/~ajs300/security/CIA.htm.

7. "Email Attack on Vendor Set Up Breach at Target," *Krebs on Security*, February 14, 2014, http://krebsonsecurity.com/2014/02/email-attack-on-vendor-set-up-breach-at-target/.

8. Sarah Pillai, "What is IPSEC and how IPSEC does the job of securing data communication," *Root.in*, July 27, 2013, http://www.slashroot.in/what-ipsec-and-how-ipsec-does-job-securing-data-communication.

9. "Racketeer influenced and corrupt organizations," 18 *U.S. Code* §96; "Fraud and related activity in connection with computers," 18 *U.S. Code* §1030.

10. Kim Zetter, "How Digital Detectives Deciphered Stuxnet, the Most Menacing Malware in History," *Wired*, July 11, 2011, http://www.wired.com/2011/07/how-digital-detectives-deciphered-stuxnet/all/; "Hack attack causes 'massive damage' at steel works," *BBC*, December 22, 2014, http://www.bbc.com/news/technology-30575104.

11. Ward Carroll, "Israel's Cyber Shot at Syria," *Defense Tech*, November 26, 2007, http://defensetech.org/2007/11/26/israels-cyber-shot-at-syria/.

12. Trey Herr, "PrEP: A Framework for Malware & Cyber Weapons," *Journal of Information Warfare* 13, no. 1 (February 2014), pp. 87–100, http://papers.ssrn.com/sol3/papers.cfm?abstract_id=2343798.

Section I

SECURING DATA, DEVICES, AND NETWORKS

Chapter 1

Understanding Information Assurance

Eric Ormes and Trey Herr

"Information Assurance" is the art and science of securing computer systems and networks against efforts by third parties to disable, intrude, or otherwise impede operations. It is the focus of most "cybersecurity" professionals in the technical community. The principal goals are to maintain an information system's Confidentiality, the secrecy of information as it is used and stored; Integrity, reliability of data and equipment; and Availability, that a computer system is ready and able to function as needed.[1] Information assurance includes writing secure software, deploying it safely, and managing it to minimize the risk of compromise.

The breach experienced by the Target Corporation in 2013 demonstrated that determined opponents are only half of the equation in cybersecurity. In that incident, the company's point of sale systems were compromised because an employee at a third-party vendor clicked on an attachment, allowing attackers to jump into the Target corporate network and move their code onto merchant systems around the country.[2] Securing the third-party vendor's systems, as well as Target's corporate network, against these sorts of attackers are information assurance challenges. This chapter describes six relevant domains: network and system security, software vulnerabilities, information sharing, federal security standards, critical infrastructure protection (CIP), and workforce training and qualification.

Network and Information System Defense

Network defense is a key tenet of information assurance. There are two main categories of defensive systems: host based (the defensive mechanism resides on a system to protect it) and network based (the defensive system focuses on looking at network traffic to protect systems).[3] Both are deployed utilizing various techniques in order to form a defensive strategy. Here are a few key concepts and ideas:

Defense-in-Depth

This is the overarching strategy employed by most organizations. Conceptually similar to medieval castles, defense-in-depth is composed of multiple defensive rings, from the outermost curtain wall to the inner ward. The strength of the design is the multiple levels of protection and redundancy, all of which must be defeated, bypassed, or neutralized before an attacker can penetrate into the inner sanctum and achieve their objective. While based upon solid concepts, defense-in-depth runs into difficulties in the virtual world, where a new vulnerability might turn even the stoutest fortress into a house of cards overnight. Newer technologies emphasize access controls and the behavior of network traffic and individuals moving in and out of the fortress, rather than relying solely on layered defenses.[4]

Deception

Using systems that appear genuine, this strategy is based upon trying to hide real network traffic and computers among convincing fakes.[5] While this is the epitome of a somewhat criticized practice known as "security through obscurity," it can provide two important capabilities to the defender, increasing the amount of work required for attackers to find valuable data and raising the possibility that they make a mistake.[6] Deception, most often implemented through network and system devices that appear to be real but are without value and can trip up attackers, called honey nets, causes so much confusion for an outside attacker regarding what is real and what is fake that it makes their task exponentially more difficult to execute. These honey nets can also lure the attacker to target fake systems and traffic instead of real ones. Since this is a defender-controlled environment, typically with various forms of detection tools that activate the moment a breach occurs, the attacker will likely tip their hand and reveal his presence. This defensive strategy is one that acknowledges the difficulty of stopping 100 percent of the threats, 100 percent of the time, and relies instead on attackers to fall for a trap and reveal themselves. So long as attackers are willing to take the bait, the strategy can be effective.

Virtualization

A virtual machine is an emulation of a computer system, a digital "replica" of a computer within a real machine, that enables the encapsulation and containment of processes as they run on the host system.[7] This means that when a program runs, whether malicious or not, it is only granted access to a set amount of resources and does not interact directly with important system processes. Therefore, it does not matter if a threat reaches the target, as it will be contained within the virtual environment. This means that the virtualized software does not care about what vulnerabilities might be present in the various other applications and programs, because once the virtual process is shut down, the malware is gone as well. This is not a foolproof method, and there are attacks—referred to as Virtual Machine (VM) escape—that could allow a malicious process to try and break out of its container and infect the host system.[8] Currently however, many of these attacks are either technically difficult or resource intensive to execute.

Vulnerabilities

In the realm of information assurance, vulnerability management is one of the most important areas for strengthening defenses.[9] Yet it generally receives scant attention from organizations working to prevent breaches. Vulnerabilities are the weaknesses that can be exploited by a threat in order to compromise the confidentiality, integrity, or availability of information. They may be purposefully included features or simple bugs in an otherwise functional design. There are three main types of vulnerabilities: physical, human, and system (software or hardware). Physical vulnerabilities can range from susceptibility to Acts of God to poor security at server facilities. People likewise pose a vulnerability to information assurance, either through willful acts as "malicious insiders" or through simple ignorance of security precautions (e.g., by clicking on attachments). There are varying controls that can be put in place to address these issues.

In software, vulnerabilities don't impede system operation. Instead, they act as a narrow window through which an exploit may be written. For example, a program that expects to retrieve a static image file but fails to check the supplied file type might return an executable software program instead.[10] Retrieving the image was intentional, but failing to check the file type allows a third party to execute malicious software. The Love Letter virus of 2000 relied on the fact that Windows 2000 and XP hid known file extensions when parsing file names from the right to the left. The virus, an executable program, thus appeared to be a .txt file, while it actually was a visual basic script (LOVE-LETTER-FOR-YOU.TXT.vbs).[11] While this design convention didn't constitute a "flaw" per se, it was used by third parties to effect unintended operations in the software. Vulnerabilities may also be introduced directly to hardware through compromises in chip design or manufacture somewhere along a supply chain.[12] While software developers have incorporated security into their development processes, thousands of vulnerabilities are still found in software every year. Many of these software-based vulnerabilities can be found on NIST's National Vulnerability Database. In 2014, over 7,900 vulnerabilities were published on the site.[13]

But despite the high number of vulnerabilities discovered every year, several of which have been rated as having a "Critical" impact to security, many organizations still do not view addressing vulnerabilities on a regular basis as part of their cybersecurity program to prevent breaches. In the Cisco 2015 Annual Security Report, 90 percent of respondents said they feel "confident about their security policies, processes, and procedures."[14] However, less than 50 percent of those polled stated that they utilized vulnerability scanning or patch and configuration management as part of their security programs.[15]

This is concerning, given data from Hewlett-Packard's Cyber Risk Report 2015 that states that the top ten vulnerabilities they saw targeted in 2014, accounting for 78 percent of the total observed, were discovered between 2009 and April 2013.[16] When considering the lack of emphasis placed on vulnerability scanning or patch and configuration management, it's not a surprise that 54 percent of Cisco respondents reported they needed "to manage public scrutiny following a security breach."[17]

Due to the complexities of software interaction, both with other programs and with hardware, it is impossible to detect all vulnerabilities prior to a piece of software being published. Encouraging the discovery, and disclosure, of vulnerabilities directly to companies can help find and patch flaws before they become used in malicious software. But this requires that vendors maintain clear disclosure policies and a good relationship with researchers and the larger security community. This sort of information can also be shared after attacks, allowing victims to band together and mitigate malicious tools rapidly.

Information Sharing

Information sharing has been a vociferously debated topic within policy circles for the past several years, a debate that has been driven largely by several versions of the Cyber Intelligence Sharing and Protection Act, finally culminating in a 2015 law. There are three possible uses for information sharing. The first is to encourage information flow from the government to private sector actors. In this "information down" scenario, federal intelligence collection and analysis capabilities are made available in some limited fashion to the private sector to improve the latter's ability to understand and defend against threats. A second use would be to encourage information sharing between organizations, either public or private.[18] A third would be to encourage "information up" from private actors to the government. In this third situation, the government acts to improve its own situational awareness of civilian networks by incentivizing private groups and firms to share their respective network activity and suspected malicious traffic.

Information sharing "up" may provide the government with an information assurance advantage, but it is not clear what direct benefit the private sector gains. Information sharing "down" may reinforce a firm's security capabilities and awareness, but is complicated by the need for clearances to share classified information with companies outside of limited pilot programs such as the Defense Industrial Base Cyber Security and Information Assurance activity.[19]

Sharing threat information between firms is already common practice in parts of the private sector. One example is the "signatures," or defining characteristic of new attacks, shared by vendors with users of their antivirus and intrusion detection systems. Another is companies collaborating directly with each other. In early 2015, Facebook announced ThreatExchange, a platform for sharing signatures, URLs, and contextual information about threats with other firms.[20] It began as an ad-hoc collaboration between companies to help stop sizable distributed denial of service attacks, and the service has evolved to combine proprietary and open source information feeds into a single data format accessible to members.[21] Yet many information assurance experts criticize the focus on information sharing as it provides little direct information assurance benefit; "information sharing allows better and faster bandaids but doesn't address the core problem," says Jeff Moss, founder of the DEF CON and Black Hat information security conferences.[22]

Federal Standards

U.S. government information assurance standards are rooted in the *Federal Information Security Management Act of 2002* (FISMA). This was the original source of responsibility for the National Institute of Standards and Technology (NIST) to develop information assurance and risk management standards for the federal government. It resulted in a set of requirements and checklists, which have received varying degrees of criticism since.[23] There have been several recent efforts to reform FISMA, including a large provision in the failed 2012 Lieberman/Collins bill (*Cybersecurity Act of 2012*, S. 2105) and the 2014 *Federal Information Security Modernization Act*, which successfully implemented reforms to reporting requirements and operational standards.[24]

Some of the 2014 changes included a shift toward the practices of the NIST Risk Management Framework (RMF).

Risk Management Framework

The RMF is a U.S. government successor to the Defense-specific Information Assurance Certification and Accreditation Process (DIACAP) that first received interim approval in 2006.[25] Formally established by the Department of Defense (DoD) in 2014, the RMF serves as a risk assessment and management program for federal organizations and is in the process of being implemented across federal civilian and national security information technology (IT) systems.[26] The program's application to the private sector is enforced for all secure facilities and firms working on government contracts.

The framework is based on a series of NIST Special Publications that lay out a common risk assessment and mitigation process, including a compendium of security controls, applicable based on an information system's risk category. These Special Publications form the basis for federal organizations to develop information assurance security plan and secure their IT environments. While the controls contained in the NIST documentation undergirding both the RMF and the Cybersecurity Framework are relatively detailed, the risk assessment process associated with their selection and application has evolved from the original FISMA approach but remains largely up to federal agencies to develop themselves.[27]

HIPAA and HITECH

One of the only major U.S. laws to set and enforce information assurance standards over any particular sector was the *Health Insurance Portability and Accountability Act* (HIPAA) passed in 1996. It included security requirements for participants and businesses covered by the Act. Its Security Rule contained provisions for administrative, physical, and technical security with rules split between required and suggested.[28] Most of the technical standards, even those "required," are written vaguely, with one example defining the standard for transmission security as a requirement for "technical security measures."[29] Enforcement of these standards was considered loose to nonexistent, and many of the final rules from the Department of Health and Human Services (HHS) did not come into effect till 2003–2006.[30]

This shifted in 2009 with the passage of the HITECH Act as part of an unrelated stimulus bill. The new law increased the civil penalties HHS could assess, required the notification of affected customers in breaches resulting in the loss of healthcare information, and expanded the application of HIPAA's Security Rule to businesses associated with covered healthcare entities.[31] Enforcement actions increased, although the core standards of the original Security Rule remain relatively nonspecific and penalties have appeared to vary more with changes in HHS leadership than with particular standards requirements for healthcare companies and business partners.[32]

Varied History of Federal Efforts

This history of federal information assurance standard setting stretches back twenty years, to midway through the Clinton administration, when the protection of critical infrastructure first rose into the national policy spotlight. Three common themes emerged throughout: the lack of specific standards, a dearth of strong enforcement mechanisms, and—where there were detailed standards—no comparable risk assessment or management programs. Until the NIST controls emerged in the mid-2000s, and in some instances afterward, government approaches focused on functional requirements—shying away from specifying the exact nature of the security tool or procedure in favor of a rule that organizations do something to achieve a particular end such as secure internet communications. Few of the standard programs came with compliance mechanisms attached and even where they did apply to the private sector, as with security provisions of the HIPAA, the regulatory body responsible was often reluctant to strictly audit and penalize nonperforming firms.

As with many things, the best information assurance strategy will depend on the context of the threat and the organization being protected. There is no single plan capable of protecting everyone. The golden rule for any organization is that the cost of the defense should not exceed the value of the information being protected. A thorough risk assessment for every organization is the only way to determine what countermeasures are best and how to design a defensive strategy. The key to understanding risk, in other words, is understanding scarce resources.[33] No organization or business can protect everything, everywhere, all of the time. Choices have to be made to prioritize some things over others. Identifying which data and systems are most vulnerable or could present catastrophic damage if they are lost or unavailable is critical to assuring information security.

Critical Infrastructure Protection

CIP is the protection of hardware and the specialized software across sixteen sectors, including chemical manufacturing, the financial services industry, and electricity generation. Each of these has been highlighted as "essential services that underpin American society."[34] CIP falls under information assurance as well. For all of its specialized challenges, the basic steps are similar: to isolate and protect key applications from the internet, to remove or patch vulnerabilities in software, and to make sure users don't break anything. There are differences between the software in your laptop and that used to control industrial systems, but the distinction has begun to shrink as industrial control systems (ICS) start to integrate internet protocol and other more common communications standards.[35] For some sectors, standards of protection and practice already exist; for example, companies involved in electrical power generation and transmission operate under security standards developed by the North American Electric Reliability Corporation.[36] For others, like financial services, they are still evolving.

There are many challenges in securing each of these diverse sectors, but two particular issues predominate. First, the vast majority of information system assets in each of the sixteen sectors are in private hands, which translates into a diversity of standards and security approaches and resistance to the various federally mandated approaches that have been put forth since the late 1990s. Second, many of these critical infrastructure sectors must secure both traditional IT systems and operational technology (OT). IT systems typically function with widely used software including Adobe Reader or Mozilla's Firefox browser. Even where more enterprise (organization-wide) applications such as e-mail or network print services are required, the software employed generally has a wide user base. OT software, by contrast, deals with monitoring and control of physical systems and equipment, like ICS.

For software associated with ICS, the design and testing process for patches to vulnerabilities can be cumbersome.[37] The embedded nature of ICS makes them difficult to access and modify, while the user base for ICS application is generally much smaller than that of IT systems, leading to niche products with software that is esoteric and difficult to change. Industrial activities often require nearly continuous operation, so taking ICS equipment offline for regular updates and patching is challenging at best.[38] ICS software also tends to be designed for long-run use, with equipment lifetimes of fifteen years or more as opposed to IT software which can change substantially in far shorter cycles. Indeed, in its first decade of existence, the Firefox browser evolved through thirty commercial versions. In addition, while the software development community in the commercial IT sector has largely moved to embrace the process of regular patching, along with the responsibilities and overhead costs associated with it, ICS developers and operators still lag behind. This means that patching is not yet a standard feature of ICS software development and use, even though vulnerabilities continue to be discovered in ICS software.[39]

Workforce Training and Certification

Dealing with these problems requires implementing technical and policy solutions. That, in turn, requires a trained and certified workforce. Developing the skills and education applicable to the field can be a challenge, however. There is a shortage of skilled information assurance professionals, especially for federal work, and disagreements over how to encourage more to enter the workforce as the continually evolving problem area has forced trade-offs between practical experience and technical expertise.[40]

A 2011 paper from the Cyber Security and Privacy Research Institute at George Washington University found that "the university model does not completely satisfy all cyber security education and training needs [as] traditional undergraduate and graduate programs tend to take several years to complete and . . . [these programs] face difficulties educating students about a rapidly changing field. . . . Academic silos prevent collaboration and integration . . . [as] most academic programs have tended to build their own tools rather than exchange resources with others, and they tend to hold firm ownership over whatever they create."[41] This need for both skills and experience raises the question of whether to emphasize practical experience and "on-the-job" training, like airline pilots, who obtain thousands of hours of flight time in progressively larger aircraft, or to treat information assurance as a certified profession like law, where professional credibility comes from grueling coursework and testing.

A popular approach, which tempers but does not resolve this debate, is the use of certifications. Short class sequences and testing are used in lieu of university-based programs, but often require work experience and annual continuing education as well. Many "purists" in information assurance feel that certifications don't genuinely show skill level, only that the applicant can pass a test.[42] After all, certifications are a business and organizations have a vested interest in making them mandatory for specific jobs. One DoD document, DoD Instruction 8570, requires particular certifications in order for individuals to hold positions like an Information Assurance Manager or an Incident Handler.[43] Without these certifications in hand, individuals would be unable to work in any of the identified positions, regardless of previous experience.

But while certifications don't necessarily prove one's ability to perform a given task, they do at least show a standardized understanding of the issues covered by the certificate program and so provide an opportunity for nonprofits and many commercial firms, like the SANS Institute, to establish common bases of knowledge. This helps create expectations within the information assurance community and can, for better or worse, provide a rapid means for employers to screen potential candidates.

While there is a hiring crunch for information assurance professionals in the federal workforce, it is possible that the problem will resolve itself. A 2014 RAND Corporation study concluded that much of the labor market shortfall could be explained by the natural lag time for educational institutions to respond to particular market demand. In the case of information assurance, the study suggests: "The difficulty in finding qualified cybersecurity candidates is likely to solve itself, as the supply of [qualified individuals] currently in the educational pipeline increases, and the market reaches a stable, long-run equilibrium."[44] This would be further helped by continued growth in the commercial information assurance labor market.

MAKING POLICY FOR INFORMATION ASSURANCE

Information assurance focuses on ensuring the confidentiality, integrity, and availability of information. It encompasses a cluster of topics, including the defense of information systems and networks against compromise, design of secure software, protection of critical infrastructure, and the challenge of educating and hiring qualified professionals. While not the most headline grabbing, these are bread-and-butter topics for security professionals and constitute the majority of defensive "cybersecurity" activity in organizations on any given day.

The challenge for policymakers is that there is little opportunity for direct intervention. The standards and techniques of network and system security are continually evolving. Federal requirements, like FISMA, can help to create consistent practices, but risk lowering the bar of "minimum acceptable" behavior and may embed inflexible requirements that are quickly outpaced by events. In information assurance, ameliorating vulnerabilities is largely a software design and patch management problem. CIP has benefited from the government's role as a trusted intermediary, and while it faces many of the same rapidly evolving threats as more conventional IT security, the OT space lags some years behind. As such, it is more likely to benefit from established standards for security behavior.

Workforce training and certification presents an intriguing opportunity for lawmakers. The federal workforce embodies a vast set of standards for education and training. Better defining the information assurance roles required by public sector organizations, and the accompanying knowledge, skills, and abilities that these positions require, could help standardize many training and certification pipelines. Either by using a single organization's workforce as a model or through some comprehensive review process, standardized roles would serve as a powerful voice in the discussion of how to constitute a professional information assurance labor pool.

CONCLUSION

At the end of the day, there are a variety of strategies for securing systems and networks in use by both public and private organizations. Developing and deploying software free from vulnerabilities, meanwhile, remains an ongoing and still largely unsuccessful struggle. Much of the difficulty in securing critical infrastructure systems is the diversity of private actors who own them and the challenge of patching software used in complex machinery and other OT. Finally, the workforce required to support all of these varied tasks and missions is still smaller than is necessary, in part because of a range of opinions on the best way to train and educate professionals in the field. Information assurance is a highly technical cluster of topics within cybersecurity and an area where many traditional policy tools are likely to have little direct and positive effect. There is much more under cybersecurity, but this chapter serves as an introduction to some of the more technical defensive issues that occupy the day-to-day focus of many organizations.

CHAPTER HIGHLIGHTS

Information Assurance focuses on ensuring the confidentiality, integrity, and availability of information. It encompasses a cluster of topics, including the defense of information systems and networks against compromise, design of secure software, protection of critical infrastructure, and the challenge of educating and hiring qualified professionals.

Strategies Vary. The best information assurance strategy will depend on the context of the threat and the organization being protected. There is no single plan capable of protecting everyone. The golden rule for any organization is that the cost of the defense should not exceed the value of the information being protected. A thorough risk assessment for every organization is the only way to determine what countermeasures are best and how to design a defensive strategy.

Vulnerability Management. In the realm of information assurance, vulnerability management is one of the most important areas for strengthening defenses. Vulnerabilities are the weaknesses that can be exploited by a threat in order to compromise the confidentiality, integrity, or availability of information.

Federal Standards. U.S. government information assurance standards are rooted in the *Federal Information Security Management Act of 2002* (FISMA). This was the original source of responsibility for the National Institute of Standards and Technology (NIST) to develop information security and risk management standards for the federal government. It resulted in a set of requirements and checklists, which have received varying degrees of criticism since. There have been several recent efforts to reform FISMA, but none have been very effective.

Critical Infrastructure Protection (CIP) is the protection of hardware and the specialized software that controls it, as well as of information systems that are deemed to be of national importance (such as those used in the financial sector). CIP falls under information assurance as well. For all of its specialized challenges, the basic steps are similar: to isolate and protect key applications from the internet, to remove or patch vulnerabilities in software, and to make sure users don't break anything.

Workforce Training and Certification. There is a shortage of skilled information assurance professionals, especially for federal work, and disagreements over how to encourage more to enter the workforce as the continually evolving problem area has forced trade-offs between practical experience and technical expertise. Certification programs do not necessarily prove one's ability, but allow for a standardization of understanding a common base of knowledge.

NOTES

1. "What is Security Analysis?" Imperial College London, http://www.doc.ic.ac.uk/~ajs300/security/CIA.htm.

2. "Email Attack on Vendor Set Up Breach at Target," *Krebs on Security*, February 14, 2014, http://krebsonsecurity.com/2014/02/email-attack-on-vendor-set-up-breach-at-target/.

3. Andrew Schneiter, Harold F. Tipton and Steven Hernandez, *Official (ISC) 2 guide to the CISSP CBK*, third ed. (Auerbach Communications, 2013).

4. Ines Brosso and Alessandro La Neve, "Adaptive Security Policy Using User Behavior Analysis and Human Elements of Information Security," in Elmer P. Dadios, ed., *Fuzzy Logic – Emerging Technologies and Applications* (InTech, 2012), http://cdn.intechopen.com/pdfs-wm/32882.pdf.

5. Aarti Shahani, "Hygiene, Honey Pots, Espionage: 3 Approaches To Defying Hackers," NPR, February 16, 2015, http://www.npr.org/blogs/alltechconsidered/2015/02/16/386669799/hygiene-honeypots-espionage-3-approaches-to-defying-hackers.

6. See, for example, "The Problem with Security Through Obscurity," http://www.diablotin.com/librairie/networking/puis/ch02_05.htm.

7. Shahani, "Hygiene, Honey Pots, Espionage."

8. Kelly Jackson Higgins, "Hacking Tool Lets A VM Break Out And Attack Its Host," *Dark Reading*, June 4, 2009, http://www.darkreading.com/risk/hacking-tool-lets-a-vm-break-out-and-attack-its-host/d/d-id/1131254?; Fahmida Rashid, "VUPEN Method Breaks Out of Virtual Machine to Attack Hosts," *Security Week*, September 5, 2012, http://www.securityweek.com/vupen-method-breaks-out-of-virtual-machine-attack-hosts.

9. Cisco Corporation, *Cisco 2015 Annual Security Report*, http://www.cisco.com/web/offers/lp/2015-annual-security-report/index.html.

10. This description of a vulnerability taken from Trey Herr, "PrEP: A Framework for Malware & Cyber Weapons," *The Journal of Information Warfare* 13, no. 1 (February 2014): 87–106.

11. "Information About the VBS.LOVELETTER Worm Virus," Microsoft Corporation, http://support.microsoft.com/kb/282832.

12. Georg T. Becker et al., "Stealthy Dopant-Level Hardware Trojans," paper presented at the Cryptographic Hardware and Embedded Systems (CHES) 2013 conference, Santa Barbara, California, August 21, 2013, http://sharps.org/wp-content/uploads/BECKER-CHES.pdf.

13. "National Vulnerability Database," https://nvd.nist.gov/.

14. Cisco Corporation, *Cisco 2015 Annual Security Report.* http://www.cisco.com/web/offers/lp/2015-annual-security-report/index.html

15. Ibid.

16. "National Vulnerability Database."

17. Cisco, *2015 Annual Security Report.*

18. For more, see chapter 2.

19. "Department of Defense (DoD)-Defense Industrial Base (DIB) Voluntary Cyber Security and Information Assurance (CS/IA) Activities," *Federal Register*, October 22, 2013, https://www.federalregister.gov/articles/2013/10/22/2013-24256/department-of-defense-dod-defense-industrial-base-dib-voluntary-cyber-security-and-information.

20. "Understanding Threats with ThreatData," *Facebook* post dated March 25, 2014, https://www.facebook.com/notes/protect-the-graph/understanding-online-threats-with-threatdata/1438165199756960.

21. Michael Mimoso, "Facebook Threat Exchange Platform Latest Hope for Information Sharing," Kaspersky, February 11, 2015, http://threatpost.com/facebook-threatexchange-platform-latest-hope-for-information-sharing/110993.

22. Sara Sorcher, "Influencers: Obama's Info-Sharing Plan Won't Significantly Reduce Security Breaches," *Christian Science Monitor*, February 25, 2015, http://www.csmonitor.com/World/Passcode/2015/0225/Influencers-Obama-s-info-sharing-plan-won-t-significantly-reduce-security-breaches.

23. Daniel M. White, "The Federal Information Security Management Act of 2002: A Potemkin Village," *Fordam Law Review* 79, iss. 1 (2011), http://ir.lawnet.fordham.edu/cgi/viewcontent.cgi?article=4687&context=flr.

24. *Cybersecurity Act of 2012*, S. 2105 (112th Congress, 2011–2013), https://www.govtrack.us/congress/bills/112/s2105/text; Sean B. Hoar, "Congress Passes The Federal Information Security Modernization Act of 2014: Bringing Federal Agency Information Security into the New Millennium," *Privacy & Security Law Blog*, December 18, 2014, http://www.privsecblog.com/2014/12/articles/cyber-national-security/congress-passes-the-federal-information-security-modernization-act-of-2014-bringing-federal-agency-information-security-into-the-new-millennium/.

25. Brigette Wilson, "Move over DITSCAP . . . The DIACAP Is Here!" (Boeing, May 11, 2006), http://cs.uccs.edu/~cs591/studentproj/projS2007/bwilson3/doc/DIACAPClassPresentation.ppt.

26. "Risk Management Framework (RMF) Overview," NIST Computer Security Division, http://csrc.nist.gov/groups/SMA/fisma/framework.html.

27. Other efforts to set standards by the state include specific security requirements and a common risk assessment process for cloud computing facilities with U.S. government data, the FedRAMP standards, and passage of the Cybersecurity Information Sharing Act (CISA) which provided liability protections for private sector groups to share information on threats and network activity with federal authorities. See Bryan Graf, "10 Steps toward FedRAMP Compliance," *Federal Computing Weekly*, October 21, 2013, https://fcw.com/articles/2013/10/21/10-steps-to-fedramp-compliance.aspx; Dianne Feinstein, "S.2588—113th Congress (2013–2014): Cybersecurity Information Sharing Act of 2014," legislation, (July 10, 2014), https://www.congress.gov/bill/113th-congress/senate-bill/2588?q=%7B%22search%22%3A%5B%22CISA%22%5D%7D&resultIndex=1.

28. "45 CFR 164.306—Security Standards: General Rules," *LII/Legal Information Institute*, accessed December 31, 2015, https://www.law.cornell.edu/cfr/text/45/164.306. Suggested rules are referred to as "addressable."

29. "45 CFR 164.312—Technical Safeguards," *LII/Legal Information Institute*, accessed December 31, 2015, https://www.law.cornell.edu/cfr/text/45/164.312.

30. Daniel Solove, "HIPAA Turns 10: Analyzing the Past, Present, and Future Impact," *GW Law Faculty Publications & Other Works*, January 1, 2013, http://scholarship.law.gwu.edu/faculty_publications/950.

31. Howard Anderson, "The Essential Guide to HITECH Act," accessed December 26, 2015, http://www.healthcareinfosecurity.com/essential-guide-to-hitech-act-a-2053.2015.

32. Joseph Goedert, "HIPAA Sanctions Coming in Rapid Order as 2015 Ends," *HDM Top Stories*, accessed December 31, 2015, http://www.healthdatamanagement.com/news/HIPAA-Sanctions-Coming-in-Rapid-Order-as-2015-Ends-51719-1.html.

33. For more, see chapter 6—"Understanding Cyber Crime."

34. White House, Office of the Press Secretary, "Presidential Policy Directive—Critical Infrastructure Security and Resilience," February 12, 2013, http://www.whitehouse.gov/the-press-office/2013/02/12/presidential-policy-directive-critical-infrastructure-security-and-resil.

35. For more on Internet Protocol, see chapter 11.

36. "CIP Standards," North American Electric Reliability Corporation, http://www.nerc.com/pa/Stand/Pages/CIPStandards.aspx.

37. For more, see chapter 4.

38. Bonnie Zu, Anthony Joseph, and Shankar Sastry, "A Taxonomy of Cyber Attacks on SCADA Systems," *IEEE Conferences on Internet of Things, and Cyber, Physical and Social Computing*, 2011, http://bnrg.cs.berkeley.edu/~adj/publications/paper-files/ZhuJosephSastry_SCADA_Attack_Taxonomy_FinalV.pdf.

39. Brian Donohue, "Bug Hunters Find 25 ICS, SCADA Vulnerabilities," *Threat Post*, October 16, 2013, http://threatpost.com/bug-hunters-find-25-ics-scada-vulnerabilities.

40. Amber Corrin, "Is there a cybersecurity workforce crisis?" *FCW*, October 15, 2013, http://fcw.com/articles/2013/10/15/cybersecurity-workforce-crisis.aspx.

41 Ronald C. Dodge, Costis Toregas, and Lance Hoffman, "Cybersecurity Workforce Development Directions," 2011, http://static1.squarespace.com/

static/53b2efd7e4b0018990a073c4/t/54203f2de4b09a2902bc6f8a/1411399469318/costis_-_cybersecurity_workforce_development_directions.pdf.

42. Jeff Atwood, "Do Certifications Matter?" *Coding Horror*, January 17, 2007, http://blog.codinghorror.com/do-certifications-matter/.

43. "DoD Approved 8570.01-M Information Assurance Workforce Improvement Program," Information Assurance Support Environment, November 10th, 2015, http://www.dtic.mil/whs/directives/corres/pdf/857001m.pdf.

44. Martin Libicki, David Senty and Julia Pollak, *Hackers Wanted: An Examination of the Cybersecurity Labor Market* (RAND, 2014), http://www.rand.org/content/dam/rand/pubs/research_reports/RR400/RR430/RAND_RR430.pdf.

Chapter 2

A Path to Collective Security

Information Sharing at the State and Local Level

David Weinstein

Information assurance is a major challenge; attackers are constantly innovating and defenders must take a variety of steps to mitigate this reality, such as investing in security technologies and training employees to raise user awareness of threats. Information sharing, while not a solution by itself, has proven to be a key component of an effective information assurance strategy. Information sharing must take place across different sectors and businesses to effectively combat threats and reduce risk. Attackers are rarely unique to a single industry or line of business. The key to defeating determined threat groups thus becomes moving faster across organizational boundaries to share information than the threats themselves can shift between targets. Sharing information on current and previous incidents between businesses and public sector groups can shorten other defenders' responses. This in turn forces a costly adaptation on the attacker's part as they switch targets but find their stock of tools and tricks rapidly depleted by even a single use. Information sharing is the connective tissue that takes information assurance away from a single, siloed activity and links defenders together into a more resilient network.

At its core, the logic of information sharing is straightforward; the observation—or misfortune—of one organization contributes to the security of others. Companies and governments that participate in information sharing communities often weigh the risks of revealing vulnerabilities or suffering reputational harm versus the benefits of gleaning insights into real-time threats. The potential for this collective security is in the information about threats, gleaned from a victim or successful defense, and shared to others.

Translating the logic of information sharing into effective practice, however, demands trust and technological integration—particularly automation. Information sharing communities, usually called Information Sharing and

Analysis Centers (ISACs) or Information Sharing and Analysis Organizations (ISAOs), must implement strict protocols for protecting the confidentiality of data contributed by their members. This confidentiality becomes even more important as these groups transition information sharing to standardized automated processes. The goal of automation is to promote widespread awareness of vulnerabilities and threats as close to the point of disclosure as possible. The potential harm is that breaches of confidentiality can happen much faster and thus be more difficult to mitigate. Information being shared through ISACs and ISAOs cannot be personally identifiable or proprietary. Guaranteeing this sort of sensitive information is not disclosed between organizations is an ongoing requirement for effective trust and integration. Instead, information sharing focuses on indicators of compromise, or threat intelligence, which can reveal vulnerabilities in a computer system or means of defeating a particular security control.

Background

In recent years, Congress has spent multiple legislative calendars drafting and amending bills such as the *Cybersecurity Information Sharing Act* (CISA) to enhance the exchange of threat intelligence between industry and government.[1] The motivation behind Capitol Hill's push for legislation is the recognition that much of the most useful information on cyber threats resides on private sector networks. Nearly 80 percent of America's critical infrastructure is owned and operated by industry, giving it a front row seat to the greatest threats to the United States.[2] This truism was sufficient to garner bipartnership support for the *Cybersecurity Act of 2015* and its inclusion in Congress' end-of-year omnibus bill.

The effective sharing of threat intelligence requires two factors: incentives and institutions. *The Cybersecurity Act of 2015* aimed to address concerns over liability associated with sharing information, something industry, including regulated and nonregulated entities, have long called for when sharing with the federal government. These calls became more pronounced in the wake of Edward Snowden's revelations about ongoing U.S. intelligence collection activities and a string of breaches at federal organizations including the Internal Revenue Service and the Office of Personnel Management. Companies were concerned that, by sharing information with the government, they might reveal network security gaps, which could be used to levy penalties or construct new regulatory regimes. In addition, firms lacked confidence regarding how the data would be handled and to what agencies it would be accessible within the federal government. In practice, organizations tend to exercise caution when sharing information with any external entity if what is shared could reveal existing vulnerabilities in their security posture. The concern is that unintentional release of this information, as the result of a data breach for example, could result in more effective attacks on the organization.

The Cybersecurity Act of 2015 aimed to quell most of the industry's primary concerns regarding liability protection that led to vigorous support from the U.S. Chamber of Commerce but vehement protestations from many privacy and civil liberties advocates. Companies are given specific procedures to abide by in order to gain the law's liability protections. The new law also includes granular details on the type of information that can be shared and with whom. These indicators of compromise, technical information illustrating how attackers defeat security controls or exploit vulnerabilities, are the currency of an information sharing program. Central to the law is the role of the National Cybersecurity and Communications Integration Cell (NCCIC) under the Department of Homeland Security (DHS), which will act as the primary interface for sharing information with the federal government.

The law is limited, however, by its focus on sharing with the federal government, with comparatively little emphasis to encourage sharing between private organizations or from the federal government down to companies. While the law establishes the NCCIC as the federal government's primary information sharing hub, it is likely to be largely ineffective in the absence of other sharing organizations across the public, private, and nonprofit sectors. The fundamental idea behind information sharing is that the observation of one can lead to the security of many. This philosophy poses a conflict for sharing organizations composed of highly competitive members and has only been amplified in recent years as executives and board members in some sectors have invested a great deal of resources in securing their systems to achieve a competitive advantage. Nevertheless, in situations when an entire sector is being targeted by similar threat vector, such as the distributed denial of service (DDoS) attacks against American financial institutions in 2012, the mutual benefit of information sharing is extremely high.[3]

In February 2015, President Obama signed Executive Order 13691 to promote public-private cooperation on cybersecurity information sharing by calling on the U.S. DHS to encourage the establishment of so-called ISAOs. ISAOs are organized along a common affinity or community of interest based on individuals, industry, geography, or even a particular event. While their standards remain largely undefined, ISAOs are intended to serve as venues for collaboration on threat intelligence and incident response established by a mutually engaged group of willing members.

ISAOs and ISACs

Although related, ISAOs are not necessarily synonymous with ISACs, which are typically organized around a particular industry and loosely governed by a common set of standards. Their governing body, the National Council of ISACs, is composed of twenty-four sector-specific organizations, including the financial sector and the multi-state ISAC (MS-ISAC), which is chartered as the "focal point for cyber threat prevention, protection, response and recovery for the nation's state, local, tribal and territorial (SLTT) governments."[4] The precise similarities and differences between ISAOs and ISACs remain under scrutiny; however, Executive Order 13691 also mandates the establishment of a Standards Organization to further define the characteristics of an ISAO.

For over a decade, information sharing on threat groups has largely occurred within ISACs aligned with a particular industry vertical such as banking and finance, retail, or internet services and often without government involvement. Certain ISACs, prominently those set up for the financial services industry and electrical utility firms, have built trusted venues for exchanging threat intelligence. These centers are established through common administrative and technical protocols, most of which adhere to standard information security controls around data protection and handling, that preserve anonymity and confidentiality for their members.

ISACs are generally funded by fees from their members which, though often nominal and rarely prohibitive, are necessary to operate and deliver an array of managed security services. One exception to this rule is the MS-ISAC, which is federally funded to assist state and local governments across the country in detecting, analyzing, and sharing threat information with their respective members like businesses, schools, and citizens. Like their private sector counterparts, the MS-ISAC offers monitoring and incident response services, but at a highly subsidized cost. For most state and local governments the MS-ISAC Security Operations Center constitutes the bulk of their information security program, without which they would not have the capacity to monitor their network for security events or respond to incidents. In this respect, most enterprise and agency information assurance professionals at the state and local level rely almost exclusively on the MS-ISAC for supporting services.

Since early 2015, however, some states have begun to decrease their dependence on the MS-ISAC's services in favor of establishing internal capacity to monitor network traffic, correlate log activity, detect attackers, remediate incidents, and share threat indicators. In many cases, governments with large and federated enterprises are compelled to supplement MS-ISAC's services with additional capacity in order to deliver high-quality services to each individual agency.

Ill-defined ISAOs, originally established in accordance with Executive Order 13691 and the *Cybersecurity Act of 2015*, present a unique opportunity to expand information sharing on cyber threats beyond industry-specific silos and across America's economic sectors and state borders. In this respect state ISAOs can be a useful model for bridging the gap between the federal information sharing institutions, such as the NCCIC, and state and local governments. Moreover, ISAOs operating on a regional basis can scale the services of ISACs for members within a particular geographic jurisdiction.

In Focus: The New Jersey Cybersecurity and Communications Integration Cell

State governments are beginning to experiment with ISAOs, a good example of which is New Jersey, which offers a unique perspective on how to operationalize an ISAO at the state level. On May 20, 2015, the State of New Jersey established the United States' first state-level Information Sharing and Analysis Organization. Named the New Jersey Cybersecurity and Communications Integration Cell (NJCCIC), the organization is designed to coordinate cyber threat information sharing between the local, state, and federal levels of government, eventually culminating with the DHS's NCCIC in Arlington, Virginia. The NJCCIC is collocated and fully integrated with the state's Emergency Operations Center.

The NJCCIC was established as a reaction to the threat intelligence divide between the State of New Jersey and the federal government. The state's lack of an institutional counterpart to the NCCIC contributed to a deficit of awareness about cyber threats impacting both government and critical infrastructure networks. A secondary motivation was the lack of collaboration between the state and private sector organizations on information assurance issues. There was intense ambiguity throughout New Jersey regarding incident reporting and response for regulated and unregulated entities. Most organizations lack a clear understanding of who to contact in the event of an incident. The NJCCIC was designed to improve coordination between government agencies like law enforcement and emergency management as well as with private sector groups and the DHS. In assessing the value of state-level ISAOs to the U.S. broader cyber threat information sharing regime, it is important to highlight the scope of their activities across three component parts: operations, analysis, and partnerships.

Operations

In New Jersey, the Integration Cell is responsible for monitoring a government agency's networks for threats and facilitating the exchange of cyber threat intelligence with trusted partners. The scope of the network monitoring spans the entire government enterprise in order to detect and block cyber threats targeting individual agencies. Once vetted, and validated by correlating the data against other sources and ruling out false positives, information about these threats is automatically shared with trusted government and private sector parties using a universal format known as the Structured Threat Information eXpression (STIX). The receiving party, like a major public utility or industry-aligned ISAC, can then consume the intelligence to both scan its networks for the threat and update its security architecture accordingly.

Analysis

The NJCCIC employs full-time intelligence analysts, each with dedicated portfolios organized by sector and threat actor. These analysts work side by side with the NJCCIC's engineers to link security reporting with other intelligence sources related to known actors and their tactics, techniques, and procedures. This enriched intelligence informs multiple activities such as information assurance policy development, standards development, incident response, patch deployment, public awareness campaigns, training curricula, and the design of more realistic exercises. Moreover, the NJCCIC analysts are well positioned to support criminal investigations based on their understanding of the cyber threat landscape within a particular jurisdiction.

Partnerships

Working with stakeholders across the state, the NJCCIC's communications, outreach, and engagement strategy is executed by Cyber Liaison Officers, each with dedicated sector-specific portfolios. This component manages all incoming and outgoing communications to include fielding incident reports from across the state and disseminating tailored cybersecurity resources in the form of vulnerability advisories, intelligence analysis, and time-sensitive alerts to the NJCCIC's over one thousand members. This is one of the larger implications of an ISAO, sharing more than just information – it can become a centerpiece of a region's repository of knowledge on information assurance issues and best practices.

Benefits of the ISAO Model

One of the primary benefits of establishing ISAOs on a regional basis is the opportunity to engage with ISACs for the benefit of their members within a particular jurisdiction. Most ISACs cater to a specific industry, rather than a single locality, so their membership may be spread across the country. In some cases, such as with Financial Services ISAC, the membership consists of both domestic and international firms. The benefit of this arrangement is that the ISAC enjoys global context for the cyber threat landscape. However, a globally distributed membership can challenge the tailored delivery of services, especially for small- to medium-sized enterprises (SMEs) like community credit unions or local merchants, most of which are limited to a single geographical jurisdiction.

Regional ISAOs, therefore, are well positioned to partner with ISACs on behalf of their members concentrated in a particular region. In New Jersey for example, the NJCCIC reached agreements with the Financial Services ISAC and the National Health ISAC to tailor globally pooled cyber threat information for their New Jersey-based members. Not only are SMEs often ill-equipped to consume the massive quantities of data shared by sector-specific ISACs, they also struggle to make informed decisions based on this information in the absence of clarifying context and additional analytic capacity. State ISAOs can fill this void by filtering the amount of information that is shared and enriching it with relevant analytics and recommendations.

Automated Indicator Sharing

There are multiple ways to govern the relationship between ISACs and ISAOs, but preserving the culture of trust that ISACs have established over the last decade is paramount. For such a construct to be effective over time, ISAOs and ISACs must adopt uniform standards for handing cyber threat information and preserving the anonymity of sources throughout the analysis and exchange process. One of these emerging standards in both real-time and shared awareness is known as automated indicator sharing (AIS). Developed by the DHS, AIS serves as an automated protocol to identify and strip out personal information and limit the period of time information is retained.[5] ISACs are increasingly employing AIS along with major corporations and public utilities, making it a useful component for strengthening public-private information sharing partnerships. New Jersey, through the NJCCIC, has already begun using AIS with the federal government as well as the financial and healthcare sector ISACs. Establishing peer-to-peer connections between each party's servers breaks down the vertical information sharing silos that hinder shared situational awareness and can help widen awareness of valuable state and local incident information.

With the ongoing implementation of the *Cybersecurity Act of 2015*, it is essential to incorporate state and local governments into the AIS dialogue. Establishing and sustaining the capability to use AIS, especially as it relates to procuring, building, and maintaining the infrastructure, will require financial support from the federal government. One valuable vehicle for this support is the State Homeland Security Grant Program, which can earmark funds for ISAO standards implementation and help support widespread adoption of AIS.

Protecting County- and Municipal-Level Governments

Perhaps the greatest benefit of a state-level ISAO is illustrated by the resources provided for county and municipal governments. If states are poorly equipped to manage the security environment of their existing networks, the situation is even worse for local governments. While local governments are eligible for the MS-ISAC's network monitoring services, the sheer number of entities outstrips the single ISAC's capacity to provide services. Multiple regional or state-level ISAO, however, would be well positioned to deliver managed security services, at least in the form of networking monitoring, to county and local governments within their states. Most counties across the United States can barely afford to purchase intrusion prevention systems, a basic information assurance tool to monitor activity on a network and detect malicious traffic. For those that have the technology, managing the ensuing onslaught of logs can be both cost and time prohibitive.

State governments, by contrast, with the proper allocation of human, technical, and fiscal resources, are in a much better position to monitor small localities' networks for cyber threats. The information gleaned from monitoring county networks can, in turn, be analyzed by the ISAO and then shared to promote broader awareness of local cyber threats. In addition to monitoring for county and local governments, state-level ISAOs should be the primary command and control mechanism for coordinating statewide cyber incident response. Today, state and local governments rely exclusively on the United States Computer Emergency Readiness Team (US-CERT) and the MS-ISAC for incident response services. Most incidents do not rise to a high enough threshold to warrant US-CERT's intervention, leaving MS-ISAC to manage a portfolio of fifty states and hundreds of municipalities. This is an overwhelming number; incident response is a resource-intensive discipline, making it operationally and fiscally prohibitive for a single ISAC to serve such a broad constituency. An alternative to this single monolithic structure is a federated model with groups organized on a regional basis. In this respect, regional and state ISAOs are well positioned to field incident reports from local, county, and states agencies and both organize response efforts and deploy resources based on the severity of the incident and the resources available.

POLICY RECOMMENDATION

Information sharing should remain a key tenet of national information assurance policies and cybersecurity debate. The years 2015 and 2016 produced encouraging signs for introducing incentives to drive private sector participation. In order to construct a more comprehensive information sharing regime, however, it is critical to address the institutional gap that exists at the state and local level. Most ISACs limit their services to specific sectors and the MS-ISAC, while an invaluable resource for many state and local governments, lacks the resources to scale its services to all interested organizations.

Regional and state-level ISAOs provide an opportunity to bridge the cyber threat intelligence divide between the federal, state, and local governments and enhance cross-sector collaboration within specific jurisdictions. Expanding the number of these organizations would help build information assurance capacity at the levels it is needed most. A logical starting point for regional and state-level ISAOs is State and Major Urban Area Fusion Centers. These centers are existing institutions that are owned and operated by state and local governments, but supported from the federal government through "deployed personnel, training, technical assistance, exercise support, security clearances, connectivity to federal systems, technology, and grant funding."[6] Their primary purpose is to assist state law enforcement and local governments while enhancing threat information sharing from intelligence and national law enforcement bodies.

By integrating regional and state-level ISAOs with the national network for Fusion Centers, state and local governments will benefit from pooled resources and access to existing services and institutional ties that are critical to the operation of an ISAO. Demonstrated in New Jersey, the colocation of law enforcement, emergency management, and homeland security professionals at all levels of government helps to coordinate response efforts and contributes to shared situational awareness. Given that each Fusion Center is unique, ISAOs will likewise enjoy sufficient latitude to develop standards and practices in accordance with state and local norms and privacy expectations. In this respect, each of these ISAOs will benefit from existing public-private partnerships within each jurisdiction.

The integration of regional and state-level ISAOs into the national network of Fusion Centers is not without significant barriers. First and foremost, states and localities continue to struggle in the fight to attract and retain qualified personnel to perform the operational and analytical tasks of an ISAO. In addition, the start-up costs associated with establishing an ISAO, while hardly exorbitant, require prudent and strategic budget forecast in an era of fiscal constraints for state and local governments. Federal assistance is a key component of any ISAO funding strategy, but the initial and sustainment costs must be shared across all levels of government. Finally, because each Fusion Center interacts with the federal government but is owned and operated by state and local entities, there are unique policy issues to consider within each jurisdiction. Chief among these policy considerations is the application of state sunshine laws and the Freedom of Information Act.

The ISAO Standards Organization that was established as part of Executive Order 13691 will serve to assist the reconciliation of some of these challenges, but it will be incumbent upon each ISAO itself to overcome the majority of the relevant organizational and policy challenges. Implementing common standards will demand leadership from the next administration and close engagement with the National Fusion Center Association and the National Governor's Association to draft a strategy and implementation plan based on identified gaps and established best practices. Thus far, the Standards Organization, through its various working groups, has proven a valuable convening authority for representatives across the various sectors. These exchanges have included ISACs, trade organizations, corporations, and government entities, each benefiting from shared insights and the diverse experience of existing information sharing models. By evaluating different information sharing techniques, privacy policies, organizational structures, and regulatory regimes, the Standards Organization is well positioned to pool lessons learned and apply historical context to the development of future voluntary standards. In this respect, the diversity of the Standard Organization's composition is critical to its value for state and local governments.

CONCLUSION

Information sharing is not without its challenges but has demonstrated value as part of larger information assurance strategies for organizations of all shapes and sizes. The critical mass of experience and acceptance within local government and law enforcement bodies with information sharing is building, demonstrated by the capable integration and proven benefits of the NJCCIC in New Jersey. Many of the obstacles to expanding similar organizations and providing robust security capacity to new localities are not rooted in technology but policy issues. Shaping the political environment to support regional ISAOs and the security benefits they can bring to state and local governments may be difficult but will prove a worthwhile endeavor.

CHAPTER HIGHLIGHTS

Information Sharing Benefits. Companies and governments that participate in information sharing communities often weigh the risks of revealing vulnerabilities or suffering reputational harm versus the benefits of gleaning insights into real-time threats. The potential for this collective security is in the information about threats, gleaned from a victim or successful defense, and shared to others. Sharing information on current and previous incidents between businesses and public sector groups can shorten other defenders' responses. Most useful information on cyber threats reside on private sector networks (nearly 80 percent of U.S. critical infrastructure is owned by industry).

Private Sector Sharing Concerns. Organizations tend to exercise caution when sharing information with any external entity if what is shared could reveal existing vulnerabilities in their security posture. The concern is that unintentional release of this information, as the result of a breach, for example, could result in more effective attacks on the organization.

Cybersecurity Act of 2015. Companies are given specific procedures to abide by in order to gain the law's liability protections and it dictates what information and with whom it can be shared (ex. indicators of compromise, technical information about the attack). Central to the law is the role of the National Cybersecurity and Communications Integration Cell (NCCIC) under the Department of Homeland Security, which will act as the primary interface for sharing information with the federal government.

Executive Order 13691. Promotes public-private cooperation on cybersecurity information sharing by calling on the DHS to encourage the establishment of so-called Information Sharing and Analysis Organizations (ISAO).

ISAO Benefits. One of the primary benefits of establishing ISAOs on a regional basis is the opportunity this presents to interact with Information Sharing Analysis Centers (ISACs) for the benefit of their members within a particular jurisdiction. Most ISACs cater to a particular industry, rather than specific locality, so their membership may be spread across the country. State ISAOs can also filter the amount of information that is shared and enriching it with relevant analytics and recommendations to smaller companies and local governments and be the primary command and control mechanism for coordinating statewide cyber incident response.

Bridging the Divide. Regional and state-level ISAOs provide an opportunity to bridge the cyber threat intelligence divide between the federal, state, and local governments, and enhance cross-sector collaboration within specific jurisdictions. Expanding the number of these organizations would help build information assurance capacity at the levels it is needed most.

NOTES

1. *Cybersecurity Information Sharing Act of 2015*, S. 754, 114th Congress, 1st sess (October 28, 2015).

2. "Critical Infrastructure Protection: Challenges for Selected Agencies and Industry Sector," *U.S. Government Accountability Office*, GAO-03-233 (Washington, DC, 2003), http://www.gao.gov/assets/240/237450.html.

3. Denise Anderson, "Brothers in Arms: How the Financial Sector Fought the Brobot Attacks," RSA Conference, Asia Pacific and Japan, 2014. http://www.rsaconference.com/writable/presentations/file_upload/trm-t07-brothers-in-arms-how-the-financial-sector-fought-the-brobot-attacks.pdf.

4. "MS-ISAC Multi-State Information Sharing and Analysis Center," *Center for Internet Security*, accessed April 1, 2016, https://msisac.cisecurity.org.

5. United States Computer Emergency Readiness Team, "Automated Indicator Sharing (AIS)," *U.S. Department of Homeland Security*, accessed April 1, 2016, https://www.us-cert.gov/ais

6. "State and Major Urban Area Fusion Center," *U.S. Department of Homeland Security*, last modified April 21, 2016,https://www.dhs.gov/state-and-major-urban-area-fusion-centers.

Chapter 3

Protecting Industrial Control Systems in Critical Infrastructure

Robert M. Lee

In 2013 a team of cyber operators working in Iran set out to target U.S. infrastructure. The operation, sanctioned by senior Iranian government members, was a sensitive but important intelligence activity.

Many of the operators relished the opportunity to target U.S. infrastructure. For most of them the story of the Stuxnet worm launched against the Natanz uranium-enrichment facility, a pride and joy of Iran, hung on their minds.[1] The authorization to finally target the U.S. infrastructure in response was as exciting as it was nerve wracking. For other members of the team, this was nothing new. The more senior among them knew better than to think espionage and sabotage in the cyber domain was a novel phenomenon. They had all been involved in one way or another in operations dating back to at least the early 2000s and likewise knew many countries carried the same sensitive secrets. The campaign to target U.S. infrastructure was important but not revolutionary. The cyber operators began by targeting energy companies. The men were good hackers but did not know much about industrial control systems (ICS) such as supervisory control and data acquisition (SCADA) networks. These sensitive and often proprietary systems using embedded technologies, operational technology, remained foreign to most. Finding the exact entry points into systems controlling industrial infrastructure could be difficult, and even more challenging was knowing what to do once they obtained access. Therefore, many operators started by targeting the energy companies themselves and their contractors. These networks carried information about the ICS of interest while utilizing more familiar information technology (IT).

However, there were members of the team who understood engineering, control systems, and physical processes. These engineers were paired off with some of the more talented cyber operators and tasked with finding particularly sensitive targets, focused on energy, water, and transportation networks deemed critical infrastructure to the United States. During the operations to compromise these energy companies and steal documents from the contractor networks, one team gained access to the Bowman Dam. The operators spent weeks researching this target. At 245 feet tall and 800 feet wide, the Arthur Bowman Dam in Oregon definitely met the criteria for critical infrastructure in the United States; being able to sabotage it could lead to the loss of thousands of lives. It was precisely what the senior leadership desired in a target. It was an opportunity to gain access to a critical infrastructure system that could provide Iran with political leverage if necessary.

The operators who worked the target were not aware the U.S. Intelligence Community was monitoring the intrusion into the dam. The Iranians also were not aware that the dam they found was actually the Bowman *Avenue* dam, a much smaller one well below the threshold of critical infrastructure located in Rye, New York, until an article hit the Wall Street Journal in 2015 documenting the entire case.[2] To their credit, the media noted that the U.S. responders were initially unaware that the dam was the one in New York as well. After all, remotely learning about ICS networks both as defenders and as attackers can be extremely difficult.

Information Assurance in ICSs

This telling of the dam intrusion story is more fiction than fact. The Iranians did target a U.S. dam in 2013 as the *Wall Street Journal* revealed in 2015 but the rest of the details are a best guess account of how things might have occurred for the Iranians.[3] The substance of the problem remains the same however, demonstrating how difficult it can be to learn about ICS networks whether for offense or defense. The U.S. Department of Justice (DOJ) has since decided to indict Iranian operators involved in the breach.[4] The purpose of opening with this story is not to paint a picture of incompetence by adversaries or defenders, but to depict the difficulties associated with the ICS networks that make up U.S. critical, and noncritical but important, infrastructure.

The DOJ has labeled the effort by the Iranian operators an attack. However, not only is this a misuse of the word *attack* but an attack was never even possible at the Bowman Avenue Dam in New York. The Bowman Avenue Dam is about twenty feet tall and shores up a small waterway. Causing the flood gates to open would have little impact. The Iranians never engaged in offensive operations so the United States would describe the intrusion as Title 50 intelligence operation. Title 50 is the portion of the U.S. Code which covers covert action and intelligence operations while Title 10 deals with traditional military activities. There is an argument that the operation could have been considered Title 10 offensive operations under the context of military preparation of the environment. However, that designation would greatly jeopardize numerous U.S. Intelligence Community operations that operate under Title 50. On their face value these operations concern an adversary but would not accurately be called offense.[5]

Instead, it is important to note two considerations. Outside the context of the U.S. Code, the Iranian operations targeting the Bowman Avenue Dam were only intelligence gathering. In addition, there was never any possibility for the Iranians, or anyone else, to attack the dam as Bowman Avenue features no control system capable of operating the flood gate remotely by any person or adversary. This small, but vital, distinction underscores challenges in the policy discussions around cyber operations targeting ICS and highlights areas that are crucial for understanding the nature of cyber defense. Technical concepts matter greatly, and these distinctions are essential to better understanding the ICS community and their systems.

This chapter lays out the Sliding Scale of Cyber Security as it applies to ICS networks such as those that run hydroelectric dams, power grids, manufacturing facilities, oil and gas pipelines, oil drilling rigs, and more. Using this Sliding Scale, policymakers and defenders alike can better understand areas for improvement. ICS security differs from IT security in a number of ways; chief among these is that ICS networks operate physical systems such as turbines and assembly lines, demanding different priorities and approaches for security. The loss of human life or significant environmental damage is a possibility when discussing critical infrastructure where ICS is involved. Improving the quality of policy discussions around these systems and the collective understanding of their defense can help encourage investments in key areas to support U.S. national security through the protection of critical infrastructure.

THE SLIDING SCALE OF CYBER SECURITY

The Sliding Scale of "Cyber Security," hereafter referred to as the "sliding scale," was created for the purpose of adding nuance to the discussion of cybersecurity, specifically information assurance, by categorizing different types of investments (see figure 3.1). These categories are *architecture*, *passive defense*, *active defense*, *intelligence*, and *offense*. Each category has an impact on the other categories or relies upon them in some interconnected way. Likewise, cybersecurity policies developed ultimately strive to impact at least one of the categories as well. Understanding the categories ensures a proper discussion on the topic as well as better informed policies and guidance. The sections below discuss each category as well as a few recent references, models, or events that fall into each as they relate to the ICSs in critical infrastructure.

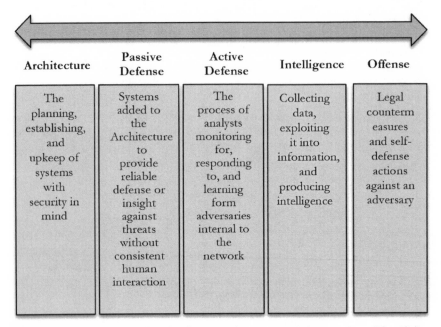

Architecture	Passive Defense	Active Defense	Intelligence	Offense
The planning, establishing, and upkeep of systems with security in mind	Systems added to the Architecture to provide reliable defense or insight against threats without consistent human interaction	The process of analysts monitoring for, responding to, and learning form adversaries internal to the network	Collecting data, exploiting it into information, and producing intelligence	Legal counterm easures and self-defense actions against an adversary

Figure 3.1 The Sliding Scale of Cyber Security. *Source*: Robert M. Lee. "The Sliding Scale of Cyber Security." The SANS Institute. August 2015, https://www.sans.org/reading-room/whitepapers/analyst/sliding-scale-cyber-security-36240.

Architecture

Architecture refers to "the planning, establishing, and upkeep of systems with security in mind."[6] This category of the sliding scale is where most security issues originate and what the other categories are often attempting to address in their relation to an adversary. For example, a software patch often addresses a vulnerability identified in a piece of software. The industrial control system computer emergency response team (ICS-CERT) at the Department of Homeland Security routinely disseminates advisories on vulnerabilities in ICSs that recommend infrastructure owners patch these systems. Patching them sometimes, but not always, eliminates an adversaries' ability to take advantage of that vulnerability to gain access to or deny access to that system. Patching and maintaining infrastructure resides in the architecture category of the sliding scale; it is not an act of defense but maintenance to the systems being defended.

The Problem—Resources Spent on Patching Insecure Systems

In IT environments, patching a system often leads to eliminating the vulnerability. However, that isn't necessarily the case in control systems. Dale

Peterson, CEO of ICS security and research firm DigitalBond, has been highlighting the ineffectiveness of patching in ICS for years. In a presentation in 2016, he made a bold claim: "90% of ICS vulnerabilities do not increase risk to the ICS."[7] This might sound controversial, but makes sense for a few different reasons.

Patching systems internal to an ICS is a difficult task. The vendors of these control systems and their software must test and validate the patches before they're distributed, or else users will void the warranty on their often multimillion dollar systems. Patching is intensive on the end users as well. After the patches are validated; they still must be tested in the specific ICS environment they are being deployed in to avoid unintended effects. This process takes time and even afterward, patching cannot be deployed except during scheduled outages of the ICS. As an example, an electric generation facility may be taken offline for maintenance about once every six months; at that time the patch is applied as late as two to three years after vulnerabilities are identified. This leaves a long time for adversaries to take advantage of the vulnerability.

Patches may also do little to solve the underlying software flaw. In a sampling of vulnerabilities, the security firm DigitalBond found that a number of vendor patches did little more than disable the exploit that had been written for them, rather than fix the underlying vulnerability.[8] Vendors would identify the code sample that researchers or adversaries were using to show a vulnerability in their software and design their fix to make sure the exploit would no longer be effective. But these corrections would not fix the flaw in the software itself, leaving adversaries to simply develop new code that could impact the system through the same vulnerability. Even more concerning, when a patch gets issued, only customers of that product are alerted, which is problematic because many vendors are interconnected and the vulnerability may impact other products and firms that never find out. As an example, one security firm identified a vulnerability in a specific software development tool.[9] ICS-CERT then issues an advisory for the vulnerability to the company that created the tool. However, many major control system vendors utilized this development tool and the vulnerability impacted all of them. Unfortunately, no advisory was issued to all of those customers and many vendors likely did not even know the vulnerability existed in their infrastructure.

Many adversaries do not need these vulnerabilities to impact ICS but there are some vulnerabilities that are more impactful than others. Internet-connected control systems that have a vulnerability to allow adversaries to directly take over the system are concerning and should be patched immediately. However, many of the vulnerabilities released are nothing an adversary would need or use. As an example, most systems within an ICS are designed so that they can interact fully. If someone using the system requests information, it is made available. If someone knows how to send a command to shut off the system, it will comply. These systems were designed for functionality not security. In some cases, an adversary can achieve their goal just by gaining access to a network; they do not need vulnerabilities in the systems to learn the control process and how to manipulate it, they merely need to use the ICS as it was designed.

Passive Defense

Passive defense can be understood as "systems added to the architecture to provide consistent protection against, or insight into, threats without constant human interaction."[10] Passive defenses are add-ons to the architecture, similar to firewalls, and thus will not be as effective when compared to better designed systems. Ideally, passive defenses should be adaptable placeholders that address security deficiencies, until a more permanent capability can be developed into the architecture. Additionally, the passive defense systems, whether software or hardware, add value but are not expected to expel every intrusion. They do not require constant human interaction, but rather provide visibility and situational awareness into the network, without necessarily blocking any adversary actions.

Passive defenses are tools. They are also the most significant focus of most security discussions including security control frameworks. A number of current standards focus heavily on passive defenses as well as architecture, including the National Institute of Standards and Technology's (NIST)'s Cybersecurity Framework and the International Society of Automation (ISA)'s ISA99—Industrial Automation and Control Systems Security standards.[11] Understanding the role these passive defenses play, their importance but not exclusive relevance, is critical.

The Problem—A Misunderstanding of Community Priorities and the ICS Environment

Technology and security vendors are creating very effective passive defenses. Endpoint security solutions, anti-malware technologies, cyber situational awareness platforms, and next-generation firewalls are commonplace in IT networks. Unfortunately, these technologies are not as commonplace in ICS networks. This is not solely an issue of vendor validation like the patches, or of security culture awareness, although those issues can complicate the matter. Instead, the bigger roadblock to adoption is a misunderstanding of the systems that the passive defenses are meant to protect.

Technology companies are continually utilizing acquisitions of smaller start-ups to bring innovative technologies into their organization. Relying on start-ups can help reduce the risk and cost of internally developing and innovating in large organizations. However, ICS organizations adopt these security technologies at a much slower rate. These operators have to critically examine new security technologies before adopting them into sensitive critical infrastructure networks. Yet, these same security start-ups need to gain customers quickly, raise funds often through venture capital, and continuously satisfy and attract new investors. This creates an underlying tension; many of these start-ups do not deeply understand one vertical in the industry, such as electric versus oil versus gas, let alone the entirety of the ICS industry. Many develop solutions that simply are not effective against the real problems in ICS networks.

As an example, a common current industry trend is the development of security tools that reside on individual computers, end points, and use faster methods to patch systems. As previously discussed, the patching issue is more fundamental to the software life cycle itself than any one technology can fix. Additionally, end point security solutions and next-generation firewalls can help alleviate traditional and untargeted malware but do not prevent a determined threat. For example, when the Iranians attempted to access the Bowman Dam network, a misconfigured system was accessible via the internet. A firewall could have helped address that visibility into the network and identified new connections. But on the system itself, if malware targeted the actual manipulation of controls required to open the sluice gate, if it had been possible, a passive defense alone would not be effective. Once the malicious software made it past the network perimeter, protected by the firewall, it could operate on the ICS network like any other user.

If it had been possible to remotely manipulate the New York dam's control system, the commands would have been legitimate control system communications. This begs the question; can't those commands be patterned and blocked against normal activity in the ICS? In fact they can. The problem is that if a passive defense system ever has a false positive, thereby blocking legitimate communications in an ICS, it could be catastrophic for system operation. And all passive defense tools still register false positives, despite marketing materials that state otherwise. Right or wrong, it is a completely different conversation to state that an adversary brought down critical infrastructure that killed people than it is to state that a defensive system the infrastructure owners bought and installed was responsible for a similarly destructive accident. Mistakes in these industries have severe consequences.

Active Defense

An active defense is "the process of analysts monitoring for, responding to, learning from, and applying their knowledge to threats internal to a network."[12] In essence, it is the effort of the human defender to identify and counter an adversary internal to the defender's network. In the context of critical infrastructure networks this process excels.

Adversaries are not as powerful and all-knowing as they are often portrayed. In ICS networks, intruders must make sense of foreign systems and understand the engineering behind physical equipment and processes in hopes of inflicting sufficient damage. At the same time, ICS networks are smaller and more static, making it less resource intensive for defenders to learn about and safeguard their environment. In short, adversaries have a more difficult time conducting the most concerning types of attacks, whereas defenders have an easier time safeguarding a well-maintained ICS than a traditional IT network.

The Problem—Getting the ICS Ready and Finding and Training the Defenders

One of the biggest challenges with performing an active defense is ensuring that the control system environment can support it. When an active defender needs access to data for review but cannot retrieve it from the network, they are effectively useless. This is a common issue in ICS networks where legacy infrastructure has made little data available to determine when an adversary is in the network. However, this is an area that can be addressed in the architecture phase of the sliding scale. Having access to the environment to determine when an adversary is in the ICS is not important solely for protecting the ICS, but also for determining what happened after the intrusion.

The ICS-CERT released their year in review for 2014 and highlighted that of 245 incidents reported, 94 of them, 38 percent, were of unknown origin.[13] In other words, the ICS-CERT and the defenders onsite could not determine how the incident occurred or how the adversary or malware gained access to the network nearly four out of every ten security incidents. That is not a problem of advanced adversaries but instead of a lack of visibility into the ICS network—a shortfall in basic data collection, event logging, and access to information on these control systems. The largest known infection vector in 2014 was spear phishing, where messages with information of specific interest to the target are used to carry infected files or malicious links; 17 percent of the reported instances were a result of spear phishing. These forty-two incidents may represent that the most common infection vector is actually spear phishing. However, most infrastructure sites do not let external e-mails into the ICS network. Users access business networks and traditional IT systems for e-mail. So this metric more than likely indicates poor data, stemming from the lack of visibility into ICS networks. This serves to highlight that the main area for seeing infections in ICS at the moment tends to be business networks connected to the control systems, including e-mail servers and file shares.

The issues of *preparing* for an active defense are appropriately handled in the architecture category, but the process of *executing* an active defense as part of the sliding scale still needs attention. After getting the environment ready and using passive defenses to gain visibility while eliminating untargeted malware, defenders have to be prepared for focused adversaries. In fact, it is naïve to assume that a human threat actor is going to be completely stopped by a passive system placed on the network. Only trained and prepared people, operating in an ICS with good architecture and passive defenses, can truly and consistently counter persistent and adaptive adversaries. However, a human versus human engagement requires trained personnel and good intelligence.

Intelligence and Offense

Intelligence is a well-understood process that involves gathering data, developing it into information, and combining that to produce assessments which can help cover gaps in understanding about an issue or adversary. Offense is often understood as the process of disrupting, denying, degrading, deceiving, or destroying a system, its data, or its communication paths. The difference between these two categories is important especially in ICS networks. The United States conducts intelligence operations worldwide but would like to greatly discourage attacks on critical infrastructure.[14]

The Problem—Mislabeling Activities Encourage Inappropriate Responses

Most incidents identified as a cyber-attack in the media, and in many instances by the security industry and government, are actually espionage efforts. Identifying intelligence operations as attacks places these legitimate activities, conducted by the United States and its allies, into question. In the ICS community, an attack can mean the loss of human life or severe damage to the operating environment. Espionage and the theft of information is concerning, but not an attack; it is an adversary's intelligence operation. Malicious software in ICS is often untargeted and incidental. This malware may pose slight harm but only accidentally and it should be addressed with changes at the architecture or passive defense stages. An attack is different, causing damage, disruption, or loss of data from manipulating a control system. Attacks on ICS are serious infractions and could potentially rise to an act of armed conflict resulting in significant repercussions for states.

Investing in capabilities that compromise ICS networks or disrupting them can have importance for national security. The ability to cripple an adversary's infrastructure in the midst of conflict is appealing especially if that infrastructure consists of sites such as integrated air defenses that guard against United States and its allied pilots and munitions. However, the ability to create destructive effects on an opponent's system is only a small piece of the puzzle. These capabilities don't contribute directly to improved information assurance of our own systems and so are more limited in their utility for defenders.

RECOMMENDATIONS—MAKE BETTER SYSTEMS AND FOCUS ON TRAINING DEFENDERS

It should be no surprise that many of the control systems used in America were built without security in mind. It is possible to blame the vendors and demand that they develop more secure products. However, vendors would be right to push back and note that two immediate challenges exist. First, when there is a request for proposals to develop new products many customers do not include any desire for security features or specifications for what is needed. This leaves the vendors having to guess as to what security measures may be important. Second, when the vendor does eventually develop more secure products, there is a price increase associated with it that the infrastructure customers often do not want to pay for, so vendors choose different, more insecure, systems. This is a long-standing issue in the community but presents opportunities for influence from policymakers as part of the evolving discussion around ICS security.

Policymakers could try to engage vendors directly, to gather information and understand ideal levers of influence such as tax incentives to develop more secure control systems sold with little to no increase in price. These incentives could also target customers, to drive purchases of better secured systems. The tax code comes with its own limitations; besides being slow to respond to new changes, not all of the affected vendors are U.S. owned or fully understand the problem. Another approach to drive incentives for good investment by vendors and customers is to create procurement requirements for government purchasing. Federal facilities, military infrastructure, and vehicles, and other government uses of control systems could all be subject to requirements for more secure ICS. By influencing bids for contracts of more secure albeit costly systems, vendors would have more direct incentives to develop these products for availability to the civilian infrastructure owners. Although there is no panacea, security technologies can provide improved security in the interim.

The good news is that the industry is already policing itself in the area of security technologies. A solid supply and demand ecosystem and critical valuations of companies and their technologies are beginning to emerge, for the most part, as needed. In this area, policy should be limited to encouraging research activities and funding, similar to the Defense Advanced Research Project Agency (DARPA)'s Rapid Isolation and Characterization Systems (RADICS) Broad Agency Announcement (BAA).[15] The RADICS BAA put forth $77 million to invest in technologies useful for ICS security especially focused on the electric grid. This has been well received by the industry so far and can help catalyze improved awareness and responsiveness in security tools.

Other ongoing policy efforts include the Energy Policy Modernization Act of 2015 that addresses physical infrastructure as well as efforts to fund research into forensic tools for ICS networks.[16] These efforts to help fund new technologies and reward companies that are performing well are useful but dangerous if taken too far. American's tax dollars are being used to fund security companies that have to compete against each other, creating an interesting dilemma. A few good efforts to encourage investment into security technologies are useful, but too much investment will create a less competitive market where companies attempting to innovate must compete against government-funded initiatives. The recommendation here is simple: a little influence goes a long way but excessive funding and well-intentioned policy could stymie innovation and disrupt the security ecosystem.

To maximize the investment outcome, policymakers attempting to help influence the security of critical infrastructure should invest in the active defense category of the sliding scale. Trained information assurance personnel, working to defend control systems, can not only help counter adversaries but also help change the security culture at ICS organizations. In the process these trained defenders can also make recommendations for better architecture and passive defense investments to get the various ICS communities into the position to have an effective active defense strategy. Finding and training the right people to be active defenders can be expensive and there are a limited number of personnel who understand ICS security.

A typical SANS Institute course, the leading cybersecurity training provider in the world, costs roughly $5,500 for a five-day training course.[17] That, bundled with time away from the office, airfare, and hotel costs can quickly mean a true cost of $10,000–$12,000 for organizations. For organizations that can afford the cost they clearly see value, as thousands of people attend SANS training, including their ICS security courses, each year. But the amount of trained personnel will always pale in comparison to the demand for skilled defenders. One training class for five days is not enough for a professional who needs to attend training on a regular basis to hone their skills and stay ahead of new threats. Organizations are being asked to invest heavily in advanced security training to counter highly capable threats. This is an area where policy could make a significant impact both in expanding access to valuable curricula and in incentivizing the development of new training pipelines.

Policymakers should also consider encouraging cybersecurity training for critical infrastructure personnel. Organizations absorb a portion of the costs as they receive value in newly capable defenders, but legislative and regulatory levers that lower the true cost of training could help to motivate organizations train a greater proportion of their staff. These trained personnel will not only help to counter adversaries and make recommendations along the sliding scale, but also help to change the security culture in the community. There will also be more informed ICS security experts who are able to influence policy discussions and create an intellectual life cycle to support furthering critical infrastructure security.

CONCLUSION

ICSs present a set of challenges to the assumptions underlying information assurance. Policymakers seeking to influence ICS security need to understand the control system operating environment using models like the Sliding Scale of Cyber Security. Utilizing this model, the most effective investments focus on architectural improvements and the active defense category. Designing and integrating more secure systems into critical infrastructure networks will have a positive impact that has the most significant return on investment of any other actions for security. Investing in the training of personnel can ensure that trained defenders are ready to help guide ICS networks, build a broader and better educated security community, and expand the number of individuals ready to identify and counter capable adversaries. The combination of more secure infrastructure and better trained defenders will drive marked improvements in ICS security. Understanding the true scope of the problem facing critical infrastructure security requires trained defenders operating in environments conducive to identifying threats and learning from them. For policymakers, expanding this community and reinforcing secure architectural practices can help improve how we protect control systems and the critical infrastructure that undergirds modern society.

CHAPTER HIGHLIGHTS

Industrial Control System Vulnerabilities. Industrial control systems (ICS) such as supervisory control and data acquisition (SCADA) networks control critical infrastructure including hydroelectric dams, power grids, manufacturing facilities, oil and gas pipelines, oil drilling rigs, and others. Finding the exact entry points into infrastructure is difficult; therefore, operators often first target the networks of associated critical infrastructure companies and their contractors. These networks have information about the ICS of interest while utilizing information technology (IT) more familiar to adversaries.

Sliding Scale of Cyber Security. Created for the purpose of adding nuance to the discussion of cyber Security, specifically information assurance, by categorizing different types of investments. These categories are: *architecture*—considering security when planning, establishing, and patching systems; *passive defense*—adding defensive security systems to the architecture without consistent human interaction; *active defense*—analysts monitoring and responding to threats on the network; *intelligence*—collecting data/processing data to get useful information; and *offense*—legal self-defense countermeasures against an enemy.

Architecture. In IT environments, patching a system often leads to eliminating the vulnerability. However, that isn't necessarily the case in control systems. The patch is often only written to prevent a particular exploit rather than address the vulnerability.

Passive Defense. Add-ons to the architecture, similar to firewalls, thus will not be as effective when compared to better designed systems. Ideally, passive defenses should be adaptable placeholders that address security deficiencies, until a more permanent capability can be developed into the architecture.

Active Defense. One of the biggest challenges with performing an active defense is ensuring that the control system environment can support it. When an active defender needs access to data for review but cannot retrieve it from the network, they are effectively useless. This is a common issue in ICS networks where legacy infrastructure has made little data available to determine when an adversary is in the network.

Intelligence/Offense. The difference between these two categories is important especially in ICS networks. The United States conducts intelligence operations worldwide but would like to greatly discourage attacks on critical infrastructure.

Recommendation. Policymakers should invest in the active defense by training ICS information assurance personnel, who can then recommend better architecture and passive defense investments for ICS facilities.

NOTES

1. Kim Zetter, "An Unprecedented Look at Stuxnet, the World's First Digital Weapon," *Wired.* November 3, 2014, accessed March 16, 2016, http://www.wired.com/2014/11/countdown-to-zero-day-stuxnet/.

2. Danny Yardon, "Iranian Hackers Infiltrated New York Dam in 2013," *Wall Street Journal*, December 20, 2015, accessed March 16, 2016, http://www.wsj.com/articles/iranian-hackers-infiltrated-new-york-dam-in-2013-1450662559.

3. Ibid.

4. "Manhattan U.S. Attorney Announces Charges Against Seven Iranians For Conducting Coordinated Campaign Of Cyber Attacks Against U.S. Financial Sector On Behalf Of Islamic Revolutionary Guard Corps-Sponsored Entities," Department of Justice, March 24, 2016, accessed March 26, 2016, https://www.justice.gov/usao-sdny/pr/manhattan-us-attorney-announces-charges-against-seven-iranians-conduct-ing-coordinated.

5. For more, see chapter 16—"Understanding Military Cyber Operations."

6. Robert M. Lee. "The Sliding Scale of Cyber Security." The SANS Institute. August 2015. https://www.sans.org/reading-room/whitepapers/analyst/sliding-scale-cyber-security-36240.

7. Dale Peterson, "Why 90% of ICS Vulnerabilities Don't Increase Risk," Proceedings of SANS ICS Summit, Florida, Orlando, https://files.sans.org/summit/2016_ICS_Security_Summit/PDFs/Why-90-Percent-of-ICS-Vulner-abilities-Dont-Increase-Risk-and-How-to-Identify-the-Important-Ones-That-Do-Dale-Peterson-Digital-Bond.pdf.

8. For an example of such an advisory see ICSA-16-077-01 here https://ics-cert.us-cert.gov/advisories/ICSA-16-077-01.

9. Dale Peterson, "Why 90% of ICS Vulnerabilities Don't Increase Risk."

10. Robert M. Lee, "The Sliding Scale of Cyber Security."

11. "Cybersecurity Framework," *NIST*, February 12, 2014, accessed March 16, 2016, http://www.nist.gov/cyberframework/; "ISA99—Industrial Automation and Control Systems Security," International Society of Automation, https://www.isa.org/isa99/.

12. Media sources have encouraged a discussion where "active defense" has been mislabeled as "hack back" or some other sort of intelligence gathering from adversary networks. This has been echoed in a few ill-placed academic papers and conference proceedings. The accurate use of active defense is exactly as it sounds: actively defending the network. No aspect of going into an adversary's network either with small tokens or actively could be construed as defense vice intelligence efforts.

13. "Year in Review FY2014," *ICS-CERT*, January 1, 2015, https://ics-cert.us-cert.gov/sites/default/files/Annual_Reports/Year_in_Review_FY2014_Final.pdf.

14. White House, U.S. International Strategy for Cyberspace, 2011—https://www.whitehouse.gov/sites/default/files/rss_viewer/international_strategy_for_cyberspace.pdf.

15. "DARPA Exploring Ways to Protect Nation's Electrical Grid from Cyber Attack," *DARPA RSS,* December 14, 2015, accessed April 18, 2016, http://www.darpa.mil/news-events/2015-12-14.

16. *Energy Policy Modernization Act of 2015,* 114th Congress, 2012 Session (September 9, 2015) Congress.gov.

17. "SANS Information Security Training," *The SANS Institute,* accessed March 16, 2016, https://www.sans.org/.

Chapter 4

Safer at Any Speed

The Roads Ahead for Automotive Cyber Safety Policy

Joshua Corman and Beau Woods

"Our dependence on connected technology is growing faster than our ability to secure it in areas affecting public safety and human life."
—*iamthecavalry.org*[1]

Failures in technology dependencies of modern automobiles harm public safety and human life. The well-publicized effects of a high-consequence failure would be likely to trigger a crisis of confidence in the stability of key markets and have a material impact on the U.S. economy. While government has resisted legislation and regulation of these technology dependencies, it must still take a role in assuring that the goals of public safety are clearly defined and effectively achieved. This chapter identifies automotive cybersecurity contributions to public safety and human life affecting public trust. It then reviews progress to date. Finally, it frames where government can use policy levers to lead, follow, and stay out of the way.

Modern vehicles are a hybrid of mechanical and cyber technologies. Today, cars roll off assembly lines with dozens of computers and sensors, communicating through wired and wireless signals. These connected technologies aim to improve safety, environmental impact, and performance for consumers as well as increasing comfort and convenience. Failures in the cyber systems that underlie these vehicles could harm public safety and human life ("cyber safety"). Highly publicized effects of high-consequence failures are likely to trigger a crisis of confidence in the stability of key markets with material effect on the American economy. While the government has resisted legislation and regulation around the dependence on these technologies across automotive manufacturers, this chapter suggests there is a narrow role for government to help improve security and lower tolerance for failure.

For a long time, consequences of cybersecurity failure were annoyances, and could be dealt with through purely information assurance. Now that cars are computers on wheels, "bits & bytes" affect "flesh & blood." Where cybersecurity impacts public safety ("cyber safety"), consequences are measured not in dollars but in deaths. These cyber safety issues merit a higher level of concern than most of those handled under information assurance.

There are clearly delineated areas where the government should lead, follow, and stay out of the way in cyber safety policy. For topics affecting public safety and the public good, regulations provide baseline assurances—outside of the technology realm. The cyber and the physical have collided, necessitating attention and an appropriate response from both the private sector and the government. The consequences of failure will be measured in lives lost from immediate impacts, and sustained harm to public safety and the U.S. economy for years to come.

Cyber Safety on the *Real* Superhighway

Responsibly securing new vehicles with so many networked technologies is essential. With proper implementation, technology innovation will save lives. Alternatively, failures will lead to loss of life and shatter public confidence in key markets, impacting the broader U.S. economy for years until safer architectures can be designed, developed, and built. All systems fail, therefore connected vehicles need to be designed and equipped to handle failure. At present, these vehicles are not tolerant of failure and vulnerabilities are becoming more evident. Car hacking is now demonstrable and increasing in volume and variety—in March 2016 the FBI issued a public service announcement on the increased risks of remote car hacking.[2] Urgency is the watchword.

Resilient systems reduce harm from failure, through preparation and sound engineering. Leveraging the multistakeholder *5 Star Automotive Cyber Safety Framework* published by iamthecavalry.org in 2014, this chapter explains the need for automakers to better prepare for failures and improve cars' resilience against both accidents and adversaries.[3] While the private sector is attempting to develop many of the required safety measures over time, some will require incentives, assistance, and coordination, while others are not likely to ever happen effectively without direct intervention from the government. For purposes of this chapter, a "policy failure" is defined as a public automotive cybersecurity incident that triggers a crisis of confidence in the connected vehicles and related markets. The range of impact from such a failure will be partly predicated on who was responsible and to what degree the event affects trust in automakers. For example, there is a substantial difference between an isolated injury caused by an accidental cybersecurity failure in one vehicle affecting only one manufacturer and an attack affecting many vehicles, and most models, from many OEMs.

The Stakes and the Race

In 2014, 32,675 lives were lost in vehicular accidents.[4] Of those accidents, 94 percent were due to human error.[5] Technology promises to significantly reduce mistakes made by tired, distracted, inexperienced, or impaired drivers. This is one reason the National Highway Traffic Safety Administration (NHTSA) has been so bullish on vehicle-to-vehicle and vehicle-to-infrastructure communications technologies alongside the push toward autonomous and semiautonomous vehicles. Beyond the lives saved, driverless vehicles and technology-assisted traffic flows could significantly cut down on congestion, fuel consumption, and pollution.

Embracing these technologies and integrating them into our daily lives makes trust in their secure design and manufacture critical. This is a precarious moment in history where cars and trucks currently on the market are increasingly prone to failures from accidents and adversaries, but are not yet prepared to handle said failures. Trust in these technologies could translate into tremendous gains in automotive efficiency and safety. Loss of this trust could mean substantial missed opportunities, loss of life, and a crisis of consumer confidence.

Collectively, we're in a race between the manifestation of cyber safety failures in connected vehicles and our ability to respond. Traditional modes of identifying, investigating, and treating automotive failures assume incidence will be low, conditions consistent, and that triggers will leave evidence. However, failures in cyber safety can spread across a fleet of vulnerable cars within seconds after a single "patient zero" is affected. By comparison, engineering and implementing new cyber safety capabilities can take years. Our physically oriented risk management approach to preventing wide-scale harm is orders of magnitude too slow to deal with this new epidemiological problem. The situation commands decisive and coordinated action between Congress, Executive Branch agencies, such as the NHTSA, insurers, the automotive industry, and other affected stakeholders.

Software and Technology Truths

As previously stated, all systems fail. This is true in physical engineering and is even more prevalent in software development. Across all types of software, the rate of flaws or defects is measured for every 1,000 lines of code (LoC). No amount of engineering effort would find every bug and indeed it wouldn't be economical to do so.[6] It only takes one flaw to create an accident or allow access to an adversary. Therefore, more code translates into more problems. To put this into context, the Windows 7 operating system has just under 40 million LoC, and despite being subject to one of the most mature security programs in the world, it still has to update a dozen or so critical and high-security flaws per month.[7] A modern vehicle has over 100 million LoC, but no automotive manufacturer has anywhere near so rigorous or sophisticated a security program.[8] Software in connected vehicles is undeniably vulnerable—increasingly so, as ever more features are added. Connectivity dramatically increases software vulnerability exposures to a greater number and variety of interactions—friendly, hostile, and unexpected. Connected vehicle software will fail—and fail often. The prudent response is to be prepared for failure and build in the capacity to tolerate and overcome this failure.

What Changed? Connectivity

The presence of software in vehicles is not new. What *is* new is the connectivity. There are a growing number and variety of ways to remotely access a vehicle's computer systems. For a time, the automotive industry took comfort in the fact that hacking a car would require physical access. For some time now, onboard systems have been exposed to remote attacks through varying means and at different ranges (see figure 4.1) through the TPMS (Tire Pressure Monitoring System), 4G LTE Wi-Fi hotspots, and even smart key receivers standard in some vehicles.[9] Worse, even "dumb cars" that are not remotely accessible become accessible with the growing number of insurance and aftermarket information collection devices—which enjoy unfettered access to the car's central network controller and everything it touches.[10]

Not only are these remote attack vectors growing in theory, increasingly researchers are showing proof-of-concept demonstrations for them.

There's No Money in Hacking Cars?

Over the course of 2015, a series of demonstrations and increasing engagement with the research community forced the automotive industry to concede that there were avenues for attackers to gain access to vehicles and wreak havoc. This wasn't enough to trigger action though; it merely shifted automaker rhetoric and rationales for inaction. They moved from denying there was a problem to claiming, "But no one would hurt you." Even some of the researchers shared this blind spot, echoing "There's no money in hacking cars."

Putting aside the point that there are plenty of ways to monetize malicious hacking of vehicles, both arguments against better security are founded on a false assumption that the only motivation for would-be attackers is

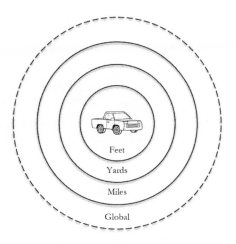

Vehicle Exposure to Cyber Intrusions	
Range	*Susceptible Vehicle Component*
Feet	Tire Pressure Monitoring Keyless Entry/Remote Start Bluetooth[2]
Yards	Wi-Fi[1]
Miles	3G/4G/5G/LTE Modem[1,2] Radio Data System
Global	Internet

These ranges represent distances in the official specification for the particular technologies. Through techniques such as targeted antennas and signal strength boosting, the distance can be amplified 10-100x.

[1] Both Wi-Fi and 3G/4G/5G/LTE imply Internet connectivity.
[2] Many of the third-party dongles, such as those used by insurance companies or rental fleets to capture driving habits, use Bluetooth or 3G/4G/5G/LTE Modems. Also, most vehicles today have connectivity through 3G/4G/5G/LTE Modem which may be "always-on" even if the owner has not subscribed, such as Cheverolet UConnect, GM OnStar, Hyundai BlueLink, BMW ConnectedDrive, etc.

Figure 4.1   Vehicle Exposure to Cyber Intrusions

Table 4.1 Sample Automotive Cyber Safety Incidents

Motivation	Real-World Example
Profit—financial	Ransomware "Pay us a Bitcoin to Start your ambulance"
Nation-state military/economic/spying	Disable military convoys or target commercial trucking and harm market confidence
Ideological and extremist	Strike fear/indiscriminant harm
Activist/protest (e.g., Anonymous, LulzSec)	Disabling public transport
Curiosity and/or collateral damage	Accidental/incidental harm
Murphy	Failure of safety systems, such as brakes

financial. There are as many motivations for attackers as are found in the human condition. Further, malicious intent is not a prerequisite to harm. In fact, every threat model should start with the adversary known as Murphy (and his famous law, which expects that anything which can go wrong, will). Table 4.1 depicts a few potential real-world examples of automotive hacking. If steps are not taken to address automotive software vulnerabilities in a timely manner then connected vehicles and fleets will be at greater risk.

Why take solace in the assumption that no one *would* hurt you? A preferable posture is one where few people *could* hurt you. "On the internet, every sociopath is your next door neighbor" says Dan Geer of In-Q-Tel.[11] Once automakers decided to connect cars to the internet, it no longer mattered what *most* would do; it becomes an issue of what any *one* person might do. Accidents are a distinct, but no less, critical class of failures. Toyota's unintended acceleration problems have been plausibly traced to poorly designed and implemented software code.[12] Investigations cited several methods by which these weaknesses and flaws could have triggered conditions that lead to death in several cases. Many of the same quality mechanisms that thwart adversaries will also help avoid, identify, analyze, and inoculate against accidental failures.

What are the consequences if an attack on connected vehicles created sudden accidents and trapped dozens in New York's Lincoln tunnel leading to deaths and injuries? What if a terrorist group such as ISIS claimed credit and threatened similar attacks against other cities in the United States? The automotive industry, Congress, and the Executive Branch would have to consider a range of factors—how many models were affected, how many lives could be lost, what's the economic impact on the targeted city, how costly is a recall, how quickly can *all* affected cars be repaired, what happens if Americans stop trusting their cars, what's the cost to jobs and the economy, and more?

This scenario is currently plausible. Remote manipulation of connected vehicles is both possible and demonstrable. Only adversaries' willing restraint is preventing such disaster from befalling us—but that is unlikely to last for long. Although all systems fail, not all systems are prepared for failure. Connected automobiles, writ large, lack the foundational capabilities to handle inevitable failures caused by accidents and adversaries. Given the very long lead times in automotive design and manufacturing cycles, waiting for proof of harm leaves everyone at risk and could shatter confidence in significant portions of the U.S. economy.

Five Foundational Cyber Safety Capabilities

In August 2014, iamthecavalry.org published its "Open Letter to Automotive CEOs."[13] The goal was to offer a multistakeholder framework for collaboration and cooperative security in automotive design between the technical security community and manufacturers. "You're masters of your domain, we're masters of our domain," the letter read, "and now that our domains have collided, we will have safer outcomes sooner, if we work together." In consultation with several stakeholder groups in the ecosystem, the proposed *5 Star Automotive Cyber Safety Framework* (see table 4.2) was intended as a starting point for free market innovation. The *Framework*'s aim is to provide for better security while allowing consumers to make informed and visible risk decisions in their own self-interest and which might unlock insurance incentives.[14]

Since it was proposed in 2014, conversation has coalesced around "the 5 Stars," both for and against, making clearer over time what the industry can accomplish on its own and what will be difficult to impossible without mandate, incentives, and/or assistance from government. For instance, two automakers have adopted the capability of third-party collaboration; meanwhile automakers without evidence capture capability regularly claim there is no evidence of car hacking. Following the descriptions, the next section maps where there has been progress, where there hasn't, and why.

Security by Design (aka "Avoid Failure")

When a company publicly describes the process it utilizes to ensure that its software is reasonably free of flaws, it demonstrates a commitment to safety.

Table 4.2 5-Star Automotive Cyber Safety Framework

Formal Language	Plain Speak (Tell us how you:)
1. Security by Design	1. Avoid *Failure*
2. Third-Party Collaboration	2. Take Help Avoiding *Failure*
3. Evidence Capture	3. Capture and Learn from *Failure*
4. Security Updates	4. Respond to *Failure*
5. Segmentation and Isolation	5. Contain and Isolate *Failure*

Do automakers publish attestations of their Secure Software Development Lifecycle, summarizing design, development, and adversarial resilience testing programs for their products and supply chain?

Plain Speak: *Help me compare your security program with others.*

This description need not divulge trade secrets, the goal is to convey confidence to the general public and to allow consumers to make informed choices among market alternatives. Software manufacturers, such as Microsoft and others, make this attestation and could serve as a model for automakers (see figure 4.2).

Using existing vetted standards, including those from the International Organization for Standardization (ISO), the National Institute of Standards

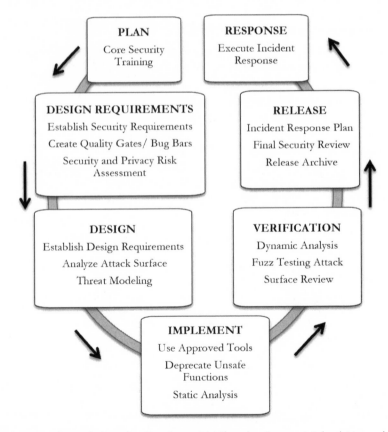

Figure 4.2   Microsoft Security Development Lifecycle. *Source*: Michael Howard and Steve Lipner, The security development lifestye: SDL, a process for developing demonstrably more secure software, Microsoft Press, 2006.

and Technology (NIST), or others in the private sector, would both accelerate an organization's maturity and ensure more predictable, normalized, comprehensive practices. Structuring well-governed and traceable hardware and software supply chains can enable more defensible products, shorter times to overcome failures, and more agile responses. This is especially true where components are of highly variable quality, security, and origin.

Reducing the elective exposure and complexity of a software product minimizes points of vulnerability and attack for adversaries to discover. There is a clear correlation between security and complexity; the longer, larger, and more intricate a system, the greater the potential source of flaws and vulnerabilities.[15] And the greater the level of exposure, the greater the "attack surface" of a system. Leveraging common libraries and better design practices can help minimize this sort of flaws and reduces the number of elective components, thereby minimizing the elective attack surface.

Firms should also employ independent adversarial resilience testing, carried out by qualified individuals independent of those who initially designed and implemented a product, to probe it for security holes. These individuals can be internal resources under a different organizational branch or third parties.

Third-Party Collaboration (aka "Take Help Avoiding Failure")

A collaboration policy that supports positive, productive interaction between the automotive industry and security researchers is a key mechanism to improve security. Researchers should be invited to contribute to automotive safety as willing allies to help discover and address flaws before adversaries and accidents can impact vehicle safety. Such coordinated exchanges are more productive and effective than other alternatives. Automakers who accept reports of vulnerabilities from outside third parties make themselves aware of potential safety flaws before adversaries discover and take advantage of them.

Using existing ISO standards for vendor-side disclosure and internal vulnerability handling (ISO 29147 and ISO 30111) accelerates a manufacturer's ability to quickly establish a more mature security program and can help ensure predictable, normalized interfaces for researchers and facilitators. After establishing a program and working out processes, positive incentives,

Do vendors have a published Coordinated Disclosure policy inviting the assistance of third-party researchers acting in good faith?

Plain Speak: *Do researchers see a "Welcome Mat" or a "Beware of Dog" sign?*

such as public recognition or cash rewards, can help shape the volume of submissions and researchers' focus as desired by the automakers. Several prominent "Hackathon," "Hall of Fame," and "Bug Bounty" programs have proven successful and continue to drive iterative improvements.

Vulnerability discoverers need an effective means to communicate bug information to vendors. Independent vulnerability disclosure coordinators have normalized the interfaces between affected manufacturers and third-party researchers. These include nonprofit organizations, bug bounty companies, and government agencies. This too can support greater efficiency, effectiveness, and participation.

Evidence Capture (aka "Capture and Learn from Failure")

Safety investigations drive substantial improvements, and records of electronic systems' operation provide visibility into root causes of failure that may otherwise remain opaque. These records can plainly show sources of error, be they malfunctions, design defects, human error, or deliberate attack. Those waiting for proof of hacking, electronic sabotage, or software failure will not find evidence without such logging and evidence collection in place. These capabilities will require more effort, over time, than other suggestions, but are central for improving safety in the long term and providing the data to underlie decision-making now and in the future.

Capturing evidence begins with standards about what, and when, data should be recorded. These should conform to existing legal standards of care around the forensics process, for example, maintain records within a chain of evidence. This process will improve the effectiveness of the NHTSA by providing a data dump for connected vehicles similar to "black box" data recorders in airplanes that can facilitate root cause investigations. The benefits of a black box for connected vehicles can be had without violating the privacy expectations of citizens across the complexities of various jurisdictions. Categories such as location data are far less important than internal system operation and recording data inputs and outputs to look for, as an example, malware delivered by an adversary. Debates over the capture of data, including GPS movement tracking or other recording of individuals,

Do manufacturer vehicle systems provide tamper evident, forensically sound logging and evidence capture to facilitate safety investigations?

Plain Speak: *If cars are hacked, will you capture evidence and improve your designs and the industry overall—similar to NTSB airplane and train black box recordings?*

can thus be decoupled from safety to avoid unnecessary entanglement. There are nonsecurity and very limited capture of passenger information stored in Event Data Recorders (EDRs) within airbags. These may be the best delivery vehicle to build upon, but ultimately, affected stakeholders will need to gather requirements, set standards, and decide the best means of implementation.

Security Updates (aka "Respond to Failure")

Security and functionality flaws must be able to be remediated, in a prompt, reliable, and secure manner. If newly discovered flaws can't be rapidly corrected, the window of exposure increases and the cost of recall, repair, and restitution can grow significantly. The recent Heart Bleed flaw put hundreds of thousands of devices at risk.[16] Without the ability to update software in the field, similar flaws in automobiles could require carmakers to undertake costly factory recalls or accept the associated consequences of perpetual, critical security issues.

While updating is a necessary capability, an insecure update design could facilitate an adversary's access or trigger accidents. Identical to software vendors, automakers need to employ an authenticity and quality verification mechanism within the software update system that preserves the integrity of updates and prevents digital tampering or unexpected failures.

While it is critical to be able to update a vulnerable system, valuable aspects such as Mean Time To Repair (MTTR) will vary among manufacturers. Service-level agreements can set and track timeline commitments. Further, automakers who commit to, and invest in, improving their MTTR will realize better safety, enabling free market choice to incentivize more rapid repair.

An effective platform for public communication to facilitate transparent and forthright interaction with consumers is crucial for any update process. Decades of experience in the software industry have taught that the best way to ensure security and safety are notification of when and where flaws exist, a description of its severity, and clear instructions on how to remediate. Absence of these may delay remediation and decrease participation rates.

Can automaker's vehicles be securely updated in a prompt and agile manner?

Plain Speak: *If my car is vulnerable, can I update immediately and securely? If not, with a physical recall? Ever?*

Segmentation and Isolation (aka "Contain and Isolate Failure")

If different systems share the same memory, computing, and/or circuitry, as most current generation cars do, then a vulnerability in one component could compromise the reliability of all. Such risks to life and limb are entirely avoidable and merit a higher standard of care. An adversary's successful attack on an infotainment system or Bluetooth connection should never have the ability to exercise control over critical functions including braking, deploying airbags, or turning the steering wheel.

Systems must be segmented and isolated to prevent small vulnerabilities and failures in one system from impacting others. Key to these processes is establishing air gaps and physical separation to ensure that noncritical systems cannot adversely impact primary, operational, and safety systems. Hacking a car's stereo should never allow an attacker to engineer a crash. While some manufacturers are planning, discussing, or implementing software-based isolation techniques, methods to circumvent these measures are routinely discovered and demonstrated, so segmentation alone may not be sufficient.

Techniques exist to assure detection of compromises to a system's integrity. Earlier detection can reduce the total duration and extent of the compromise as well as help drive remediation. In some cases, a "fail safe" or "safe mode" (sometimes called "limp home mode") can be an automatic fallback safety mechanism. Understanding when a system has been compromised and being able to minimize the risk of adversary activity is critical to building resilience into a connected vehicle's design. Choices about how to segment and design these "fail safe" modes should be scrutinized with experienced threat analysis as they may introduce new opportunities for adversaries by intentionally reducing functionality.

The potential for harm from the systems embedded in connected vehicles merit increased rigor and a high level of assurance. Third-party review and validation of architecture, implementation, and adversary resilience testing can raise confidence in design processes. Operating system choices, including the use of mandatory access control architectures, which enforce rules on how different processes can interact with systems, further reduce risk.[17]

Does the manufacturer publish the physical and logical isolation measures they have implemented to separate critical systems from noncritical systems?

Plain Speak: *I don't care if my stereo is hacked—I care that malware can also cut the brakes. Tell me how you separate systems.*

Performing well in this space is difficult. Microsoft is among the best in the world, hitting all 5 stars in its market but despite this, the company still has to issue a dozen or so critical or high-value security updates per month. Automotive manufacturers, building even bigger software platforms, have comparatively little experience with information assurance or cybersecurity as well as substantially higher consequences from failure. In many ways, the lack of these five foundational elements has kept policymakers and involved citizens collectively "spinning our wheels" with no mechanism for evidence capture allowing there to be no evidence of a problem. Meanwhile, automotive software is increasingly exposed and vulnerable, with few security improvements on the horizon.

Where Does the Automotive Industry Stand?

The *5 Star Automotive Cyber Safety Framework* captured examples of existing investments, as well as aspirational capabilities. Some automakers have already implemented parts of the framework, either independently or because of the document.

Security by Design—Zero

No automakers have made public attestations of their software development cycle or security practices as yet. The Society of Automotive Engineers published a cybersecurity technical design standard in January 2016, which advocates many of the elements of Security by Design.[18] This is a positive step forward to build upon and to monitor whether, and how, automakers implement the standard. The newly formed Auto-ISAC has prioritized publishing a voluntary set of best practices, but will allow individual original equipment manufacturers (OEMs) to make "risk-based" decisions on where and how to conform with them. It is unclear if any of these judgments will be shared with consumers.[19]

Third-Party Collaboration—Only Two, So Far

Shortly after the *5 Star Framework* was published, Tesla announced its first coordinated disclosure program. Six months later, the firm added a $1,000 prize, later raised to $10,000.[20] In January 2016, General Motors followed suit and announced its own disclosure program.[21] Other OEMs are participating and investigating coordinated disclosure via the Commerce Department's National Telecommunications and Information Administration Safety Working Group. In addition, NHTSA, the Department of Transportation, and 18 automakers signed a pledge in 2016 to work more closely with the security community.[22]

Evidence Capture—Zero

Automakers are unlikely to independently design and implement a mechanism to capture evidence of failure without a mandate and a standard as the research and development costs of developing a means to capture data would be costly and redundant if developed by each manufacturer, harming the economic competitiveness of the early adopters. Many have expressed if there was a shared burden across all carmakers, it clearly makes sense to do it. To be of use in a "black box" role, such a device would require data collection and design standards which balanced privacy with evidence capture interests and was tolerant of accidents and crashes. Some manufacturers claim to have similar processes in place, but none, when pressed, have plans for court-admissible, forensically sound evidence capture for security relevant data.[23]

Security Updates—A Handful, but Slow Adoption

Security updates are a lynchpin for responding to failure, allowing manufacturers to rapidly distribute patches for software flaws securely, even over an insecure network to their consumers. Tesla employs secure over-the-air (OTA) updates, some years and models of BMW have it for certain components, and Ford has announced it will adopt OTA as a standard update mechanism.[24] Other car manufactures have and will begin to offer some limited OTA updates. As evidenced in 2015, some models of Jeep lack OTA, but have a manual, owner-installed update mechanism through a USB stick in the infotainment system.[25] This method is much slower and has low participation rates. There are pure economic incentives to adopt secure OTA updates, as the cost of a recall is significantly reduced—and the brand damage and stigma with routine software updates is very different.[26] Some manufacturers and suppliers are resistant so this might be an area in need of new incentives to accelerate adoption.

Segmentation and Isolation—Very Slow Adoption (and not made public)

To the authors' knowledge, no automakers have made public statements on design practices around segmentation or isolation. Tesla has taken deliberate steps to isolate its infotainment unit from critical systems in the vehicle, by separating cables for different systems cabling (BUSes) and isolating software using virtualization.

Regulatory Climate and Context

The momentum of the federal government in recent years—even within regulatory agencies—has been toward a light touch or even deregulatory approach. Both the Food and Drug Administration (FDA), for medical technology, and the NHTSA, for automotive technology, have been reluctant to stifle innovation regardless of which party controlled Congress or the White House. While there are good reasons to avoid excessive or burdensome regulations, few would argue for nothing at all. Removing requirements for seat belts and kitchen sanitation codes for commercial restaurants, or eliminating safety inspections for commercial airlines are all highly unlikely. In areas affecting public safety and the public good, regulations can provide baseline assurance. This consideration should force a reevalution and rationalization of the balance between "too little" and "too much" legislation or regulation. The following section frames a core set of foundational safety and security capabilities for handling failures in connected vehicles and defines the appropriate role for the federal government.

RECOMMENDATIONS

Establish an Evidence Capture Task Force

While the auto industry may prefer self-regulation, a consistent and effective standard for evidence capture will require the involvement of Congress and the NHTSA. The Cybersecurity Act of 2015[27] necessitated the formation of the Health and Human Services (HHS) Task Force to improve cybersecurity in healthcare. A similar task force, led by the NHTSA, should be created to design and develop a standard for an automotive "black box." The resulting device should be implemented across all vehicle types, to be mandated at a later date. The fact that government *can* introduce unintended consequences doesn't eliminate the need to act where required. Instead, it should highlight the need for a multistakeholder process to contribute to the design and use of such a "black box."

The evidentiary capture task force should include participants from NIST, representatives from the automotive industry—especially those with EDR expertise, security researchers, legal and evidentiary experts, privacy advocates, academia, and more.[28] It should have a narrow and specific remit focus on the evidence capture problem and should be implemented over 3–6 months. At its conclusion, the task force should submit a report to Congress and a recommended timeline for mandatory inclusion of the capture mechanism in all vehicles or identify incentives to drive widespread voluntary adoption. Most stakeholders will benefit from having a standard and effective evidence capture mechanism, but without centralized design and execution, they may be developed too late or too poorly to avoid unneeded loss of life and damaged confidence in connected vehicles, markets, and desired benefits.

Establish a Cyber Safety Label Task Force

Requiring that automotive manufacturers be transparent with consumers about their security design and safety practices could catalyze and accelerate cyber safety investment and trust in the U.S. automotive industry. Rather than a prescriptive approach from government, labeling provides a mechanism for free market forces to drive better security behavior by manufacturers. Until the industry is able to capture a sufficient corpus of evidence on which designs and defensive measures work best, the goal should not be to mandate or *pre*scribe automaker security, but to mandate they *de*scribe the choices and programs they have invested in. This can and should take place in parallel with the evidence capture task force.

Congress should establish a special task force to lead the development of a new label law, similar to the Monroney Labels which detail information about vehicle crash safety and emissions performance. The exact nature of the information on a cyber safety label and its contents should be developed by this task force, with active participation by industry groups. In addition a law will likely be needed to mandate the label's use and display by manufacturers.

A label provides consumers information about the manufacturers, allowing them to differentiate between high- and low-security automakers when select-ing new vehicles—similar to crash ratings and fuel economy information buyers utilize today. This could shift consumers toward newer, more capable vehicles and reduce the number of older, comparatively less safe, vehicles on our roads. Fleet purchasers can also leverage information to evaluate the full cost of ownership, such as downtime for hardware replacement versus manual patches or OTA updates. Labeling would allow insurers to more easily assess the relative risk of different software and manufacturers, for example, patchable versus unpatchable systems. With an informed consumer, the Federal Trade Commission (FTC) will be better poised to tenably execute its responsibilities under the "FTC Act" to protect individuals against decep-tive acts or misrepresentation by manufacturers that could lead to harm.[29]

Incentivize Coordinated Vulnerability Disclosure and Report Handling

While all five capacities of the framework should be considered minimum foundational requirements, Coordinated Disclosure programs drive the security learning curve by enabling the larger security research community to help auto manufacturers find and remediate flaws. Accepting reports of defects from friendlies (researchers, mechanics, hobbyists, and others) allows for more individual bugs and varieties of flaws to be found. Armed with this information, automakers can track trends to inform smart future design choices and hardening in a continuous improvement loop. Without these programs, manufacturers have spent years bearing a false confidence and burning precious time. Over the course of ninety days after GM announced its vulnerability disclosure program, fifty-five reported bugs were resolved, with more fixed every day. Many of these may never have been discovered or previously reported for fear of legal retaliation or being ignored.[30]

Exclusions to the Digital Millennium Copyright Act (DMCA) coming into effect in October 2016 will reduce legal hurdles to security research and reporting on vehicles.[31] With GM as an illustration, receiving dozens of new reports within three days of its program launch, there will likely be a wave of similar security reports to manufacturers.[32] If Congress and/or NHTSA prepare automakers in advance of this coming wave, it would substantially increase the likelihood of high trust, high collaboration exchanges, and graceful triage and response.

In combination with evidence capture capabilities, reports from nontechnical experts are also valuable. NHTSA provides the capability for drivers and others to report potential safety issues. These can be difficult for automakers to reproduce, diagnose, and identify root causes, because software failures don't currently leave evidence in the same manner as physical failures. Disclosure from third parties, including drivers, helps encourage formal evidence capture by automakers—when users report problems, it raises awareness for manufacturers to identify the root cause of failure. With the capability to capture evidence and analyze data from vehicles after these reports, automakers are much more likely to accurately identify the source of the safety problem, or to narrow down for more precise identification in future investigations.

Mandate Cyber Safety Procurement Requirements for Government Fleet Purchasing

The U.S. government acts as a purchaser, not just a regulator, of vehicles. Where mission critical services depend on vulnerable, exposed, automobile systems the government can use its role as buyer to influence the automotive marketplace without added regulation. Law enforcement, emergency response, dignitary protection, homeland defense, and combat operations all pose unique threat and risk scenarios but all represent as yet unexplored possibilities for more secure procurement requirements. If there were mission exposures and/or homeland emergencies affected by compromised connected vehicles, this could prevent vital government missions and services from being reliable.

Exploration of this front has not yet catalyzed changes to procurement requirements. Congress should establish a task force or study to investigate the impact of vulnerability and exposure across the various missions of the federal government. While conversations have taken place between DOT, DHS, and the private sector, there are not, as of yet, cybersecurity requirements built into GSA purchasing guidelines. Irrespective of other advances at the pace of industry, the government can—and should—make tactical risk decisions in its own interest as a consumer who is dependent on these technologies.

SUMMARY OF RECOMMENDATIONS

- Congress should create a task force to define evidence to be captured and a forensically sound mechanism to do so, to support learning from failure.
- Congress should create a task force to design and mandate an automotive cyber safety label, to unlock free market forces.
- Congress should incentivize automakers to develop and implement processes to accept and handle vulnerability reports, to reduce time to identify flaws.
- Congress should require the government use its role as an automobile buyer, to ensure mission effectiveness is not undermined by cybersecurity flaws. A summary of recommendations based on the 5-Star framework is displayed in table 4.3.

Table 4.3   Summary of Recommendations

5-Star Capability	Private Sector	NHTSA	Congress
1. Anticipate and Avoid Failure	Lead	Assist	Follow
2. Take Help Avoiding Failure	Assist	Assist	Lead (by Incentivizing)
3. Capture and Learn From Failure (Auto Black Box)	Assist	Assist	Lead (by Task Force)
4. Respond to Failure	Lead	Assist	Follow
5. Contain and Isolate Failure	Lead	Assist	Follow

CONCLUSION

Cyber threats to the automotive industry are real, despite the lack of acknowledgment and response from automakers. However, it is human nature to wait for failures and then respond. Sometimes the cost of waiting is much higher than the cost of preparing and this is one of those cases. Rewind the clock by a century. Only after the Cuyahoga River in Ohio caught fire (and stayed on fire) for the thirteenth time did the nation act to address pollution. A "river on fire" was required to tip the consciousness into action.[33] To avoid a similar fire in this instance, policymakers should work with industry to drive the recommendations embedded here—a standard and implementation process for evidence capture, labels and greater transparency for automakers' security practices, and support for coordinated vulnerability disclosure across all manufacturers. Though automotive bills have been introduced to Congress and committees that have provisions similar to those proposed here, none have yet met the measure of these recommendations. Each of the three proposals in this chapter stems from a broader, foundational, automotive safety framework. They are the start, not the end goals, of better security practices in a vital American industry that touches nearly all of modern life. Knee-jerk responses are often malformed and introduce unintended consequences. Inadequate preparation for failure can amplify the consequences and the long manufacturing cycles and lifespans of durable goods can prolong response times and exposure windows. Automotive safety has vast opportunities for improvement, and equally immense consequences if not acted upon. Only a combination of public and private action can ensure the auto industry travels down a productive path moving forward, ensuring we are safer, sooner, together.

CHAPTER HIGHLIGHTS

Automotive Cybersecurity. Modern vehicles are a hybrid of mechanical and digital technologies as they have dozens of computers and sensors, communicating through wired and wireless signals. At present, these networked vehicles are not tolerant of failure and vulnerabilities are becoming more evident. Car hacking is now demonstrable and increasing in volume and variety.

Connectivity Leads to Exposure. Previously, hacking a car would require physical access. Now, onboard systems are exposed to remote attacks through the TPMS (Tire Pressure Monitoring System), 4G LTE Wi-fi hotspots, and even smart key receivers in some vehicles. Worse, even "dumb cars" become accessible with the growing number of insurance and aftermarket information collection dongles—which enjoy unfettered access to the central network controller and everything it touches.

5 Star Automotive Cyber Safety Framework. (1) Describe the design and development processes that assure cyber safety; (2) accept reports from third parties of potential safety flaws; (3) adopt a "black box" for automobiles to capture evidence of failures in a forensically sound, privacy preserving manner; (4) have a method for prompt, secure, and agile software updates; and (5) isolate core safety components from other components.

Create Evidence Capture Task Force. Closing the evidence gap requires significant improvements in how data is collected and analyzed regarding computing system behavior in connected vehicles. Congress or the Executive Branch should establish a task force to facilitate design of a standard for Evidence Capture and a mandatory timeline to enforce its use.

Create Cyber Safety Labeling. No mechanism exists for consumers to make themselves aware of cost and safety implications of automakers' cybersecurity choices. Free market forces are predicated on the visibility of such decision-making criteria. Congress should create a task force to design and mandate a product label that supports informed choice and public trust.

Incentivize Coordinated Vulnerability Disclosure and Handling. Third-party reporting of design and implementation flaws accelerates elimination and mitigation in existing products, and avoidance in future designs. The auto industry has been slow to embrace this idea. Congress or the Executive Branch should establish a task force to define incentives for automakers to establish vulnerability handling programs.

Make Cyber Safety a Government Buying Requirement. Mission critical services must be resilient against attacks, accidents, or other cyber safety failures. The government can use its purchasing power to select vehicles on the basis of their cyber safety capabilities.

NOTES

1. This quote and some of the material for this chapter has previously been made available through the "I Am The Cavalry" website and related publications.

2. FBI PSA "Motor Vehicles Increasingly Vulnerable To Remote Exploits," March 17, 2016, http://www.ic3.gov/media/2016/160317.aspx.

3. "Five Star Automotive Cyber Safety Program," iamthecavalry.org, https://www.iamthecavalry.org/domains/automotive/5star/.

4. National Center for Statistics and Analysis, *2014 Crash Data Key Findings* (Washington: National Highway Traffic Safety Administration), http://www-nrd.nhtsa.dot.gov/Pubs/812219.pdf.

5. Santokh Singh, *Critical reasons for crashes investigated in the National Motor Vehicle Crash Causation Survey* (Washington: National Highway Traffic Safety Administration), http://www-nrd.nhtsa.dot.gov/pubs/812115.pdf.

6. "Code Review Metrics," The Open Web Application Security Project, last modified January 14, 2014, https://www.owasp.org/index.php/Code_Review_Metrics.

7. "Codebases: Millions of lines of code," *Information is Beautiful*, last modified September 24, 2015, http://www.informationisbeautiful.net/visualizations/million-lines-of-code/.

8. Ibid.

9. Ishtiaq Rouf et al., "Security and Privacy Vulnerabilities of In-Car Wireless Networks: A Tire Pressure Monitoring System Case Study," http://www.winlab.rutgers.edu/~Gruteser/papers/xu_tpms10.pdf.

10. Karl Koscher et al., "Experimental Security Analysis of a Modern Automobile," *IEEE Symposium on Security and Privacy* (2010), http://www.autosec.org/pubs/cars-oakland2010.pdf.

11. Dan Geer, "Shared Risk at the National Scale," http://web.stanford.edu/class/msande91si/www-spr04/slides/geer.pdf.

12. NASA Engineering and Safety Center, *Appendix A. Software: Technical Support to the National Highway Traffic Safety Administration (NHTSA) on the Reported Toyota Motor Corporation (TMC) Unintended Acceleration (UA) Investigation* (Hampton, VA: NASA), http://www.nhtsa.gov/staticfiles/nvs/pdf/NASA_FR_Appendix_A_Software.pdf.

13. "A Open Letter to the Automotive Industry: Collaborating for Safety," August 8th, 2014, https://www.iamthecavalry.org/wp-content/uploads/2014/08/IATC-Open-letter-to-the-Automotive-Industry.pdf.

14. The full overview of the definitions and details of this framework are at: www.iamthecavalry.org/5star/.

15. Dan Ward, *Cybersecurity, Simplicity, and Complexity: The Graphic Guide to Making Systems More Secure Without Making Them Worse*, New America, March 2016, https://static.newamerica.org/attachments/12685-the-comic-guide-to-cybersecurity-and-simplicity/Comic%20Vfinal.5e00364a8df04b7e835ad030046dc5da.pdf.

16. Dan Goodin, "Critical crypto bug in OpenSSL opens two-thirds of the Web to eavesdropping," *Ars Technica*, April 7, 2014, http://arstechnica.com/security/2014/04/critical-crypto-bug-in-openssl-opens-two-thirds-of-the-web-to-eavesdropping/.

17. "Formal Methods" of engineering and more secure protocols merit consideration. Evaluation examples may be instructive (e.g., "Common Criteria EAL 5+").

18. *SAE J3061 Cybersecurity Guidebook for Cyber-Physical Vehicle Systems*, SAE International, January 14, 2016, http://standards.sae.org/j3061_201601/.

19. Global Automakers and Alliance for Automobile Manufactures, *Framework for Automotive Cybersecurity Best Practices* (Washington: 2016), https://www.globalautomakers.org/system/files/document/attachments/framework_auto_cyber_best_practices_14jan2016_id_10376.pdf.

20. Eduard Kovacs, "Tesla Increases Bug Bounty Payout After Experts Hack Model S," *Security Week*, August 10, 2015, http://www.securityweek.com/tesla-increases-bug-bounty-payout-after-experts-hack-model-s.

21. Sean Gallagher, "GM embraces white-hat hackers with public vulnerability disclosure program," *Ars Technica*, January 8, 2016, http://arstechnica.com/security/2016/01/gm-embraces-white-hats-with-public-vulnerability-disclosure-program/.

22. And the FDA's January 2016 Post Market Guidance draft strongly encourages such programs—Food and Drug Administration, Postmarket Management of

Cybersecurity in Medical Devices: Draft Guidance for Industry and Food and Drug Administration Staff (Washington: US Department of Health and Human Services, 2016), http://www.fda.gov/downloads/medicaldevices/deviceregulationandguidance/guidancedocuments/ucm482022.pdf.

23. Importantly—this is not at all the same as proposed "automotive IDS" solutions which do not capture the right type of data, are not forensically sound, and are not court admissible.

24. Alex Brisbourne, "Tesla's Over-The-Air Fix: Best Example Yet of The Internet of Things?" *Wired*, http://www.wired.com/insights/2014/02/teslas-air-fix-best-example-yet-internet-things/; and "BMW Fixes Security Flaw in its In-Car Software," January 30, 2015, http://www.reuters.com/article/bmw-cybersecurity-idUSL6N0V92VD20150130. Benjamin Zhang, "Tesla Wants to Take Self-Driving Cars to a Whole New Level," *Business Insider*, January 11, 2016, http://www.businessinsider.com/elon-musk-on-tesla-over-the-air-software-update-summon-feature-2016-1.

25. Andy Greenberg, "After Jeep Hack, Chrysler Recalls 1.4M Vehicles for Bug Fix," *Wired*, July 24, 2015, http://www.wired.com/2015/07/jeep-hack-chrysler-recalls-1-4m-vehicles-bug-fix/.

26. "Over-The-Air Software Updates to Create Boon for Automotive Market, HIS Says," *IHS Inc.*, September 3, 2015, http://press.ihs.com/press-release/automotive/over-air-software-updates-create-boon-automotive-market-ihs-says.

27. "Health Care Industry Cybersecurity Task Force," US Department of Health and Human Services, http://www.phe.gov/preparedness/planning/CyberTF/Pages/default.aspx.

28. Other participants should include: insurers and claim investigators, the National Transportation and Safety Board (NTSB), privacy advocates and civil society, legal and evidentiary experts, and potential Department of Justice or Federal Trade Commission (FTC) representatives.

29. "Federal Trade Commission Act, Section 5: Unfair or Deceptive Acts or Practices," in *Consumer Compliance Handbook*, (Washington: The Federal Reserve Board, 2015), https://www.federalreserve.gov/boarddocs/supmanual/cch/ftca.pdf.

30. "General Motors," HackerOne, https://hackerone.com/gm.

31. David Kravets, "US Regulators Grant DCMA Exemption Legalizing Vehicle Software Tinkering," *Ars Technica*, October 27, 2015, http://arstechnica.com/tech-policy/2015/10/us-regulators-grant-dmca-exemption-legalizing-vehicle-software-tinkering/.

32. John Stoll, "GM to Use External Reports to Strengthen Cybersecurity," *Wall Street Journal*, March 22, 2016, http://www.wsj.com/articles/gm-to-use-external-reports-to-strengthen-cybersecurity-1458656166.

33. Jonathan H. Adler, "Fables of the Cuyahoga: Reconstructing a History of Environmental Protection" (2002). Faculty Publications. Paper 191. http://scholarly-commons.law.case.edu/faculty_publications/191.

Chapter 5

Bad Code

Exploring Liability in Software Development

Jane Chong

Liability is a no-brainer when it comes to malfunctioning machines embedded with error-ridden software: think cars that accelerate uncontrollably or radiation therapy machines that blast holes through patients.[1] But liability for insecure software is a different story. For decades, the idea of holding software vendors financially responsible for the harms that arise from shoddy, easily exploited code has remained just that—an idea. Though frequently renewed and rehashed, the liability debate has stalled so dramatically that it no longer makes sense to engage the topic without examining features of the impasse itself.[2]

This chapter uses the term "software security" to denote designing, building, testing, deploying, and patching software to reduce vulnerabilities and to ensure the software's proper function in the face of malicious attack. Not all coding errors are vulnerabilities; vulnerabilities are a subset of software defects—implementation bugs and design flaws—that offer malicious third parties an opportunity to attack a security boundary. They can be introduced at any phase of the software development cycle. Indeed, in the case of design flaws, they can enter the picture before software development ever begins.[3]

Most security breaches are made possible by vulnerabilities, yet poor-quality software remains the market norm.[4] Experts have long attributed this state of affairs not to the technical challenges of producing safer code, formidable though they are, but to social acceptance of software insecurity.[5] Despite decades of valiant brainstorming by legal scholars, security experts, and hopeful plaintiffs—and an annual slew of high-profile software security failures—unnecessarily insecure software continues to flood the market and leave end users without legal remedy. Periodically major players in the industry will come together to fund a security initiative of some kind, but these efforts are purely the product of corporate goodwill.[6]

This chapter provides a brief overview of the legal and market failures that account for the no-liability status quo. It then turns to a somewhat less conventional explanation for our collective failure to change this status quo: two ideas, that software is special and that secure software is hard, have helped feed resistance to the idea of penalizing manufacturers for their code and have proven powerful in ensuring liability discussions remain largely confined to the theoretical plane.

But to insist that software is by its very nature incompatible with a liability framework is to fundamentally misunderstand what a liability regime needs to look like. Broadly construed, legal liability comes in many possible shapes and sizes. The chapter thus concludes by proposing some concrete examples of starting principles for constructing a liability regime that strikes a balance between industry incentives and end-user needs. The central idea, and ultimate objective, is to reconsider how we think about software development, and to open up a new conversation about the things that our software has yet to be.

The No-Liability Status Quo

There are two major dimensions to the present no-liability status quo. One is a story of legal battles lost. The other is an account of misaligned market forces. Both are key to understanding why insecure software and preventable defects are the norm, not the exception.

Legal Failure

For a while it looked like history would go the other way: early on, scholars predicted that software vendors would eventually be inundated with lawsuits, resulting in "catastrophic" consequences for the industry.[7] But the opposite has happened. Fast forward thirty years, and software users, not vendors, bear the costs of insecure software. And it is not for lack of theorizing. Legal and security experts have proposed everything from the creation of new torts, such as the negligent enablement of cyber crime and professional computer malpractice, to the establishment of insurance regimes to pay for the resulting costs to software vendors.[8] Most of this has been to little effect.

Once upon a time commentators speculated that the contract-making principles embodied in the Uniform Commercial Code (UCC)—a set of model laws adopted at least in part by all the states to govern commercial transactions—could be used to "pierc[e] the vendor's boilerplate" and create a legal framework that would equally benefit vendors and users, licensors and licensees.[9] One commentator predicted as early as 1985: "The courts have adequate means to protect software vendees from unconscionable contract provisions and the UCC makes requirements for effective disclaimers of warranty clear, so that the UCC will adequately protect software vendees and will not serve as a vehicle for manufacturers to limit their liability."[10] Instead, because the UCC is built on freedom-to-contract principles that assume roughly equal bargaining power between the buyer and the seller, the UCC has served as just that: a liability-limitation vehicle.

End Use License Agreements

Today, just as yesterday, the disgruntled user has two choices when it comes to the mass-market End Use License Agreements (EULAs) bundled with virtually all software products—take it or leave it.[11] Software vendors typically shunt all the risks associated with their products onto users through these boilerplate license agreements, which the courts have generally treated as enforceable contracts since the mid-1990s.[12]

The courts have accepted the fiction that end users are free to accept, reject, or negotiate the terms of the EULAs that accompany the software that they buy.[13] Software vendors are, as a result, virtually bulletproof, as they may simply contract away responsibility for the deficiencies of their products with sweeping disclaimers.[14] This has prompted one commentator to dub the EULA the "legislative license."[15] In other words, thanks to a long line of court decisions, "the law of the software license has come largely to be defined by each software license itself."[16]

Boilerplate license agreements are not the only obstacle for users seeking compensation in contract when a third party exploits the vulnerabilities in their software. Today much application software is free. This bars recovery under contract law (as well as under certain consumer protection statutes) because generally courts will not hold software providers liable for harms brought about for products or services for which users did not offer some form of payment—or what lawyers call "consideration."[17]

Negligence

Recognizing the many obstacles to liability within the private-ordering framework, scholars have searched outside of the contract realm for ways to hold software providers accountable for the harms that users sustain as a result of insecure code. In light of the type of oversight being alleged of software vendors who employ poor security practices—failure to develop their software in such a way as to prevent reasonably foreseeable harms to end users—early on, the most logical avenue for a tort action seemed to be a negligence claim. Negligence typically requires establishing four elements: that the software vendor owed the user a duty, that the vendor breached that duty, that the breach caused the user injury, and that harm was caused by the injury to the user as a result of that breach. But each of these elements poses special challenges in the software context.

The difficulties begin with the threshold inquiries. What, exactly, is a software vendor's duty to the user when it comes to precluding or patching vulnerabilities? And at what point, if any, can vulnerabilities be deemed to rise to the level of a breach of that duty? These questions, though fuzzy, are not impossible to answer. As this chapter will explain, coding is not finger-painting; there are best practices and rules of thumb for building out better, more secure software; conversely, certain coding practices are universally frowned upon and could theoretically form the basis for a negligence claim—for example, failing to use industry standard encryption methods. But in the absence of a legislative or regulatory scheme concretizing what end users may expect of their software providers, courts have been reluctant to make the kinds of technical assessments necessary for creating and enforcing vendor duties.

It has become common for courts to sidestep the duty question altogether in favor of ruling on injury. The injury requirement has proven problematic for user suits of all stripes in cases involving the compromise of sensitive customer data—not just tort actions but also suits brought under consumer protection laws, and not merely where attackers target end users by way of software vulnerabilities but also where hackers target companies actually holding customer data. To start, most jurisdictions have adopted the economic loss doctrine, which prohibits tort recovery for pure economic loss—that is, loss that does not involve personal injury or which flows from damage to the product itself—on the theory that risk allocation for economic losses is best addressed under a contract framework. The doctrine has placed a bar on software tort actions even in cases not involving a malicious third party and where the software defect was alleged to be obvious and easily correctable.[18]

The economic loss doctrine aside, the nature of the injury inflicted on end users when they suffer the exposure of their personal information is in other, more essential respects an impediment to legal recovery. This is well illustrated by recent trends in corporate data breach litigation, involving damage incurred by consumers not by way of hacks on user software but rather attacks on institutions and companies entrusted with sensitive customer data. For example, in a case involving the physical theft of a life insurance representative's laptop containing unencrypted customer information, where the plaintiffs feared but had not yet actually suffered identity theft, the D.C. Circuit affirmed the dismissal of the plaintiffs' negligence and gross negligence claims. The court reasoned that the injury was speculative and that the security expenses the plaintiffs had been forced to incur to guard against the misuse of their data arose not out of any injury but rather anticipation of future injury.[19] Cases of this kind are important to the software liability discussion because they highlight how deficient our legal vocabulary is when it comes to even articulating and cognizing security-specific harms.

Finally, even where plaintiffs are able to establish a cognizable security-related injury, they may be unable to prove the requisite causation. This, too, is well illustrated by data breach cases where courts have dismissed the negligence actions of plaintiffs who suffer identity theft in the wake of massive thefts of sensitive company-held customer data for failure to tie the theft to the particular breach in question.[20] Tracing an injury to a software vulnerability within a security environment belonging to and maintained by the user poses only more complications.

Market Failure

The seductive centerpiece of the argument against imposing legal liability on software vendors is that security is properly left to market forces. The theory goes that if code creates sufficient hazards for people and businesses, this should generate demand for more secure code, or for patching practices and antivirus products that adequately address security holes. Needlessly imposing liability, on the other hand, will only increase costs, slow development, and stifle innovation.

The problem with this theory—which retains its tenacious grip on the public imagination despite years of evidence to the contrary—is that it assumes end users will push for a solution when in fact we have proven to be active contributors to the problem. Not only are users relatively apathetic about software security, we systematically disregard it in favor of functionality.[21] We accept defective software because defective software works most of the time.[22] Moreover, so insatiable is our appetite for more and improved features that we have only encouraged the industry's "fix-it-later" culture.[23] Thus software companies look for bugs late in the development process and knowingly package and ship buggy software with impunity, relying on timely release and incremental patching as a primary security strategy.[24] Features, and speed to market, effectively trounce security.

These practices spell disaster for end users, who are generally slow in acknowledging vulnerabilities, patch too infrequently, and persist in running outdated software.[25] Researchers have found that users are sluggish about deploying security fixes, even in the case of critical vulnerabilities, and that 75 percent of targeted attacks could be prevented through regular patching.[26] Indeed, some of the most infamous malware exploited vulnerabilities for which patches were readily available. These include Code Red in 2000, which caused an estimated $1.2 billion in network damage, and SQL Slammer in 2003, an even faster-spreading piece of malware that completely shut down the internet in South Korea and led to outages and slowdowns throughout Asia.[27] Secure software development and user security practices exist as linked but separate challenges in the information assurance environment.

On top of everything else, users do not fully absorb the costs of their bad habits, a reality that only exacerbates negative externalities for all members of a highly interconnected cyber ecosystem.[28] Unlike the malicious software of yesteryear, which would typically disrupt the operation of the infected machine in a noticeable fashion, modern malware more commonly infects one machine and uses the host to attack another.[29] Consider the many high-profile attacks on financial institutions and other corporate entities made possible by user machines co-opted into botnets that are used to launch DDoS attacks unbeknownst to the rightful users.[30]

According to Bruce Schneier, perhaps the most prominent voice in the long-running call for vendor liability, "If we expect software vendors to reduce features, lengthen development cycles, and invest in secure software development processes, they must be liable for security vulnerabilities in their products."[31] This view is not predicated on the premise that market forces are merely inadequate in effecting the kind of industry-wide changes required for improved security. The idea is that those forces actively push in the opposite direction.

The No-Liability Gridlock

U.S. end users are generally bereft of means for legally recovering from vulnerability-related software harms. And a host of readily identifiable end-user practices help explain why free market forces have not pressured the industry into sweeping self-regulation. But these points do not account for why no fix is in sight, and why the idea of subjecting software to a liability regime provokes such fierce opposition. Underlying that opposition are powerful preconceptions about what software is and whether secure software is viable.

Software Is Special

Software is more than a good or service. Code is a language and a medium. Thus, the argument goes, clumsily imposed liability rules could place significant and unacceptable burdens on software speech and application-level innovation. In her book on the relationship between internet architecture and innovation, Barbara van Schewick offers a description of the nexus between software applications and human potential that could also double as an explanation for the perceived values at stake in the debate over the wisdom of imposing liability for coding defects. She writes:

> The importance of innovation in applications goes beyond its role in fostering economic growth. . . . [T]he Internet, as a general-purpose technology . . . creates value by enabling users to do the things they want or need to do. Applications are the tools that let users realize this value. For example, the Internet's political,

social or cultural potential—its potential to improve democratic discourse, to facilitate political organization and action, or to provide a decentralized environment for social and cultural interaction in which anyone can participate—is tightly linked to applications that help individuals, groups or organizations do more things or do them more efficiently, and not just in economic contexts but also in social, cultural, or political contexts.[32]

Accounts of this kind, of the special social significance of code for social expression and self-determination, do some work in explaining the state of software liability law. Although software liability critics and proponents speak most often in terms of market forces and industry incentives, the increasingly important subtext of this debate is the vaunted status and multidimensional significance of code as a kind of totem for social creativity and technological progress. It is not unusual to muse on whether code is art, and to debate whether Steve Jobs was an artist.[33] Little wonder, then, that we are unwilling to impose what many see as a kind of tax on code as embodied in software—a product that we have internalized as the manifestation of innovation and the currency of creativity itself.

Software Security Is Hard

To illustrate the need for a liability regime, liability advocates often draw comparisons between the dangers of software and the dangers of those products for which we have difficulty imagining a no-liability regime—for example, exploding Coke bottles or stroke-inducing painkillers or cars outfitted with faulty ignition switches.[34] But to insist that software defects and, say, vehicle defects should be governed by substantively similar legal regimes is to ignore many distinctions relevant to the question of whether liability is warranted and what form it should take. For starters, automobile defects almost invariably risk bodily injury and property damage. In contrast, "software" is a category comprising everything from video games to aircraft navigation systems, and the type and severity of harms arising from software vulnerabilities in those products vary dramatically.

Liability skeptics, for their part, point not only to the uniqueness of software but also to the special challenges of software security as an argument for exempting software programs from traditional liability rules altogether. This argument tends to rely on a narrow conception of what a regulatory regime can achieve but is one worth understanding.[35]

Gary McGraw, presently Chief Technical Officer at Cigital (and not a liability skeptic), attributes software's growing security problems to what he has dubbed the "trinity of trouble": connectivity, extensibility, and complexity.[36] To this list, we can add Daniel Geer's well-known contribution, the problem of software "monoculture."[37] Together, these factors help explain at a systemic level what makes software security difficult to measure, difficult to achieve, and seemingly difficult to penalize.

First, increasing *connectivity* between computers makes all systems connected to the internet increasingly vulnerable to software-based attacks. The resulting security issues are only exacerbated by the fact that old platforms not originally designed for the internet are pushed online despite not supporting security protocols or standard plug-ins for authentication and authorization.

Second, system *extensibility* allows for an incrementally evolving system and increasing functionality, but also makes it difficult to keep the constantly adapting system free of software vulnerabilities.[38] This flexibility in function gives rise to software uses and conditions which may never have been envisaged by a developer.

Third, software systems are increasing exponentially in *complexity*, resulting in thousands of bugs in multi-million-line codes and unexpected interactions between individual applications.[39] As Fred Brooks pointed out in his famous 1986 paper distinguishing between essential and accidental complexity, some complexity can be eliminated by way of code optimization. But in other respects complexity is an "essential property" of software that comes with unavoidable technical and management difficulties and leads to product flaws.[40]

Finally, *monoculture*, or system uniformity, predisposes massive numbers of users to devastating attacks. As Geer has put it, "The security situation is deteriorating, and that deterioration compounds when nearly all computers in the hands of end users rely on a single operating system subject to the same vulnerabilities the world over."

For all of these reasons, software of nontrivial size and complexity cannot presently be made vulnerability free or even simply catastrophe free. But that does not foreclose the feasibility of a carefully constructed liability scheme. Liability skeptics battle a straw man when they make arguments like this one, from computer security authority Roger Grimes: "If all software is imperfect and carries security bugs, that means that all software vendors—from one-person shops to global conglomerate corporations—would be liable for unintentional mistakes."[41] This conclusion relies on a caricature of liability that ignores the fact that an attempt to systematically hold vendors accountable for vulnerabilities could build in realistic constraints to prevent exposing the industry to crushing liability.

The Many Levers of Liability

Though critics see liability as a kind of nuclear option, proponents understand liability as a multifaceted weapon—a many-levered machine—that could be calibrated to effectively promote the development of more secure software without imposing undue costs on the industry. An effective software liability regime would be one that takes the many unique features of software into account when it comes to designing rules, creating duties, or imposing standards.

Practices That Warrant Regulation or Incur Liability

Classical command-and-control regulation is too restrictive and inflexible to form a viable foundation for a software security regime. And because security must be "baked" into the development life cycle, rather than "bolted on" after deployment, and because even the most carefully considered development process yields vulnerabilities, an effective liability or regulatory regime cannot equate to simple testing or patching requirements; nor can it revolve around penalizing software vendors for the number or severity of vulnerabilities discovered in a given piece of software. Indeed, such absolutes could reveal more about the software's popularity than its inherent insecurity.

The objective must be to influence vendor design and development choices without unduly restricting them. This balance might be struck by imposing on software vendors certain self-certification or public reporting requirements that make transparent and easily understandable to consumers their adherence to or departure from industry standards and best practices. Best practices, in turn, could constitute an affirmative defense against regulatory fines, and might range from periodic independent security audits to participation in what David Rice, Apple's global director of security, describes as a ratings system for software security, an analogue to the National Highway Traffic Safety Administration's rating system for automobile safety.[42] This general approach echoes the voluntary programmatic initiatives implemented by the U.S. government in the realm of environmental regulation; these have ranged from requiring firms to set their own environmental objectives, to publicly recognizing firm participation in environmental programs, to identifying and labeling environmentally responsible products for consumers.

As individual end users and businesses migrate to the cloud, there is also an argument to be made for shifting the focus of the interminable liability debate as it applies to client-side software (run on the end-user's computer) to server-side applications like increasingly popular cloud-based software services (Software as a Service—SaaS).[43] Centrally hosted and accessed by users over the internet, SaaS applications are already subject to a variety of federal and state privacy and data management laws and regulations governing online services that collect personal information from users. Such laws impose consequences on vendors for misrepresentation and failure to institute reasonable security measures for maintaining and transmitting user data.[44] In addition, entities contracting with cloud vendors have some room to negotiate contractual provisions for risk allocation and mitigation in the event of a security breach. But over the long term, incentivizing secure SaaS product development may require, among other things, the enactment of legislative restrictions on indemnification provisions and other limitations of liability in subscription software agreements.

Fines and Taxes

Holding software providers accountable for their code need not entail exposing them to unlimited private lawsuits. Indeed, a legislative or regulatory regime need not turn on the creation of a private right of action at all.

Government-imposed fines and forfeitures are one obvious alternative. Take the federal legislative and regulatory obligations presently imposed on telecommunications carriers, which are subject to capped forfeiture penalties levied by the Federal Communications Commission under Section 503(b) of the *Communications Act* in the event that they fail to employ reasonable data security practices to protect consumers' personal information.[45] Most states, too, have enacted legislation that penalizes companies for failing to safeguard sensitive user information. These laws governing responsible third-party data retention and breach disclosure practices offer a useful model for imposing narrowly circumscribed security duties on software providers.

An Indiana law, for instance, requires that the owner of any database containing personal electronic data disclose a security breach to potentially affected consumers but does not require any other affirmative act. The terms of the statute are decidedly limited—it provides the state attorney general enforcement powers but affords affected customers no private right of action against the database owner and imposes no duty to compensate affected individuals for inconvenience or potential credit-related harms in the wake of the breach.[46] Similarly, laws or regulations imposing best practices on the software industry could take the form of fines or fees levied by the government rather than individual end users. Requirements could range from the narrow, such as basic patching or government disclosure obligations, to the more substantive and onerous, such as vulnerability assessment and penetration testing procedures.

Taxes are a second means of avoiding the floodgates problem associated with a traditional liability regime. The idea of levying a Pigovian tax on software, which attempts to correct the cost of insecure code to the market, is not so counterintuitive if we accept that all software contains vulnerabilities and generates negative externalities. Rice has analogized vulnerabilities to pollution and called for a tax to encourage the development of safer, "cleaner" software.[47] But rather than assessing taxes as a function of the magnitude or severity of vulnerabilities in a particular piece of software, as Rice suggests, they could be assessed against all software vendors (or vendors of a specified size) on a percentage of revenue basis, with deductions available for implementing healthy security practices.

Liable Entities

Not all software providers can or should be subject to liability or regulation. Most notably, imposing liability on contributors to free open source software is an incoherent proposition, one that would jeopardize the progression and availability of collective resources and have problematic First Amendment implications. Whether or not you believe that the process by which open source software evolves actually constitutes its own security mechanism—a view that lost considerable support in the wake of Heartbleed—the fact is that open source software offers users both the cake and the recipe. Users are free to examine the recipe and alter and distribute it at will. By offering users the ability to access and modify the source code, open source software hands off responsibility to users.[48]

The calculus should change when it comes to proprietary applications, however, as the security of the code does not lie with users but remains instead entirely within the control of a commercial entity. The fact that much proprietary software is "free" should not foreclose liability: a narrowly tailored rule might provide that where users are "paying" for a software product or service with their data, a data breach that is deemed the result of unreasonable security practices could be grounds for government-imposed fines.

Drawing a liability line between open source and proprietary software is not without complications. Consider two forms of proprietary relicensing schemes that make use of open source code. First, companies can buy exceptions to a license governing open source code in order to incorporate the code into their proprietary products without being bound by the license's ordinary redistribution requirements. Second is the open core model, under which a company may maintain an open source version of their software for free and offer an enhanced, proprietary version for a fee. But mere use of open source software cannot become a liability escape hatch; a commercial vendor's decision to make use of open source resources should not materially alter its security obligations.

CONCLUSION

The software liability debate has retained its basic shape over the years, but the harms giving rise to the debate have evolved in that time. The earliest software liability discussions focused on embedded software errors that led to physical injury or death.[49] With the explosion in cyber crime and cyber-espionage, and rising fears of related terrorism, attention has converged on the vulnerabilities lurking in shoddy code.[50] Yet if the decades of paralysis on the liability question are any indication, software vendors will remain free of the repercussions of the vulnerabilities they ship—until, perhaps, the losses and costs shouldered by users materially change. Ultimately, it may take nothing short of our collective transition to the cloud and the dramatic expansion of the "Internet of Things"—and malicious attacks on smart toasters, door locks, automobiles, and pacemakers that result in readily cognizable, physical harm—to bring us full circle and tip the liability scales against software vendors. But we have options beyond the wait-and-see approach and should assess them on their merits, not reject them as a matter of course.

CHAPTER HIGHLIGHTS

Socially Acceptable Bad Code. Most security breaches are made possible by vulnerabilities, yet poor-quality software remains the market norm. Experts have long attributed this state of affairs not to the technical challenges of producing safer code, formidable though they are, but to social acceptance of software insecurity.

End Use License Agreements (EULAs). These contracts have long been bundled with virtually all software products and force users to "take it or leave it." Software vendors typically shunt all the risks associated with their products onto users through these boilerplate license agreements, which the courts have generally treated as enforceable contracts since the mid-1990s. Software vendors are, as a result, virtually bulletproof, as they may simply contract away responsibility for the deficiencies of their products with sweeping disclaimers. Software users, not vendors, bear the costs of insecure software.

Understanding Negligence. Negligence typically requires establishing four elements: that the software vendor owed the user a duty, that the vendor breached that duty, that the breach caused the user injury, and that harm was caused by the injury to the user as a result of that breach. But each of these elements poses special challenges in the software context.

Market Failure. Not only are users relatively apathetic about software security, we systematically disregard it in favor of functionality. The appetite for more and improved features has encouraged the industry's "fix-it-later" culture. Thus software companies look for bugs late in the development process and knowingly package and ship buggy software with impunity, relying on timely release and incremental patching as a primary security strategy. Users are sluggish about deploying security fixes, even in the case of critical vulnerabilities (research shows 75 percent of targeted attacks could be prevented through regular patching).

Limiting Liability. The objective must be to influence vendor design and development choices without unduly restricting them. This balance might be struck by imposing on vendors certain self-certification or public reporting requirements that make transparent and easily understandable to consumers their adherence to or departure from industry standards and best practices. Best practices, in turn, could constitute an affirmative defense against regulatory fines, and might range from periodic independent security audits to participation in a ratings system for software security. That said, not all software providers can or should be subject to liability or regulation. Most notably, imposing liability on contributors to free open source software is an incoherent proposition.

NOTES

1. For example, in 2013, Toyota announced a massive settlement to resolve hundreds of suits alleging software bugs caused sudden vehicle acceleration. Paul M. Barrett, "Toyota Waves the White Flag on Sudden-Acceleration Lawsuits," *Bloomberg*, December 16, 2013, http://www.bloomberg.com/bw/articles/2013-12-16/toyota-enters-settlement-talks-over-sudden-acceleration-lawsuits; Between 1985 and 1987, software errors in the Therac-25, a state-of-the-art medical linear accelerator, were linked to at least six radiation overdoses. The resulting lawsuits against Atomic Energy of Canada Limited, which held rights to the software design, were settled out of court. Nancy G. Leveson and Clark S. Turner, "An Investigation of the Therac-25 Accidents," *IEEE Computer* 26, no. 7 (July 1993), doi: 10.1109/MC.1993.274940.

Portions of this chapter have previously appeared in a modified form as series on *The New Republic* and *Lawfare*, https://www.lawfareblog.com/bad-code-whole-series.

2. For a recent example, see Jessica Twentyman, "Calls to Make Software Designers Liable for Security Weakness," *Financial Times*, April 10, 2015, http://www.ft.com/intl/cms/s/0/4569a00e-c272-11e4-ad89-00144feab7de.html#axzz41VamYhch.

3. Relative to bugs, which tend to be localized coding errors that may be detected by automated testing tools, design flaws exist at a deeper architectural level and can be more difficult to find and fix. Gary McGraw, *Software Security: Building Security In* (Upper Saddle River: Pearson Education, Inc., 2006), 191.

4. Huseyin Cavusoglu, Hasan Cavusoglu and Jun Zhang, "Security Patch Management: Share the Burden or Share the Damage?" *Management Science 54* (April 2008). doi: 10.1287/mnsc.1070.0794; Byung Cho Kim, Pei-Yu Chen, and

Tridas Mukhopadhyay, "The Effect of Liability and Patch Release on Software Security: The Monopoly Case," *Production & Operations Management* 20, no. 4 (July/Aug. 2011): 603.

5. See, e.g., Mike Fisk, "Causes & Remedies for Social Acceptance of Network Insecurity," in *Proceeding of the Workshop on Economics and Information Security, University of California, Berkeley*, May 16–17, 2002.

6. "Avoiding the Top 10 Software Security Design Flaws," *IEEE Cyber Security*, http://cybersecurity.ieee.org/2015/11/13/avoiding-the-top-10-security-flaws; in April 2014, the public learned that a two-year-old OpenSSL vulnerability—dubbed the "Heartbleed" bug—had exposed half a million secure web servers to data theft and illicit tracking. Twice in 2015, researchers revealed that "Stagefright" flaws in the Android operating system had made nearly a billion user phones susceptible to remote hijacking; After Heartbleed sent the web reeling, the Linux Foundation launched the Core Infrastructure Initiative "to harden the security of key open source projects" with the backing of major industry players like Google and Microsoft. Core Infrastructure Initiative, accessed March 6, 2016. https://www.coreinfrastructure.org.

7. Lawrence B. Levy and Suzanne Y. Bell, "Software Product Liability: Understanding and Minimizing the Risks," *Berkeley Technology Law Journal* 5 (1990), doi: 10.15779/Z38695K.

8. Michael L. Rustad and Thomas H. Koenig, "The Tort of Negligent Enablement of Cybercrime," *Berkeley Technology Law Journal* 20 (2005): 1553, doi: http://dx.doi.org/doi:10.15779/Z38JX0S; see, e.g., "Chatlos Systems v. National Cash Register Corp," 479 F. Supp. 738, 740 n. 1 (D.N.J. 1979); Harold Lee, "Can the Insurance Industry Patch Our Software?" *UCLA Journal of Law and Technology* (2004).

9. Douglas E. Phillips, "When Software Fails: Emerging Standards of Vendor Liability Under the Uniform Commercial Code," *The Business Lawyer 50*, no. 1 (November 1994): 151, http://www.jstor.org/stable/40687574; a different, controversial model code, the Uniform Computer Information Transactions Act (UCITA), is the first to specifically govern software licensing, but has been harshly criticized for its proindustry bias and is of little use to the injured user because it validates mass-market license agreements. See Michael L. Rustad, "Making UCITA More Consumer-Friendly," *John Marshall Journal of Computer and Information Law* 18 (1999): 549, 560.

10. Bonna Lynn Horovitz, "Computer Software as a Good under the Uniform Commercial Code: Taking a Bite Out of the Intangibility Myth," *Boston University Law Review* 65 (1985).

11. David McGowan, "Free Contracting, Fair Competition, and Article 2B: Some Reflections on Federal Competition Policy, Information Transactions, and 'Aggressive Neutrality,'" *Berkeley Technology Law Journal* 13 (1998): 1213; W. Kuan Hon, Christopher Millard, and Ian Walden, *Stanford Technology Law Review* 16, no. 1 (2012): 92–94 (describing the contractual liability of SaaS providers).

12. Rustad and Koenig, "The Tort of Negligent Enablement," 1565.

13. The question of whether the UCC is applicable at all, under the theory that software is not a good or that the transaction is not a sale, is long-running and has reemerged with a vengeance with the rise of cloud-based software services. See

Edward G. Durney, "The Warranty of Merchantability and Computer Software Contracts: A Square Peg Won't Fit in a Round Hole," *Washington Law Review* 59 (1984): 516–20.

14. See, e.g., *ProCD, Inc. v. Zeidenberg*, 86 F.3d 1452–57 (7th. Cir. 1996) (shrink-wrap license was an enforceable contract under the UCC); *NMP Corp. v. Parametric Tech. Corp.*, 958 F. Supp. 1536, 1547–48 (N.D. Okla. 1997) (rejecting breach of contract claim alleging defective where licensing agreement "clearly and unambiguously disclaims all other warranties, express or implied, including any warranty of merchantability or fitness for a particular purpose").

15. Douglas E. Phillips, *The Software License Unveiled: How Legislation by License Controls Software Access* (New York: Oxford University Press, 2009), 3.

16. Ibid.

17. See, e.g., In re Facebook Privacy Litig., 791 F. Supp. 2d 705, 715 (N.D. Cal. 2011) aff'd, 572 F. App'x 494 (9th Cir. 2014) ("Plaintiffs do not allege that they paid fees for Defendant's services. . . . Because Plaintiffs allege that they received Defendant's services for free, as a matter of law, Plaintiffs cannot state a [Unfair Competition Law] claim under their own allegations"). This is presumably Bruce Schneier's point when he observes that "[f]ree software wouldn't fall under a liability regime because the writer and the user have no business relationship; they are not seller and buyer." This is correct only with respect to liability within the private-ordering contract realm.

18. See, e.g., *Shema Kolainu-Hear Our Voices v. ProviderSoft, LLC*, 832 F. Supp. 2d 194, 208 (E.D.N.Y. 2010).

19. *Randolph v. ING Life Ins. & Annuity Co.*, 973 A.2d 702, 708 (D.C. 2009).

20. See, e.g., *Slaughter v. AON Consulting, Inc.*, No. CIV.A. 10C-09-001FSS, 2012 WL 1415772, (Del. Super. Jan. 31, 2012).

21. Charles C. Mann, "Why Software Is So Bad," *MIT Technology Review*, July 1, 2002, https://www.technologyreview.com/s/401594/why-software-is-so-bad.

22. Watts S. Humphrey, "Defective Software Works," *Carnegie Mellon University Software Engineering Institute*, January 1, 2004, http://www.sei.cmu.edu/library/abstracts/news-at-sei/wattsnew20041.cfm. Some variation of this argument probably explains why so many programmers produce suboptimal code, usually recycling the suboptimal code of others in the process; Bernard Meisler, "The Real Reason Silicon Valley Coders Write Bad Software," *Atlantic*, October 9, 2012, http://www.theatlantic.com/national/archive/2012/10/the-real-reason-silicon-valley-coders-write-bad-software/263377 (lamenting the quality of API documentation).

23. Ibid.

24. "A Lemon Law for Software?" *Economist*, March 14, 2002, http://www.economist.com/node/1020715.

25. See, e.g., Symantec Corporation, *Internet Security Threat Report* 20 (April 2015): 103, https://www4.symantec.com/mktginfo/whitepaper/ISTR/21347932_GA-internet-security-threat-report-volume-20-2015-social_v2.pdf.

26. Eric Rescorla, "Security Holes . . . Who Cares?" 12th USENIX Security Symposium, Washington, D.C., August 2003, https://www.usenix.org/legacy/event/sec03/tech/full_papers/rescorla/rescorla.pdf; James A. Lewis, "Raising the Bar for

Cybersecurity," *Center for Strategic & International Studies*, February 12, 2013, http://csis.org/files/publication/130212_Lewis_RaisingBarCybersecurity.pdf.

27. "The Cost of 'Code Red': $1.2 Billion," *USA Today*, August 1, 2001, http://usatoday30.usatoday.com/tech/news/2001-08-01-code-red-costs.htm#more; David Moore et al., "Inside the Slammer Worm," *IEEE Computer Society* (2003), doi: 1540-7993/03.

28. Ross Anderson and Tyler Moore, "The Economics of Information Security: A Survey and Open Questions," *Science* 314, October 27, 2006.

29. Michel Van Eeten and Johannes M. Bauer, "Emerging Threats to Internet Security: Incentives, Externalities and Policy Implications," *Journal of Contingencies & Crisis Management* 17, no. 4 (December 2009), doi: 10.1111/j.1468-5973.2009.00592.x.

30. Testimony of Joseph Demarest, Assistant Director, Cyber Division Federal Bureau of Investigation, before the Senate Judiciary Committee, Subcommittee on Crime and Terrorism, July 15, 2014, https://www.fbi.gov/news/testimony/taking-down-botnets.

31. Bruce Schneier, "Liability Changes Everything," *Schneier on Security*, November 2003, https://www.schneier.com/essays/archives/2003/11/liability_changes_ev.html.

32. Barbara van Schewick, *Internet Architecture and Innovation* (Cambridge: MIT Press, 2012), 359.

33. See, e.g., Paul Graham, *Hackers & Painters: Big Ideas from the Computer Age*, O'Reilly, (2004); Joshua Rothman, "Was Steve Jobs an Artist?" *New Yorker*, October 13, 2015, http://www.newyorker.com/culture/cultural-comment/was-steve-jobs-an-artist.

34. *Escola v. Coca Cola Bottling Co. of Fresno*, 150 P.2d 436 (Cal. 1944); Alex Berenson, "Merck Jury Adds $9 Million in Damages," *New York Times*, April 12, 2006, http://www.nytimes.com/2006/04/12/business/12vioxx.html?fta=y; Chris Woodyard, "GM Ignition Switch Deaths Hit 124," *USA Today*, July 13, 2014, http://www.usatoday.com/story/money/cars/2015/07/13/gm-ignition-switch-death-toll/30092693.

35. "RSA 2012: Are Software Liability Laws Needed?" *Infosecurity*, March 2012, https://www.schneier.com/news/archives/2012/03/rsa_2012_are_softwar.html.

36. McGraw, *Software Security: Building Security In*, 5.

37. Daniel Geer et al., "Cost of Monopoly," last modified September 27, 2003, cryptome.org/cyberinsecurity.htm.

38. Web browsers, for example, support plug-ins that enable users to install extensions for new document types.

39. A 2009 NASA report commissioned to identify and address risk associated with increasing complexity of NASA flight software defines complexity simply: "how hard something is to understand or verify" at all levels from software design to software development to software testing. Daniel L. Dvorak, "NASA Study on Flight Software Complexity," NASA Office of Chief Engineer (2009), http://www.nasa.gov/pdf/418878main_FSWC_Final_Report.pdf. For example, in 2013, Microsoft instructed users of Windows 7 to uninstall the 2823324 security update when unexpected interactions between the update and certain third-party software rendered some users' computers unbootable. Dan Goodin, "Microsoft Tells Windows 7 Users to

Uninstall Faulty Security Update," *Ars Technica,* April 12, 2013, http://arstechnica.com/security/2013/04/microsoft-tells-windows-7-users-to-uninstall-faulty-security-update.

40. Fred P. Brooks, Jr., "No Silver Bullet—Essence and Accidents of Software Engineering," *IEEE Computer* 20, no. 4 (1987), doi:10.1109/MC.1987.1663532.

41. Roger A. Grimes, "Vendors Should Not Be Liable for Their Security Flaws," *InfoWorld,* July 24, 2012, http://www.infoworld.com/article/2617937/security/vendors-should-not-be-liable-for-their-security-flaws.html.

42. Blake Glenn, "Geekonomics Author David Rice: 'They're Not Trying to Make Bad Software,'" *Commerce Times,* October 15, 2008, http://www.ecommercetimes.com/story/64810.html.

43. Terrence August, Marius Florin Niculescu, and Hyoduk Shin, "Cloud Implications on Software Network Structure and Security Risks," *Information Systems Research* 25, no. 3 (2014), doi: http://dx.doi.org/10.1287/isre.2014.0527.

44. For example, in 2014, the mobile messaging app developer Snapchat entered into a twenty-year consent decree with the Federal Trade Commission for misrepresentation and privacy violations following a hack of 4.6 million usernames and their phone numbers.

45. 47 U.S.C. § 503(b)(1)(B); 47 C.F.R. § 1.80(a)(2).

46. Ind. Code Ann. §§ 24-4.9-3-3.5(d)–(e), 24-4.9-4-1(a).

47. David Rice, *Geekonomics: The Real Cost of Insecure Software* (Boston: Pearson Education, Inc., 2008), 313.

48. Whether software is properly considered "open source" turns on more than access to the source code. Among other things, the program must permit distribution in source code and compiled form, and allow distribution of modifications and derived works under the same terms as the original software license. Open Source Initiative, accessed March 7, 2016. https://opensource.org/docs/osd.

49. Robert D. Sprague, "Software Products Liability: Has Its Time Arrived?" *Western State University Law Review* 19 (1991): 137.

50. Michael D. Scott, "Tort Liability for Vendors of Insecure Software: Has the Time Finally Come?" *Maryland Law Review* 67 (2007): 425; Kevin R. Pinkney, "Putting Blame Where Blame Is Due: Software Manufacturer and Customer Liability for Security-Related Software Failure," *Albany Law Journal of Science and Technology* 13 (2002): 43.

Section II

COMBATING CYBER CRIME

Chapter 6

Understanding Cyber Crime

Sasha Romanosky and Trey Herr

Cyber crime covers a wide range of activities that include theft, fraud, and harassment; stealing valuable intellectual property as part of industrial espionage; committing financial fraud and credit card theft; and disrupting internet services for ideological goals ("hacktivism"). The crimes target both firms and consumers, and while they rarely result in physical harm or property damage, there can still be severe consequences.[1] For example, many data breaches are caused by criminals hacking into private corporations and government agencies in order to steal personal information. The compromised data may include individuals' names, addresses, social security numbers, dates of birth, driver's licenses, passport numbers, credit card numbers, and other financial data. The information can then be used to commit crimes including unemployment fraud, tax fraud, loan fraud, and payment card fraud.[2] Individual harms stemming from these breaches include direct financial loss, the burden of increased loan interest rates, denial of utility services, civil suits, or even criminal investigations.[3] The resulting costs incurred by firms might include forensic investigations, consumer redress, disclosure fees, and litigation—and sums can reach over $200 million.[4]

Overall, the chapter frames this complicated topic as a discussion of two markets: one of information assurance, occupied by victims (e.g., firms and consumers), and one of threats, where buyers and sellers of malicious software and stolen information trade their goods.[5] Policy solutions that attempt to reduce victim harms and cyber crime address more than just device or network security, they seek to influence the incentives and behaviors of illicit actors and victims through criminal, civil, and administrative law. The motivating question is: how can government interventions affect the incentives of actors in each of these markets in order to reduce losses, and bring about more efficient investment in security?

THE MARKET FOR THREATS

What drives cyber crime? The majority of computer-enabled or -supported crime is financially motivated and is thus the result of a rational cost-benefit analysis on the part of attackers.[6] Both the cost of acquiring and implementing malware and the security posture of potential firms can influence target selection by criminal groups. Successful cyber-attacks can therefore be considered a result of mismatched investment in security. Attackers constitute a market for "threat," counterbalanced with a victim's market for security. In these markets, there exist two principal goods: malicious software and stolen data.

Goods

Malicious software used by criminals to gain access to a victim's information systems is composed of three parts, each of which can be developed, bought, and sold independently of each other: a propagation method, exploits, and a payload.[7] These different components are exchanged using various transaction types, in some cases rented, while in other cases sold outright.[8] One of the most popular means to distribute malware is via phishing e-mails—fake e-mails which appear to be from a legitimate sender and are distributed to a wide audience. These phishing mails can be propagated by large collections of zombie computers called botnets (see Botnet description in figure 6.1). Botnets are usually rented rather than sold, and an individual maintains the machines in each "herd" of computers or small group that continually infects new machines in order to offset lost computers or expand their herd.[9]

Stolen data comes in an even greater variety of forms; for example, credit card numbers are stolen, bundled, and sold through an ever-evolving mix of illegal underground marketplaces.[10] In addition, thieves may use the loot themselves, while in other cases the stolen data is sold to security researchers or to corporations such as banks looking to detect fraudulent accounts.[11] These markets for malware and stolen data are supported by several types of actors, described below.

Actors

Criminal organizations vary in size, purpose, and sophistication. Some are focused exclusively on espionage and have developed the means to distribute work internally, with different teams assigned to research and identify future potential targets, passing off their work to others for the development of malicious code, and yet more teams to package and deploy it.[12] Other groups, organized along the existing social networks of offline criminal

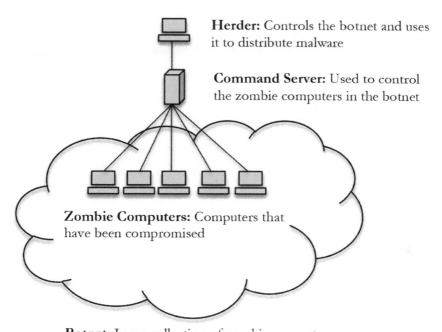

Herder: Controls the botnet and uses it to distribute malware

Command Server: Used to control the zombie computers in the botnet

Zombie Computers: Computers that have been compromised

Botnet: Large collection of zombie computers

Figure 6.1 Botnet Diagram

organizations, pursue a wide range of criminal activities, using information obtained to conduct traditional identity theft, extortion, and financial fraud.[13]

Some groups retain a single function. For example, the process of "carding" (using stolen credit card information to reproduce cards and withdraw funds before the cards or their accounts are frozen) has emerged as a specialty activity in some circles. Small numbers of more knowledgeable "carders" tasked with stealing or otherwise securing credit card information then distribute these to large numbers of money mules (otherwise unknowledgeable low-level individuals spread across regions and countries), who then withdraw funds from ATMs.[14] The goal for carder groups is to use purchased credentials to extract as much cash out of these accounts as possible, as quickly as possible, before banks begin to disrupt the process. Several of the largest groups devoted to stealing funds from stolen bank accounts with replicated credit card information are vertically integrated, responsible for every step of the fraud process from theft to withdrawal.[15]

The market for threats assumes largely financially motivated groups, and does not consider strategically motivated actors who pursue political or military goals without regard for financial benefit. These activities, which may involve attempting to achieve destructive digital or kinetic effects, fall more closely under the military cyber operations topic rather than cyber crime. For financially motivated actors, however, there are established market mechanisms, a means to determine available buyers and sellers, to price the goods themselves, and establish the reputation and some means of transaction between actors.[16]

Market Dynamics

Much like the market for a used car or a new toaster oven, the market for cyber threat shares several underlying characteristics: trust, reputation, price, and competition. Unlike cars and toasters, however, buying and selling malicious software and stolen data takes place under a necessary veil of secrecy.

As there are few external means to compel buyers to provide payment, or sellers to provide their wares in the event of a fraudulent transaction, reputation plays a pivotal role. Some markets adopt a reviewer process much like Amazon, where other customers can comment on their experience with different malware components. In writing about purchasing freejoiner, a malicious payload that can steal personal data, for example, one such customer commented, "Purchased a freejoiner 2 and left very happy," while another wrote, "Thank you for a FreeJoiner, is the best program in its class I have ever seen."[17] Some underground websites may compliment these user reviews with site moderators who verify products and transactions to track high-quality sellers and remove scammers. Customer satisfaction matters; sellers of credit card information may offer bonuses if users buy certain quantities or offer freebies to make up for already deactivated accounts.[18]

Another dynamic to consider is the price of goods within this marketplace. The cost of e-mail account credentials, for example, has fluctuated in the past decade, ranging between $4 and $30 in 2007 and dropping to $0.50 to $10 in 2015.[19] This drop in prices may indicate oversupply, a surplus of available accounts, or less demand for e-mail as a means of developing and sustaining attacks. Prices for custom features and revisions are added on top of the initial purchase by sellers who expect repeat business or who are selling a tool to users as part of a service. The "Pinch" malicious payload offers users a means to steal data from targeted systems in a variety of configurations. Though at one point Pinch's source code was posted online, the tool continued to be updated and sold on a regular basis for up to $30 per user.[20]

Competition plays a role in the market for threats as well. Where buyers can select between different sellers, the traditional competitive mechanics that decrease price and increase quality come into play, especially for malicious software components. One example is the evolution of SpyEye, a rival to the popular ZeuS malware which has primarily been used to target banking systems for user credentials but now includes a host of other features.[21] Early versions of ZeuS were relatively simple, but the emergence of SpyEye at a lower price point in the same forums to target the same customers resulted in a feature arms race between the two payloads, with developers rushing to add more features to each in an effort to attract and maintain customers.[22] In 2010, just over a year after SpyEye's emergence, the two actually merged, with ZeuS folding into its rival's brand.[23]

INFLUENCING THE MARKET

There are often two opportunities for policy interventions—*ex ante*, or before the event, and *ex post*, after the event. *Ex ante* opportunities to shape the market for threat rest primarily on altering the market dynamics explained above. While targeting price seems an obvious first step, there are multiple by-products to consider. Attempting to increase the price of malicious software components may make it less attractive for low-skilled attackers to acquire capabilities and could reduce overall demand, but such an increase may also incentivize new sellers to join the market, thereby increasing the variety or sophistication of what is available. For stolen information, there are similarly multiple effects from any action; attempting to increase the price of stolen information may reduce the number of individuals willing to make purchases, but could increase the perceived value of such information, incentivizing more elaborate attempts to steal new credentials and card data.

An alternative approach may be to attack the reputation mechanisms, disrupting the tenuous chains of trust that link buyers and sellers for malicious software and stolen information. For example, law enforcement agents sometimes pose as sellers and falsify reviews, but can also set up alternative markets in an effort to drive users onto a smaller and smaller number of controlled platforms.[24] Sowing distrust by seeding outdated or useless credit card or personally identifying information could also help disrupt these criminal markets as buyers are faced with an increasingly uncertain environment in which to spend limited resources.

Operating in a market is difficult, especially when it takes place in a more clandestine context with few mechanisms to enforce transactions or guarantee contracts. The traditional information asymmetry between the seller who holds a good and the buyer who seeks to obtain it is made that much more burdensome as the market for cyber threats is fundamentally a den of thieves. With mechanisms to establish the reputation of, and trust in, buyers as willing agents and sellers as purveying the goods they advertise already fragile, law enforcement activities to disrupt these processes may yield outsize effects.

Ex post options are more common but somewhat more restrictive, focusing on punitive criminal measures for buyers and sellers as well as intermediaries like forum operators who provide a marketplace for these interactions. A conventional alternative to attacking the market for threats directly is to apply penalties to the activities taking place and seek to prosecute buyers and sellers.

The primary legal vehicle for U.S. cyber criminal law enforcement is the *Computer Fraud and Abuse Act* (CFAA), originally enacted in 1986 and amended several times since.[25] The CFAA criminalizes conduct in two general categories: access to computer systems and activities on them. The nine main violations include "exceeding authorized access" to a computer system, trespassing on a government computer, and causing damage by intentional access either recklessly or with negligence.[26] There are limitations to the law, however. This includes a running debate within the courts over the definition of "authorized" access where there are at least three competing definitions: (a) behavior taken to bypass existing and clearly evident security measures, (b) any activity, including that by otherwise authorized users, which exceeds the authorized scope of operations on that computer system, and (c) actions taken to obtain access to information in excess of that for which use of the computer system was originally granted.[27]

THE MARKET FOR SECURITY

There are many forms of government intervention that can be adopted in order to induce companies (and individuals) to invest in an appropriate level of information assurance, and optimize (but not necessarily eliminate) any harms caused by the kinds of criminal activities previously described.

Ex Ante versus Ex Post

As mentioned, two familiar interventions are *ex ante* safety regulation (mandated standards), and *ex post* liability.[28] *Ex ante* regulation is considered a heavy-handed prevention mechanism that enforces a minimum standard of care in order to prevent or reduce harm (e.g., fire codes that define wall thickness and materials used in clothing or homes). These standards are useful when the harms are thought to be extreme (i.e., either catastrophic or miniscule) but widely distributed, affecting large numbers of individuals. Obviously, catastrophic harms (e.g., nuclear disasters) are worth preventing through regulation, but so are minor harms that are spread across thousands or millions of individuals. The reason is that the harm to any one individual may be small, but in the aggregate, it may be worth the burden of increased prevention.

Regulation can also be useful when the source of the harm is unknown. For example, in the case of health risks (e.g., pollution) or data breaches, often the offending company may not be known, and so it becomes worthwhile to mandate specific controls to prevent avoidable harms. However, its effectiveness is hampered when the regulated inputs are only loosely correlated with the harmful outputs. For example, mandating two-factor authentication and encryption on Health IT systems may be ineffective if health professionals share login information and remained logged in to applications, resulting in medical identity theft.

Nevertheless, monitoring compliance to a regulation may well be easier for an enforcement agency than estimating the amount of harm caused by a particular event. For example, it may be much easier to verify that a company has implemented basic security controls and passed a security audit than it is to measure the total loss from identity theft. This leads into a separate question of what manner of policy reforms are feasible rather than most effective.

Ex post liability, on the other hand, is meant to allow injured parties to recover any losses through civil litigation. The cost of defending against a lawsuit and the threat of future suits are expected to force companies to internalize any losses, inducing them to increase security prevention measures. Liability, however, becomes ineffective if the harms are either incalculable, unverifiable, or when the injuring party is unknown. Identity theft and privacy harms, for example, often suffer from these limitations; while courts have granted standing for plaintiffs in some cases of credit monitoring, these claims are more frequently dismissed where they argue increased potential risk of identity theft or fear of future harms.[29] However, a liability regime has the advantage of allowing firms to manage their information assurance (generally, any prevention measures) on their own, in ways that are most efficient for them. When they do properly bear the cost of their actions, they will naturally seek ways to reduce their total cost of any harmful behavior.[30]

Data Breach Disclosure Laws

As a result of losses stemming from data breaches, most states in the United States (as well as other countries) have enacted laws that require organizations to notify individuals when personally identifiable information has been lost or stolen. A primary goal of the laws is to empower consumers to take action in order to mitigate losses. A secondary goal is to force firms to internalize more of the cost of a data breach, thereby inducing them to increase their investment in security measures.[31]

The impact of these laws has yet to be fully examined, but existing research provides mixed conclusions; one study demonstrated an improvement in firm practices, while another found only marginal reduction in the rate of consumer identity theft.[32] Critics argue that such laws inflict unnecessary costs for both firms and consumers if indeed firms already bear most of the loss, or when lost data is recovered before it is even accessed.[33] Moreover, when the risk of harm is low, unnecessary notification may desensitize individuals, preventing them from acting when a serious threat does exist.[34] Further, consumers may be unable to properly respond to breach notifications, as the notices may present a substantial cognitive and psychological barrier to taking action, also causing them to underreact.[35] Alternatively, news media and the burgeoning market of identity theft prevention services may breed panic and confusion, causing consumers to overreact by unnecessarily purchasing such products, increasing their expected costs.[36]

Cyber Insurance

Since the first data breach disclosure law was passed in 2003, thousands of breaches have been publicly disclosed, increasing costs to firms—costs against which they are preferring to insure (see table 6.1 for examples of corporate data breach). What has followed is a powerful and unforeseen consequence of fueling a market for cyber insurance.[37]

The defining characteristics of cyber insurance are: interdependent security, correlated failure, and information asymmetry. Some of these properties are common to all insurance markets, while others—and their combined effects—are unique to the risks of networked computing systems and cyber-insurance. First, interdependent security reflects the degree to which the security of one computer network is affected by the compromise of another system (the breached system is said to impose a negative externality on the victim). For example, the security of Reagan National Airport in Washington, D.C., may be compromised if luggage from San Francisco International Airport is not properly screened.[38] Correlated failures are where a single malicious event causes failures across a host of systems; the loss of power at security monitoring company like ADT could compromise the security of residences in surrounding neighborhoods, for example. Finally, information

Table 6.1 Data Breach History

Year	Data Breach	Number of Records Compromised	Estimated Cost to Firm
2003	TJX Companies Inc.	94 million	$5 million
2011	Sony Corporation	77 million	$15 million
2012	Global Payments Inc.	1.5 million	$121.2 million
2013	Target Corporation	70 million	$11 million
2014	eBay	145 million	$46 million
2014	The Home Depot	56 million	$33 million
2014	JP Morgan Chase	76 million	$250 million
2015	Anthem Inc.	80 million	$100 million

All findings can be accessed at the U.S. Securities and Exchange Commission website under Company Filings. https://www.sec.gov/edgar/searchedgar/companysearch.html.

asymmetry in the context of insurance reflects the familiar moral hazard and adverse selection problems; companies behave in a riskier manner when fully protected from loss and insurance carriers have difficulty differentiating between high- and low-risk clients.

Cyber insurance policies generally cover three categories of loss: first-party losses, regulatory fines and fees, and third-party liability. First-party coverage includes losses stemming from outages or business interruption costs incurred due to a data breach, privacy violation, or security incident. For example, breach notification costs, credit monitoring, public relations, forensic investigations, call center support, business interruption, and in some cases even extortion. Regulatory fines and fees cover sanctions brought by state or federal agencies (e.g., by the FTC or SEC). Third-party liability coverage includes settlements, judgments, and defense costs due to civil litigation. Naturally, these policies also include many exclusions, such as discrimination, criminal, or deliberate acts, patent infringement or violations of trade secrets, or acts of war, invasion, or insurrection.

The data collected by insurance carriers affords them a unique advantage over any other entity—even government agencies—when it comes to assessing the benefits of different information assurance controls and practices. Recall that the critical questions are: which security controls are most effective at reducing risk? Is it better to have a firewall or an intrusion detection system? Is two-factor authentication really better than a single-factor one? If so, by how much, and how much of a discount in premium should a policyholder enjoy? To date, no single firm or government agency has been able to answer these basic, yet fundamental, questions.

Insurance companies are perfectly positioned because they possess the necessary data. Using their security assessment forms, policy and claims data, they can correlate the information assurance controls of an insured entity with loss outcomes. With sufficient data, the carrier could rank order security controls by effectiveness. This would, in effect, determine which information assurance measures are most effective at reducing loss. These answers could be invaluable at driving information assurance research, the market for cyber-insurance, and ultimately the security posture of U.S. critical infrastructure.[39]

Alternative Policy Devices

Taxes, subsidies, and nudging are additional methods of inducing efficient behavior. Taxes and subsidies are often thought to produce equivalent outcomes whether a policy maker taxes bad behavior or subsidizes good behavior (and in this way, each are considered efficient policies). However, taxes (or any form of sanction) will be less efficient as the cost of applying those sanctions increases. For example, a subsidy can simply be paid to those who comply, while noncompliance must be detected and enforced, which can be costly. Sanctions may be preferred to subsidy if the *threat* of sanctioning is credible, because the desired behavior is achieved at no cost.[40] Some have even suggested a "reversible reward" in which a subsidy is offered for compliance, but then in the event of noncompliance that same reward is used to penalize (perhaps through litigation or other sanction), thereby doubling the incentive mechanism.[41]

Nudging has become a very popular form of public policy.[42] It is a form of choice architecture that specifically exploits (rather than ignores) human cognitive biases in order to achieve outcomes that are thought to be in the best interests of the individual. For example, if students are more likely to fill up on foods that are presented first in a cafeteria lineup, then simply presenting healthier foods before fattening ones should create healthier plates, without eliminating personal choice. Indeed, there is no reason nudging cannot be applied to the private sector for the purpose of appropriate information assurance investment; after all, companies (and government agencies) are run by people.

SECURITY AS INVESTMENT

Information assurance as the means to prevent compromise to a computer or network is fundamentally a question of security investment as firms seek to reduce the likelihood of an attacker stealing sensitive data or disrupting operations. On one hand, underinvestment is less costly, it yields a greater number of successful attacks and is suboptimal as firms lose valuable information and customers over the inability to protect their data and systems. On the other hand, overinvestment can be similarly damaging as companies expend scarce resources with little to no return on improved security. An effort to thwart every single attack is likely impossible as there are no perfectly secure systems, especially given the necessary involvement of human operators. Framing security as an investment, therefore, proposes that the purpose of government intervention is to support a market that encourages companies to find the optimal point between the cost of attacks and benefit of defensive information assurance measures.

Many consumer rights organizations and privacy advocates argue that companies are not spending enough on information assurance. In their eyes, this may be justified by the increasing rates and scale of software vulnerabilities and data breaches. This argument rests on two conditions. First, it assumes that consumers cannot—or should not—take measures to protect their own data and computing devices. Like pedestrians looking to cross a busy roadway, do consumers, themselves, not also bear some responsibility for taking appropriate precautions when browsing the internet, and protecting their personal data? Certainly, there are many circumstances when individuals are harmed through no fault of their own (e.g., theft of one's personal information from a data breach). However, there are also many situations where individuals *are* or *could be* empowered to take measures to protect their data (such as practicing proper browsing habits, the appropriate disclosure of personal information, password hygiene, laptop and data record storage, etc.). And so discussions regarding policies or regulations to force firms to increase cybersecurity should also be balanced with discussions of inducing *consumers* to take appropriate security and privacy precautions.

The second concern is that the argument that companies do not invest enough implicitly assumes that a world where companies *did* properly invest would experience *zero* data breaches or security incidents. Effectively, "appropriate" security, by that argument, implies "absolute" security. But as we have heard many times, perfect security is only achievable with zero utility (i.e., a broken computer is perfectly secure but entirely useless). Therefore, if we recognize that perfect security is neither practical nor efficient, and we instead seek to have both companies and individuals bear some responsibility for their actions, and invest in an efficient level of precaution (i.e., one that balances the incremental costs with incremental benefits), then this would describe a world in which both data breaches and security incidents existed.

The point is simply that the existence of security incidents could, in fact, reflect a state of efficient security investment. Just because we see some volume of data breaches or security incidents does not *necessarily* imply that companies (or individuals) are not *already* spending an efficient amount on security. While increased spending may reduce security incidents, that additional cost of investment may be larger than the benefit from that investment. If efficiency is the primary goal, then before we answer the question of *"how* should we encourage companies to invest more?" we must first ask, *"should* we encourage companies to invest more?"

While some policymakers may applaud firms for managing information assurance just as with any other kind of risk they face (product, employee, corporate, etc.), there is an important consequence to this action. Namely, that by doing this, firms will (can and should) act in their own best interest. While this behavior is appropriate, these actions may ignore any harms they cause to consumers. That is, when firms cause harms to others but don't bear the burden of those costs, they act in a manner that is not in society's best interest.

In sum, the goal of a policymaker should be to optimize—not minimize—security incidents. That is, he or she should seek to balance the cost of a security measure with its benefit. Thus, the existence of data breaches and security incidents does not *necessarily* imply that companies are not investing in an efficient level of security. In fact, an absence of successful attacks leading to breach would likely imply excessive spending. People, like companies, are self-interested; we make decisions to maximize our returns and so should not expect companies to do otherwise (or begrudge them when they do). The challenge of stymieing cyber crime is finding the point where reasonable security investment yields appreciable returns, and effective information assurance techniques can act to deter most attackers and prevent catastrophic incidents.

CONCLUSION

Structuring a policy response to cyber crime that encourages efficient investment in security and disrupts the market for threats is a difficult proposition, but progress is possible with an approach that recognizes the scarce resources available to both attackers and defenders. An important consideration for policy reform is the role of independent researchers and academics, who play an important function in identifying vulnerabilities and testing the security of information systems. These activities, like penetration testing and vulnerability disclosure, can sometimes appear uncomfortably similar to criminal activity at a high level, so a degree of nuance is required for any legal reforms that may impact their activities. Combating cyber crime requires looking at the whole board, considering the incentives of actors in the market for threats and the market for security by influencing attackers and defenders alike.

CHAPTER HIGHLIGHTS

Defining Cyber Crime. Cyber crime covers a wide range of activities that include theft, fraud, and harassment; stealing valuable intellectual property as part of industrial espionage; committing financial fraud and credit card theft; and disrupting internet services for ideological goals ("hacktivism"). The crimes target both firms and consumers, and while they rarely result in physical harm or property damage, there can still be severe consequences.

Smart Investments. Both the cost of acquiring and implementing malware and the security posture of potential firms can influence target selection by criminal groups. Successful cyber-attacks can therefore be considered a result of mismatched investment in security.

Disrupting Criminal Markets. To combat cyber crime, one approach may be to attack the reputation mechanisms, disrupting the tenuous chains of trust that link buyers and sellers for malicious software and stolen information.

Leveraging Insurers. The data collected by insurance carriers affords them a unique advantage over any other entity—even government agencies—when it comes to assessing the benefits of different information assurance controls and practices.

Shared Responsibility. Discussions regarding policies or regulations to force firms to increase cybersecurity should also be balanced with discussions of inducing consumers to take appropriate security and privacy precautions.

Optimizing Government Intervention. Framing security as an investment proposes that the purpose of government intervention is to support a market that encourages companies to find the optimal point between the cost of attacks and benefit of defensive information assurance measures.

NOTES

1. However, in some cases of cyber stalking and online harassment, outcomes can be tragic. "The Top 6 Unforgettable Cyberbullying Cases |NoBullying|," NoBullying Bullying CyberBullying Resources, April 23, 2013, accessed March 2, 2016, http://nobullying.com/six-unforgettable-cyber-bullying-cases/.

2. Dan Goodin, "IT Contractor Caught Stealing Shell Oil Employee Info," The Register, October 7, 2008, accessed March 2, 2016, http://www.theregister.co.uk/2008/10/07/shell_oil_database_breach/; Robert McMillan, "United Healthcare Data Breach Leads to ID Theft," *Computer World*, http://www.computerworld.com/article/2535131/security0/unitedhealthcare-data-breach-leads-to-id-theft-at-uc-irvine.html; Mary Hogan, "Arrests Made in ID Theft Case," *The Sealy News*, September 23, 2008, accessed March 3, 2016, http://www.sealynews.com/news/article_8fb9ad7b-6776-5251-ab26-b0863106007f.html.

3. Synovate, "Federal Trade Commission-2006 Identity Theft Survey Report," *Hawley's Condensed Chemical Dictionary*, November 15, 2007, accessed March 2, 2016, doi:10.1002/9780470114735.hawley07141; Katrina Baum, "Identity Theft, 2004," April 2006, Bureau of Justice Statistics.

4. For example, Target has incurred $252 million in costs due to its data breach. Kevin M. McGinty, "Target Data Breach Price Tag: $252 Million and Counting | Privacy & Security Matters," *Privacy Security Matters*, February 26, 2015, accessed March 2, 2016, http://www.privacyandsecuritymatters.com/2015/02/target-data-breach-price-tag-252-million-and-counting/.

5. Ross Anderson and Tyler Moore, "The Economics of Information Security: A Survey and Open Questions," *University of Cambridge Computer Laboratory*, accessed March 2, 2016, http://www.cl.cam.ac.uk/~rja14/Papers/toulouse-summary.pdf.

6. Gary Becker, "Crime and Punishment: An Economic Approach," in *Essays in the Economics of Crime and Punishment*, 169–93 (New York: Journal of Political Economy, 1968).

7. Trey Herr, "PrEP: A Framework for Malware & Cyber Weapons," *The Journal of Information Warfare* 13, iss. 1 February 2014, 87–106.

8. Jamie Cifuentes, "Rent, Buy, or Lease? Exploit Toolkits A La Carte," *Security Watch*, March 19, 2013, http://securitywatch.pcmag.com/none/309324-rent-buy-or-lease-exploit-toolkits-a-la-carte.

9. Tim G., "Renting a Zombie Farm: Botnets and the Hacker Economy," *Symantec,* August 8, 2014, accessed March 2, 2016, http://www.symantec.com/connect/blogs/renting-zombie-farm-botnets-and-hacker-economy.

10. Thomas J. Holt, and Eric Lampke, "Exploring Stolen Data Markets Online: Products and Market Forces," Taylor & Francis, March 17, 2010, accessed March 4, 2016, doi:10.1080/14786011003634415.

11. Brian Krebs, "Taking Down Fraud Sites Is Whac-a-mole," *Krebs on Security* RSS, April 15, 2015, accessed March 2, 2016, http://krebsonsecurity.com/2015/04/taking-down-fraud-sites-is-whac-a-mole/.

12. FireEye, Supply Chain Analysis: From Quartermaster to Sunshop, Report, 2014, accessed March 4, 2016, https://www.fireeye.com/content/dam/fireeye-www/global/en/current-threats/pdfs/rpt-malware-supply-chain.pdf.

13. Roderic Broadhurst, Peter Grabosky, Mamoun Alazab, and Steven Chon, "Organizations and Cyber crime: An Analysis of the Nature of Groups engaged in Cyber Crime," *International Journal of Cyber Criminology* 8, iss. 1 (January–June 2014), 1–20, http://www.cybercrimejournal.com/broadhurstetalijcc2014vol8issue1.pdf.

14. Brian Krebs, "Peek Inside a Professional Carding Shop," *Krebs on Security* RSS, June 4, 2014, http://krebsonsecurity.com/2014/06/peek-inside-a-professional-carding-shop/.

15. Vaibhav Garb, Sadia Afroz, Rebekah Overdorf, and Rachel Greenstadt, "Computer Supported Cooperative Work," *SpringerReference*, accessed March 3, 2016, doi:10.1007/springerreference_61822.

16. For more, see chapter 7—"Disrupting Malware Markets."

17. Thomas J. Holt, "The Market for Malware," Speech, Def Con 15, Riviera Hotel and Casino, Las Vegas, August 4, 2007, accessed March 4, 2016. https://www.defcon.org/images/defcon-15/dc15-presentations/dc-15-holt.pdf.

18. Raymond Hil, "Computer Crime Is Slicker Than You Think," *Dynamics Southwest*, accessed March 2, 2016, http://www.dynamicssouthwest.com/computer-crime-is-slicker-than-you-think/.

19. Candid Wueest, "Underground Black Market: Thriving Trade in Stolen Data, Malware, and Attack Services," *Symantec*, November 20, 2015, accessed March 2, 2016. http://www.symantec.com/connect/blogs/underground-black-market-thriving-trade-stolen-data-malware-and-attack-services.

20. Thomas J. Holt, "The Market for Malware," Speech, Def Con 15, Riviera Hotel and Casino, Las Vegas, August 4, 2007, accessed March 4, 2016, https://www.defcon.org/images/defcon-15/dc15-presentations/dc-15-holt.pdf.

21. Brian Krebs, "SpyEye vs. ZeuS Rivalry," *Krebs on Security* RSS, April 10, 2015, accessed March 2, 2016, http://krebsonsecurity.com/2010/04/spyeye-vs-zeus-rivalry/.

22. Sean Martin, "The Making of a Cybercrime Market," *CSO*, August 11, 2014, accessed March 2, 2016, http://www.csoonline.com/article/2463175/data-protection/the-making-of-a-cybercrime-market.html.

23. Brian Krebs, "Revisiting the SpyEye/ZeuS Merger," *Krebs on Security* RSS, February 11, 2011, accessed March 2, 2016, http://krebsonsecurity.com/2011/02/revisiting-the-spyeyezeus-merger/.

24. Elinor Mills, "Q&A: FBI Agent Looks Back on Time Posing as a Cyber-criminal," *CNET*, June 29, 2009, accessed March 02, 2016, http://www.cnet.com/news/q-a-fbi-agent-looks-back-on-time-posing-as-a-cybercriminal/.

25. For more, see chapter 8—"The Computer Fraud and Abuse Act: Structure, Controversies, and Proposals for Reform."

26. "18 U.S.C. §§ 1030(a)(1), (a)(2), & (a)(4)," LII/Legal Information Institute, accessed March 2, 2016, https://www.law.cornell.edu/uscode/text/18/1030; "18 U.S.C. §§ 1030(a)(3)," LII/Legal Information Institute, accessed March 3, 2016, https://www.law.cornell.edu/uscode/text/18/1030; "18 U.S.C. §§ 1030(a)(5)(B) & (a)(5)(C)," LII/Legal Information Institute, accessed March 3, 2016, https://www.law.cornell.edu/uscode/text/18/1030.

27. Alden Anderson, "The Computer Fraud and Abuse Act: Hacking Into the Authorization Debate," *Jurimetrics Journal* Volume 53 (Summer 2013), 447–66, http://www.americanbar.org/content/dam/aba/publications/Jurimetrics/summer2013/anderson.authcheckdam.pdf.

28. See generally, William Landes and Richard Posner, *The Economic Structure of Tort Law* (Cambridge: Harvard University Press, 1987); Steven Shavell, "Economics and Liability for Accidents," *New Palgrave Dictionary of Economics*, 2nd Edition (Macmillan, 2008); Charles Kolstad, Thomas Ulen, and Gary Johnson, "Ex Post Liability for Harm vs. Ex Ante Safety Regulation: Substitutes or Complements?" *American Economic Review* 80, iss. 4, September 1990, 888–901.

29. Sasha Romanosky, David Hoffman, and Alessandro Acquisti, "Empirical Analysis of Data Breach Litigation," *Journal of Empirical Legal Studies* 11, 2014, 74–104. doi: 10.1111/jels.12035.

30. See Romanosky et al. (2009) for a full discussion of how these interventions have been applied to breaches of personal consumer information.

31. Deborah Majoras, statement before the Committee On Commerce, Science, And Transportation, June 16, 2005.

32. Samuelson Law, Technology, & Public Policy Clinic, "Security Breach Notification Laws: Views from Chief Security Officers," December 2007, https://www.law.berkeley.edu/files/cso_study.pdf; Sasha Romanosky, Rahul Telang, and Alessandro Acquisti, "Do Data Breach Disclosure Laws Reduce Identity Theft?," *Journal of Policy Analysis and Management* Volume 30, iss. 2, 2011, 256–86. http://papers.ssrn.com/sol3/papers.cfm?abstract_id=1268926.

33. Thomas Lenard and Paul Rubin, "Slow Down on Data Security Legislation," *Progress Snapshot* 1.9, August 2005, https://www.techpolicyinstitute.org/files/ps1.9.pdf.

34. Ibid.

35. Sasha Romanosky and Alessandro Acquisti, "Privacy Costs and Personal Data Protection: Economic and Legal Perspectives of Ex Ante Regulation, Ex Post Liability and Information Disclosure," *Berkeley Technology Law Journal* 24, iss. 3 (2011), http://papers.ssrn.com/sol3/papers.cfm?abstract_id=1522605.

36. For more, see chapter 9—"Breach Notification Laws: the Policy and Practice."

37. A version of this chapter appeared in Sasha Romanosky, Comments to the Department of Commerce, April 26, 2013, http://www.ntia.doc.gov/files/ntia/romanosky_comments.pdf.

38. Geoffrey Heal and Howard Kunreuther, *Environmental Assets and Liabilities: Dealing with Catastrophic Risks,* Technical paper no. 2008-11-06, November 2008, http://opim.wharton.upenn.edu/risk/library/WP2008-11-06_GH,HK_EnvAssets.pdf.

39. For more, see chapter 10—"Cyber Insurance: A Market-Based Approach to Information Assurance."

40. Donald A. Wittman, "Liability for Harm or Restitution of Benefit?," *The Journal of Legal Studies* 13, iss. 1 (1984), 57.

41. Omri Ben-Shahar and Anu Bradford, *"Reversible Rewards,"* *American Law and Economics Review* 15 (2013), 156.

42. Robert Sugden, "On Nudging: Improving Decisions About Health, Wealth, and Happiness by Richard H. Thaler and Cass R. Sunstein," *International Journal of the Economics of Business* 16, iss. 3 (2009), http://www.tandfonline.com/doi/abs/10.1080/13571510903227064.

Chapter 7

Disrupting Malware Markets

Trey Herr and Ryan Ellis

Decoding the structure, participants, and interactions of the malicious software market is imperative to informed policy.[1] The key to understanding the behavior of cyber criminal groups is their access and incentives to use malicious tools. The framing and language of the market is a means to describe how groups build, buy, and deploy these tools. It defines the diffusion of capabilities between different organizations over time, the various specializations of participants, and guiding logic of malicious tools and their use as an ecosystem.

This market also has defensively focused participants such as Google and Microsoft who purchase vulnerability information to improve their software before it can be used to develop malicious tools. The interaction of malicious and defensive groups is a focus of recent policy efforts to regulate the spread and use of malware through the Wassenaar Arrangement.[2] Malicious software are the tools of the trade in disrupting internet services, stealing personal information, extorting funds from users, and cyber crime of all sorts. For example, Carberp, a malicious software package used to target banks and financial account credentials, is rented to users and combined with other services to target particular organizations. The criminal marketplace described in chapter 6 is a mechanism to derive value from stolen goods as well as to purchase these tools. This market is important because it is a means to transfer capabilities between groups and may enable new attacks as well as the spread of exploits. This chapter covers the full range of potential buyers but emphasizes nonstate groups.

Describing the malware market is a process of explaining who participates in buying and selling these tools and how these transactions take place. Using this structure as a jumping off point to identify opportunities for disruption, this discussion of the malware market becomes a mapping exercise to identify points of systemic weakness. The following sections provide a brief description of malware, outline key market forces, and provide an overview of the participants. In conclusion, the chapter offers several policy recommendations on how best to intervene in the market.

What Is Malware?

Malware are software tools used to gain access to a computer system or network. These are composed of subsidiary malicious software components; describing each briefly helps explain the market because each component can be bought and sold separately. Breaking down malware is similar to differentiating between various types of cars. While a convertible, SUV, and sedan are all automobiles, they also have distinct functions and design of varying levels of interest to consumers.

The automobile metaphor can translate well to malware components; combining engines, wheels, and frames in various combinations creates a wide array of end products. Differentiating between malware components can help explain the resources and skill required to engineer various types of malware and highlight where defensive and malicious market actors are competing to purchase and use the same goods. Each of these components can also be combined differently to create particular services, so distinguishing between individual malware components helps explain the goods of the malicious software marketplace:

1. a *propagation method*—the method through which malware spreads onto a particular target device;
2. an *exploit*—code that takes advantage of a particular flaw in order to allow malware to execute some specified action; and
3. a *payload*—code that defines how the malware will impact the target, payloads can have multiple functions and may be used to communicate remotely with an attacker.[3]

This Propagation, Exploit, Payload approach is the PrEP framework for malware.[4] In it, each component has a different function.

Propagation Method

Malware requires a way to move from its origin into a target. This process, *propagation*, can take a number of different forms. It may involve broad-scale methods, such as sending a batch of infected e-mails to a huge number of potential targets; or more narrow means, such as loading malware onto a portable thumb drive and dropping it in a parking lot.[5] The design of a propagation method can limit the extent of its spread. An e-mail purporting to be from a coworker may contain a compromised attachment which, if opened, will infect your computer. Including relevant details or suggesting the attachment is a document of specific interest could make you more likely to click on the e-mail but others less so. Malware's propagation can be limited by a number of various other factors, including technical features—some may only work in conjunction with a particular operating system or software version. Propagation may be a long-term and ongoing effort to gain access to target systems. For example, the so-called Equation Group malware, identified by Kaspersky Labs as a state-developed platform, used a number of different methods to try and assure access to a target even after computers had been wiped and reformatted.[6]

Exploits

Aiding propagation methods are *exploits*. Exploits are software programs—code—that take advantage of vulnerabilities found in computer software or systems. Exploits leverage these flaws to allow malware to execute particular commands. Vulnerabilities are common; they are present in software, "as a result of faulty program design or implementation."[7] These flaws can also be deliberately introduced by an adversary in order to provide a "backdoor" for later access.[8] One of Stuxnet's propagation methods utilized an exploit in the Windows Print Spool network service to spread itself between computers. From an infected machine, Stuxnet would submit a specially formatted print request to another, uninfected, machine. Instead of supplying data to print, the infected computer would send malicious code, spreading Stuxnet across a network of computers.[9] While the vulnerability in this example was in the network print service, an exploit had to be written to take advantage of it for Stuxnet. Discovering vulnerabilities—that is, flaws that can be reliably and usefully exploited—is not trivial. Further developing exploits targeting these flaws for use in malware is an uncertain and potentially expensive process.[10] Importantly, exploits are not intrinsically or necessarily malicious but have an array of potential uses. For example, there is cottage industry of companies who conduct mock attacks in order to pinpoint weaknesses in organization's networks. What distinguishes these penetration testing firms from criminals and state attackers is intent. While both are relying on the latest research and techniques to exploit a vulnerability, penetration testing firms seek to identify workable exploits in order to alert an impacted organization to a pressing concern.

Payload

A *payload* is the core content of malware, a piece of software designed to achieve some predefined goal, such as deleting data or manipulating hardware to cause physical destruction. A payload can be quite complex, combining diverse elements potentially engineered by multiple people at different points in time.[11] Payloads often dictate the identity of malware, such as a keylogger, code targeting banks, or "spyware" intended to gather information and spy on its targets. There is a subtle, but important, distinction between exploit and payload, and failing to distinguish the two can cause some analytic confusion. The two are logically distinct both in sequence and form: exploits are written to take advantage of a particular vulnerability present in target software, while payloads are written to achieve a particular effect. Exploits open the door for malicious code to execute on a target system. The Stuxnet payload was designed to infect industrial control systems running Iranian centrifuges but it was spread using, among other techniques, an exploit manipulating the Windows networking service. While the payload was the package being spread, the exploit was responsible for fooling other computers to accept a print request carrying the malware.

THE MARKET FOR MALWARE

The existence of a market for the exchange, purchase, and sale of malware components is not novel.[12] In 1995, Netscape initiated one of the very first bug bounty programs.[13] They agreed to offer (modest) cash rewards to anyone who reported a flaw in their new web browser, Netscape Navigator 2.0. Today, bug bounty programs are commonplace. Hundreds of companies operate bounty programs, rewarding researchers who discover flaws in their software or websites.[14] Major tech companies—including Google, Apple, Facebook, and Microsoft—operate large and thriving bounty programs. More recently, the Department of Defense (DoD) joined the fray. It announced its own version of a bug bounty program, dubbed "Hack the Pentagon." Under the pilot program, DoD will pay researchers for bugs impacting its public websites.[15]

Yet, vendors and website operators are not the only ones purchasing malware components—far from it. Intelligence agencies, military organizations, and criminal groups also purchase malware components. Newly discovered vulnerabilities and novel exploits can aid espionage, sabotage, and law enforcement activity. Zero-days are incredibly useful: they are exploits that take advantage of previously unknown flaws and are difficult to detect or mitigate, allowing them to operate with near impunity.

There are essentially two overlapping markets for malicious software and they are linked together, but each with some analytical distinctions. The "defensive market" is home to software vendors and firms working to obtain software vulnerabilities in order to develop patches. The "offensive market" is home to states and criminal groups, actors purchasing components and services in order to compromise computer systems. There are many common goods between the two—vulnerabilities, for example, are simply information and can be rediscovered by many parties or traded at no marginal cost and provide value to vendors and attackers alike. The "defensive market" buys through different mechanisms, however, with greater transparency through competitions and even some publicly available bug bounty leaderboards. The "offensive market" resembles a more traditional illicit marketplace with highly opaque transactions and a larger role for intermediaries to manage uncertainty and reputation across participants.

Another key difference between the markets relates to the intentions of the actors purchasing the component. In the defensive market, flaws are purchased in order to correct the vulnerabilities. In the offensive market, however, newly discovered flaws and exploits are resources that will be concealed and used to gain access to targeted systems. In the defensive market, vulnerabilities are problems to be solved; in the offensive market, they are resources to be used. These two markets, as discussed below, are entwined: they compete for labor and commodities (malware components, mostly exploits). In many ways, the defensive market is a reaction to, and an attempt to subvert, the perceived dangers introduced by the offensive market.

The growth of demand in the offensive market is troubling. The offensive market for malware, in some ways, enables the proliferation of sophisticated malicious cyber capabilities. The market provides nation-states, criminals, and other powerful tools to conduct espionage, sabotage, and several other criminal activities. The market also enables poorly equipped states to gain access to highly capable espionage malware. While the canonical state threat, including America's NSA or Israel's Unit 8200, is generally accorded a high degree of technical capability, other less sophisticated actors, such as the intelligence bodies from the Republic of Sudan and Ethiopia, are able to purchase capabilities they might not otherwise have access to.[16] For example, Hacking Team, a prominent Italian company whose internal e-mail system and documentation was leaked onto the web in May 2015, uses a regular stream of new exploits purchased from within this market to support its core malware product called Galileo RCS or Remote Control System. The RCS can be used to spy on a variety of desktop and mobile phone operating systems. Customers can purchase a license to increase the number of computers and phones they collect information from at any given time. Companies, including Hacking Team, even offer training, customization, and maintenance features for more advanced users through this market.

A range of policy interventions to disrupt the market for malware is possible—including the continued support and growth of the defensive market. However, before considering the utility and limitations of different policy approaches, a detailed understanding of the composition and structure of the market is necessary. Previous empirical and theoretical work has examined aspects of pricing, different types of transaction, and other issues linked to market structure.[17]

Market Forces

Supply

Malware components are products of engineering effort—building a payload or writing an exploit takes time, skill, and with exploits some factor of luck. The vulnerabilities on which exploits depend come from software and must be discovered. These vulnerabilities are information and so may be rediscovered by multiple parties and, once made known to the vendor, can be patched and their value to a potential exploit reduced. There are numerous copies and alternatives available for payloads and propagation methods on the market. There is a tremendous variety in the underground forums where buyers select malware components and related services. Vulnerabilities can be reused by anyone with a capable exploit, but their value decreases the longer time passes after the software flaw was discovered.

The source of supply varies by malware components. The supply of exploits is driven by both flaws in vendor software and the labor and talent of individuals working to discover these flaws. Propagation methods are numerous; an example is the herds of infected computers known as botnets. Marshaling these machines and renting them is a nontrivial process and may depend on the skill and preexisting resources of the seller. Payloads are largely developed by individuals or small groups and may be purchased, captured, or even stolen. The variation in their purpose means that groups with different skill levels may be unsuccessful at adapting the tools of others or creating their own for complex tasks.

Each of these components can be reused and their respective value changes over time. Payloads are designed for a specific purpose so adapting them may take substantial engineering effort, but they retain value even after discovery. This reuse process is made more difficult if the payload in question is well-obfuscated or designed for a particular goal such as Stuxnet, which has seen no apparent reuse or direct copies. By contrast, Zeus, a popular malware family used to target banks and financial institutions, was leaked online in 2011 without cryptographic obfuscation.[18] Less than six months later, several new malware families had integrated some or all of the Zeus code and seen sales growth as a result.[19]

Exploits are fungible: they can be integrated with different malware components and adapted from one tool to another. But they are also highly perishable: their value decreases after use, discovery, and subsequent patching. One of the major espionage platforms discovered in the past several years, Duqu, utilized an exploit in the Windows operating system to escalate privileges on a target machine and enable payload execution.[20] Less than a year after the announcement of its discovery, the same exploit was integrated into two major exploit kits and used in attacks against a range of targets.[21] Propagation methods vary in how easily they can be repurposed, but their value changes more as a function of access. Larger botnets may be more valuable as they can target victims from a variety of different IP addresses, thereby providing better means to bypass traffic filtering and other defenses.

Payloads, exploits, and propagation methods describe the basic building blocks of malware but the malicious software market also contains more finished goods such as the exploit kit, which combines a variety of exploits and a propagation method.[22] The level of skill required to use these finished goods is lower, presenting users with a "plug-and-play" or "malware-as-a-service" type offering.[23] With an exploit kit, for example, the customer need only supply a payload to create fully functioning malware. These finished goods may be a complete malicious software package more akin to a financial management dashboard, such as GammaGroup's FinSpy, a fully capable surveillance package that allows organizations to collect data on and from computing devices including recording video from webcams, logging keystrokes, and reading e-mail content.[24]

Demand

The determinants of demand in the offensive market are inconsistent. Some groups appear to select targets based on the tools that are available to them, while others find tools to satisfy strong preferences between victims. The implication for groups that focus on the tools available to them is that demand is shaped by the security posture and configuration (e.g., vulnerabilities present and unpatched) in victim firms. Target focus implies a willingness to develop or purchase and modify components to fit the needs of a narrowly defined target set or even a singular firm. Where this latter decision-making process dominates, the defensive capability of the victim may prevent the direct purchase/reuse of a set of malware components from the market, forcing a more extended development process on the part of threat groups. This tool focus translates to victim firm security posture/configuration driving demand where attacks are more opportunistic, but where the potential target is more important than the tool employed, a different calculus reigns. Demand may be more directly influenced by the availability of goods as supply includes both basic malware components (propagation methods, exploits, and payloads) and vendors who assemble components and resell them and even some who offer complete services from malware to managing stolen goods.[25]

Demand on the defensive side is a mix of rational investment in security by vendors and the politics of disclosure. Programs from software vendors to pay researchers for vulnerability information, so-called bug bounties, were once a controversial idea opposed vehemently by large companies such as Oracle and Microsoft. In the past half-decade however, they have become a fixture for how many firms, including Microsoft, discover and fix flaws in their products. When companies announce new programs, such as General Motors did in early 2016, it can drive researchers to find and disclose new bugs in these products. Providing cash rewards for software vulnerabilities can create greater demand to find the flaws and help direct the supply of vulnerability information to vendors rather than offensive actors.

Intermediaries and Trust

For offensively minded participants, how do you establish trust in a den of thieves? Reputation mechanisms are the devices by which two parties in a transaction establish a basis of trust to guarantee the desired exchange of goods or services for compensation.[26] Understanding the potential for fraud, buyers must evaluate the relative quality and character of the good being purchased. Conventional marketplaces have developed a number of reputation and transaction enforcement mechanisms—many centered on civil law and information disclosure. The malware market is no different. It, too, needs to account for information asymmetries and lack of trust.[27]

In this offensive marketplace, intermediaries serve two functions. They can act as both buyer and seller, aggregating goods and pricing information.[28] This allows intermediary firms to sit in between basic component vendors, such as researchers developing exploits, and customers demanding more complete services including fully capable espionage tools. For example, Hacking Team is an intermediary that may participate directly in the market as a buyer in order to expand their wares. The Italian company also functions as a supplier, for at least a portion of the market, to resell more developed products that are intended largely for states, but may also involve some more sophisticated criminal groups. This mix is interesting as some state organizations may be less capable than nonstate actors. These intermediary firms can also help to manage reputations and lower transaction costs, although this function is largely contained to the offensive market. Intermediate firms such as brokers, who negotiate between vulnerability discoverers and buyers, act as trusted middlemen to facilitate sales and guarantee both the functionality of goods (for the buyer) and payment (for the seller). By creating stable relationships between buyers and sellers, intermediaries help manage transactional uncertainty and potentially provide a network for first-time buyers and sellers.

There are also systems relying on a "vouching" protocol, not unlike friend of friend chains in other illicit environments, which allows existing trusted networks to add nodes at the edges by brokering introductions between previously disconnected parties.[29] These can be interpersonal, especially among more experienced buyers and sellers, or even institutional, as organizations emerge to facilitate transactions and payment between distrustful parties. Independent crowd-sourced mechanisms, generally managed by websites or forums where many of these transactions occur, appear very similar to the rating and buyer feedback tools found on mainstream e-commerce sites such as Amazon and eBay.[30] Users post information about the quality of code and services received, complain about poor customer support, and call out fraudulent transactions or failure to receive the promised product.

In the defensive market, intermediaries may provide information assurance resources and managed security services, or they may directly purchase vulnerabilities. Verisign's iDefense Vulnerability Contributor Program, for example, purchases vulnerability and exploit information with the intent of disclosing it to vendors after a delay, sometimes substantial, in which subscribers have exclusive access.[31] Defensive intermediaries participate in the market by affecting the stock of goods, for example, by disclosing vulnerabilities to vendors publicly, purchasing vulnerability information through bug bounties, or impacting some other market force. There is also a cottage industry of companies that, for a fee, will conduct mock attacks on organizations' networks to pinpoint weaknesses; these penetration testing firms employ exploits in the same manner as a criminal or state attacker and often have an interest in the latest research in order to be most effective but can purchase exploits more cheaply since they don't require exclusive access.

Supply-Side Actors—Malware Component and Service Vendors

These are suppliers selling very specific malware components, a payload focused on the extraction of user credentials for example, or services integrating multiple components such as exploit kits. Exploit sales typically originate from small groups or freelancers who have discovered a vulnerability, written basic proof-of-concept code, and made the decision to sell instead of disclose it to the vendor.[32] Suppliers in the high end of the market are a highly fragmented ecosystem of skilled individuals who focus on the development and sale of new exploits for well-secured software or high-value targets.[33] Companies selling exploits such as ReVuln and Exodus Intelligence generally operate on a subscription service model similar to the cellphone data plan structure; governments and other intermediaries pay a certain amount every year in exchange for a fixed number of exploits. By one estimate, among the whole of the market there are at least half a dozen such firms capable of selling more than 100 new exploits a year to both governments and nonstate actors, with an average list price between $40,000 and $160,000.[34]

There is little evidence of payload or propagation method sales to governments except as more complete service offerings like the Galileo RCS and associated customer support from intermediaries, although this is likely due in part to the difficulty in observing interactions between states and suppliers. Reputation typically relies on common points of contact and acquired reputation.[35] Suppliers at the low end of market are selling both malware components such as payloads and propagation methods and vulnerabilities, although rarely those unknown to the vendor (zero-days).[36] These suppliers also offer services such as click fraud, intended to drive visitor traffic through particular ads, and pay-per-install, where threat groups can pay according to the vendor's success at infecting different users.[37] Interaction usually transpires via Internet Relay Chat or through a shifting collection of forums including Agora, Darkode, and Abraxas.

Offensive Buyers

States

State intelligence and military organizations can be highly resourced actors with specific objectives that exist only partly in information security. In the marketplace, they're most commonly represented by organic law enforcement or intelligence capacity and may be subject to the cultural predilections and shaping behaviors of these institutions. States are capable of employing, and have demonstrated interest in, destructive payloads but also have the human capital and time to develop components internally rather than exclusively through purchase or reuse. The capabilities of certain states are such that their technical superiority moves in advance of the market and their use creates a proliferation challenge—spreading more sophisticated components to other threat actors. Less skilled actors can then try to reengineer these components into their own tools although, again, this is a challenging task depending on the difficulty of deciphering the code obtained.[38]

Nonstate Actors

This category covers the canonical information security threat—criminal groups, gangs, and malicious individuals—all threat actors who are not states. This cross-section of actors is heterogeneous: they have different motives and capabilities. As such, it is difficult to offer a general, common, decision-making process for these groups. Yet, they almost certainly have access to fewer human or material resources than states. Nonstate actor interactions are rarely overt and unlike states their goals are generally oriented toward financial gain. This category may include organizations with a political or otherwise ideological agenda but the sophistication of the tools employed is typically on the lower end of the spectrum.

Defensive Buyers

Vendors may also be buyers in the market through vulnerability purchase programs. While not purchasing with malicious intent, vendors can impact the incentives of potential suppliers by offering alternatives to existing brokers and buyers. This in turn can reduce the quantity of goods available in the market. These programs take a variety of forms and many reward more than stand-alone vulnerabilities; compensation is also given out for novel attack and defense techniques. Firms such as Google and Facebook organize "bug bounties" (also known as Vulnerability Reward Programs), designed to encourage researchers to disclose vulnerabilities directly in return for prestige and a cash reward. Google, for example, advertises rewards between $100 and $20,000 for information about qualifying vulnerabilities in its software or major services.[39] Some companies, including HackerOne and BugCrowd, sit in between organizations and vulnerability researchers, managing these bounty programs for software firms.[40] There are also competitions where researchers are given set amounts of time to find vulnerabilities in major commercial software and prove their effectiveness with a rudimentary exploit. In 2015 Pwn2Own, a competition held in Canada, paid out prizes totaling more than $400,000 for vulnerabilities in the Chrome, Safari, Internet Explorer, and Firefox browsers as well as other software.[41] Hewlett-Packard planned to sponsor a similar competition in 2016, but reneged after concerns that changes to the Wassenaar Arrangement, an international export control regime, might impose penalties or unmanageable legal costs on the event.[42] States may be present in the defensive market, through bug bounty programs such as the one announced by the DoD, but they are still uncommon.

Intervening in the Market

The market represents a means for groups, both offensive and defensive, to gain access to capabilities they might not otherwise. Over time, this sort of exchange has allowed a great deal of specialization in the offensive market, creating potential benefits to criminal groups able to create economies of scale for the development of tools for information theft and fraud. Intervening in this market may prevent the sale or exchange of components necessary for groups to target vulnerable organizations, presenting opportunities for policymakers to disrupt the market for threats. This section highlights two such interventions.

Shrink the Attack Surface: Attack Demand

As discussed previously, some percentage of adversary groups are limited to attacking targets suitable for the tools they have access to. These limits might be financial or related to human capital, but they constrain the potential set of malware these groups can use. For these tool-focused groups, demand is generated by weaknesses in potential targets such as poorly implemented security applications or weakly protected databases. Many of these attacks use vulnerabilities for which patches exist, called N-day (the software flaw has been known to the original vendor for "N" days). To attack demand means incentivizing more secure organizational practices, for example, consistent patching. These best practices might be based on an existing standards body such as the National Institute of Standards and Technology (NIST) Cybersecurity Framework.[43]

As long as software is complex, it will contain flaws that can be exploited, but improving implementation and making it simpler to be secure can help attack demand for particular types of malware. Adding new functions and complexity allows malware to thrive. So, then, how do we shrink the attack surface? In general, developing methods to encourage secure design and limit unneeded functionality is the optimal solution. How can policy play a constructive role? Transparency regarding the design and capabilities of products allows consumers to make informed choices. Spurring greater investment in processes like the Cyber Independent Testing Lab (CITL), which provides a security rating systems for software products, can help bring market power to bear for consumers to select products they can securely implement.[44] In time, this UL may also encourage the design of more secure software, as customers select between vendors. But this is an issue of attacking supply rather than demand.

Drain the Swamp: Reduce Supply

Targeting supply effectively involves making malware costlier—scarce, harder to produce, and more difficult to execute. Despite increasing spending and interest, malware is still relatively simple in terms of its construction. In other words, although software is becoming increasingly complex, in terms of lines of code, malware remains behind the evolutionary curve.[45] If the key enabling component for malicious software are vulnerabilities, their source is the insecurity of software. There are legal and regulatory mechanisms to drive more robust incentives for vendors to design more secure products. Chief among these is liability for software vendors, using a framework from civil law to tie financial responsibility for the security of products to their manufacturers.[46] Liability, however, will not lead to perfect software. Indeed, flaws will inevitably remain.

Providing cash incentives for researchers can also help encourage them to discover and disclose vulnerabilities in major commercial software packages and common libraries would help drain the pool of flaws available for adversary groups. These funds should be directed at more than simply finding current bugs, attempting to discover new techniques for identifying vulnerabilities and methods of exploitation to push defenders ahead of the offensive cycle. The process is similar to an arms race, an innovation cycle between attacker and defender. Driving more offensive innovation into the defensive market makes it accessible to software vendors for patching and mitigation. These purchases should also include purchasing exploit techniques.[47] The same vulnerability can potentially be taken advantage of in a number of ways. Purchasing, and disclosing to software vendors, entire classes of exploit techniques can reduce the number of individual patches necessary.

CONCLUSION

The malware market is a framework to understand how groups buy, build, and use malicious tools—a collection of often disparate communities and online forums rather than a single marketplace. Defensive actors, for example, vendors such as Mozilla, attempting to buy vulnerabilities to patch their products, purchase these goods through very different mechanisms than offensive actors such as state intelligence organizations and criminal groups. Understanding the marketplace is critical to understanding malicious software and its use by states or nonstate groups, as an ecosystem. Exploits, one malware component, have a shelf life as useful goods determined by the rate at which the vulnerabilities they take advantage of are slowly discovered and patched by vendors. Other goods, such as payloads, have no such half-life but vary dramatically in the skills required to engineer them. The market has a set of repeating behaviors that are still not widely understood but two initial recommendations should be considered: (1) attempt to reduce the demand for particular types of malware by improving organizational security practices and (2) attack supply by reducing the availability of vulnerabilities and novel exploit techniques. There are opportunities for the policy community to work with industry to shape the market and, hopefully, reduce its harms on all.

CHAPTER HIGHLIGHTS

Malware. Tools used to gain access to a computer system or network for malicious ends like disrupting internet services, stealing personal information, extorting funds from users, and committing other types of cyber crime. Payloads, exploits, and propagation methods describe the basic building blocks of malware, but the malicious software market also contains more finished goods such as the exploit kit, which combines a variety of exploits and a propagation method. The level of skill required to use these finished goods is lower, presenting users with a "plug-and-play" or "malware-as-a-service" type offering.

Malware Markets. The "defensive market" is home to software vendors and firms working to obtain software vulnerabilities in order to develop patches. The "offensive market" contains most state organizations like intelligence agencies as well as nonstate actors like criminal groups. This offensive market is home to actors who are purchasing components and services in order to compromise computer systems. Vulnerabilities can be rediscovered by many parties or traded at no marginal cost and provide value to vendors and attackers alike. The "defensive market" buys through different mechanisms, however, with greater transparency through competitions and public bug bounty leaderboards. The "offensive market" resembles a more traditional illicit marketplace with highly opaque transactions and a larger role for intermediaries to manage uncertainty.

Offensive Demand. The determinants of demand in the offensive market are inconsistent, as some groups appear to select targets on the basis of the tools available to them, while others find tools to satisfy strong preferences between victims. The implications for tool-focused groups are that demand is shaped by the security posture and configuration (e.g., vulnerabilities present and unpatched) in victim firms. Target focus implies a willingness to develop or purchase and modify components to fit the needs of a narrowly defined target set or even a singular firm.

Recommendations. Incentivize more secure organizational practices (consistent patching), increase transparency regarding the design and capabilities of products (consumers can make informed choices), and spur greater investment in security rating systems for software products. The key enabling component for malicious software is the vulnerability; thus the focus should be on providing incentives for researchers to discover and disclose them.

NOTES

1. Selected portions of this chapter have previously appeared in Trey Herr, "Malware Counter-Proliferation and the Wassenaar Arrangement," in 2016 8th International Conference on Cyber Conflict: Cyber Power (CyCon, Tallinn, Estonia: IEEE, 2016). http://dx.doi.org/10.2139/ssrn.2711070.

2. For more, see chapter 15—"Countering the Proliferation of Malware."

3. William A. Owens, Kenneth W. Dam, and Herbert S. Lin, eds., *Technology, Policy, Law, and Ethics Regarding U.S. Acquisition and Use of Cyberattack Capabilities* (Washington, DC: National Academies Press, 2009), http://www.nap.edu/catalog/12651.

4. Trey Herr, "PrEP: A Framework for Malware & Cyber Weapons," *The Journal of Information Warfare* 13, no. 1 (February 2014): 87–106.

5. "Microsoft Security Intelligence Report—Zeroing in on Propagation Methods" (Microsoft, 2011), https://www.microsoft.com/en-us/download/details.aspx?id=27605; Michael Hanspach and Michael Goetz, "On Covert Acoustical Mesh Networks in Air," *Journal of Communications* 8, no. 11 (2013): 758–67, doi:10.12720/jcm.8.11.758-767.

6. "Equation Group: Questions and Answers" (Kaspersky Lab, February 2015), https://securelist.com/files/2015/02/Equation_group_questions_and_answers.pdf.

7. Owens, Dam, and Lin, *Technology, Policy, Law, and Ethics Regarding U.S. Acquisition and Use of Cyberattack Capabilities.*

8. R.J. Danzig, "Surviving on a Diet of Poisoned Fruit," *Center for a New American Security,* July 21, 2014, http://www.cnas.org/surviving-diet-poisoned-fruit.

9. Nicolas Falliere, Liam O. Murchu, and Eric Chien, "W32. Stuxnet Dossier" (Symantec, 2011), http://www.h4ckr.us/library/Documents/ICS_Events/Stuxnet%20Dossier%20(Symantec)%20v1.4.pdf.

10. Brian Fung, "The NSA Hacks Other Countries by Buying Millions of Dollars' Worth of Computer Vulnerabilities," *The Washington Post*, August 31, 2013, https://www.washingtonpost.com/news/the-switch/wp/2013/08/31/the-nsa-hacks-other-countries-by-buying-millions-of-dollars-worth-of-computer-vulnerabilities/.

11. Nicolas Falliere, Liam O. Murchu, and Eric Chien, "W32. Stuxnet Dossier."

12. See, for example, Böhme, Rainer. "Vulnerability Markets." In Proc. of 22C3, 27:30, 2005. https://www.wi1.uni-muenster.de/security/publications/Boehme2005_22C3_VulnerabilityMarkets.pdf.

13. Joan E. Rigdon, "Netscape Is Putting a Price on the Head Of Any Big Bug Found in Web Browser," *The Wall St. Journal,* October 11, 1995.

14. For a partial listing of programs, see: HackerOne, https://hackerone.com/; BugCrowd, "Reward Programs," https://bugcrowd.com/programs/reward; Bugsheet, "Bug Bounties & Disclosure Programs," http://bugsheet.com/directory.

15. Andy Greenberg, "Pentagon Launches Fed's First 'Bug Bounty' Program for Hackers," *Wired*, March 2, 2016, http://www.wired.com/2016/03/pentagon-launches-feds-first-bug-bounty-hackers/.

16. Cora Currier and Morgan Marquis-Boire, "A Detailed Look at Hacking Team's Emails About Its Repressive Clients," *The Intercept*, July 7, 2015, https://theintercept.com/2015/07/07/leaked-documents-confirm-hacking-team-sells-spyware-repressive-countries/.

17. Lillian Ablon, Martin C. Libicki, and Andrea A. Golay, *Markets for Cybercrime Tools and Stolen Data: Hackers' Bazaar* (Rand Corporation, 2014), http://www.rand.org/content/dam/rand/pubs/research_reports/RR600/RR610/RAND_RR610.pdf; Chris Grier et al., "Manufacturing Compromise: The Emergence of Exploit-as-a-Service," in *Proceedings of the 2012 ACM Conference on Computer and Communications Security* (ACM, 2012), 821–32, http://dl.acm.org/citation.cfm?id=2382283; Kurt Thomas, Danny Yuxing Huang, et al., "Framing Dependencies Introduced by Underground Commoditization," 2015, http://damonmccoy.com/papers/WEIS15.pdf.

18. Dennis Fisher, "Zeus Source Code Leaked," *Threatpost | The First Stop for Security News*, May 10, 2011, https://threatpost.com/zeus-source-code-leaked-051011/75217/.

19. Damballa, "First Zeus, Now SpyEye. Look at the Source Code Now!" *Day Before Zero*, August 11, 2011, https://www.damballa.com/first-zeus-now-spyeye-look-the-source-code-now/.

20. Guillaume Bonfante et al., "Analysis and Diversion of Duqu's Driver," January 8, 2014, http://arxiv.org/pdf/1401.6120.pdf.

21. Julia Wolf, *CVE-2011-3402: Windows Kernel TrueType Font Engine Vulnerability,* March 8, 2013, https://cansecwest.com/slides/2013/Analysis%20of%20a%20Windows%20Kernel%20Vuln.pdf.

22. Elizabeth Clarke, "The Underground Hacking Economy Is Alive and Well | Security & Compliance Blog | Dell SecureWorks," December 26, 2013, http://www.secure-works.com/resources/blog/the-underground-hacking-economy-is-alive-and-well/.

23. Aditya K. Sood and Richard J. Enbody, "Crimeware-as-a-service—A Survey of Commoditized Crimeware in the Underground Market," *International Journal of Critical Infrastructure Protection* 6, no. 1 (March 2013): 28–38, doi:10.1016/j.ijcip.2013.01.002.

24. Colin Anderson, "Considerations on Wassenaar Arrangement Control List Additions for Surveillance Technologies," accessed March 11, 2015, https://cda.io/r/ConsiderationsonWassenaarArrangementProposalsforSurveillanceTechnologies.pdf; Nicole Perlroth, "FinSpy Software Is Tracking Political Dissidents," *The New York Times*, August 30, 2012, sec. Technology, http://www.nytimes.com/2012/08/31/technology/finspy-software-is-tracking-political-dissidents.html.

25. Huang et al., "Framing Dependencies Introduced by Underground Commoditization," 2015.

26. Michael Yip, Craig Webber, and Nigel Shadbolt, "Trust among Cybercriminals? Carding Forums, Uncertainty and Implications for Policing," *Policing and Society* 23, no. 4 (2013): 516–39.

27. On the transactional challenges of a market for flaws, see Charlie Miller. "The Legitimate Vulnerability Market." Workshop on the Economics of Information Security, 2007, http://www.econinfosec.org/archive/weis2007/papers/29.pdf.

28. Ibid.

29. Marti Motoyama et al., "An Analysis of Underground Forums," in *Proceedings of the 2011 ACM SIGCOMM Conference on Internet Measurement Conference* (ACM, 2011), 71–80, http://dl.acm.org/citation.cfm?id=2068824.

30. T. J. Holt, "Examining the Forces Shaping Cybercrime Markets Online," *Social Science Computer Review* 31, no. 2, September 10, 2012: 165–77, doi:10.1177/0894439312452998.

31. Stefan Frei, "The Known Unknowns" (NSS Labs, December 2013), https://library.nsslabs.com/reports/known-unknowns-0.

32. Vlad Tsyrklevich, "HACKING TEAM: A ZERO-DAY MARKET CASE STUDY," July 22, 2015, https://tsyrklevich.net/2015/07/22/hacking-team-0day-market/; Kim Zetter, "Hacking Team Leak Shows How Secretive Zero-Day Exploit Sales Work," *WIRED*, July 24, 2015, http://www.wired.com/2015/07/hacking-team-leak-shows-secretive-zero-day-exploit-sales-work/.

33. Jaziar Radianti, "Eliciting Information on the Vulnerability Black Market from Interviews" (Fourth International Conference on Emerging Security Information, Systems and Technologies, IEEE, 2010), 93–96, doi:10.1109/SECURWARE.2010.23.

34. Frei, "The Known Unknowns."

35. Charlie Miller, "The Legitimate Vulnerability Market: Inside the Secretive World of 0-Day Exploit Sales," in *In Sixth Workshop on the Economics of Information Security* (Citeseer, 2007), http://citeseerx.ist.psu.edu/viewdoc/summary?doi=10.1.1.139.5718.

36. Jaziar Radianti and Jose J. Gonzalez, "Dynamic Modeling of the Cyber Security Threat Problem: The Black Market for Vulnerabilities," *Cyber-Security and Global Information Assurance: Threat Analysis And Response Solutions*, 2009, http://www.igi-global.com/chapter/dynamic-modeling-cyber-security-threat/7408.

37. Team Cymru, "A Criminal Perspective on Exploit Packs," May 2011, https://blog.qualys.com/wp-content/uploads/2011/05/team_cymru_exploitkits.pdf.

38. Sariel Moshe and Jacqueline Keith, "Recycle, Reuse, Reharm: How Hackers Use Variants of Known Malware to Victimize Companies and What PayPal Is Doing to Eradicate That Capability | PayPal Engineering Blog," *PayPal Engineering*, November 19, 2015, https://www.paypal-engineering.com/2015/11/19/recycle-reuse-reharm-how-hackers-use-variants-of-known-malware-to-victimize-companies-and-what-paypal-is-doing-to-eradicate-that-capability/.

39. "Google Vulnerability Reward Program (VRP) Rules," *Google Application Security*, 2015.

40. Ben Popper, "A New Breed of Startups Is Helping Hackers Make Millions — Legally," *The Verge*, March 4, 2015, http://www.theverge.com/2015/3/4/8140919/get-paid-for-hacking-bug-bounty-hackerone-synack.

41. Dan Goodin, "All Four Major Browsers Take a Stomping at Pwn2Own Hacking Competition," *Ars Technica*, March 20, 2015, http://arstechnica.com/security/2015/03/all-four-major-browsers-take-a-stomping-at-pwn2own-hacking-competition/.

42. Michael Mimoso, "Citing Wassenaar, HP Pulls out of Mobile Pwn2Own," *Threatpost*, September 4, 2015, https://threatpost.com/citing-wassenaar-hp-pulls-out-of-mobile-pwn2own/114542/.

43. "Framework for Improving Critical Infrastructure Cybersecurity" (NIST, February 12, 2014), http://www.nist.gov/cyberframework/upload/cybersecurity-framework-021214.pdf.

44. Bruce Schneier, "Essays: Cyber Underwriters Lab?—Schneier on Security," *Communications of the ACM*, April 2001, https://www.schneier.com/essays/archives/2001/04/cyber_underwriters_l.html; Dennis Fisher, "Cyber UL Could Become Reality Under Leadership of Hacker Mudge," *Threatpost*, June 30, 2015, https://threatpost.com/cyber-ul-could-become-reality-under-leadership-of-hacker-mudge/113538/.

45. William Jackson, "DoD Cyber Fast Track Program to Fund Small-Scale Hacker Reasearch," *Defense Systems*, August 5, 2011, https://defensesystems.com/articles/2011/08/04/black-hat-darpa-mudge-fast-track-hackers.aspx.

46. For more, see chapter 5—"Bad Code: Exploring Liability in Software Development."

47. Michael Mimoso, "Don't Build a Bounty Program; Build an Incentive Program," *Threatpost*, February 16, 2015, https://threatpost.com/dont-build-a-bounty-program-build-an-incentive-program/111103/; Microsoft, "New Bounty Program Details," *Security Research & Defense*, June 19, 2013, https://blogs.technet.microsoft.com/srd/2013/06/19/new-bounty-program-details/.

Chapter 8

The Computer Fraud and Abuse Act

Structure, Controversies, and Proposals for Reform

Paul Ohm

In 1984, the U.S. Congress enacted the Computer Fraud and Abuse Act ("CFAA"), defining a set of federal crimes directed at computer hacking and other forms of unauthorized access on computers and computer networks.[1] Amended nine times since then, today the CFAA is an essential tool used by law enforcement for the investigation, prosecution, and deterrence of computer crime. At the same time, a litany of high-profile and arguably abusive prosecutions have led observers to recommend a significant narrowing of the statute.

This chapter reviews the structure, controversies, and proposals for reform of the CFAA. As currently written, the CFAA is an overbroad statute, one that vests too much prosecutorial discretion in law enforcement. Congress should narrow the CFAA, perhaps by enacting one of the many "Aaron's Law" proposals from the past two Congresses. At the same time, because we live in a time plagued with cyber insecurity, and because the CFAA plays a role in protecting our security online, the statute should retain its essential, core features.

BASIC STRUCTURE OF CFAA

To clear up one important and frequently repeated misconception: the statute is neither merely a "hacking statute" nor a "computer trespass statute." It instead defines (at least) seven separate federal crimes, in the seven subsections of 1030(a):

- (a)(1): prohibiting the obtaining of information protected for reasons of national defense or foreign relations.

123

- (a)(2): broadly prohibiting *access "without authorization"* to computers. (a)(2)(C) is regarded the most broadly defined crime in the statute and is often characterized as a broad "computer trespass" prohibition.
- (a)(3): prohibiting access to certain U.S. government computers.
- (a)(4): prohibiting using unauthorized access to computers to commit fraud. This provision is often analogized to the mail fraud and wire fraud statutes.
- (a)(5): prohibiting causing damage to computers. The provision most often charged against classic "computer hackers." Defines three separate crimes that differ in the intent that must be proved and whether the hacker accesses the affected computers or attacks them from afar.
- (a)(6): prohibiting password trafficking. Rarely charged and charged often in conjunction with 18 U.S.C. 1029's prohibition on trafficking in access control devices.
- (a)(7): prohibiting extortion involving threats to a computer. Rarely charged.

The two subsections that probably are charged most often, and thus receive the most commentary, are (a)(2)(C) (computer trespass) and the three crimes defined in (a)(5) (damage). The base prohibition of (a)(2)(C) is only a misdemeanor, punishable by a maximum of one year in prison. The maximum sentence increases to a five-year felony in cases involving "purposes of commercial advantage or private financial gain," (c)(2)(B)(i), "in furtherance of any criminal or tortious act," (c)(2)(B)(ii), or if "the value of the information obtained exceeds $5,000" (c)(2)(B)(iii).

The base prohibition of (a)(5) is a ten-year felony for intentional damage (c)(4)(B), five-year felony for reckless damage (c)(4)(A), or a misdemeanor for all other damage, (c)(4)(G). The felony versions of (a)(5) can be enhanced if any one of six enhancement factors are present, (c)(4)(A)(i), including loss aggregating at least $5,000 in value, physical injury to any person, a threat to public health or safety, or damage involving a computer used in furtherance of justice, national defense, or national security. By statute, both the FBI and the U.S. Secret Service share responsibility for investigating CFAA violations.

KEY CONTROVERSIES

CFAA prosecutions have often led to criticism and debate. Many of these episodes have revolved around attempts to define what "authorization" means in the law. These controversies have come to a head in recent years, most importantly around the prosecution of Aaron Swartz, a prominent young internet developer and activist who took his own life after being indicted under the

CFAA for downloading millions of academic articles.[2] The death of Swartz focused great attention on potential CFAA reform.[3]

In addition to focusing on the debate over authorization, this section will also review two other areas of contention over the CFAA. First, it discusses the distorting effect of allowing the CFAA to be enforceable not only through criminal law but through civil lawsuit. Second, it analyzes whether companies should be granted CFAA immunity for "hacking back" against intruders into their networks.

"Authorization"

For every crime defined in the CFAA, culpability depends on prosecutors proving that the defendant acted either "without authorization" or "in excess of authorized access." Courts and commentators have long struggled with assigning precise meaning to these terms, which essentially remain undefined in the statute.

Code-Based, Contract-Based, and Norms-Based Theories

Professor Orin Kerr has proposed a tripartite approach to defining authorization under the CFAA, a structure that has been cited by many courts.[4] CFAA authorization can be defined by reference to code, contract, or norms.

- A *code-based* authorization is one defined and regulated by software. A password prompt is the paradigmatic example. A person who guesses or steals a password can be said to be "without authorization" to use the system.
- A *contract-based* authorization is one defined by contract. A user who agrees to use a system but only for a particular purpose might be said to act "in excess of authorized access" if he uses the system for a different purpose.
- A *norms-based* authorization is one defined by established social norms. Many computer viruses and worms, for example, exploit security software in ways unintended by system architects, which some relevant community (say computer security experts) would consider a breach of social norms. The virus or worm authors might be said to have violated those norms.

Until recently, most commentators agreed that a code-based definition is appropriate and sound, as a matter of both correct statutory interpretation and good public policy. Contract-based authorization has been much more controversial, particularly when the "contract" in question are voluminous website terms of service that are not read by the users they claim to apply to. Norms-based theories have rarely been embraced by courts or commentators, at least until the recent past. All three theories are undergoing reevaluation, in response to recent prosecutions.

Reconsidering the Clarity of Code-Based Lines

Not too long ago, many commentators agreed that code-based theories of authorization were a proper and sound way to define authorization in the CFAA. This agreement has been challenged by the dawning realization by many that the line between code-based and norms-based theories is less bright than it once seemed. Take *United States v. Morris* for example.[5] The famous "Morris Worm" that spurred the first CFAA prosecution involved an exploit of "SENDMAIL," a low-level protocol still in use today for sending e-mail between systems. The Morris Worm took advantage of a flaw in SENDMAIL implementations to propagate, spreading between computers at a time when systems administrators considered this use to be an abuse of the software, establishing a reasonably clear norms violation. But whether the worm subverted a "code-based" flaw seemed much more difficult to say, nearly devolving into a basically philosophical debate about what it meant for a computer to permit an action. For its part, the Second Circuit, in upholding the conviction of the worm's author, spoke mostly about social norms, devising a test still cited today that asks whether the software subverted the "intended function" of the code.

Another much more recent prosecution has helped crystallize the latent ambiguity in the code-based theory. In 2012, prosecutors charged John Kane and Andre Nestor for violating the CFAA.[6] According to prosecutors, Kane discovered a vulnerability in the software for certain video poker machines. Through a complex and unlikely set of button presses, Kane was able to dramatically increase his cash payouts on these machines, and racked up nearly a half-million dollars in earnings. To CFAA experts, the theory of the case seemed to spotlight a latent problem with code-based theories: in many cases, whether code is "circumvented" or instead "used not as intended" is only in the eye of the beholder.[7] The clean clarity of the code-based theory suddenly began to seem quite muddy.

Terms of Service and Lori Drew

Many have criticized the expansive use of contract-based theories of the CFAA, focusing into three, related major objections. First, critics assail the widespread use of boilerplate terms of service for websites. It is one thing to say that a terms of service document might serve as a binding contract, but quite another thing to claim that it somehow delineates the boundaries of criminal culpability. These critics echo a broader critique of boilerplate and clickwrap contracting, pointing to studies of user behavior (almost everybody clicks through) and the dense legalese usually embraced in these documents.[8]

Second, critics of a broad contract approach to CFAA liability point to absurdities that might result from this theory, given the minor and insignificant contractual terms users supposedly agree to every day. Website contracts supposedly obligate users to use their real names rather than pseudonyms and prohibit children under thirteen from using most major social networking services, even though millions of users violate terms like these each and every day. The problem is that these commonly disregarded minor transgressions become elevated to criminal violations under aggressive contract-based theories of CFAA authorization.

Third, critics argue that a contract-based theory essentially empowers private parties to draw the boundaries of criminal law, a rare and perhaps unprecedented delegation of a quintessentially legislative role to nongovernmental actors.

The prosecution of a woman named Lori Drew rested on contract-based theories of authorization and inspired critiques like those above. Drew allegedly encouraged or helped her teenaged daughter create a MySpace account for a boy who did not exist for the express purpose of harassing her daughter's classmate, a girl named Megan Meier. After the "boy" showed initial interest in and ultimately rejected Meier, the distraught girl committed suicide. After local Missouri prosecutors decided they could not press charges against Drew, the U.S. Attorney in Los Angeles, the home district for MySpace, brought a CFAA prosecution, premised entirely on a contract-based theory of authorization: Drew's actions violated several terms of the MySpace Terms of Service, which prohibited among other things, using untruthful information during account registration and harassing other people.

After a jury voted to convict Drew, the district court judge dismissed the case holding that the breach of these inconsequential terms of service could not support a conviction.[9] To rule otherwise, the judge reasoned, would render the CFAA unconstitutionally void for vagueness. The U.S. Attorney chose not to appeal. The Ninth Circuit has cut back significantly on the validity of contract-based theories of the CFAA in a case called United States v. Nosal.[10] In a sweeping opinion, the Ninth Circuit reversed a conviction against a man for convincing his former coworkers to take data from their employer's computer network, with the purpose of creating a new firm, all in breach of the man's contract not to compete. In the opinion, the Ninth Circuit held that "the phrase 'exceeds authorized access' . . . does not extend to violations of use restrictions," as a matter of statutory interpretation and with reference to both the void for vagueness and rule of lenity doctrines.

The Recent Embrace of Norms-Based Theories

Although code-based and contract-based theories have received the great bulk of attention, both from prosecutors and commentators, in the very recent past, academics have begun to shift their attention to norms-based theories of the CFAA. One wonders if litigants and judges might follow the academics, as they have before with this law, and begin to focus on norms. We should hesitate before going too eagerly down this path. The problem with norms-based theories is their inherent lack of standards and concomitant unpredictability. In a recent article, many of the conclusions take on a "know it when you see it" approach to locating and documenting norms.[11] As with any similar standard, people will likely disagree not only about what norms a community holds but even about what community is the relevant one for analysis.

The Abuse of Expansive Prosecutorial Discretion: weev and Aaron Swartz

The government sometimes defends the potentially vast scope courts have granted to the meaning of "authorization" in the CFAA by pointing to its own wise exercise of prosecutorial discretion. In a world of limited resources, the argument goes, the government will not investigate much less press charges against those who violate minor terms of service or breach an ambiguous online social norm. It is better to have a criminal hacking statute that overcriminalizes conduct, relying on law enforcement to select the worthy cases from a larger pool, rather than undercriminalize conduct, leaving some blameworthy conduct unpunishable.

CFAA critics respond, in part, by pointing to two recent cases that suggest the need to resist blind deference to prosecutorial discretion. The fact that the government pursued these cases, they say, suggests that the government will not hesitate to use the CFAA in overbroad and aggressive ways, particularly against defendants who espouse unpopular views.

Andrew Auernheimer: "weev"

A case that has served as a rallying cry was the prosecution of Andrew Auernheimer, also known as weev. Prosecutors charged weev under the CFAA for systematically downloading information about the early adopters of iPads from AT&T's website.[12] This information was available on AT&T's public-facing website, but access required a little intelligent guessing about AT&T's use of URLs. To many, this case rested on a theory of CFAA authorization entirely premised on norms violations, because any information available on a public website could not be said to be protected by code. After he was convicted and served more than a year in federal prison, the Third Circuit dismissed the case for improper venue and, to date, prosecutors have not brought new charges.

Many saw this case as an overreach. Even though the affected iPad users might have justifiably felt harmed by the public outing of their e-mail addresses and maybe even their "early adopter" purchasing habits, their ire should have been directed at AT&T for designing an insecure website, much more than at weev for exploiting it, so the argument went.

Critics were also suspicious about the government's motive. Weev is a notorious figure, a self-described "troll" who has engaged in a long string of destructive attacks on vulnerable victims. His infamy was also widely publicized, most notably in a long profile in the New York Times magazine.[13] Until the AT&T incident, he had bragged about his exploits with impunity. Many wondered whether the FBI had found a way through the CFAA to finally punish this public menace for his past sins.

Aaron Swartz

But it was the case against Aaron Swartz that truly brought the CFAA to the front of public and Congressional attention, at least for a while. Swartz was a brilliant computer programmer and civic activist who had helped create the real simple syndication (RSS) protocol and founded the website Reddit before the age of twenty.[14] Active in movements to challenge what he saw as abuses of copyright law, he launched a secret effort to download millions of academic articles sitting behind the paywall of an academic publishing clearing house known as JSTOR. Many universities negotiate broad site licenses to download articles from JSTOR, and these agreements often permit unrestricted access to users of university networks. Swartz, an employee at Harvard at the time, took advantage of the open MIT network across town to download JSTOR articles.

In many ways, the case against Swartz was far stronger than that against weev. For as soon as MIT and JSTOR detected the bulk download activity, they implemented code-based countermeasures, such as IP and MAC address blocking, many of which were subsequently circumvented by Swartz. The evidentiary case against Swartz was also compelling, particularly because it involved surveillance video showing Swartz entering a network wiring closet to hide a laptop used for the download.

Critics were dismayed, nevertheless, by the prosecution's choice to pursue Swartz. Importantly, the case struck a nerve because it focused on two paradigmatic institutions for access to knowledge—university campuses and academic publishing—and many sympathized with the idea that "freeing" scientific research was a noble cause, even though it is still today unclear exactly what Swartz intended to do with the downloaded articles. It is also clear that many critics blame prosecutors for Swartz's decision to commit suicide.[15] Many have been critical of what they claim were prosecutors pressing too hard and negotiating too aggressively and hostilely against a relatively young and vulnerable defendant.

Civil Liability

The CFAA has also been criticized for its dual civil-and-criminal nature. The CFAA is not only a criminal law, but also one that provides for civil liability. According to the statute, "Any person who suffers damage or loss by reason of any" of the profited acts in the CFAA may sue for damages and injunctive relief against the violator.[16]

Since the dawn of the CFAA, numerous civil litigants have sued for relief under this statute. The most common pattern is a lawsuit by a company against a competitor or former employee or both for theft of valuable company information. In fact, most of the important CFAA contract-theory cases involve companies complaining about faithless employees who have departed for a competitor, with trade secrets or other valuable documents in hand. In essence, the CFAA has been treated as a "trade secrets light" cause of action. Critics contend that these cases go far beyond the original intent of the statute and are being used to replace a far more carefully delineated body of trade secrets law.

The problem with these lawsuits, critics contend, is that courts interpret the meaning of a statute with both criminal and civil application consistently across these contexts.[17] Thus, a judge in a civil case interpreting the meaning of the words, "without authorization," will also be creating law for future criminal cases. They often engage in this kind of interpretation, however, without the benefit of briefing by those engaged in criminal prosecution, and sometimes without even appearing to realize that what they are saying may extend to a very different context. Also, because of the rate at which cases are brought, over time civil lawsuits have tended to lead while criminal lawsuits have tended to lag the development of the law. Especially early in the development of the CFAA, much of the early understanding came from short and vaguely reasoned opinion of judges in civil cases.

Hacking Back

A final area of debate around the CFAA is over the legality of what information security experts call "Active Defense," but what is often known more colloquially as "Hack Back." The question is whether an information assurance professional charged with defending a corporate or government network is permitted to pursue an unauthorized intruder back to a source computer, perhaps deploying offensive hacking tools and techniques to retrieve stolen data or disable the attack.

The legal problem is that the CFAA provides no textual defense for unauthorized access or damage to a computer in order to practice self-defense. Section 1030(f) allows "any lawfully authorized investigative, protective, or intelligence activity of a law enforcement agency," so government-deputized hack back may be legal. But law enforcement agencies rarely, if ever, authorize private hack back, so the question remains. Some observers have argued that the CFAA should be interpreted to include a common-law argument for self-defense, drawing analogies to self-defense of the home.[18]

There are several problems with this reasoning. Most importantly, most active defense methods involve actions that go well beyond the analogies being drawn. No one has yet found a precedent in common law to permit a homeowner to pursue a thief into a house across town, much less across the country. Second, it is far-fetched to believe that in enacting an extremely detailed criminal statute, one which micromanages definitions and actions in excruciating detail, Congress would have left such a broad and fundamental exception subject to common-law development without at least mentioning the possibility.

No court has embraced a hack back defense to the CFAA, and none should. Beyond the legal arguments already advanced, there are practical reasons to fear that such an exception would unnecessarily muddy investigations into what today is considered clearly culpable activity. It would also sanction reckless behavior that could give rise to many innocent victims. At the very least, these issues are the kind of policy considerations that should be debated in Congress rather than in the first instance in the courts.

CONGRESSIONAL ACTION: PAST, PRESENT, AND FUTURE

Congress has amended the CFAA at least nine times since it originally drafted the law. It is fair to say almost every amendment has expanded the scope of conduct covered by the law or increased penalties for violations. This steady drumbeat has been abetted by a tendency by lawmakers to focus on the last failed investigation or court battle and by very effective lobbying by the Department of Justice (DoJ) and its champions on Capitol Hill. The outpouring of grief and activism following the death of Aaron Swartz seemed at least temporarily to breathe life into attempts to narrow the CFAA. Several narrowing proposals were introduced, although the initial wave of attention seems to have died down in the ensuing years.

A History of Expansion Without Contraction

Throughout its history, the CFAA has almost always been expanded and never contracted. Perhaps the most important shift came in 1986, when a relatively narrow CFAA was expanded to cover not only "federal interest computers" but also any "protected computers," a term that has been given a vast meaning by courts.[19] Today, the term is properly understood to apply to any device with a processor that can access the internet, and probably many devices that do not. Congress amended the CFAA again in the USA PATRIOT Act following the September 11th terrorist attacks.[20] These amendments extended the CFAA more explicitly than before to application to acts occurring outside the United States if the affected computer "is used in a manner that affects interstate or foreign commerce or communication of the United States."[21] *The PATRIOT Act* also increased some maximum sentences for certain violations.

Botnets

Many more recent amendments have responded to the rise of so-called botnets, those "zombie armies" of personal computers on the internet under control of a malicious third party and controlled as a group when commanded. Botnets are often used to launch massive distributed denial of service attacks against a single target, disabling web services and denying access to legitimate users. In 2008, at DoJ's behest, Congress amended the same provisions relating to (a)(5) to declare it a felony to cause "damage affecting 10 or more protected computers during any 1-year period," without requiring proof of the $5,000 damage threshold.[22]

Aaron's Law

At least for a while, reaction to Swartz's death spurred a vocal push to amend the CFAA, with particular attention on narrowing contract-based theories. Several bills were introduced under the name "Aaron's Law," and some of these seemed for a time to have a chance of being enacted. Aaron's Law was originally introduced in 2013 just months after Swartz's death and reintroduced in 2015. No version of the bill has been voted on by any Congressional committee to date. The various versions of Aaron's Law would all attempt to clarify and narrow the meaning of "authorization" by restricting it to "technological or physical measures that are designed to exclude or prevent unauthorized individuals."[23] This would appear to embrace a "code-based" approach to interpreting the CFAA.

One problem with these proposals is that they perhaps have not kept up with the latest debates over the CFAA. Some commentators now think that the way to strike the proper balance between an important law enforcement tool is not to embrace "code-based" solutions but rather to look toward "norms-based" understandings. By referring to "technology or physical measures that are designed to exclude or prevent," Aaron's Law might close the door on some norms-based theories.

A potential irony of the Aaron's Law movement is that the case against Swartz was primarily a code-based case, not a contract-based case. In other words, even under Aaron's Law, the Justice Department could still have prosecuted Swartz. For this reason, the Electronic Frontier Foundation has proposed at least two other reforms to the CFAA in the wake of Swartz's death, each tied much more closely to the facts of his case: a reduction in the maximum sentences for many CFAA crimes, and an exception for "tinkerers, security researchers, innovators, and privacy seekers."[24] To date, these proposals have not been incorporated in the "Aaron's Law" amendments that have been proposed.

Removing the Civil Liability Provision of 1030(g)

Lost amid the attention on shoring up the definition of authorization is another sensible proposal for revision that should be less contentious yet still meaningful. Congress should amend the CFAA to take away a civil right of action. As a tool for civil litigants, the CFAA is an unnecessarily duplicative tool. Most cases that have been litigated have presented obvious trade secrecy causes of action. The only thing added by the CFAA is, perhaps, federal jurisdiction and a lower evidentiary requirement. As described above, many of the distortions in the law have been the product of civil litigants pursuing agendas quite separate from the criminal deterrence at the heart of the original law. The statute would be a more focused, arguably successful statute if stripped of its dual role.

CONCLUSION

At the heart of the CFAA lies a confusing and poorly defined concept—authorization. Prosecutors have frequently overstepped the bounds of sensible discretion in the cases they have chosen to bring that have sought to exploit this vagueness and expand this definition. The DoJ has also pushed too hard to expand the law contributing to the overbreadth and ambiguity. Still, without a major overhaul, the CFAA can be sensibly reformed to constrain its ambiguities. Once amended, the law can serve as an important weapon in the fight against computer crime and as a piece of a broader strategy to bring better security and privacy to the internet and mobile networks.

CHAPTER HIGHLIGHTS

Computer Fraud and Abuse Act (CFAA). In 1984, the U.S. Congress enacted the CFAA, defining a set of federal crimes directed at computer hacking and other forms of unauthorized access to computers and computer networks. Amended nine times since then, today the CFAA is an essential tool used by law enforcement for the investigation, prosecution, and deterrence of computer crime.

CFAA Crime Culpability. For every crime defined in the CFAA, culpability depends on prosecutors proving that the defendant acted either "without authorization" or "in excess of authorized access." Courts and commentators have long struggled with assigning precise meaning to these terms, which essentially remain undefined in the statute.

Defining CFAA Authorization. A tripartite approach to defining authorization under the CFAA, a structure that has been cited by many courts. CFAA authorization can be defined by reference to code, contract, or norms: (1) *code-based* authorization is defined and regulated by software (e.g., Password prompt); (2) *contract-based* authorization is defined by contract (e.g., user agrees to use a system but only for a particular purpose); and (3) *norms-based* authorization is defined by established social norms (e.g., bypassing security software in ways unintended by system architects).

Embracing Norm-Based Authorization. Although code-based and contract-based theories have received the great bulk of attention, both from prosecutors and commentators, in the very recent past, academics have begun to shift their attention to norms-based theories of the CFAA. Litigators should hesitate before going too eagerly down this path. The problem with norms-based theories is their inherent lack of standards and concomitant unpredictability.

Hacking Back. There is debate around the CFAA over the legality of what information security experts call "Active Defense," but what is often known more colloquially as "Hack Back." The question is whether an information assurance professional charged with defending a corporate or government network is permitted to pursue an unauthorized intruder back to a source computer, perhaps deploying offensive hacking tools and techniques to retrieve stolen data or disable the attack. CFAA provides no textual defense for unauthorized access or damage to a computer in order to practice self-defense; however, allowing hack back would also sanction reckless behavior that could give rise to many innocent victims.

Removing Civil Liability. Congress should amend the CFAA to take away a civil right of action. As a tool for civil litigants, the CFAA is unnecessarily duplicative. Most cases that have been litigated presented obvious trade secrecy causes of action. The only thing added by the CFAA is, perhaps, federal jurisdiction and a lower evidentiary requirement.

NOTES

1. Codified today at 18 U.S.C. § 1030.
2. Henry Farrell, "Remembering Aaron Swartz," *Crooked Timber*, January 12, 2013, http://crookedtimber.org/2013/01/12/remembering-aaron-swartz/.
3. Brian Fung, "The Justice Department Used This Law to Pursue Aaron Swartz. Now It's Open to Reforming It.," *Washington Post*, February 7, 2014, sec. The Switch, https://www.washingtonpost.com/news/the-switch/wp/2014/02/07/the-justice-depart-ment-used-this-law-to-pursue-aaron-swartz-now-its-open-to-reforming-it/.
4. Orin S. Kerr, *Cybercrime's Scope: Interpreting "Access" and "Authorization" in Computer Misuse Statutes*, 78 New York University Law Review 1596 (2003).
5. *United States v. Morris*, 928 F.2d 504 (2d. Cir. 1991).
6. Kevin Poulsen, "Use a Software Bug to Win Video Poker? That's a Federal Hacking Case," *Wired*, May 1, 2013, http://www.wired.com/2013/05/game-king/.
7. James Grimmelmann, "Computer Crime Law Goes to the Casino," Concurring Opinions, May 2, 2013, http://concurringopinions.com/archives/2013/05/computer-crime-law-goes-to-the-casino.html.
8. Lorrie Faith Cranor et al., "Are They Worth Reading? An in-Depth Analysis of Online Advertising Companies' Privacy Policies," in *2014 TPRC Conference Paper*, 2014, http://papers.ssrn.com/sol3/papers.cfm?abstract_id=2418590.
9. *United States v. Drew*, 259 F.R.D. 449 (C.D. Cal. 2009).
10. *United States v. Nosal*, 676 F.3d 854 (9th Cir. 2012) (en banc).
11. Orin S. Kerr, "Norms of Computer Trespass," *Columbia Law Review* 116, (forthcoming 2016).
12. *United States v. Auernheimer*, 748 F.3d 525 (3d Cir. 2014).
13. Mattathias Schwartz, "The Trolls Among Us," *New York Times*, August 3, 2008, http://www.nytimes.com/2008/08/03/magazine/03trolls-t.html?_r=0.
14. Justin Peters, *The Idealist: Aaron Swartz and the Rise of Free Culture on the Internet* (New York: Simon and Schuster Inc., 2016).
15. Lawrence Lessig, "Prosecutor as Bully," *LESSIG Blog, v2*, accessed April 28, 2016, http://lessig.tumblr.com/post/40347463044/prosecutor-as-bully; David Kravets, "Obama Won't Fire Aaron Swartz's Federal Prosecutors," *Ars Technica*,

January 8, 2015, http://arstechnica.com/tech-policy/2015/01/obama-wont-fire-aaron-swartzs-federal-prosecutors/.

16. Fraud and related activity in connection with computers, 18 U.S.C. § 1030(g) (2002).

17. Jonathan Mayer, Cybercrime Litigation, 164 Penn L. Rev. ___ (forthcoming 2016), https://jonathanmayer.org/papers

18. An archive of a blog-based debate over the hack back self-defense argument is available online at Steptoe, "The Hackback Debate," *Steptoe Cyberblog,* November 2, 2012, http://www.steptoecyberblog.com/2012/11/02/the-hackback-debate/.

19. Computer Fraud and Abuse Act of 1986, Pub. L. 99–474, 100 Stat. 1213.

20. Uniting and Strengthening America by Providing Appropriate Tools Required to Intercept and Obstruct Terrorism Act of 2001, Pub. L. No. 107–56.

21. Fraud and related activity in connection with computers, 18 U.S.C. § 1030(e) (2)(B), (2002).

22. Identity Theft Enforcement and Restitution Act of 2008 (Title II of Former Vice President Protection Act of 2008, Pub. L. 110–326).

23. Aaron's Law Act of 2016, S. 1030, 114th Congress (2016).

24. Parker Higgins, "Critical Fixes for the Computer Fraud and Abuse Act," Electronic Frontier Foundation, January 29, 2013, https://www.eff.org/deeplinks/2013/01/these-are-critical-fixes-computer-fraud-and-abuse-act.

Chapter 9

Breach Notification Laws

The Policy and Practice

Sasha Romanosky

This chapter examines data breaches and breach notification laws, discussing the stages of a data breach as well as incentives by firms and consumers with regard to protection of personal information. A data breach is a security incident where personally identifying or otherwise sensitive information is made available to unauthorized third parties, copied, or stolen. The chapter introduces the components of state data breach notification laws and discusses the ways in which they have evolved along with emerging threats. The chapter then considers federal breach notification bills and how they might provide an improvement over state laws. Combining each of these elements, the final section concludes by noting the importance of four key considerations relevant to policy interventions generally and breach notification specifically. The chapter highlights the distinction between security versus privacy, understanding harms, appropriate forms of redress, and potential consequences of these notification laws.

Firm Incentives to Invest in Security

In response to Presidential Executive Order 13636, many federal agencies were tasked with helping to improve the information assurance posture of the nation's critical infrastructure.[1] As part of this effort, the National Institute of Standards and Technology (NIST) developed a comprehensive suite of best practices that eventually became the NIST Cybersecurity Framework.[2] While this was, and still is, an important deliverable, there remains a key issue—private sector adoption of these standards and practices. In effect, the Framework answers the question, "how do we improve the protection of information technology (IT) systems and data?" but does not address the question, "why should we improve it?" To be clear, the latter was not

NIST's challenge, yet the problem remains: what incentives exist for firms to improve their information assurance and how do we create better incentives in the market for security?

Consider figure 9.1 that describes distinct stages of a data breach.[3] Such a diagram can be useful in order to help identify incentives by relevant stake-holders, and opportunities for policy interventions that may help correct or adjust these incentives. First, conditional on a firm engaging in some level of data protection, it may suffer a data breach (either accidentally by human error, through theft, or cyber-attack). Once a breach has occurred, the firm may become aware of it, either from their own security controls, or alerted by customers, employees, or law enforcement.[4] State laws may require the firm to notify affected individuals. Once notified, these individuals may take action (such as enrolling in credit monitoring) to reduce any anticipated harm. And finally, the individual may (or may) not suffer any resulting harm. Of course, avoiding harm is not guaranteed even with reasonable defensive efforts.[5]

Given the stages of a breach identified by figure 9.1, there are two stages that are most relevant to understanding firm incentives: the first stage (investment in security controls *ex ante*) and the fifth stage (individual actions taken *ex post* that seek to reduce loss), discussed next.

Incentivizing Action

One of the key factors driving a firm's incentive to invest in effective security controls is the cost incurred from a breach. The more costly it could be, the more resources the firm is likely to use to prevent it.[6] So what do we know about the cost of a data breach? Recent research, looking at a dataset of over 12,000 cyber events covering data breaches, privacy violations, and phishing attacks over the years 2005–2015, pegged the cost of a breach at less than $200k per event.[7] The research analyzed the characteristics of the incidents (such as the cause and types of information compromised), as well as the breach and litigation rates, by industry. This finding differs from some surveys that place the average figure at $6.5 million.[8] The difference is explained because of the large variation in losses incurred across incidents. For example, while Target suffered more than $250 million from their breach in 2013, the vast majority of breaches are substantially less costly.[9]

Consumers play a role as well, by protecting their data, and responding to breach notifications. A 2016 paper surveyed over 2000 individuals within the United States and found that most respondents (77 percent) were very satisfied with firm actions taken postbreach, and that 62 percent of respondents accepted offers of free credit monitoring.[10] That is, despite claims and fears of customer attrition, 89 percent of respondents from this survey continued to patronize the

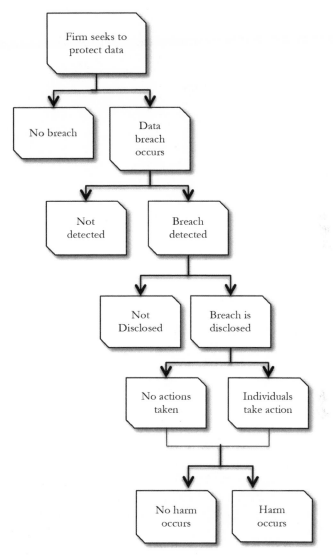

Figure 9.1 **Stages of a Data Breach**

firms that had been breached. These findings are both surprising and revealing because from the small amount of available evidence, only a small fraction of consumers accept these offers of free credit monitoring.[11] Indeed, in some cases, less than 10 percent of consumers respond.[12] The more recent 62 percent figure is encouraging, suggesting that consumers may well be taking the kinds of action that legislators of the breach notification laws intend.

One of the primary motivations that firms have for avoiding data breaches is reputational damage (a component of total costs). While this is a very ambiguous term, one interpretation could simply mean lost business.[13] When respondents were asked whether they would stop patronizing the company following the breach, only 11 percent said yes. That is, the vast majority of consumers maintained their relationship with the breached firm. Together, these results (modest cost of a breach, and satisfied consumers postnotification) suggest that firms currently have very little incentive to improve their security practices. Based on this review of the stages of a data breach and discussion of the incentives by firms and consumers to mitigate loss, the next chapter examines the primary legal means by which these incidents have been regulated: state-level breach notification.

INTRODUCTION TO BREACH NOTIFICATION LAWS

There are many alternative ways to regulate a firm's behavior. *Ex ante* (before the event) regulation seeks to impose minimum standards of care in order to prevent accidents or harm from occurring at all. For example, fire safety and building codes prevent the spread and magnitude of damage in the event of a fire. On the other hand, *ex post* (after the event) liability simply allows injured parties to seek redress for any harms incurred by an injuring party. While *ex ante* regulation is useful to prevent widespread or catastrophic harms, *ex post* liability is useful when both parties (the injurer and injured) are known, and any harm is cognizable or quantifiable.[14]

A third alternative is information disclosure, which does not address any firm behavior directly, nor provides immediate relief to victims, but instead leverages economic incentives in the market by forcing the firm to disclose the potential for harm to those conceivably affected by an event. This "sunshine effect" drives the firm to improve its practices in order to avoid a costly incident, and empowers victims to take action and mitigate loss.[15] However, disclosure works best when the disclosed information is timely, actionable, and consumers are both aware and concerned enough to take action. Nevertheless, such disclosure has been the prominent policy mechanism by which data breaches (and privacy breaches) have been regulated in the United States.

California first adopted a state breach notification law in 2003, while Kentucky was the most recent of forty-seven states to adopt it in 2014.[16] In general, these laws require entities that possess personally identifiable information to notify those affected when this data has been improperly disclosed. While there is some variation across state laws, they generally include the following provisions: covered entities (e.g., businesses, persons, and government agencies), covered data (e.g., name, address, and credit card number), trigger for notification, notification method and requirements, exceptions, and penalties.[17] This chapter examines these in more detail below, followed by a discussion of evolving trends in the laws.

Entities and Covered Data

The entities covered by these laws may include business, individuals, and government agencies. That is, it is these businesses and agencies which bear the burden of notifying affected parties in the event that personal information in their possession, or licensed to another party, is compromised. Typically, personal information is considered to be first and last name, in addition to another kind of personally identifiable information, such as address, driver's license or passport number, financial or medical account information. The kinds of data covered by these laws are becoming ever more inclusive.

Trigger Requirements

Some states require notification simply for unauthorized disclosure, which is a relatively low threshold, for example, the loss or theft of a computer that happens to contain personal information. Other states require that there be a reasonable risk of actual harm, which represents a higher threshold for disclosure, for example, such as fraud resulting from theft of information. Importantly, the assessment of the risk of harm, however, is typically left to the firm itself. This distinction in threshold of harm is contentious because it is unclear which approach is most effective in reducing costs for both firms and consumers. Disclosure of all breaches affords consumers an opportunity to mitigate harm. However, this can also lead to consumers becoming desensitized to the notices, causing them to ignore important recommendations (e.g., applying for credit monitoring).[18] One compromise that is sometimes used is to assign the higher threshold (e.g., notification only in the case of reasonable risk of identity theft), but then also requires notification to a state agency, such as the state's attorney general, regardless of the threshold.[19]

Notification

Typically, state breach disclosure laws require that notification be provided in writing, by phone, or by electronic means, and must be issued as soon as practical and without unreasonable delay of discovery of the breach. Some states even impose additional requirements, requiring that notification occur no longer than thirty (Florida), forty-five (Ohio), or ninety (Connecticut) days from breach detection.[20] There is an important tension concerning the timing of these notifications, however. On one hand, individuals may feel, as a matter of principle, that they should be told as soon as possible. Indeed, there is evidence to suggest that people incur less financial loss from identity theft when they are notified sooner.[21] On the other hand, it takes time for firms to identify the precise cause and scope of a breach, and so a notification letter sent too quickly may be incorrect or misleading. It is, therefore, an unresolved issue as to what is the optimal time for disclosure.

Exceptions

Some states provide exceptions for disclosure in the event that the covered entity is already required to notify under other state or federal statutes, such as the Gramm-Leach-Bliley Act, or the Health Insurance Portability and Accountability Act that provide their own notification requirements.[22] In addition, some states may also provide notification exceptions if the compromised information was encrypted, redacted, or if there is an active law enforcement investigation. The approach with these exceptions is to attempt not to overburden individuals with notices when the risk of potential identity theft is very low, or when it may interfere with law enforcement.

Penalties

Penalties for violations can result in civil fines ranging from hundreds or thousands of dollars per day, up to hundreds of thousands of dollars in cases of extreme delay. For example, in Florida, any entity that violates the statute "is liable for a civil penalty of $1,000 per day up to 30 days following any violation and $50,000 per 30 day period thereafter up to a maximum total of $500,000."[23] In addition, some states provide a private right of action that allows individuals affected by the breach to sue companies for nondisclosure. To be clear, these penalties impose fines only for the act of not properly disclosing a breach, and are not meant to provide relief to affected individuals due to any financial harm. Any injuries alleged by private individuals are redressed through traditional legal methods.[24]

An important characteristic of these state laws (like many others) is that they apply to covered entities that possess or license information about residents of the state with the enacted law, regardless of where the breach occurred. For example, a firm suffering a breach affecting residents of Pennsylvania must comply with Pennsylvania state law, even if the origin of the breach was a server located in another state. While straightforward, this can be problematic for some firms who must distinguish among affected individuals, by state, in order to determine whom to notify. Indeed, this is a main criticism by firms regarding these state laws—that they incur unnecessary legal costs in order to properly understand, and comply with each state's law.

Evolution of Data Breach Notification Laws

When initially drafted, these state laws were quite limited with regard to the scope of personal information and entities covered, as well as the form and presentation of the notification. In recent years, however, many states have revised or are planning to revise their existing laws. Indeed, in 2015, thirty-three states introduced revisions to their breach notification laws, which cover a range of issues.[25] For example, they expand the definition of covered entities (e.g., government agencies, contractors, and third parties who possess, but do not own the data, and service providers), as well as covered information (i.e., to include fingerprints, voice prints, DNA, e-mail addresses, tax or other identification numbers, electronic signatures, online usernames and passwords, and birth or marriage certificates).[26]

The format of the actual notification has also been the subject of consumer criticism and therefore innovation by state legislators. For example, California has amended its law to require companies to provide a clear description of the incident, the type of information compromised, and contact information for credit bureaus. In addition, it also amended its law to require that the notice include specific sections and topic areas. Namely, the following headings: "What Happened," "What Information Was Involved," "What We Are Doing," "What You Can Do," and "For More Information." The hope is that by clearly enumerating these categories, consumers will be less confused, be able to more readily assess their risk of identity theft, and take appropriate action to reduce any harms. Understanding the most effective way to communicate risks of harm to individuals (in any industry) is an unsolved problem and it is unclear whether there actually exists an optimal format or style of notice. The issue is exacerbated by the problem that the ideal outcome is itself unclear. That is, what is it that we most want to achieve? Is it simply to have each recipient of a notice understand the terms of a letter? Or that they each be able to properly assess their individual risk of harm? Or that whenever free credit monitoring is offered, 100 percent of recipients comply? Or something else?[27]

Are Breach Notification Laws Effective?

There exists little evidence concerning the effectiveness of state breach notification laws. One research paper examined their effect on consumer-reported identity thefts and the authors found that the notification laws reduced consumer identity theft by 6 percent.[28] Is this a good outcome? It is difficult to say, because there is no formal or informal threshold over which one could definitively prove the effectiveness of a state law. Yes, rate of consumer identity theft is one potentially useful measure, but perhaps other measures should be found. In principle, the effect of these notification laws is to force firms to increase their investment in security controls and to encourage consumers to take action to prevent economic harm.[29] It is worth noting, however, that these two measures seek to reduce data breaches *and* consumer harms. Therefore, estimating the effect of breach notification laws directly on actual security incidents may also be a useful exercise.

Unfortunately, however, while adoption of these laws has been increasing since 2003, so have the reported rates of data breaches and privacy violations.[30] One possible explanation is that the underlying breach rate has remained constant, but the laws have simply forced the public disclosure of a greater percentage of them. Alternatively, the increased breach rate may be due to more frequent cyber-attacks. The point being that identifying (not to mention measuring) intended and unintended effects of policy interventions can be quite difficult and requires proper empirical analysis.

Could a Federal Breach Notification Law Help?

In addition to state efforts to disclose data breaches, many federal bills have also been written over recent years, with multiple competing bills being introduced in the 114th Congress.[31] However, none have yet passed both chambers of the U.S. Congress. The main provisions of the federal bills have generally mirrored those of the state laws (i.e., kinds of covered entities, scope of personal information, form and requirement for notification, etc.). However, there exist a number of important differentiators concerning a federal proposal.

One of the main criticisms with the current set of state laws concerns the many variations among them that force firms to investigate and comply with each state's unique requirements. A federal law could help by alleviating these unnecessary burdens and costs. However, there are a number of important caveats.

First, whether state law or federal law, these policies only address post-breach activity and therefore do nothing to directly prevent the incident itself.[32] In fact, one may argue that a federal statute would simply reduce firm expenses in the event of a breach, thereby reducing their total (*ex post*) mitigation costs, and ultimately reduce its overall investment in information security. In other words, the less a firm has to spend mitigating the cost of a breach, the less it will invest beforehand to prevent it.

Second, with uniformity of obligations under a federal law comes preemption of state laws. And while the singular statute would certainly ease the burden on firm compliance, the possibility exists that any federal statute would be a much weaker version of any single state law, such as with California, which has one of the most expansive privacy protection laws. For example, a federal law might set the threshold of notification to only those breaches for which a reasonable expectation of harm exists (e.g., such as when the breach is caused by a hack directed at personal information specifically). While some may argue that this is an appropriate trigger (lest consumers be bombarded with excessive notifications and begin ignoring them all), it suffers from the concern that many breaches would go unreported because they are deemed too low a risk. The concern in this is the same as faced by law enforcement and the intelligence community—it is difficult to be sure ahead of time which events will provide critical evidence of systematic patterns of criminal or malicious behavior.

Another concern is that the scope of personal information or covered entities may not adequately reflect the appropriate variety of personal information sufficient to capture the full range of data breaches and privacy violations. For example, the *Data Security and Breach Notification Act of 2015* would restrict notification to breaches that pose an actual risk of financial harm.[33] While ostensibly useful, financial harm is just one kind of adverse outcome. This approach would ignore other kinds of privacy harms that may occur from the compromise of personal information. The loss or theft of, for example, voting records; HIV status; criminal, medical, employment, and biometric information may well have grave consequences that are not financial at all.

On the other hand, a federal law that does not preempt state laws would create, in effect, yet one more breach notification law that must be followed. And it is difficult to see how this approach could be beneficial for anyone, except possibly in cases where there exists a gap in coverage (e.g., definition of personal information) in all but a few states.

Caution should be taken, however, with adopting a federal statute that preempts state laws in a manner that weakens the overall scope of state laws in regard to the kinds of information affected. If it is true that federal statutes are much slower to evolve to the changing threats of how personal information is collected, used, shared, and consequently hacked, then this suggests that state legislatures are in a better position to drive breach notification laws.

One possible advantage to a federal statute, however, could lie with uniform, national reporting. If a federal law were to require reporting of all breaches (possibly limited to some minimum number of records compromised, but regardless of threshold of harm) to a single agency, then this could provide data which might be used to empirically associate breaches with state-level information security practices and rates of identity theft.

POLICY CONSIDERATIONS

As a policy intervention, information disclosure is an appealing approach. It is a light-handed form of intervention that can be enacted at relatively low cost.[34] However, it requires that the information disclosed be informative, actionable, and presented in an effective manner for the target audience. Therefore, in light of the criticisms of these laws and relatively little empirical results showing beneficial outcomes, is there room for improvement?[35]

Regulate Security or Privacy?

A key issue concerning the protection of personal information is the distinction between security and privacy and how each of those can or should be governed. In the context of this chapter, *privacy* generally refers to a normative construct or state of mind in how we "feel" private, or feel a loss of privacy when our personal information has been improperly disclosed.[36] In effect, one may define privacy as the extent to which one has control over one's personal information or behaviors, as opposed to *security* which can be considered an attribute of an IT system and objectively measured and tested. Examples may include whether or not a particular kind of communication is allowed between two computers, or how many forms of authentication are required to gain access to one's online bank account. The distinction is important for the purpose of composing corporate or public policies (state or federal laws). A corporation may choose and require that no e-mail network traffic should originate from servers other than those specifically designated, or that no computers from a development network should communicate directly with machines on the finance network. These are distinct and configurable rules that can be easily determined, applied, and enforced. The outcomes are deterministic, and firms are likely in the best position to determine which rules should be applied, in which locations, on their networks.

On the other hand, privacy rules are much more difficult to create because it is not clear (or at least consistently clear) which approach is preferred and, therefore, which policy to design. While one policy may be socially optimal, another may be privately optimal, while another may be considered more consumer friendly.[37] For example, policies (laws) may be designed to favor the firm and allow them complete access to consumer data, and the ability to innovate using these data (e.g., to offer differential prices based on consumer attributes). On the other hand, a separate law may be designed to favor consumers and prevent firms from collecting consumer information to begin with. However, under which circumstances is one approach better than the other, and by which measures is this to be evaluated?

In addition, privacy matters are famously contextual: the same rule that allows firms to present online ads to social media users may be savored by one user (who really does value the advertisement) and hated by another (because they feel the delivery of advertisements is intrusive).[38] Further, while one may approve of sharing medical information (for instance) with one's doctor, sharing this same information with one's employer may be objectionable.

Understanding Harms from Data Breaches

When seeking to regulate any harmful activity, of primary importance is understanding the type and magnitude of harm borne by injured parties. Given the previous discussion concerning security versus privacy, the challenges of assessing harm from a data breach become most evident when examining data breach litigation and actual attempts by plaintiffs to seek redress for alleged harms. For example, previous research examined over 200 federal breach lawsuits, and identified almost 90 unique causes of action ranging from tort (negligence and strict liability, trespass to chattels, unjust enrichment), contract, and state and federal statutes.[39] This huge variation in legal claims is telling, because it suggests that the legal system is currently ill-equipped to adequately capture the kinds of harms that plaintiffs allege.

But this should not be unexpected. As has been made clear, privacy harms are personal, emotional, and, yes, even financial. They are also highly contextual—the same activity (e.g., data collection or online tracking) by a firm may represent a privacy intrusion for one person, while another person may be entirely unaffected. Further, data breaches may be thought of as being similar to environmental accidents, where any specific injurer may not be known with certainty, and where the harm may only manifest after many years. They are also similar to common fraud, where the loss is immediate and quantifiable, and related to privacy invasions, where the disclosure of personal information is itself the harm (such as with a person's HIV status). But they are also unlike any of these because the potential risks to individuals from inferences drawn by retailers, employers, insurance companies, or government agencies from the disclosure of disparate pieces of personal information are unpredictable and uncertain.

Providing Redress

While privacy goal of breach notification laws has not been to provide redress to affected individuals, any new legislation that seeks to regulate data breaches (in whatever form that may take) should be mindful of the great degree of variation in harms (as just discussed), and therefore how it addresses any remedies.

For example, while the consequences of data breach involving credit card information may be easily mitigated with credit monitoring or reissuing the compromised payment cards, potential harms from other breaches are not so easily prevented. The data breach by the Office of Personnel and Management involving approximately 25 million records in 2015 is a clear example because included in the compromised files were fingerprints, complete employment, and medical and criminal records, and there is very little that credit monitoring can do to assuage the risks.[40] What is even more concerning is that there are no clear means available to mitigate the theft and misuse of this information. This chapter aims to raise awareness of the matter, because it is a significant problem that will likely only increase in time as more, and different kinds of, data is lost and stolen.

An Unintended Consequence?

A final concern that has been raised with breach notification laws (federal or otherwise) is the potential for the laws to stifle corporate innovation.[41] One may argue that the more expensive it is for firms to collect and use information about consumers and consumer behavior, the less incentive they have to innovate using this information. Additional costs originate from the burden of notification, as well as first- and third-party expenses incurred as a direct or indirect result of public disclosure of a breach. Innovation come in the form of entirely new services or applications, such as distant familial associations discovered from genetic testing, or social media research uncovering important patterns of sickness or social movements. Or it may come from improved algorithms that better detect the likelihood of purchases, criminal activity, or an individual's financial risk.

Importantly, despite this suggestion of reduced innovation, it has yet to be empirically shown. This is not to suggest that the effect does not exist, but rather that no rigorous empirical analysis has revealed evidence of it. It is these uncertainties that demonstrate the necessity for additional research on the effects of not just breach notification laws (such as additional outcome measures, or innovation), but also other similar bills that seek to regulate cybersecurity and privacy practices.

CONCLUSION

Data breach notification affords an attractive, yet complicated policy device. On one hand, a law could be implemented at relatively low cost to taxpayers (i.e., it wouldn't require the burden of enforcing a list of mandatory standards, or incur the social cost of litigation). On the other hand, the details of such a proposal are fraught with difficulties and uncertainties. For example, given the evolving set of attack vectors, and degree to which new kinds of personal information are being collected and used, it is likely necessary to consider that any proposed breach legislation be nimble enough to account for these new trends. Further, it is unclear what should be the optimal time delay for which to notify individuals of a breach. Disclosure too soon risks communicating bad information and jeopardizing law enforcement investigations, while disclosure too late prevents individuals from acting right away to reduce any loss. The trigger threshold of disclosure is also unsettled. Notifying everyone for any event reduces an individual's ability to differentiate low from high risks, potentially causing them to ignore all notifications. On the other hand, requiring notification only for the most severe breaches prevents potentially useful insight to be drawn from incidents. One potential solution, however, could lie with requiring notification to individuals for the more severe breaches, while requiring notification to a state or federal agency for all breaches. Breach notification is deceptively simple, with minute changes in the manner, timing, and requirements of notification likely to have a substantial impact on any law's potential efficacy.

CHAPTER HIGHLIGHTS

Data Breach. A security incident where personally identifying or otherwise sensitive information is made available to unauthorized third parties, copied, or stolen.

Motivation to Mitigate Data Breach. A key factor driving a firm's incentive to invest in effective security controls is the cost incurred from a breach. The costlier it could be, the more resources the firm is likely to use to prevent it. A primary motivation for avoiding data breaches is reputational damage (a component of total costs). Based on the modest cost of breaches, consumer reaction to notifications, and the difficulty in assessing harm, the data suggest that firms currently have very little incentive to improve their security practices.

Regulating Firm Behavior. There are many alternate ways to regulate a firm's behavior. *Ex ante* (before the event) regulation seeks to impose minimum standards of care in order to prevent accidents or harm from occurring at all. *Ex post* (after the event) liability simply allows injured parties to seek redress for any harm incurred by an injuring party. A third alternative is information disclosure, which does not address any firm behavior directly, nor provide immediate relief to victims, but instead leverages economic incentives by forcing the firm to disclose the potential for harm to those conceivably affected by an event.

Data Breach Notification Law. These laws require entities that possess personally identifiable information to notify those affected when this data has been improperly disclosed. While there is some variation across state laws, they generally include the following provisions: covered entities (i.e., businesses, persons, government agencies), covered data (i.e., definition of "personal information"), trigger for notification, notification method and requirements, exceptions, and penalties.

Crossing State Lines. An important characteristic of state laws (like many others) is that they apply to covered entities that possess or license information about residents of the state with the enacted law, regardless of where the breach occurred.

Breach Law Effectiveness. There exists little evidence concerning the effectiveness of state breach notification laws. In principle, the effect of these notification laws is ostensibly to force firms to increase investment in security controls and to encourage consumers to take action to prevent economic harm. One of the main criticisms with the current set of state laws concerns the many variations that force firms to investigate and comply with each state's unique requirements. A federal law could help by alleviating these unnecessary burdens and costs but might also create a weaker standard.

Policy Intervention. Information disclosure about data breaches is an appealing approach. It is a light-handed form of intervention that can be enacted at relatively low cost. However, it requires that the information disclosed be informative, actionable and presented in an effective manner for the target audience.

NOTES

1. See Office of the Press Secretary, "Executive Order—Improving Critical Infrastructure Cybersecurity," *The White House,* February 12, 2013, https://www.whitehouse.gov/the-press-office/2013/02/12/executive-order-improving-critical-infrastructure-cybersecurity.

2. See "Cybersecurity Framework," *National Institute of Science and Technology,* last updated April 18, 2016, http://www.nist.gov/cyberframework/.

3. Clearly, this is a simplified diagram, which is designed to highlight the key decision point states of interest.

4. Trustwave, "Global Security Report," United States, 2015, https://www2.trustwave.com/rs/815-RFM-693/images/2015_TrustwaveGlobalSecurityReport.pdf.

5. Notice that even if the breach had neither been detected nor disclosed, it may (or may not) still result in harm. For clarity, however, we suppress these paths from the diagram.

6. One may consider that firms seek to minimize total costs by optimizing the level of security, where total cost is increasing in the cost of controls, and decreasing in the cost of a breach. See Romanosky et al., "Data Breaches and Identity Theft: When is Mandatory Disclosure Optimal?" Workshop on the Economics of Information Security, 2010, available at http://www.econinfosec.org/archive/weis2010/papers/session1/weis2010_romanosky_pres.pdf.

7. S. Romanosky, "Costs and Consequences of Cyber Incidents" (in review).

8. Ponemon Institute, "2015 Cost of Data Breach Study" United States, May 2015.

9. See Michael Kassner, "Data breaches may cost less than the security to prevent them," *TechRepublic,* April 9, 2015, http://www.techrepublic.com/article/data-breaches-may-cost-less-than-the-security-to-prevent-them/.

10. L. Ablon, P. Heaton, D. Lavery, S. Romanosky. "Consumer Attitudes Toward Data Breach Notifications and Loss of Personal Information," *RAND Corporation,* 2016.

11. Ponemon Institute, "2015 Cost of Data Breach Study."

12. Paul, "Amid Rampant Data Theft, Consumers Left Breached and Burned Out," *The Security Ledger,* May 4, 2015, https://securityledger.com/2015/05/amid-rampant-data-theft-consumers-left-breached-and-burned-out/.

13. This property has yet to be formally defined. Does it refer to lost stock market price, lost market share, a composite of both, or something entirely?

14. For more, see chapter 6—"Understanding Cyber Crime."

15. S. Romanosky, R. Telang, and A. Acquisti, "Do Data Breach Disclosure Laws Reduce Identity Theft?" *Journal of Policy Analysis and Management,* Vol. 30, No. 2, 2011, pp. 256–86.

16. District of Columbia, Guam, Puerto Rico, and the Virgin Islands also have similar laws, while New Mexico, South Dakota, and Alabama do not. See "Security Breach Notification Laws," *National Conference of State Legislatures,* January 4, 2016, http://www.ncsl.org/research/telecommunications-and-information-technology/security-breach-notification-laws.aspx for a full list of all state laws.

17. See *Comparison of US State and Federal Security Breach Notification Laws,* Steptoe & Johnson, LLP, January 21, 2016, http://www.steptoe.com/assets/htmldocuments/SteptoeDataBreachNotificationChart.pdf for a comprehensive description of all state laws.

18. Samuelson, "Security Breach Notification Laws: Views from Chief Security Officers," *Samuelson Law, Technology & Public Policy Clinic,* University of California-Berkeley School of Law, (2009).

19. As with the Alaska breach notification statute, Alaska Stat. § 45.48.010 et seq.

20. See "Security Breach Notification Laws," *National Conference of State Legislatures,* January 4, 2016, http://www.ncsl.org/research/telecommunications-and-information-technology/security-breach-notification-laws.aspx for specific statutes.

21. Federal Trade Commission (2007b). FTC Identity Theft Survey Report: 2006. Federal Trade Commission and Synnovate.

22. See http://www.aba.com/Tools/Function/Technology/Pages/datasecuritynotification.aspx, and http://www.hhs.gov/hipaa/for-professionals/breach-notification/index.html.

23. See Fla. Stat. § 501.171, and Reid J. Schar and Kathleen W. Gibbons, "Complicated Compliance: State Data Breach Notification Laws," *Bloomberg,* August 9, 2013, http://www.bna.com/complicated-compliance-state-data-breach-notification-laws/.

24. For more, see S. Romanosky, D. Hoffman, and A. Acquisti, "Empirical Analysis of Data Breach Litigation," *Journal of Empirical Legal Studies,* Vol. 11, No. 1, 2014, pp. 74–104.

25. See "2015 Security Breach Legislation," *National Conference of State Legislatures,* December 31, 2015, http://www.ncsl.org/research/telecommunications-and-information-technology/2015-security-breach-legislation.aspx.

26. For example, Connecticut, Oregon, Montana, and Wyoming are all expanding their definition of personal information. See Jim Halpert and Michelle J. Anderson, "State breach notification laws—updates from the 2015 session, 6 action steps for companies," *DLA Piper,* July 20, 2015, https://www.dlapiper.com/en/us/insights/publications/2015/07/state-breach-notification-laws/ for more information.

27. This is a familiar problem with financial disclosure notices, and the Financial Consumer Protection Bureau recently posted a list of suggestions that it feels would make for better notices. See http://www.consumerfinance.gov/newsroom/cfpb-finalizes-rule-to-promote-more-effective-privacy-disclosures/.

28. S. Romanosky, R. Telang, and A. Acquisti, "Do Data Breach Disclosure Laws Reduce Identity Theft?" *Journal of Policy Analysis and Management*, Vol. 30, No. 2, 2011, pp. 256–86.

29. The driving mechanism is that to the extent that firm actions harm consumers, public notification would force firms to internalize more of these costs, increasing their incentive to invest because of the greater marginal benefit of increased investment.

30. S. Romanosky, "Costs and Consequences of Cyber Incidents," *Journal of Cybersecurity* (accepted with minor revisions).

31. See "Senators introduce bipartisan data breach bill," *The Hill,* http://thehill.com/policy/cybersecurity/239057-sentors-introduce-bipartisan-data-breach-bill.

32. Of course, we previously described how they may indirectly induce firms to increase investment which may reduce the probability of a future breach.

33. See David Lazarus, "Federal data-breach bill would replace dozens of stronger state laws," *Los Angeles Times,* April 21, 2015, http://www.latimes.com/business/la-fi-lazarus-20150421-column.html.

34. For example, compared to *ex post* litigation that consumes a great deal of public and private resources.

35. Thomas M. Lenard and Paul H. Rubin, "Much Ado about Notification," *Regulation,* Vol. 29, No. 1, (Spring 2006), 44–50; S. Romanosky, R. Telang, and A. Acquisti, "Do Data Breach Disclosure Laws Reduce Identity Theft?" *Journal of Policy Analysis and Management,* Vol. 30, No. 2, (2011), pp. 256–86.

36. That is, we distinguish between privacy feelings in regard to a data breach versus privacy issues related to constitutional matters.

37. Where "socially optimal" implies that the aggregate of all firm and consumer costs (benefits) are minimized (maximized), while privately optimal implies that only the welfare of one party (i.e., the firm) is maximized.

38. See Helen Nissenbaum, *Privacy in Context: Technology, Policy, and the Integrity of Social Life* (Stanford Law Books, 2009).

39. For more, see S. Romanosky, D. Hoffman, and A. Acquisti, "Empirical Analysis of Data Breach Litigation," *Journal of Empirical Legal Studies*, Vol. 11, No. 1 (2014), pp. 74–104.

40. See Cybersecurity Resource Center, "What Happened," U.S. Office of Personnel Management, https://www.opm.gov/cybersecurity/cybersecurity-incidents/.

41. It has also been argued that a federal law may stifle innovation among state laws that seek to find the optimal balance of characteristics. See "Data Security and Breach Notification Bill Would Harm Consumers," *Open Technology Institute,* https://static.newamerica.org/attachments/2799-resources-for-the-public-on-the-data-security-and-breach-notification-act-of-2015/OTI-Data-Security-Breach-Pros-Cons.633b635562f24c9aa68b41690237ee0e.pdf. Thomas M. Lenard and Paul H. Rubin. "Much Ado about Notification." Regulation, Vol. 29, No. 1 (Spring 2006), 44–50.

Chapter 10

Cyber Insurance

A Market-Based Approach to Information Assurance

Robert Morgus

Prominent members of the cybersecurity insurance industry believe the market is thriving.[1] From the perspective of insurers, this is undoubtedly the case. Estimates suggest that the insurance industry collects around $5 billion in premiums each year, with some estimating that this number could rise to $7 or $8 billion in the near future.[2] However, Greg Vernaci, Senior Vice President at AIG, also noted that cybersecurity insurance is "more than just an insurance project" as insurance firms become engaged to help customers mitigate risks to their information technology (IT).[3] This is an area for improvement—if structured correctly, the market for cybersecurity insurance holds immense potential to push the adoption of best practices and standards for information assurance.

Buying, building, and maintaining complex information systems generate risk. In the past, companies running these systems have sought to mitigate risk through smart procurement practices and offline alternatives to their digital infrastructure. At the same time, policy and lawmakers have sought to manage the risk to private firms and government organizations by designing light-handed security requirements through regulation and law.[4] Smart procurement and policy approaches are potentially useful tools but fail to address the key security vulnerability of most computer systems: people.

The crux of the challenge in developing good security practices comes down to organizational and human behavior. Poor security practices and insufficient investment by the U.S. Office of Personnel Management in their information assurance processes and training are largely responsible for the loss of tens of millions of records.[5] Sony was felled via a basic social engineering attack.[6] Humans were the weaknesses in the system that threat actors sought to exploit.

Mitigating human foibles and countering insecure organizational behavior is where insurance can play a role, managing risk through more than just technical security standards. There are procedural fixes and policies that seek to address the human-centered cybersecurity vulnerability. Indeed, a suite of security best practices have been developed and promoted by groups and engineering bodies including the Center for Internet Security's Critical Controls and the Internet Engineering Task Force, respectively. But these standards often go unheeded or are poorly implemented. The root of this problem is not technical, but behavioral, and exists on a large scale. There are a variety of mechanisms to influence social and organizational behavior through public policy including regulation, the tax code, and litigation. This chapter focuses on a market-based solution, insurance premiums, in comparison to two often-used public policy tools: regulation and legislation.

How Does an Insurance Market Drive Good Security Behavior?

Policymakers are quick to gravitate toward regulation, legislation, or executive order for solutions to large problems. However, in the case of incentivizing best practices in information assurance, a market-based solution holds greater potential benefit. Markets may be less susceptible to emotional and cognitive biases than regulation or legislation. Further, markets are complex systems, which grants them a great deal of adaptability, especially in comparison to rigid bureaucracies. Finally, insurance can have the same positive effect as regulation or legislation as a means of driving best practices in security and effective risk management by organizations.

Markets Are Less Susceptible to Cognitive Biases Than Regulation or Legislation

Regulation and legislation rely on the human decision-making of a select few, that is, lawmakers and administrative agency officials. Behavioral economics, the practice of examining the implications of cognitive flaws on human decision-making, illuminates several biases that plague human decision-making.

- The availability bias: reliance on available and recently discovered information, rather than complete information;[7]
- The hindsight bias: a tendency to overestimate the probability of an improbable event occurring again because it just occurred;
- Confirmation bias: human tendencies to "discount true information contrary to prior beliefs";

- The optimism bias: a habit of "overestimate[ing] the probability of a good outcome"; and
- Status-quo bias: the irrational tendency to cling to the current state of affairs.

All of these cognitive biases are present in human decision-making about regulation and legislation but they are concentrated in a small number of decision-makers.[8] Markets, by contrast, rely on the decisions of many, thus are less susceptible to biases of individual or small group decision-making. As James Cooper argues, regulators (and by extension legislators) "who suffer from these cognitive flaws are likely to commit systematic errors while forming policies."[9] The presence of numerous actions to move the needle means that markets most often regress to the mean, averaging out cognitive biases.

A Market Is a Complex, but Adaptive, System[10]

Although markets are less susceptible to cognitive biases than legislation or regulation, they are nonetheless more agile in response to fundamental changes to environmental conditions than their more cumbersome government-based counterparts. It is in the interest of insured firms to release, and insurance companies to collect, information about breaches and security postures as both parties share incentives to identify and implement best practices. The market is thus more data driven and adaptive in regulating behavior in comparison to government regulation and legislation.[11]

In addition to structured data, markets function as a great aggregator of tacit, or local, knowledge held by individual firms. As firms innovate, their products are either imitated by rival firms or countered by internal innovations.[12] This is a surefire sign of a complex adaptive system at work, as "in complex adaptive systems the component parts have the ability to change their behavioral repertoire in response to their environment or each other."[13]

This is how markets function, but what makes it relevant to cybersecurity insurance as a regulatory tool? Due to misaligned incentives, government agents rarely hold an advantage over private actors in gathering information about private activities.[14] Government agencies, lawmakers, and regulators have limited resources with which they are able to gather information. For insurers, on the other hand, information is crucial to business. It is integral to accurately structuring policies, assessing risk across different customers, and vetting claim applications.[15] Insurers can also use this information to drive better security behavior within clients, reducing risk, and therefore the potential for a claim. To be clear, insurance should not necessarily be relied upon to create standards, but can sit alongside well-researched and -developed standards to augment and encourage their adoption.

WHAT IS CYBERSECURITY INSURANCE?

Insurance, writ large, is a form of risk transfer that allows companies to shift the liability associated with incidents to a third party, known as an underwriter. Insurance has been used to protect individuals from massive health-related expenses, to cover the liability of toy manufactures, and even to protect the potential future value of an athlete.

Cybersecurity insurance is not radically different. It is specifically designed and targeted insurance offered by a number of mainstream insurance vendors to firms with the aim of helping "mitigate losses from a variety of cyber incidents, including data breaches, business interruption, and network damage."[16] As the U.S. Department of Homeland Security notes, "A robust cybersecurity insurance market could help reduce the number of successful cyber attacks by: (1) promoting the adoption of preventative measures in return for more coverage; and (2) encouraging the implementation of best practices by basing premiums on an insured's level of self-protection."[17]

Finding an effective blend of technical defensive measures and behavioral best practices that are not financially overwhelming remains a challenge for many firms. Where the risk borne from connectivity is difficult to acceptably self-insure, cybersecurity insurance provides a means to transfer risk to insurers who then bear the financial liability for any resulting, covered, incident.

Insuring against breaches and other security incidents has been touted as a way to help identify and enforce good security standards while simultaneously allowing firms to offload liability for major attacks.[18] As the cybersecurity community has developed better risk management programs, and in keeping with the steady drumbeat of security incidents at firms of all shapes and sizes, insurance has become a target for security investment.[19]

Insurance Markets as a Risk Management Lever and Standards Enforcer

Insurance holds the same (or greater) potential as a risk management lever and a standards enforcer than government action through two sticks, coverage requirements and policy exclusions, and two carrots, premiums and policy limits.

On cybersecurity insurance applications, the potential customer is asked a number of standardized questions designed to map current security practices and organizational process. These questions help frame the cost of baseline coverage. This coverage then comes with certain minimum requirements, allowing insurers to become standard setters for firms and organizations seeking coverage. Insurers can then deny coverage should the potential customer not meet the insurer's standards. A potential precursor to outright denial of applications is the strategic use of policy premiums and limits. A policy premium is the price an insured firm pays the insurer for coverage. A policy limit is the maximum amount an insurer agrees to pay out in the event of an incident. By instituting high premiums and low limits on firms that do not adhere to good security behaviors, insurers can offer the carrot of lower premiums and higher limits for better behavior. In the case of cybersecurity insurance, as firms adopt better IT security controls and practices, premiums can drop and limits can go up. Data from insurance applications helps inform insurers about what security controls firms use.

Policy exclusions can operate with a similar standard-setting purpose. Policy exclusions are clauses written into insuring agreements stipulating certain types of events that are not covered by the insurer. Current common exclusions include events caused by war and terrorism to events that cause physical damage or bodily harm and are outlined in greater detail later in this chapter. Although many policies contain an average of just over twenty-four exclusions, many of these are crafted without information assurance standards and best practices in mind.

By better syncing these practices and standards with exclusions, events caused by nonadherence to best practices or security standards will go uncovered. When these events go uncovered, the liability for such events sits squarely on the insured firm. Without insurance to cover that liability, firms will be penalized financially, encouraging corrective behavior to mitigate and transfer risk.

Transferring risk to an insurer does not cause that risk to vanish. Instead, the insuring firm distributes the risk of one client among a pool of other firms, charging each a fee, or premium, associated with the likelihood of their making a claim for some amount. Selecting terms and financial limits of coverage involves the insurer's assessment of the likely frequency and severity of potential costly events to their customers ensuring the firm retains a profitable mix of risk types and prices their products accordingly.

Risk Pool

For insurance firms, selecting clients and determining the scope of coverage requires understanding the nature of risk for each applicant company. The goal of an insurance firm is to construct a pool of clients whose collective contribution (in the form of premiums) is equal to or greater than the probable cost of payouts for claims. The mechanics of a risk pool function, in part, because no one party can be sure if they will need to submit a claim, but most will not, thereby providing financially viable coverage to the few claimants and an incentivizing profit to the insurer.

Premiums

For an insurer, the risk of any one client experiencing an incident resulting in a claim is spread among this pool of different customers. Each of these customers contributes funds to the pool in the form of a premium. These can be a flat fee common to all customers or an equitable rate based on the risk profile of each customer. Judging this risk in order to set the price of the premium requires assessing the frequency and severity of the potential losses for each insured in the pool in a given year. This calculation allows firms to adjust premiums based on the risk profile associated with each individual customer—a more computationally intensive but financially advantageous approach for insurers.[20]

This is not to imply that insurers are happy to simply take on the risk of their insured and let it sit. Indeed, insurers are as interested in risk, and risk management, as their customers. As the same risk mitigation tools and management techniques are being found wanting for businesses, however, they are even more inadequate for the needs of insurance firms. Insurance firms that do not trust their own ability to understand and quantify the risk of current and potential clients will be unlikely to offer many policies that transfer this risk onto themselves. Cybersecurity insurance providers are struggling to assess the risk of organizations being insured and have thus generally been conservative in specifying the conditions under which coverage may be offered.[21] This is one possible explanation for low advertised coverage limits, which, to date, have generally not exceeded $100 million.[22] For context, coverage limits for general corporate liability insurance often reaches into the billions of dollars.

COVERAGE TYPES

Cyber insurance covers an array of different, and at times overlapping, policy types. The lack of common verbiage from provider to provider means that the actual content of these different policies can overlap. Coverages are broken into first- and third-party types, a distinction common in other insurance areas. First-party coverage involves claims made to the insurer from the insured. This type of insurance is most useful for companies that are users, but not necessarily producers, of technology. Third-party coverage protects people and businesses that produce, monitor, administer, or are otherwise responsible for the technology that caused damage.

To better understand first- versus third-party coverage, think of a homeowner whose roof collapses under the weight of heavy snowfall. Typical homeowner's insurance covers the damage caused by a severe winter storm. First-party coverage responds to the claim made by an insured directly to the insurance company. Third-party coverage considers claims from the contractors who built the roof or the architects who designed it—if the homeowner sues either of these other groups, both the contractors and architect would need third-party coverage to help cover damages from the suit. Third-party cybersecurity insurance works this same way, offering companies that design, produce, monitor, or administer IT protection from claims by individuals or businesses that use their products or services. Many existing policies offer some combination of first- and third-party coverages.

Many plans do not profess to cover many of the categories outlined below and indeed, no one single plan covers all of them. This first- versus third-party analysis is drawn from a collection of insurance applications and related documentation from U.S. and European markets between 2008 and 2016. While not complete, this sample serves to elucidate important trends in the types of coverage and exclusion in the evolving market for cybersecurity insurance.

First-Party Coverage—Incident Response, Business Interrupt, and Crisis Management

Most of the policies examined for this chapter cover event/incident response costs. The definition provided for event/incident response costs is relatively standardized and includes the costs of investigation, similar to postevent forensics and hiring an outside security consultancy to assess whether the damage can be reversed.[23] Notably, 79 percent of plans cover loss associated with restoring stolen, damaged, altered, deleted, or corrupted data while only 50 percent cover the loss associated with restoring systems due to physical damage caused by an incident. The remaining plans, while covering the cost of investigating what happened, do not cover the loss associated with the incident.

Nearly 80 percent of the sampled policies cover losses associated with an event which interrupts service. These interruptions include language covering, "network security wrongful acts," and similar insurance jargon for what the IT security community often calls a network security failure and includes malicious acts that compromise the confidentiality, integrity, or accessibility of systems.[24] A critical determining factor for claims decisions are the context in which a network security failure takes place, whether as a result of an external adversary or accident. Only a small minority of policies cover business interruption due to system failure regardless of whether the failure was caused by a malicious act.[25] In the broader context of business interruption coverage, policies are generally voided if the insured does not adhere to certain IT maintenance and security standards.

While many policies include crisis management expenses in incident response coverage, generally covering the cost of deciphering what happened, only a small number include the cost of rebuilding systems. Crisis management additionally tends to provide monetary relief for the insured to seek outside public relations resources to manage, maintain, or restore public confidence in the insured firm.[26]

Third Party—Data Privacy, eMedia, and Failure to Deliver Service Incidents

Ninety-three percent of plans examined for this chapter include data privacy breach third-party coverage. For data breach coverage, in addition to covering defense/regulatory expenses and damages, some plans also cover the cost of notifying third-party victims of the data breach. Of the plans covering data breaches, 71 percent include the notification cost. One hundred percent of plans covering data privacy incidents include both defense/regulatory expenses and damages. Most insurers define a data breach as the loss, unauthorized alteration, inappropriate publication, or theft of data held by a firm on its computerized system.

Sixty-four percent of surveyed plans cover the defense/regulatory expenses associated with an eMedia wrongful act. An eMedia wrongful act, a term used by many insurers, includes negligence that results in misappropriation of content and infringement of copyrights, or other intellectual properties. Only 57 percent cover the damages due to an eMedia wrongful act. Thirty-eight percent of plans cover defense/regulatory costs and damages incurred from failure by an insured firm to deliver promised services to a third party. As is the case with most business interruption coverage, plans that cover failure to deliver services feature a long list of exceptions. Coverage here is for costs to customers and business partners, rather than the originating firm.

An Area for Expanded Coverage—Physical Damage

Exclusions are clauses in insurance policies that identify specific events not covered by the policy. Notably, an event does not need to be excluded in order for the insurer to claim noncoverage but these generally result in litigation to resolve disputed claims. The policies examined for this chapter ranged from seven to thirty-nine specific exclusions, averaging twenty-four. One of the most common was covering physical damage, an area of increasing interest with the spread of embedded computing systems in devices including home appliances and cars, the rise of the Internet of Things (IoT).

Many cyber insurance policies exclude physical damage. This damage is separate from coverage for IT assets such as servers and computers. Eighty-six percent particularly exclude bodily injury from coverage, while others do not address it directly. Zero percent of policies examined for this chapter explicitly cover these types of damages and may not cover physical damage outside of IT or network assets or bodily injury until something, like continued litigation, forces the issue. Some insurance representatives have claimed that general corporate liability coverage may cover physical damage or injury caused by a cyber-attack, though these claims have yet to be borne out.

This lack of specific coverage is a problem for insurance-seeking firms in sectors where cybersecurity can have an impact on physical safety, for example, healthcare devices, automotive manufacturing, or power generation.[27] Incidents at these types of firms have the potential to cause physical damage, injure workers, or undermine confidence.[28] Society's tolerance for negligence on the part of manufacturers in these industries is low as the security of these devices is paramount: "[if] you brick a pacemaker, you brick a human."[29]

Secure coding standards exist, and, though they are in a nascent stage, best security practices for firms where cybersecurity and physical safety converge are available or in development.[30] Both design and operational security standards are tools that insurers could use to price and manage risk of insured firms. Secure coding standards are a means through which insurers can assess the risk of companies based on their product acquisition and, to mitigate that risk, push firms toward the adoption of more secure technologies. Cyber-physical security best practices are standards around which insurers can price premiums, which can in turn drive adoption.

POLICY RECOMMENDATIONS

The key to achieving any of the broader security benefits of cyber insurance is a large and sophisticated insurance market. The most commonly cited recommendation to drive growth in this market is to create an incident data repository that can help insurance firms gather and share actuarial data supporting their effort to accurately price risk. This chapter makes three more pointed additions, suggesting that policymakers promote growth by recommending that the primary state-level regulatory bodies require coverage types to meet demand, regulate the use of exclusions, and advocate for a definitions repository at the national level to encourage a common language between policies and insurers.

Recommendation 1: Product Regulation to Match Supply with Demand

The presence of a wealth of litigation is often a trigger for firms to seek a way to shift liability and there is a king's ransom to be found around the areas of privacy, security, and data breach notification. This expansion of litigation could be followed by more widespread demand for insurance policies, but should lead to companies demanding policies that more comprehensively cover their risks. In the United States, insurance regulation occurs primarily at the state level, which means that these regulators are tasked with overseeing several parts of the insurance industry including company and producer licensing, market interactions, and policies themselves.

While regulating insurance firms and ensuring a fair market are important, more relevant for matching insurance policy supply with demand is product regulation. Some current gaps and ambiguities in coverage that insured firms seek, such as the physical damage exception, could be regulated out. However, any product regulation of this type must happen in close consultation with insurers and would require unambiguous mechanisms to prevent significant inflation of premiums. These mechanisms could come in the form of legislative incentives outlined in recommendation 3.

Recommendation 2: Product Regulation to Promote More Effective Exclusions

Rather than focusing exclusions on event perpetrators, policy tools that specify coverage should focus on inadequate or missing controls, thereby excluding coverage for events attributable to a lack of good security practice. Clauses in applications and exclusions sections of policies should be tailored to address behavioral miscues most commonly at the root of incidents: insider threats, weak security controls, and bad patch management.[31] Insurers can use these exclusions and application requirements as a means to maximize the broader social benefit of the cyber insurance market.

Insider threats come in intentional and unintentional form. Intentional insider threats are those that stem from employees with malicious intent while those that are unintentional are essentially employee errors. Due to the difficulties of identifying intentional insider threats, it is reasonable for insurers to continue to exercise careful discretion when deciding to cover them. This doesn't remove insurer's responsibility to require that their customers are taking basic steps to prevent incidents, including keeping records of their data, controlling access, and maintaining logs to show the chain of custody for important files. The broad category of "weak security controls" includes the absence of identity management, poor plans to securely administer mobile devices, overly complex access permissions, and weak password requirements. To nudge firms toward instituting stronger security controls, insurers can exclude coverage for events that occur in conjunction with weak security controls, while explicitly outlining what controls must be in place on applications and insuring agreements.

Perhaps the most pressing behavioral issue causing cybersecurity vulnerabilities are bad patch management practices. Incrementally, supported software requires update to ensure that found vulnerabilities in that software are protected from exploitation. The 2015 Verizon Data Breach Investigations Report suggests that, "99.9% of exploited vulnerabilities had been compromised more than a year after the associated [common vulnerability exposure] was published."[32] To nudge firms toward better patch management, insurers should exclude incidents from coverage where they resulted from attacks leveraging known exploits for which patches were available but had yet to be applied (within a reasonable time frame).

Recommendation 3: Creation of a Definitions Repository to Normalize Language

Policy and application language, including the use of terms and their definitions across coverage and exclusion previsions, should be normalized across the cyber insurance industry and with the language of information assurance professionals. This harmonization of terms will bring several positive benefits. It will grant organizations' leadership and security managers greater clarity on what is expected of them from insurance policies. Clear language can contribute to better decision-making, ensure that requirements of insurers can be clearly translated into organizational practice, and clarify disclosure from customers so insurers will better understand the risk pool they are accumulating.

There are two issues at stake here. How can language be harmonized across the different cybersecurity insurers, and how can the language that cybersecurity insurers use be harmonized with the information assurance industry? Creating common terms and language within the cybersecurity insurance industry would require intrastate regulatory cooperation wherein state regulators agree upon a relatively coherent language to describe cybersecurity events and insurance provisions for coverage and exclusion. Such coordination could occur through the National Association of Insurance Regulators, the "standard-setting and regulatory support organization" that is made up of chief insurance regulators from all 50 states plus the District of Columbia and U.S. territories.[33]

In order to harmonize language between information assurance and cyber insurance, an Insurance Laboratory should be established within the National Institute of Standards and Technology (NIST) to consult with insurers as they formulate policies. Incentives for insurers could help drive participation, potentially tying access to an actuarial database to membership in the Lab. In addition, a cybersecurity insurance definition repository could be constructed which insurers could use to populate their policies with harmonized terms and definitions.

CONCLUSION

There is a broader social welfare that could stem from the cyber insurance industry driving better security practices through regulating organization's security standards in the short term and providing impetus for more secure software development and hardware design in the future. This latter benefit could mean bringing actual enterprise IT security behavior closer to the pre- scribed best practices through a shift in liability toward manufacturers. Many of these standards contained in recommendations from the SANS Institute, Institute of Electrical and Electronics Engineers (IEEE), and NIST already exist but have been implemented narrowly or not at all.[34] The precursor to leveraging these externalities is a thriving marketplace for insurance with selective use of exclusions and a thorough risk assessment process by insur- ers. Although the market for cybersecurity insurance certainly exists and is at a relatively mature stage, it nonetheless faces several limitations which pre- vent it from generating maximum social welfare. Important areas of coverage, such as physical damage, remain poorly covered. Due to a large degree of uncertainty around how to assess the consequences of potential incidents and quantify the cost of risk, coverage limits generally remain low. In addition, risk management mechanisms at the disposal of insurers—namely premiums, conditions, and exclusions—do not yet adequately align with and promote established best practices for the enterprise IT security industry. Risk plays a crucial role in the insurance process. Cybersecurity insurance is a growing yet still somewhat nascent industry where great potential remains. A healthy insurance market may help identify and encourage adoption of security best practices across the private sector, helping to improve the security posture of companies across different industries, both large and small.

CHAPTER HIGHLIGHTS

Cyber Insurance. Insurance, writ large, is a form of risk transfer that allows companies to shift the liability associated with incidents to a third party, known as an underwriter. Cyber insurance aims to help firms "mitigate losses from a variety of cyber incidents, including data breaches, business interruption, and network damage." As the U.S. Department of Homeland Security notes, "A robust cybersecurity insurance market could help reduce the number of successful cyber attacks by: (1) promoting the adoption of preventative measures in return for more coverage; and (2) encouraging the implementation of best practices by basing premiums on an insured's level of self-protection."

Benefits. Information is crucial to business. It is integral to accurately structuring policies, assessing risk across different customers, and vetting claim applications. Insurers can use this information to drive better security behavior within clients, reducing risk, and, therefore, the potential for a claim. Insuring against breaches and other security incidents has been touted as a way to help identify and enforce good security standards while simultaneously allowing firms to offload liability for major attacks.

Challenges. Each cybersecurity policy is linked by a common risk of failure in cybersecurity at a covered firm. Finding an effective blend of technical defensive measures and behavioral best practices that are not financially overwhelming remains a challenge for many firms.

Risk Management Levers. Insurance holds the same (or greater) potential as a risk management lever and a standards enforcer than government action through two sticks, coverage requirements and policy exclusions, and two carrots, premiums and policy limits.

Coverage Types. First-party coverage involves claims made to the insurer from the insured. This type of insurance is most useful for companies that are users, but not necessarily producers, of technology. Third-party coverage protects people and businesses that produce, monitor, administer, or are otherwise responsible for the technology that caused damage.

Recommendations. (1) Attempt to match insurance policy supply with demand by regulating coverage gaps (ensure that insured firms do not have important concerns excluded); (2) regulate products to effectively use exclusions (e.g., excluding coverage for insider threats, weak security controls, or poor patching management) for social benefit; and (3) create common terms and language across the cybersecurity insurance industry to ensure that requirements of insurers can be clearly translated into organizational practice for the insured companies.

NOTES

1. The author would like to thank Kyumin Park for his help in gathering the data behind this chapter.

2. Just Security and New America, "Beyond Breaches: Cyber Insurance," YouTube video, 1:22:24, posted by *Just Security*, October 26, 2015, accessed March 29, 2016, Minute 13:40, https://www.youtube.com/watch?v=wJcBFjpWr5M.

3. Ibid., minute 14:30.

4. See, for example:

In the case of adware, Committee on Commerce, Science, and Transportation, "Software Principles Yielding Better Levels of Customer Knowledge Act," *United States Senate 109th Congress*, June 12, 2006, accessed March 29, 2016, https://www. gpo.gov/fdsys/pkg/CRPT-109srpt262/html/CRPT-109srpt262.htm.

In the case of terrorism, National Association of Insurance Commissioners, "Terrorism Risk Insurance (TRIA)," *The Center for Insurance Policy and Research*, accessed March 29, 2016, http://www.naic.org/cipr_topics/topic_tria.htm.

5. Sean Gallagher, "Why the 'biggest government hack ever' got past the feds," *ArsTechnica*, June 8, 2015, accessed March 29, 2016. http://arstechnica.com/security/2015/06/why-the-biggest-government-hack-ever-got-past-opm-dhs-and-nsa/.

6. "The Hack of Sony Pictures: What We Know and What You Need to Know," *Trend Micro,* December 8, 2014, http://www.trendmicro.com/vinfo/us/security/news/cyber-attacks/the-hack-of-sony-pictures-what-you-need-to-know.

7. Daniel Kahneman, *Thinking, Fast and Slow* (New York: Farrar, Straus and Giroux, 2011).

8. James C. Cooper, "Behavioral Economics and Biased Regulators," *Mercatus Center,* November 2013, 2, accessed March 26, 2016, http://mercatus.org/sites/default/files/Cooper_BehavioralEconomicsandBiasedRegulators_MOP_111913.pdf.

9. Ibid.

10. Sheri M. Markose, "Computability and Evolutionary Complexity: Markets As Complex Adaptive Systems (CAS)," *University of Essex,* September 2003, accessed March 29, 2016. http://repository.essex.ac.uk/3730/1/dp574.pdf.

11. Ben-Shahar, Omri and Kyle D. Logue, "How Insurance Substitutes for Regulation," *CATO Institute,* Spring 2013, http://object.cato.org/sites/cato.org/files/serials/files/regulation/2013/3/v36n1-10.pdf.

12. Sheri M. Markose, "Computability and Evolutionary Complexity: Markets As Complex Adaptive Systems (CAS)," *University of Essex,* September 2003, accessed March 29, 2016. http://repository.essex.ac.uk/3730/1/dp574.pdf.

13. Robert L. Axtell, "Hayek Enriched by Complexity Enriched by Hayek," *Department of Computational Social Science, George Mason University,* October 2014, 1, accessed March 29, 2016, http://www.css.gmu.edu/~axtell/Rob/Research/Pages/Hayek_&_Complexity_files/Axtell%20on%20Hayek.pdf.

14. Omri Ben-Shahar, and Kyle D. Logue, "How Insurance Substitutes for Regulation," *CATO Institute,* Spring 2013, 36, http://object.cato.org/sites/cato.org/files/serials/files/regulation/2013/3/v36n1-10.pdf.

15. Omri Ben-Shahar, and Kyle D. Logue, "How Insurance Substitutes for Regulation," *CATO Institute,* Spring 2013, 38, http://object.cato.org/sites/cato.org/files/serials/files/regulation/2013/3/v36n1-10.pdf.

16. Department of Homeland Security, "Cybersecurity Insurance," last modified February 17, 2016, accessed March 29, 2016, https://www.dhs.gov/cybersecurity-insurance.

17. Ibid.

18. Ranjan Pal, Leana Golubchik Konstantinos Psounis, and Pan Hui, "Will Cyber-Insurance Improve Network Security? A Market Analysis," *Infocom,* 2014, http://www-bcf.usc.edu/~kpsounis/Papers/cyberinsurance_infocom2014.

pdf; Ranjan Pal, "Improving Network Security Through Cyber Insurance," *University of Southern California*, December 2014, http://www-scf.usc.edu/~rpal/thesis.pdf; Melissa Stevens, "3 Ways Cyber Insurance Will Improve Security Performance," January 15, 2015, accessed March 29, 2016, https://blog.bitsighttech.com/cyber-insurance-will-improve-security-performance.

19. Deloitte, "Cyber Insurance: One Element of Risk Management," *Deloitte,* March 8 2015, accessed March 29, 2016, http://mobile.deloitte.wsj.com/riskand-compliance/2015/03/18/cyber-insurance-one-element-of-a-cyber-risk-management-strategy/; Susan Kelly, "Data Breaches Spur Demand for Cyber Liability Coverage," *Treasury & Risk,* January 15, 2015, accessed March 29, 2016, http://www.treasury-andrisk.com/2015/01/15/data-breaches-spur-demand-for-cyber-liability-cove; Marsh Company, "Benchmarking Trends: As Cyber Concerns Broaden, Insurance Purchases Rise," *Marsh & McLennan Companies*, https://www.marsh.com/us/insights/benchmarking-trends-cyber-concerns-broaden-insurance-purchases-rise.html.

20. Nicolas Zahn and Costis Toregas, "Insurance for Cyber Attacks: The Issue of Setting Premiums in Context," *Cyber Security Policy and Research Institute*, January 7, 2014, accessed March 29, 2016, http://static1.squarespace.com/static/53b2efd7e4b0018990a073c4/t/54b932b8e4b0bf25db81bc33/1421423288790/Cyberinsurance+Paper+Final.pdf.

21. Ira Scharf, "The Problem With Cyber Insurance," *Dark Reading*, June 17, 2014, accessed March 29, 2016, http://www.darkreading.com/risk/the-problem-with-cyber-insurance/a/d-id/1269682.

22. Jim Finkle, "Ace offers $100 million cyber policies with added services, scrutiny," *Reuters,* September 24, 2015, accessed March 29, 2016, http://www.reuters.com/article/us-ace-ltd-cyberinsurance-idUSKCN0RO2LD20150924.

23. See, for example, AIG, "CyberEdge PC," *American International Group Inc.* Specimen Draft: April 25, 2014, accessed March 29, 2016, 2. http://www.aig.com/Chartis/internet/US/en/CyberEdge%20PC%20Policy%20Final%202014_tcm3171-595897.pdf.

24. For more, see chapter 1—"Understanding Information Assurance."

25. See, for example, QBE, "QBE Cyber Response Cyber and Data Security Insurance Policy," *QBE Insurance Group,* accessed March 29, 2016, http://www.qbeeurope.com/documents/casualty/pi/professions/cyber/cyber-response-insurance-policy.pdf.

26. See, for example, "The Hartford CyberChoice 2.0." *The Hartford*, 2008, accessed March 29, 2016, http://www.hfpinsurance.com/hfpfiles/pdf/cc00h003.pdf.

27. For more, see chapter 3—"Protecting Industrial Control Systems in Critical Infrastructure" and chapter 4—"Safer at Any Speed: The Roads Ahead for Automotive Cyber Safety."

28. Kim Zetter, "An Unprecedented Look at Stuxnet, the World's First Digital Weapon," *WIRED*, November 3, 2014, accessed March 29, 2016, http://www.wired.com/2014/11/countdown-to-zero-day-stuxnet/; Kim Zetter, "A Cyberattack Has Caused Confirmed Physical Damage for the Second Time Ever," *WIRED,* January 8, 2015, accessed March 29, 2016, http://www.wired.com/2015/01/german-steel-mill-hack-destruction/. Though the reporter that participated in the stunt hack of the Jeep vehicle did not come to any harm, the demonstration proved the concept that

an outside agent could completely remotely control a connected vehicle, placing the occupant(s) in harm's way. See Andy Greenberg, "Hackers Remotely Kill a Jeep on the Highway, With Me In It," *Wired*, July 21, 2015, accessed March 29, 2016, http://www.wired.com/2015/07/hackers-remotely-kill-jeep-highway/.

29. Joseph Marks, "Encryption ad wars," *Politico*, March 10, 2016, accessed March 29, 2016, http://www.politico.com/tipsheets/morning-cybersecurity/2016/03/encryption-ad-wars-cyber-heads-to-austin-remembrance-of-crypto-wars-past-213146.

30. Robert Seacord, "Top 10 Secure Coding Practices," *CERT*, March 1, 2011, accessed March 29, 2016, https://www.securecoding.cert.org/confluence/display/seccode/Top+10+Secure+Coding+Practices. For ICS, see ICS-CERT, "Recommended Practices," *ICS-CERT*, accessed March 29, 2016, https://ics-cert.us-cert.gov/Recommended-Practices.

For cars, see Association of Global Automakers, Inc, "Framework for Automotive Cybersecurity Best Practices," *The Association of Global Automakers,* January 19, 2016, accessed March 29, 2016, https://www.globalautomakers.org/system/files/document/attachments/framework_auto_cyber_best_practices_14jan2016_id_10376.pdf and chapter 3 of this volume.

For medical devices, see U.S. Food and Drug Administration, "Cybersecurity," *U.S. Department of Health and Human Services*, last updated February 8, 2016, accessed March 29, 2016, http://www.fda.gov/MedicalDevices/DigitalHealth/ucm373213.htm.

31. Alliey Collar, "Most Common Causes of Data Breaches," *Orion,* March 10, 2014, accessed March 29, 2016, http://www.oriontech.com/most-common-causes-of-data-breaches/.

32. Verizon, "2015 Data Breach Investigations Report," *Verizon Enterprise,* 2015, 15, accessed March 29, 2016, http://www.verizonenterprise.com/DBIR/2015/.

33. National Association of Insurance Commissioners, "About," *NAIC,* accessed March 29, 2016, http://www.naic.org/index_about.htm.

34. See, for example, SANS Institute, "Best Practices," *SANS Institute*, last updated March 8, 2016, accessed March 29, 2016, https://www.sans.org/reading-room/white-papers/bestprac; M. Ramachandran, "Recommendations and Best Practices for Cloud Enterprise Security," *IEEE,* December 15, 2014, accessed March 29, 2016, http://ieeexplore.ieee.org/xpl/articleDetails.jsp?reload=true&arnumber=7037794; Joint Task Force Transformation Initiative, "Security and Privacy Controls for Federal Information Systems and Organizations," *The National Institute of Standards and Technology*, April 2013, accessed March 29, 2016, http://nvlpubs.nist.gov/nistpubs/SpecialPublications/NIST.SP.800-53r4.pdf.

Section III

GOVERNING THE SECURITY
OF THE INTERNET

Chapter 11

Understanding Internet
Security Governance

Trey Herr and Heather West

Senator Ted Stevens once infamously described the internet by saying that "it's not a big truck . . . it's a series of tubes."[1] Though the simplicity of this analogy drew some mockery at the time, there's actually a degree of truth to both parts of it.

Secure web transactions can actually be described as an armored truck moving through a dangerous world. When a web browser makes a secure connection to a web server (e.g., a bank), the packets of information that go between the browser and the server are endowed with cryptographic protections that are like the locks on the truck or the ID card the driver carries— they prevent bad actors from reading the data or impersonating the bank.

The internet can also be described as a series of tubes. The name is important: The internet is an "inter-network," a collection of loosely coordinated networks operated by different people. This means that our armored truck driver has to stop and ask for directions as he goes ("Which network is next closest to where I'm going?"). It's also important to make sure that the driver receives credible directions from the bank, and not a potential bad actor.

Another aphorism useful in cybersecurity is: "If you build it, they will come." The security community uses this statement to talk about attacks. An insecure system on the internet is far more vulnerable to attack, because the barriers to entry are so low. In addition, attackers come in far more guises than those presented by Hollywood. Of course, criminals steal passwords and personal information, but governments collect intelligence and suppress dissent, jealous spouses track financial information, and companies engage in elaborate corporate espionage.

However, there's also a more positive sense to the phrase. When two parties make a secure connection over the internet, they negotiate the specific type of security technology to use. This means that a browser can add support for new technologies (like new encryption methods) and utilize the improved protocol as soon as a web server that also supports the technology is encountered. This dynamic can result in very fast changes in the quality of security applied to the internet. For example, between June 2015 and February 2016, usage of the insecure digital signatures (based on the SHA-1 algorithm) dropped from 70% to less than 2% of web transactions.[2] This change means that 40 billion transactions a day became more secure.

A major challenge to creating sound internet policy is the global nature of the internet. At a technical level, the internet works the same way everywhere and companies rely on these correlations to achieve economies of scale and serve a global market. Divergent global policies erode these benefits. The diversity of goals around the world make it a challenge to establish norms around security. When considering internet policies, it's important to keep a global perspective, both in the sense of establishing consistent global rules that support one global internet, and being cognizant of how a given policy might apply in a different context.

—Richard Barnes, September 2015
Firefox Security Lead at Mozilla

INTERNET SECURITY GOVERNANCE

Internet Security Governance covers the policy challenges that arise from building and governing security in the internet's architecture and key protocols. It is not a description of security for computers and networks (Information Assurance),[3] the pursuit of criminal groups and other threat actors (Cyber Crime),[4] or how to manage the negotiated structure and key functions of the internet (Internet Governance). Internet Security Governance is a cluster of defensively oriented technical and legal issues that cross national boundaries and/or involve security of the underlying protocols and hardware that make up the internet. These include international agreements, such as the Wassenaar Arrangement, and the process of drafting, approving, and promulgating security standards for implementation across the internet.

Securing the internet, a fragile network of networks, is a complicated task filled with stopgap solutions that have become de facto permanent out of necessity rather than their provision of ideal security. Perfect security is an impossible dream; people make mistakes and building, as well as implementing, secure software is difficult. This is in addition to the fact that the adversary may be highly capable and can adapt to changing defenses.

However, security that is effective for most parties at most times is possible. To find a focus amid this vast array of issues, we center on encryption—a process used to establish trust and secure data across networks of every stripe and purpose. To be clear, this is only one of many complex topics in the security environment but encryption is critical to commerce and secure communications over the internet. Without it, any information transiting a network would be vulnerable to manipulation or theft by a third party. Using encryption as a focal point, the chapter highlights several elements of Internet security governance including the underlying technology, diversity in national and cultural approaches, and key governance challenges.

Securing the Internet

The internet is a globally interconnected system of computer networks using shared protocols to facilitate communications between billions of devices— computers, servers, sensors, and a multitude of other machines. Each of these is connected to a smaller network—a school, a business, a government, or some other public or private entity. While a single individual runs some of these, others are huge intranets maintained by teams of experts.

Each local network is linked by some set of electronic, wireless, or optical networking technology and protocols. Across these links are delivered multifarious forms of digital information, from the simple HTML webpage, to encrypted e-mail, a "smart" thermostat's status messages, to highly sophisticated applications rivaling anything found on a single computer. The internet is an all-purposes network of networks connecting diverse arrays of devices and applications, each with different needs but sharing a common dependence on core principles and protocols.

Initially, internet protocols (IPs) didn't build in security, as all members of a then-experimental network knew each other and it was more important to create a proof of concept than a complete system. The earliest users of the internet were a small collection of academics at schools like Stanford and MIT. As this early academic network grew into the modern commercial internet, the lack of security changed—as it had to. Suddenly the internet was home to services like eBay and Amazon; people were banking online and needed to trust that when they sent their data to a website, it would remain safe. Now, there are hundreds of thousands of interconnected networks and billions of connected people—some of them well intentioned, and others not.[5] As a result, a global conversation has begun on how best to build security into or on top of the existing protocols of the internet. A key piece of that security puzzle is the process of encryption.

Encryption

Cryptography affords a measure of security to data in the event it is lost, stolen, or otherwise compromised, employing mathematical operations to convert legible information into digital gibberish. The power of these mathematical techniques to obscure data provides a way to secure not only information moving around the internet but also that stored on individual computers and servers around the world.

There are two places information can be at any given time—in motion or at rest. Data at rest describes the pictures stored on your phone, the document on a computer, or files backed up in the cloud. Data in motion is each of these things as they move around the web, along with a bevy of phone calls, tweets, and e-mails. Encryption provides security against theft or compromise of information and can help guarantee that data hasn't been tampered with, so that you can trust that a message received from someone hasn't been faked by an attacker.

For many years, the only way to encrypt data and share it between parties was through use of a shared secret, the key. Much as if you were to invent a secret alphabet you would need to tell your friend how to read it before writing to them, "symmetric encryption" involves exchanging a shared key between two parties who want to communicate in secret, before they can talk.[6] This runs the risk that an attacker might steal the key and copy it, allowing them to open the encrypted information as well and thus defeating the purpose.

Along came American cryptologists Whit Diffie and Martin Hellman who, unknowingly extending the work of three British intelligence analysts from the 1970s, developed a way to exchange encrypted data without the use of a shared key.[7] Instead of a single key, Diffie and Hellman's "asymmetric encryption" relies on a pair of keys, one public and one private, used by every person who wants to encrypt and securely exchange data. The two keys, linked mathematically, are used to alternately lock and unlock the same file, allowing one person to encrypt with the recipient's public key, and send it to be unlocked by the recipient's private key (see figure 11.1 for a description of public key encryption). This way, the public keys could be shared and known to the world while the private keys remained secret, thus solving the challenge of how to exchange a shared key and avoiding the risk someone might steal and copy it. One of the challenges in implementing encryption across different protocols and standards that make up the internet is the presence of a diversity of stakeholders and networks. Lots of people own the boxes, servers, cabling, and infrastructure which makes up the internet and even more have opinions about the software which runs on top. Getting even a small portion to agree can be a challenge.

Internet Architecture

Historically, the internet did not have a centralized method of governance. Instead, each network within the larger internet (short for internet working) has the ability to set its own policies, while overarching standards are laid

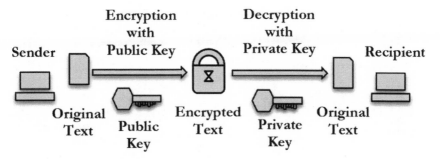

Figure 11.1 Public-Key Encryption

out according to an international multistakeholder process, with different meetings and organizations for technical and policy-oriented topics.[8] The layout of these networks is defined not by a handful of global elites but rather the networks themselves informally agreeing to interconnect and route traffic between each other. This way, to pass traffic from D.C. to Amsterdam, you don't have to lay a cable from one city to the other, needing only to find another internet service provider (ISP) or series of them who can carry your data the full distance. This interconnection process might mean the message you are sending to Holland gets routed through multiple different neighboring networks, until it reaches its destination. This kind of agreement actually causes the network to be more robust, creating many more potential routes for data to transit, rather than a nationalized or top-down model for routing.

At its highest level, the internet is a series of Internet Exchange Points (IXPs) joined by radio, copper cable, and fiber-optic links. These are the physical infrastructures that carry content from ISPs and Content Delivery Networks (CDNs) and determine where that content is routed between networks.[9] An ISP is a company that provides internet service, be that to individual homes or whole continents; chains of ISPs form the routing layer for data to move across the web. CDNs are large collections of servers, spread across the globe to distribute content. This makes it possible for companies to serve large amounts of data. An example would be the 24 gigabytes a second Netflix delivers to users during peak hours (1.3 petabytes a day).[10] This physical layer is what makes it difficult to argue the internet is an entirely new and unregulated space as the hardware associated with moving bits has to be in or on the ground somewhere. The internet was designed such that there are many routes that traffic can take to get from one point to any other, however; while these IXPs are important, networks do also interconnect outside of them, so ISPs and CDNs are able to connect directly to each other. These connections are multitudinous, with major ISPs and CDNs (some companies play both roles) having thousands of formal and informal, paid and unpaid interconnection agreements. This means that even if one route fails, any point should still be reachable by another link or connection.

The underlying architecture of the internet is not secure but the possibility of security has been present since its inception owing to flexibility in the way technologies are combined and layered. While a wholesale reengineering is unlikely, there are a number of interim solutions which have been developed, refined, and applied to secure the internet. The next section details several attempts to design a more secure content delivery and navigation system for the internet and its users.

Standards and Protocols Evolving for Security

The core protocols of the internet were developed decades ago, in the 1970s and 1980s. Since 1993, new standards and tweaks to old ones have been formalized through the Internet Engineering Task Force (IETF), a nonprofit organization composed of hundreds of technical experts and computer scientists.[11] These IETF standards range from highly detailed and technically complex issues to relatively simple language agreements and organizing conventions. The four standards below make up the internet's basic DNA, each with a core function and purpose in making the internet work.

Transmission Control Protocol/Internet Protocol: The Backbone

One of many standards adopted and updated by IETF, Transmission Control Protocol/Internet Protocol (TCP/IP) plays an important role as the backbone protocols of the internet. Each transaction over the internet is a series of "packets"—that is, a specifically formatted unit of data that is carried over a series of networks. This packet includes control information, user data, and the "payload"—the actual content or message being carried. TCP/IP defines the standard construction and transmission of these packets.

TCP/IP was developed and optimized for reliability, not security, so each lacks authentication and encryption capabilities. The security provided to data in motion by encryption is important for a number of reasons including that it prevents third parties from watching your traffic or manipulating it to, for example, inject in malware or ads. Changing the protocols themselves presents enormous challenges, so instead, in a pattern replicated across many internet security solutions, another protocol was created to secure the existing one.

Secure Socket Layer/Transport Layer Security: Securing the Backbone

Enter the secure socket layer (SSL). Netscape Communications created the original SSL in 1994, when it became apparent that there was no way to securely transfer data across the internet.[12] The first specification, version 1.0, was so heavily criticized by the security community for using weak cryptographic algorithms that it was never released for public use. As the protocol matured, it became part of the IETF's standards-track, engaging the broader technical community in refining and improving it. Through this process, SSL continued to evolve into transport layer security (TLS) in 1999 and through the most recent version, TLS 3.0, which remains in draft form.

SSL/TLS works to protect a user's data in motion between their computer and a webserver, using a shared symmetric key to establish a secure tunnel between the two. This tunnel both protects the data inside from observation by others on the web, encrypting each packet, and also works to verify to which internet service users are connecting. The protocol uses a public-key system to authenticate that both parties are who they claim to be. When the user connects to a service like Google, the webserver has to present a certificate that the user trusts to authenticate the identity of the service. Establishing that a certificate is trusted relies on a network of Certificate Authorities (CA) who independently act to verify the owners of different websites and services are who they claim to be.[13]

IPv4 is the version of the IP that has been standard since 1983. However, it is slowly being replaced by a new version, IPv6. This updated standard has introduced the use of both encryption and a means to authenticate (or prove the identity of) between users for all protocols and connections running over IP. The adoption of IPv6 provides a more resilient technical basis than SSL/TLS for secure channels over the insecure internet and is building security at a lower level. Rather than SSL/TLS, which runs on top of IP, IPv6 builds that same secure tunnel functionality in from the start. The standard was formalized by IETF in 1998 but the push for adoption, even though recently picking up speed, has generally been slow, with Google finding just under 10.5 percent of users accessing their service via IPv6 connections as of February 2016.[14]

Border Gateway Protocol: The Map

The connections between so many different networks over the internet requires that each must use the same protocols, that is, speak the same language. The typical means of communicating information about how to navigate in and between these networks is the Border Gateway Protocol (BGP). BGP acts as a sort of travel guide to different networks using a distributed database of IP locations, essentially maps of the internet and subsidiary networks. BGP updates these lists of routes as networks change shape, accepting newly advertised routes from other routers by default.

While an efficient way to map out and navigate the networks, this implicit trust between BGP routers harkens back to the day when all online players knew each other. There is no mechanism of authenticating whether routes being offered are legitimate so it raises the risk that routing data could be disrupted or manipulated. This routing information is not encrypted and, as a 2006 memo from the IETF emphasized, "There are no mechanisms internal to BGP that protect against attacks that modify, delete, forge, or replay data, any of which has the potential to disrupt overall network routing behavior."[15] BGP's trust allows for automatic, decentralized, and scalable routing across the internet's many networks, but also leaves it subject to disruptions by adding or manipulating data in the routing tables.

Securing BGP remains a thorny problem and while several technical proposals have been put forward, discussion and adoption have been virtually nonexistent.[16] Incentivizing change is hard and many network owners believe the system is granted some safety by its relative obscurity and that their familiarity with each other will help defend against a new, malicious user. While the protocol's insecurity looms large, to date, the majority of BGP incidents have been failures of capacity and not-yet-malicious attacks.[17]

Domain Name Service: The Address Book

The Domain Name System (DNS) serves as the internet's address book: if I want to connect to "example.com," where should my packets get sent, and how will they get there? If BGP serves to give computers directions on how to move data across networks, DNS tells them where in the world to go. Every host on the internet has a range of IP numbers from which their content is served. This system was designed from the outset for usability and robustness, but not for secure and authenticated transactions. DNS acts to translate the URL in a browser bar, www.microsoft.com, into an IP address like 65.52.240.200. For most, this translation process happens without our intervention but there is no guarantee that the DNS server translating a URL into an IP address isn't acting maliciously. While the web is built on DNS, it's a protocol with one major security flaw: there is no guarantee for the end user that the records received are the records sent from the actual source, which means that responses to DNS queries can be forged or manipulated in transit to redirect browsers to connect to a malicious website, add malicious content to a page, or to route e-mail to an attacker's computer.

The importance of DNS as a means of efficiently accessing information and applications on web servers meant this posed a serious challenge. Work began as early as 1995 to create a series of extensions to DNS that would provide authentication for each interaction by encrypting them with a particular key.[18] This process, called Domain Name System Security Extensions (DNSSEC), authenticates individual DNS server records first by a central server called the DNS root zone, and then through a chain of trust to pass an authenticated record from the root to child zones and down to the recipient.

Standards and Protocols as a Mail Service

 The **Transmission Control Protocol** is the mail service. It decides how your data will be packaged and sent.

The **Secure Sockets Layer** is the security tape on the box that protects your package from being stolen or compromised.

 The **Border Gateway Protocol** is the map that tells the route for how the package will get to its destination.

The **Domain Name Service** is how you find the coordinates of where your package will be delivered. It provides you the street address.

Figure 11.2   Standards and Protocols Mail Service Metaphor

Using this chain of trust,[19] DNSSEC can provide authentication of the origin of DNS data and assurance that the content of the DNS transaction has not been manipulated in transit. For a visual representation of the full standard and protocol process see figure 11.2.

UNDERSTANDING THE CULTURE(S)
OF SECURITY GOVERNANCE

What is cybersecurity? Well, that's part of what this book sets out to explain but there's tremendous disagreement between different countries on use of the term. More than a cultural gap, these distinctions have taken on political significance as the range of issues between the United States and countries like China and Russia impede the adoption of useful security standards, development of norms, and potentially impact the way the internet is built and operated. Below we highlight several differences between states ranging from issues like law enforcement access to data, stances on encryption, and content filtering.

Russia

Where the United States broadly talks about cybersecurity, Russia uses the term Information Security to connote protection from online threats as well as controls on information and interactions that take place online. Both refer to the same protection of architecture but the Russian phrase also includes law enforcement's ability to retrieve information about individuals and their affairs. This negatively impacts the freedom for firms to offer, or employ as standard, forms of encryption that are not easily compromised in response to government requests. It also supports data localization policies—the requirements that an internet service firm offering their product in a particular country must also store all user data generated by citizens of that state in the same country. As of 2015, Russia requires firms who collect data on Russian users to store that data in servers in Russia.[20] While the law doesn't affect firms' ability to transfer the data abroad or share it with other companies, it does impose a political requirement, with technical and legal implications, for all who choose to comply and continue doing business in the country.[21]

China

The Chinese government has several priorities when it comes to the internet including the maintenance of economic growth, preserving social stability, supporting ongoing and future military activities, and countering the development of international norms which might undermine any of these goals.[22] This broad swath of activities is covered under the term information security (信息安全, xinxi anquan), while topics like the protection of computers and networks is considered a subset and referred to as network security (网络安全, wangluo anquan).[23] Unlike Russia's focus on data retention and access by agents of the country, Chinese censors have constructed a remarkably flexible arrangement of filtering, blocking, and surveillance technologies, collectively dubbed the Great Firewall of China.[24] The emphasis is on real-time monitoring and "shaping" of discussions to control the flow of information from sources outside the country and about sensitive events or phrases within the country.[25] Encryption, especially for data in motion like SSL/TLS, can frustrate these efforts so at different[26] points[27] Chinese officials have used the Great Firewall to block encrypted connections to networks outside of China. While there are a large number of groups with diverse interests as to how internet security is governed in China, preservation of Chinese Communist Party (CCP) influence and political stability appear to be of paramount importance.[28]

United States

The United States has been home to much of the innovation and commercial development which brought about the internet's arrangement of protocols, hardware, and security standards as we know them today. Part of the challenge in governing this array of issues has been for the United States to work with countries that may be suspect of or outwardly hostile to this predominance. While support for an open and secure internet is rhetorically part of U.S. policies, attempts to undermine security standards and the availability of strong encryption tools have provided evidence to some who doubt the sincerity of such a narrative.[29] Existing domestic legal protections for free speech have provided a bulwark against censorship and domestic content filtering, but concerns over law enforcement access to data, especially abroad, have generated proposals that may compromise security.[30] Table 11.1 provides an information security governance comparison of China, Russia, and the United States.

The Practice of Governing Internet Security

Governing the technical architecture of the internet, across national and cultural boundaries, is a network of responsibilities. In some cases, these are filled by public institutions and clear statutory mandate while others are handled by private companies and informal arrangements. An ongoing challenge for the collective governance of internet security is the array of private owners and nongovernmental standards bodies. Coordination between this multiplicity of stakeholder groups has yielded a diverse and economically empowering system of interconnection and commerce but whose variegated nature and diverse incentives can inhibit widespread adoption of progressive security measures.

Below are three major examples of this governance environment. Each issue impacts a different facet of interstate cooperation and technical coordination. CAs govern the trust network which underpins encryption for data in motion, including the SSL/TLS protocols. MLATs or Mutual Legal Assistance

Table 11.1   Country Information Security Governance Comparison

Country	Information Security Goal	Controversial Measures
China	Maintain social stability for regime; influence population	Conducts filtering, blocking, and surveilling, and restricts information flow to public
Russia	Control public information and interactions	Compels foreign companies to store data on local servers
United States	Open and secure internet; against censorship	Law enforcement wants backdoors to encrypted technologies potentially compromising security

Treaties govern the cooperative investigation and coordinated prosecution of criminals across jurisdictions. The Wassenaar Arrangement is an example of multilateral cooperation attempting to restrict the flow of malicious software to repressive regimes and criminal groups, though with little success.

The CAs System

CAs act to certify that internet services using SSL/TLS encryption are communicating in secret and are who they claim to be. The CA system is the network of companies and, in some cases nonprofit groups, that issue, sign, and publicly share digital certificates to certify the owner of a public key (the internet service) by issuing a certificate signed with their private key (the CA). CAs are one of the central trust mechanisms on the internet so any vulnerabilities at the CA level impact a significant portion of the internet's data in motion that is presumed to be secure.

These CAs figure prominently in the setup of the Public-Key Infrastructure (PKI) on the internet, providing the trusted entity that can authenticate interactions for secure exchange of content. Based on this authentication, browsers and servers can negotiate a symmetric key (as opposed to the asymmetric key used for the certificate authenticating the exchange) to ensure that the content exchanged is safe from both prying eyes and manipulation by malicious third parties. This PKI system has become a truly distributed and global trust mechanism. Each browser manufacturer decides which CAs it considers trusted, and includes a list with the browser (and likely includes the option to add more CAs or even certificates signed by the user's own organization for an internal network). Because of the role it serves as a trusted list of certificates, a CA compromise means that its customer's communications may no longer be provably secure.

Law Enforcement: Clarifying Cooperation

MLATs are a mechanism for countries to share information related to ongoing investigations in circumstances where foreign assistance is necessary for a domestic prosecution. They provide a legal basis for international law enforcement activity like extradition and the seizure of assets.[31] As crime related to information technology has become a more substantial part of the legal landscape, the language of these documents has struggled to keep up. A key issue is most MLAT's limited or nonexistent provisions for balancing privacy protections against government interest in data and distinguishing between content and metadata in shared information.[32]

These sort of ambiguities can impede cooperation between countries whose legal systems differ in their privacy protections. It also imposes a burden on an already limited federal organizational capacity to understand the validity of requests for information and respond appropriately within the framework of U.S. law. The President's Review Group on Intelligence and Communications Technologies found that requests "appear to average approximately 10 months to fulfill, with some requests taking considerably longer. Non-U.S. governments seeking such records can face a frustrating delay in conducting legitimate investigations."[33] The effect of this is to dissuade the use of MLATs as a means to exchange data between law enforcement groups and prosecutors. And yet providing a clear and responsive channel for international legal information requests is precisely what the MLATs are intended for.

Improving the MLAT process should start with reducing the cost associated with each request to other governments and by U.S. law enforcement bodies by creating a secure digital means to submit and update information. It should also reform the language found in existing agreements through two processes. The first is to clarify the balance of privacy expectations against government interest in information and to introduce technically significant distinctions such as between the content of communications and the metadata related to their address and routing. The second process is to set clear expectations of what the United States will and will not turn over. As a jurisdiction that covers a substantial number of data storage and internet communications services, American firms will be a popular target for data requests from the security and law enforcement services of other countries. A clearly structured and responsive MLAT system will help attenuate (though not remove) the incentive for foreign governments to put into place extraordinary requirements like data localization and dissuade other more exotic and costly legal mechanisms.

Regulating Security Away

One of the venues pursued by nations in trying to structure the security environment is export controls targeting malicious software components. The Wassenaar Arrangement is an international export control regime brought into force in 1996 to cover sophisticated military and dual-use technologies including jet engines and advanced sensors.[34] The arrangement does not constitute new law in and of itself, rather it is a standing mechanism to define common expectations among nations and a basis on which to harmonize different domestic laws.[35] In 2013, the Arrangement was modified to cover technologies like deep packet inspection tools (DPI) and "intrusion software"—malicious software designed to extract or modify data and system processes.[36] Part of the intent behind the change, proposed the French and UK governments, was to deter the sale of surveillance software and technologies to repressive regimes.[37]

The resulting changes, however, as well as the subsequent rule proposed to harmonize American law with the Arrangement, by the U.S. Department of Commerce, were both written such that they cover both these surveillance products and a range of defensive tools and information. These include software used for penetration testing by defensive security firms like Metasploit Pro, a popular framework developed by H.D. Moore and now maintained by Boston-based information security company Rapid7. There are serious challenges in using export controls as a means to govern internet security, especially when focusing on software code, for which there exists an overwhelming variety of means to exchange ideas and tools across borders.

Leveraging a set of regulations whose original intent was to restrict the flow of products like missile guidance systems and avionics and using U.S. laws which also cover the sale of nuclear energy components and firearms unnecessarily equates a great deal of information security research with deviant behavior. More importantly, the imposition of a large and complicated legal regime on the information security community, whose value has come in great part from the agility to coordinate and collaborate in unexpected ways, may seriously harm efforts to improve internet security in the United States and abroad.[38]

CONCLUSION

Internet Security Governance covers those security topics that are defensive in nature (e.g., not related to the active interdiction of threats) and are multilateral and/or international in scope. This includes formal interstate relations like the Wassenaar Arrangement and MLAT process as well as private sector-led efforts like the network of CAs underpinning encrypted communications on the web. While the focus of these issues involves global standards, the influence of diverse national value systems and approaches to the topic cannot be underestimated.

Perhaps the most challenging realization is the sheer diversity of stakeholders and priorities involved with the development and adoption of security standards. This process has generated tremendous technical achievements but somewhat fragile institutions whose operation is necessary to a secure and functioning internet. The recommendations contained here are a starting point: to reform the MLAT process to lower response times and clarify expectations and treatment of digital information, to modify the language of and deemphasize export control regulations as a means of controlling security products, and to help industry and technologists reinforce the security of the CA system, maintaining the flexibility and responsiveness of private ownership. Improvement should come carefully and be rooted in the same nonstate organizations and private actors who have been largely responsible for the internet's achievements thus far.

CHAPTER HIGHLIGHTS

Internet Security Governance. Internet Security Governance is the discussion of defensively oriented technical and legal topics that cross national boundaries and/or involve security of the underlying protocols and hardware that make up the internet.

Securing the Net. The underlying architecture of the internet is not secure, but the possibility of security has been present since its inception owing to flexibility in the way technologies are combined and layered.

Encryption is Key. Encryption is critical to commerce and secure communications over the internet. Without it, any information transiting a network would be vulnerable to manipulation or theft by a third party.

Internet Protocols. The core protocols of the internet were developed decades ago, in the 1970s and 1980s. Since 1993, new standards and tweaks to old ones have been formalized through the Internet Engineering Task Force (IETF), a nonprofit organization consisting of hundreds of technical experts and computer scientists.

Multiple Stakeholders. While the wide variety of stakeholders in the internet has led to a diverse and economically empowering system of interconnection, it can also inhibit widespread adoption of progressive security measures.

Legal Considerations. Imposing a burdensome legal regime on the information security community may seriously harm that community's ability to improve internet security in the United States and abroad.

NOTES

1. "Your Own Personal Internet," *Wired.com*, June 30, 2006, accessed March 1, 2016, http://www.wired.com/2006/06/your_own_person/.

2 Time Series for CERT_CHAIN_SIGNATURE_DIGEST_STATUS, Bin(s) 4 (in%). Chart, accessed March 1, 2016, https://ipv.sx/telemetry/general-v2.html?channels=nightly%20aurora%20beta&measure=CERT_CHAIN_SIGNATURE_DIGEST_STATUS&target=4.

3. For more, see chapter 2—"A Path to Collective Security: Information Sharing at the State and Local Level."

4. For more, see chapter 6—"Understanding Cyber Crime."

5. "Internet Users," *Internet Live Stats*, last modified 2016. http://www.internetlivestats.com/internet-users/.

6. David Simmer, March 14, 2014, "Crypto Primer," *David Simmer Blog,* https://www.davidsimner.me.uk/2014/03/crypto-primer.

7. "GCHQ Trio Recognised for Key to Secure Shopping Online," *BBC News*, October 5, 2010, http://www.bbc.com/news/uk-england-gloucestershire-11475101.

8. For more, see chapter 14—"Multistakeholder Approaches to Cybersecurity Challenges."

9. "Global Traffic Map 2010," *Telegeography*, 2010. https://www.telegeography.com/assets/website/images/maps/global-traffic-map-2010/global-traffic-map-2010-x.jpg.

10. Steven Wu, Allen Wang, et al., "Evolution of the Netflix Data Pipeline," *The Netflix Tech Blog*, February 15, 2016, http://techblog.netflix.com/2016/02/evolution-of-netflix-data-pipeline.html.

11. Vint Cerf, "IETF and the Internet Society," *Internet Society*, July 18, 1995, http://www.internetsociety.org/internet/what-internet/history-internet/ietf-and-internet-society.

12 A. Freier, P. Karlton, and P. Kocher, "The Secure Sockets Layer (SSL) Protocol Version 3.0," August 2011, https://tools.ietf.org/html/rfc6101.

13. For more, see chapter 13—"Certificate Authorities: Modernizing the Internet's Chain of Trust."

14. "IPv6 Adoption," *Chart*, Google, accessed February 26, 2016, http://www.google.com/intl/en/ipv6/statistics.html.

15. Murphy, "BGP Security Vulnerabilities Analysis," *International Engineering Task Force*. January 2006, http://www.ietf.org/rfc/rfc4272.txt.

16. Cengiz Alaettinoglu, "BGP Security: No Quick Fix," *Network Computing*, February 26, 2015, http://www.networkcomputing.com/networking/bgp-security-no-quick-fix/a/d-id/1319235.

17. Sebastian Anthony, "Brace for the BGPocalypse: Big Disruptions Loom as Internet Overgrowth Continues," *ExtremeTech*, August 13, 2014, http://www.extremetech.com/extreme/187954-brace-for-the-bgpocalypse-big-disruptions-loom-as-internet-overgrowth-continues.

18. Steven Bellovin, "Using the Domain Name System for System Break-ins,"*Department of Computer Science and Engineering*, June 1995, doi:10.5040/9781472564184.ch-001.

19. Nick Sullivan, "DNSSEC: An Introduction." *CloudFlare*, October 7, 2014, https://blog.cloudflare.com/dnssec-an-introduction/.

20. Howard Amos, "Apple to Store Users' Personal Data in Russia," *The Moscow Times*, September 10, 2015, http://www.themoscowtimes.com/business/article/apple-to-store-users-personal-data-in-russiareport/529865.html.

21. Sergei Blagov, "Russia Clarifies Looming Data Localization Law," *Bloomberg BNA*, August 10, 2015, http://www.bna.com/russia-clarifies-looming-n17179934521/.

22. Derek Reveron, *China and Cybersecurity: Political, Economic, and Strategic Dimensions, Publication*, April 12, 2012, https://www.usnwc.edu/Academics/Faculty/Derek-Reveron/Documents/China-and-Cybersecurity-Workshop-Report-final.aspx.

23. Amy Chang, "Warring State: China's Cyber Security Strategy," *Center for a New American Security*, December 2014, http://www.cnas.org/sites/default/files/publications-pdf/CNAS_WarringState_Chang_report_010615.pdf.

24. Geremie R. Barme and Sang Ye, "The Great Firewall of China," *Wired*, June 1, 1996, http://archive.wired.com/wired/archive/5.06/china.html.

25. Jonathon Zittrain and Benjamin Edelman, "Empirical Analysis of Internet Filtering in China," *Berkman Center for Internet and Society*, March 20, 2003, http://cyber.law.harvard.edu/filtering/china/.

26. Charles Arthur, "China Tightens 'Great Firewall' Internet Control with New Technology," *The Guardian*, December 14, 2012, http://www.theguardian.com/technology/2012/dec/14/china-tightens-great-firewall-internet-control.

27. "China Blocks Virtual Private Network Use," *BBC News*, January 26, 2015, http://www.bbc.com/news/technology-30982198.

28. Amy Chang, "Warring State: China's Cyber Security Strategy," *Center for a New American Security*, December 2014, http://www.cnas.org/sites/default/files/publications-pdf/CNAS_WarringState_Chang_report_010615.pdf.

29. John Kerry, "An Open and Secure Internet: We Must Have Both," *U.S. Department of State*, May 18, 2015, http://www.state.gov/secretary/remarks/2015/05/242553.htm; Matthew Green, "Hopefully the Last Post I'll ever Write on Dual EC DRBG," *A Few Thoughts on Cryptographic Engineering*, January 14, 2015, http://blog.cryptographyengineering.com/2015/01/hopefully-last-post-ill-ever-write-on.html; Andi Wilson, Danielle Kehl, and Kevin Bankston, "Domed to Repeat History? Lessons From the Crypto Wars of the 1990s." *New America RSS*, June 17, 2015, https://www.newamerica.org/new-america/doomed-to-repeat-history-lessons-from-the-crypto-wars-of-the-1990s/.

30. Michael J. Gan, "First Amendment Rights and the Internet," *National Education Association* Update 3, no. 3 (September 1997), http://www.nea.org/assets/docs/HE/vol3no3.pdf.; Keith Wagstaff, "FBI Director: Encryption Is a 'massive Challenge'" *CNBC*, July 8, 2015, http://www.cnbc.com/2015/07/08/fbi-director-says-encryption-poses-law-enforcement-challenge.html.

31. Virginia M. Kendall and T. Markus Funk, "The Role of Mutual Legal Assistance Treaties in Obtaining Foreign Evidence," *Litigation 40, no. 2* (Winter 2014), http://www.americanbar.org/content/dam/aba/events/criminal_justice/CSR_MLAT_LetterRogatory.authcheckdam.pdf.

32. Jonah Force Hill, "Problematic Alternatives: MLAT Reform for the Digital Age," *Harvard National Security Journal,* January 28, 2015, http://harvardnsj.org/2015/01/problematic-alternatives-mlat-reform-for-the-digital-age/.

33. Richard A. Clark, Michael J. Morell, Geoffrey R. Stone, Cass R. Stein, and Peter Swire, "Liberty and Security in a Changing World," December 12, 2013, 227. https://www.whitehouse.gov/sites/default/files/docs/2013-12-12_rg_final_report.pdf

34. "List of Dual Use Goods and Technologies and Munitions List," in *Export Controls for Conventional Arms and Dual Use Goods and Technologies*, 1–228. Proceedings of The Wassenaar Arrangement, Austria, Vienna. Vienna, 2015. http://www.wassenaar.org/wp-content/uploads/2015/08/WA-LIST-15-1-2015-List-of-DU-Goods-and-Technologies-and-Munitions-List.pdf.

35. Innokenty Pyetranker, "An Umbrella in a Hurricane: Cyber Technology and the December 2013 Amendment to the Wassenaar Arrangement," *Northwestern Journal of Technology and Intellectual Property* 13, no. 2 (2015): 1–30, http://scholarlycommons.law.northwestern.edu/cgi/viewcontent.cgi?article=1235&context=njtip.

36. Jennifer Grannick, "Changes to Export Control Arrangement Apply to Computer Exploits and More," *The Center for Internet and Society*, January 15, 2014, http://cyberlaw.stanford.edu/publications/changes-export-control-arrangement-apply-computer-exploits-and-more.

37. Tim Maurer, Edin Omanovic, and Ben Wagner, "Uncontrolled Global Surveillance: Updating Export Controls to the Digital Age," *Digitale Gesellschaft*, March 2014, 1–46, https://digitalegesellschaft.de/wp-content/uploads/2014/03/Uncontrolled-Surveillance_March-2014_final.pdf.

38. Trey Herr and Paul Rosenzweig, "Cyber Weapons & Export Control: Incorporating Dual Use with the PrEP Model," *Journal of National Security Law Policy*, Fall 2015. http://jnslp.com/2015/10/23/cyber-weapons-export-control-incorporating-dual-use-with-the-prep-model/; Stephanie Horth, Joanna Bronowicka, and Ben Wagner, "Overview of Recent Developments in the Export Controls of Surveillance Technologies in Europe," *Centre for Internet Human Rights*, December 2015, https://cihr.eu/export-controls-policy-paper/.

Chapter 12

A Holistic Approach to the Encryption Debate

Aaron Brantly

National security intelligence is based on estimates derived from all-source information run through a rigorous analytical process. While movies and television often portray this intelligence cycle as a single swift movement from a spy's hidden camera to the panicked faces in the oval office, the reality is far more complex. The intelligence collection and analysis process requires multiple agencies with different technical and human capabilities to work together within the context of domestic and international law. The more accurate and timely the information, the higher the estimated value of the resulting intelligence product to decision-makers. Rarely is a single piece of intelligence alone reliable or accurate enough to obviate the weight of combined all-source intelligence.

Encryption is the process of converting useful information to nearly random data through a series of mathematical operations. It is the means by which to secure data against observation, theft, or corruption. A backdoor in an encryption program compromises this mathematical process to provide a third-party-guaranteed access to unencrypted data at all times. Calls to provide backdoors into encryption on popular software platforms have been described as a means to stave off intelligence failures and circumvent investigative roadblocks. Yet the demand for weakened encryption fails to consider the larger implications that such backdoors would have. The debate often focuses on security versus privacy, the notion that the protection of individual communications should not be of greater value than national security or the needs of law enforcement to solve a crime.

However, this framing of security versus privacy is inaccurate and over-simplifies the importance and reality of encryption as it is currently used. This chapter examines the argument for and against backdoors in encryption and provides intelligence, law enforcement, and policymakers with a potential path forward while highlighting the international dimensions of the issues involved. The debate over encryption necessarily centers on economic, technical, and security questions ranging from user privacy to the systemic security of weapons systems and global markets. The trade-offs are largely political in nature and should be examined with an appreciation of the consequences associated with a deliberate weakening of encryption on individual security (citizens), economic security (businesses, markets, and the economy at large), and the country's national security.

The argument that backdoors are the only way to provide certain data for investigative and intelligence purposes is a shortsighted and imperfect solution to technological advances largely beyond the control of any single national government. Rather than pushing to weaken encryption standards or implementation, policymakers should focus on improvements to investigative and intelligence collection and analysis techniques. These changes would advance state's core security interests in a rapidly changing global technical environment and provide long-term solutions to an evolving information security landscape.

A Long-Running Debate

Encryption is not a new concept. As long as the written word has been used to convey information, there has been a recurring search for secure communications. The Chinese, Greeks, Romans, and Egyptians used encrypted messages.[1] During the Civil War, code books were used to hide orders and information passing between battlefield commanders.[2] Between World Wars I and II, the British broke Japanese and American ciphers to read conversations between diplomats in both countries about ongoing naval negotiations. The British ability to read private communiqués gave them a significant advantage when negotiating fleet size and tonnage.[3] During World War II Germany successfully used the Enigma cipher machine to coordinate a campaign of submarine warfare against allied merchant convoys prior to its compromise by scientists including Alan Turing at the famed Bletchley Park.[4]

Each of these forms of encryption was susceptible to various attacks. The computing machine developed to break the Enigma cipher, called Colossus, became the first programmable electronic computer. During the Cold War period, the advance of computer technology and significant developments in mathematics facilitated an evolution in both encryption and decryption techniques. Many of these methods are based on prime number and pseudo-random number generators. The structural and mathematical vulnerabilities present in historical methods of encryption are increasingly challenging for users and have been replaced by modern mathematical approaches, such as elliptic curves, for increased security and mathematical resistance to attack.[5]

From World War II until the 1990s, encryption technology was covered under export control law in the United States and a number of other Western nations as a weapons technology. Through the American International Traffic in Arms Regulations (ITAR) and international Coordinating Committee for Multilateral Export Controls (CoCom), the export of encryption technology to the Soviet bloc or general public was strictly controlled. This included journal articles, textbooks, and other materials related to modern cryptography.

Control over encryption began to relax in the early 1990s as businesses pushed to integrate secure technologies into their products in excess of what was allowed by export control laws and privacy advocacy groups pushed back on policies designed to provide guaranteed access to intelligence organizations. In the United States, an agreement between the National Security Agency (NSA) and the Software Publishers Association initially moved cryptography off of export lists designed for weapons technologies and to the Commerce Department with other civilian products with potential military use (so-called "dual use").[6] The trend to relax controls on cryptography began to accelerate with the development of Netscape's Secure Socket Layer (SSL) encryption. Designed to secure internet communications, SSL uses a combination of public and symmetric-key cryptography with a variety of key sizes.[7]

Previous limits on these key sizes have been written into U.S. law and, for a time, reciprocated around the world through CoCom.[8] A common American symmetric-key cipher, called Digital Encryption Standard (DES), had been limited to 40-bit keys in the 1970s for any software exported outside of the United States even though the theoretical key length was substantially greater and thus much harder to break. This relaxation of encryption controls culminated in 1996 with Executive Order 13026 changing the designation of encryption products and placing them under the Commerce Department jurisdiction permanently.[9] Of the more comical aspects of encryption prohibitions, one impacted students who touched on advanced number theory and various forms of encryption mathematics. These students were prohibited from taking their textbooks outside the country or from having foreign students in their classes.[10] Although today some encryption technology still remains under regulatory control, the majority does not.

Compromising Communications in the United States: Clipper and CALEA

As encryption has become increasingly widespread, governments have attempted to introduce "backdoor" or other vulnerabilities into systems implementing encryption. Controversial in countries around the world, these efforts have yielded mixed results. Two of the more prominent examples of efforts by the U.S. government to "backdoor" encryption and communications are the Communications Assistance for Law (CALEA) and the Clipper Chip. Both the law and the device pose significant privacy and legal concerns but while CALEA is still active, the Clipper Chip was defunct from the start.

In 1993, the White House and NSA announced the Clipper Chip as a built-in backdoor for telecommunications companies providing voice communication. The device was designed and promoted through interagency working groups and factsheets as well as supported by a National Institute of Standards (NIST) report.[11] Clipper was intended to provide a permanent means of access for the U.S. government to the communications of all devices using the chip. The chip had technical flaws, illustrated through security research by computer scientist Matt Blaze.[12] Adding to this was substantial public resistance from notable cryptographers and security experts focusing on privacy and ethical issues, as well as the economic concerns that would affect businesses and the actual success of such products in a global market. By 1996, the Clipper Chip proposal and other similar devices were outdated.[13]

During the Clipper debate, as an alternative to a permanent technical solution, the law enforcement advocates in Congress passed the CALEA Enforcement Act. The law requires firms who manufacture or purchase telecommunications equipment to establish either a hardware or software backdoor in their devices that allows for law enforcement to listen into communications. Hardware implementations are known as "hard switches," while software implementations are known as "soft switches." The type of switch is important as it has ramifications for the volume and type of data that transits a given switch. Soft switches often facilitate more expansive forms of communication than originally outlined in the 1994 law.

CALEA hinders the market potential of U.S. telecommunications providers, reduces incentives to develop certain technologies in the United States, and does not provide a foolproof solution.[14] Moreover, there is significant controversy over CALEA's applicability to internet communications over broadband including a legal challenge from the American Council on Education in 2006 on the constitutionality of CALEA and several lawsuits by the Electronic Frontier Foundation against the Federal Communications Commission. In all cases the courts have ruled in favor of the government. As technology has evolved, the coverage of CALEA remained expansive. Modern CALEA implementations effectively allow for DPI, monitoring every piece of data which passes through an internet switch or router and dramatically expanding the potential content that might be intercepted.[15] Debates over encryption and national security must consider the historical context and lessons to be drawn from innovation, economics, and technical complexity.

Encryption as Open Innovation

Encryption at its most basic is mathematics, protecting information with a puzzle difficult to solve without specific information. As soon as one mathematician creates an encryption scheme, another usually attempts to solve it. This fosters a dynamic cycle of innovation that functions best in an open and collaborative ecosystem of intellectual exchange. As the fatal flaws of the Clipper Chip illustrate, the creation of new cryptographic tools within a closed or noncollaborative environment might keep the algorithm secret, but not make it safe. The mathematics of modern encryption is extremely robust and has largely kept pace with advances in computing and Moore's law, meaning keys can take in excess of a billion years to find and break if designed and implemented properly.[16] Novel encryption techniques which are developed without scrutiny by the public and the larger cryptographic community are found time and time again to lack sufficient mathematical rigor or software development quality and thus are vulnerable to compromise. While advances in computational power may threaten existing algorithms and smaller key lengths, they do not minimize the ability for mathematicians to innovate and adapt to a changing technical environment.

Much of the encryption debate centers on the hope that backdoors and other methods of cryptographic tools will provide law enforcement and intelligence agencies with a permanent means to intercept communications between criminals, terrorists, and even potentially state actors. This hope is likely in vain, however. Encryption technology is not isolated to the halls of the NSA—universities, corporations, NGOs, governments, and hobbyists all have access to the fundamental building blocks of cryptography and there is a diverse community of developers and security researchers building new tools around the world daily. While backdoors into encryption like the Clipper Chip might possibly have captured individuals with few options or subject to strict domestic laws, today there are dozens of encryption programs and devices produced globally.[17] There is significant evidence that al-Qaeda, ISIS, and other terrorist organizations have either developed or are in the process of developing their own encrypted communications channels.[18] Just as mathematicians innovate and adapt to advances in computing power, terrorists and criminals adapt and innovate as well.[19] In many ways it was inevitable that encryption would be let out of the bottle. But now that it is out, it is extremely difficult to contain without creating significant negative effects.

The Economics of Encryption

Weakening encryption in any form has significant economic ramifications. In the United States, the impact could be substantial on both companies and their customers. Beyond keeping communications private, encryption plays a critical role in safeguarding the intellectual property upon which much of the modern economy depends—securing financial transactions and personal data like healthcare records. This information is the lifeblood of a modern economy. In 2012, Amazon.com averaged approximately 306 transactions per second or 26 million per day, each of which relied on encryption to ensure the safe transit of data.[20] Many uses of encryption are government mandated or encouraged, from the Department of Education to the Department of Health and Human Services. These requirements tend to focus on particular forms of information like educational records and medical histories. A failure to protect data of this nature could lead to increases in fraud, identity theft, discrimination, and more.

The economics of compromising hardware are also challenging. Although historically U.S. technology firms controlled large swaths of the global market in software and computing hardware, this control, and the location of computer hardware manufacturing, has begun to diversify.[21] The distribution of global hardware production in particular has created three challenges for direct U.S. manipulation of cryptographic devices. Deliberately introducing flaws would necessitate that devices return to the United States for manipulation or risk having the technologies that alter encryption fall into the hands of potential adversaries if the compromise is conducted abroad. In addition, because the production of technology is conducted globally, manipulating software or hardware would require modifications in existing supply and manufacturing chains. The mandated implementation of a technology like the Clipper Chip would have resulted in a far slower development process and lower profit margins if production had to be shifted to a financially suboptimal location because of the legal requirement. Lastly, if market alternatives were developed, the deliberate weakening of encryption in U.S.-made products would provide a significant market advantage to non-U.S. manufacturers. What foreign state, company, or individual in a crowded market would willingly submit their data to surveillance and potential loss?

State and local initiatives in the United States to deliberately weaken encryption, such as those proposed in New York and California, would create a further fragmented domestic market.[22] Individuals who continue to want devices that safeguard their personal information would simply cross state lines to purchase hardware products that allowed secure encryption. Moreover, state laws would be ineffective at preventing online services that leverage encryption from crossing state and international boundaries without significant interference in the basic operation of the internet.

The impact of deliberately weak encryption would also have global ramifications. The revelations of Edward Snowden showed that the application of CALEA and expansive interpretations of other U.S. laws provide law enforcement and intelligence agencies very robust access to global communications.

These revelations significantly hindered U.S. firm's competitiveness abroad and likely led to billions of dollars of lost revenue.[23] In turn these losses in revenue prompted companies such as Apple and Google to begin developing products that could circumvent these legal restrictions and requirements. This has raised the ire of various leaders including the Director of the FBI, James Comey, and the Director of the Central Intelligence Agency, John Brennan.[24]

The net economic benefits of encryption in protecting data across industries greatly outweigh the potential security gain achieved through the deliberate weakening of standards. Yet the economic argument alone is insufficient to dissuade significant debate on the potential introduction of backdoors into encryption implementations. The next section builds on the economic argument by deconstructing the technical arguments associated with law enforcement and intelligence requests to deliberately weaken encryption.

Technical Complexity of Building Secure Code

While the math underpinning cryptography is sound, and community reviewed, the implementation of encryption in software and for digital communications is generally less robust. There are numerous reasons, ranging from economic to the technical, that suggest the deliberate introduction of vulnerabilities into encryption tool and software is more than a faint possibility. For example, general estimates on vulnerabilities in most software indicate that for every one thousand lines of code (LoC) there are between twenty and forty vulnerabilities.[25] When software is run through a secure software development lifecycle (SDLC) the number of vulnerabilities drops to three to five. If we assume a program, like the Firefox browser, has 10 million LoC then we should expect it to have roughly 200,000–400,000 potential vulnerabilities. If our Firefox example is manufactured through a rigorous SDLC process, there still remains an estimated 30,000–50,000 bugs, even if many of these are likely to be the same type of bug in different parts of the program.[26] While these are rough estimates, the scale of the coding problem remains and the complexities inherent to software development remain. The successful incorporation of encryption into a complex device or application ecosystem complicates its usage and exposes data, through these vulnerabilities, to a large number of potential avenues for compromise.

This underlying complexity makes the successful implementation of cryptography extremely difficult. al-Qaeda's efforts to build their own encrypted communications tool provide a stark example of this problem. As al-Qaeda attempted to reconstitute itself, avoid intelligence agencies, and build an online communications network, it published instructions for would-be jihadists to communicate using a self-developed encrypted chat program called Asrar Al'Mujahideen.[27] The application, first released in 2007, has remained buggy and vulnerable to attack by intelligence organizations. The encryption within the application was reasonable; however, the software wrapped around it continually exposed users to compromise and surveillance. Indeed, over the near decade since its inception, al-Qaeda has updated the software several times but has been so unsuccessful that it has now largely fallen by the wayside. While the fundamental mathematics of cryptography is extremely strong, the implementation of encryption into software is challenging. This reality is underscored by vulnerabilities with the popular software library such as OpenSSL, whose Heartbleed vulnerability was discovered years after the relevant section of code's creation.[28] Intentionally adding vulnerabilities to the development of software is a reasonable means to weaken security for all who use it.

The deliberate introduction of vulnerabilities into software can also have unknown ramifications and provide new vectors for potential attack. Because such vulnerabilities being "placed" in software require additional code to implement, even more potential weaknesses are being introduced. As the rapidly expanding market for malware indicates, there is a strong demand from criminal groups and states for the tools to gain access to potentially useful vulnerabilities.[29] The ability to seek out and find deliberately embedded vulnerabilities is likely to get significantly easier if these sorts of mandatory backdoors come into more common use.[30] Policymakers and the public are left with a dilemma. There is a genuine national security and often law enforcement need for access to communications content and other encrypted data. There are also strong economic and technological reasons why encryption, manipulated by governments, introduces unnecessary risk into markets and their products.

Putting Together the Puzzle

No matter how much we wish the law enforcement and intelligence agencies functioned like Jack Bauer from *24*, the reality is that their work, while extremely necessary, is not so sexy, fast, or simple. Deliberately weakening encryption opens the door for state and nonstate actors to wreak havoc beyond the horrific loss of life in isolated incidents of terrorism or murder. It establishes a legal and policy mechanism with consequences that stretch to the very heart of our national security. This is not a security versus privacy debate, it is debate over temporary security versus systemic security, where one affects limited populations in temporally constrained events, while the other is a widespread degradation of national security. The instinct for policymakers may be to seek easy answers to complex problems but the result is substantial harm to personal, economic, and national security. The debate over the future of encryption in technology requires delicacy and care, lest we risk far greater harm than we sought to protect against.

Access to one device through the deliberate weakening of security is largely unnecessary in the service of larger investigative or intelligence goals where the internet and communications technologies have provided a bevy of new sources of data on threat groups and their behavior. A common theme arises in investigative training and analysis across federal, state, and local law enforcement and intelligence agencies—while some aspects of adversary's lives remain hidden behind encrypted walls, the vast majority of data associated with their behavior has become increasingly pervasive and available.[31] Those who would seek to do harm now typically walk around with homing beacons that function even in the absence of active geolocation settings through the triangulation of cellular towers. They share information through e-mail, applications, social media, metadata, and more in ways that exponentially increase the potential available volume of data.

Most of these "breadcrumbs" are accessible even well after a crime has been committed and the volume of forensic evidence available extends beyond the information captured in a hard drive or phone. It is the chain of personal data generated over years of owning devices and using various services. Has a jihadist ever tweeted a picture with metadata describing their location? Has a criminal ever shared documents with contact data embedded in it or visited a website that logs computer IP addresses? The volume, velocity, and variety of data now available for intelligence officials and law enforcement far exceeds that of any other point in human history. There is a wealth of information to be gleaned from adversary's use of networked information systems, especially cellphones. Even if a single device is protected by some difficult to defeat locking mechanism, there are a range of other sources of significant information.

Another solution to the broader harm engendered by weakening encryption standards is to systemize and provide rigorous oversight for law enforcement to hack systems and devices of interest. This "lawful hacking" is an approach outlined in a 2014 paper by a group of computer scientists and privacy scholars.[32] Rather than enable the general security harm of a weakened standard or compromised telecommunications platform, lawful hacking encourages targeted compromise of laptops, mobile phones, and computer networks using existing vulnerabilities. While the paper doesn't speak to the activities of the intelligence community, it is likely that similar lessons could be drawn where strong policy guidance can provide a platform for targeted collections operations against software and hardware encryption systems. The failure to consider encryption within the broader investigative process or intelligence cycle is to overlook significant opportunities available to develop good information about targets of investigation and collection. There is no disputing that undermining encryption implementations by various corporations might provide temporary solutions, but it is a broad sword approach which cuts across the public's core interests.

CONCLUSION

Encryption plays a vital role in governing the security of the internet and connected device. This role will only grow in importance over the coming decades. Moreover, we are at the beginning of a development cycle as society grows increasingly dependent on, and thus must trust, the embedded systems of the Internet of Things (IoT). At the same time, there is a pressing need for open lines of communication, novel investigative techniques, and intelligence collection and analysis processes. What we should be seeking is not a single backdoor to make investigative and intelligence processes easier, but the provision of funds to enable investigators and intelligence agencies to utilize the thousands of vulnerabilities already available on systems. This will preserve an adversarial investigative and intelligence collections process. By focusing on improving the way we gather information, countries can adapt intelligence and law enforcement processes not only to single device and software platforms under the purview of U.S. laws and regulations but the entire future ecosystem of technology spread across the globe. Our collective aim should be security for all.

CHAPTER HIGHLIGHTS

Encryption. Encryption is the process of converting useful information to nearly random data through a series of mathematical operations. It is the means by which to secure data against observation, theft, or corruption.

The Encryption Debate. The debate centers on economic, technical, and security questions ranging from user privacy to the systemic security of weapons systems and global markets. The trade-offs are largely political in nature and should be examined with an appreciation of the consequences associated with a deliberate weakening of encryption on individual (citizens), economic (businesses, markets and the economy at large), and national security.

Government Circumvention of Encryption. As encryption has become increasingly widespread, governments have attempted to introduce "backdoors" or other vulnerabilities into systems implementing encryption. Controversial in countries around the world, these efforts have yielded mixed results. Two of the more prominent examples of efforts by the U.S. government to "back door" encryption and communications are the Communications Assistance for Law (CALEA) and the Clipper Chip.

Both the law and the device pose significant privacy and legal concerns, but while CALEA is still active, the Clipper Chip was defunct from the start. In 1993, the White House and National Security Agency (NSA) announced the Clipper Chip as a built-in backdoor for telecommunications companies providing voice communication.

Courts Support CALEA. In all cases the courts have ruled in favor of the government. As technology has evolved, the coverage of CALEA remained expansive. Modern CALEA implementations effectively allow for Deep Packet Inspection (DPI), monitoring every piece of data which passes through an internet switch or router and dramatically expanding the potential content that might be intercepted.

Weak Encryption May Fail. Much of the encryption debate centers on the hope that backdoors and other methods of cryptographic tools will provide law enforcement and intelligence agencies with a permanent means to intercept communications between criminals, terrorists, and even potentially state actors. This hope is likely in vain, however, because there are dozens of encryption programs and devices produced globally. There is significant evidence that al-Qaeda, ISIS, and other terrorist organizations have either developed or are in the process of developing their own encrypted communications channels.

Consequences of Weakening Encryption. Deliberately weakening encryption opens the door for state and nonstate actors to wreak havoc. It establishes a legal and policy mechanism with consequences that stretch to the very heart of our national security. Access to one device through the deliberate weakening of security is largely unnecessary in the service of larger investigative or intelligence goals where the internet and communications technologies have provided a bevy of new sources of data on threat groups and their behavior.

NOTES

1. David Kahn, *The Codebreakers: The Story of Secret Writing* (New York: Scribner, 1996).

2. David W. Gaddy, "Rochford's Cipher: a Discovery in Confederate Cryptography," *Cryptologia,* 16 (4), 1994.

3. J. H. Maurer and C. M. Bell, *At the Crossroads between Peace and War: The London Naval Conference of 1930* (Annapolis: Naval Institute Press, 2014).

4. F. H. Hinsley and A. Stripp, *Codebreakers: The Inside Story of Bletchley Park*, Oxford England (New York: Oxford University Press, 1994).

5. Nick Sullivan, "A (relatively Easy to Understand) Primer on Elliptic Curve Cryptography," *Arstechnica*, October 24, 2014, accessed March 28, 2016, http://arstechnica.com/security/2013/10/a-relatively-easy-to-understand-primer-on-elliptic-curve-cryptography/.

6. National Software Council, "A White Paper on U.S. Encryption Policy," Alexandria, VA, 1995, https://saltworks.stanford.edu/assets/druid:tx020jf4250.pdf.

7. For more on public versus private key, see chapter 11—"Understanding Internet Security Governance."

8. Whitfield Diffie and Susan Landau, "Privacy on the Line: The Politics of Wiretapping and Encryption," *MIT Press*, 2010.

9. Executive Order 13026 of November 19, 1996, *Administration of Export Controls on Encryption Products,* Vol. 61, Washington, D.C., https://www.gpo.gov/fdsys/pkg/FR-1996-11-19/pdf/96-29692.pdf.

10. Information obtained from presentation by Major Natalie Vanetta, 01/10/2016 given at the 2016 Law Enforcement Summit, New York. Major Vanetta was a student at the time and was told upon entering classes with books containing works on encryption that she was not allowed to travel externally to the country. Students from foreign classes complained about not being able to participate in certain classes.

11. *Fact Sheet: Public Encryption Management*, White House, 1994, https://epic.org/crypto/clipper/white_house_factsheet.html; Earnest F Brickell, Dorthy E Denning, Stephen T. Kent, David P. Maher, and Walter Tuchman, 1993, *SKIPJACK Review*, *NIST*, https://epic.org/crypto/clipper/skipjack_interim_review.html.

12. Matt Blaze, *Protocol Failure in the Escrowed Encryption Standard, the 2nd ACM Conference* (New York: ACM, 1994).

13. Whitfield Diffie, "The Impact of a Secret Cryptographic Standard on Encryption, Privacy, Law Enforcement and Technology" (hearings before the Subcommittee on Telecommunications and Finance of the Committee on Energy and Commerce, U.S. House of Representatives, 103rd Congress, 1st Session, April 19 and June 9, 1993).

14. There are still certain communications platforms inaccessible to CALEA. Certain forms of data in transit and certain forms of data at rest fall outside of CALEA.

15. Nate Anderson, "Deep Packet Inspection Meets 'Net Neutrality, CALEA," *Ars Technica*, July 25, 2007, http://arstechnica.com/gadgets/2007/07/deep-packet-inspection-meets-net-neutrality/; "FAQ on the CALEA Expansion by the FCC," September 19, 2007, https://www.eff.org/pages/calea-faq.

16. See https://howsecureismypassword.net; Elaine Barker, William Barker, William Burr, William Polk, and Miles Smid, 2012, *Recommendation for Key Management - Part 1: General. National Institute of Standards*, http://csrc.nist.gov/publications/nistpubs/800-57/sp800-57_part1_rev3_general.pdf.

17. Bruce Schneier, Kathleen Seidel, and Saranya Vijayakumar, 2016, "A Worldwide Survey of Encryption Products," 1st ed.

18. Aaron F. Brantly and Muhammad Al-'Ubaydi, "Extremist Forums Provide Digital OpSec Training," *CTC Sentinel*, May 2015, 1–11.

19. Ibid.

20. Jay Yarrow, "Amazon Was Selling 306 Items Every Second at Its Peak This Year," *Business Insider*, December 27, 2012, http://www.businessinsider.com/amazon-holiday-facts-2012-12.

21. Jason Dedrick and Kenneth Kraemer, "Globalization of Innovation: The Personal Computing Industry," April 24, 2008, accessed March 28, 2016. http://papers.ssrn.com/sol3/papers.cfm?abstract_id=1125025.

22. *Proposed Assembly Bill 8093*, New York State Senate, 2015-2016 Regular Session, June 6, 2015, http://legislation.nysenate.gov/pdf/bills/2015/A8093; Cyrus Farivar, "Yet Another Bill Seeks to Weaken Encryption-by-Default on Smartphones," *Ars Technica*, January 21, 2016, http://arstechnica.com/tech-policy/2016/01/yet-another-bill-seeks-to-weaken-encryption-by-default-on-smartphones/.

23. Claire Cain Miller, "Revelations of N.S.A. Spying Cost U.S. Tech Companies," *The New York Times*, March 21, 2014, http://www.nytimes.com/2014/03/22/business/fallout-from-snowden-hurting-bottom-line-of-tech-companies.html.

24. Cara McGoogan, "The FBI Director Wants to Stop End-to-End Encryption (Wired UK)," *Wired.com*, December 10, 2015, http://www.wired.co.uk/news/archive/2015-12/10/fbi-director-calls-for-encryption-end; Alina Selyukh and Steven Henn, "After Paris Attacks, Encrypted Communication Is Back in Spotlight," *NPR.org*, November 16, 2015, http://www.npr.org/sections/alltech-considered/2015/11/16/456219061/after-paris-attacks-encrypted-communication-is-back-in-spotlight.

25. Watts S. Humphrey, "The Quality Attitude," *Software Engineering Institute*, March 1, 2004, http://www.sei.cmu.edu/library/abstracts/news-at-sei/wattsnew20043.cfm.

26. "Simplified Implementation of the Microsoft SDL," *Microsoft*, 2016, https://www.microsoft.com/en-us/download/details.aspx?id=12379.

27. Eric Schmitt and Michael S. Schmidt, "Qaeda Plot Leak Has Undermined U.S. Intelligence," *The New York Times*, September 29, 2013, http://www.nytimes.com/2013/09/30/us/qaeda-plot-leak-has-undermined-us-intelligence.html.

28. Andrew W. Appel, "Verification of a Cryptographic Primitive: SHA-256," *ACM Trans. Program. Lang. Syst.* 37 (2), ACM: 1–31, 2015.

29. For more, see chapter 7—"Disrupting Malware Markets."

30. Matthew Green, "A History of Backdoors," *A Few Thoughts on Cryptographic Engineering*, July 20, 2015, http://blog.cryptographyengineering.com/2015/07/a-history-of-backdoors.html.

31. Robert M. Clark, *Intelligence Analysis: A Target-Centric Approach* (Washington, DC: CQ Press, 2004); Kim Zetter, "NSA Hacker Chief Explains How to Keep Him out of Your System," *Wired.com,* January 28, 2016, http://www.wired.com/2016/01/nsa-hacker-chief-explains-how-to-keep-him-out-of-your-system/.

32. Bellovin et al., "Lawful Hacking: Using Existing Vulnerabilities for Wiretapping on the Internet," 2014, http://scholarlycommons.law.northwestern.edu/cgi/viewcontent.cgi?article=1209&context=njtip.

Chapter 13

Certificate Authorities

Modernizing the Internet's Chain of Trust

Adrienne Allen

Trust is fundamental to the internet's operation and growth. Without trust, billions of users would not be able to share or believe information, conduct online transactions, or take part in everyday activities such as logging on to Facebook. Broadly defined, trust is the "psychological state comparing the intention to accept vulnerability based upon positive expectation of the intentions or behavior of another."[1] On the internet, trust takes the form of individual entities accepting vulnerability by entering into a variety of relationships to provide or consume goods and services.

Trust is also globally shifting to become more peer driven. Public relations firm Edelman released its 2016 Trust Barometer in February, noting authority figures that have traditionally held greater power and influence than those lower in the hierarchy have begun to lose influence in favor of the masses. Peers are more inclined to rely on each other's opinions to guide their actions, instead of consulting those in a higher authority. This "new pyramid of influence" results in a lack of trust, where peer networks determine acceptable terms and conditions, and can influence popular opinion for or against authority figures. Today, the world pays more attention to the behavior of authority figures and systems; they are subject to the influence of the mass of peer networks.

One of the central mechanisms to the internet's system of trust is the digital certificate, which authenticates the identity of a website or online service, and the network of Certificate Authorities (CAs) that validate these certificates. Users worldwide rely on this system every day to decide whether or not they trust the *identity* of a certain website, to complete a secure transaction with their bank, file online taxes, or buy goods and services. When CAs function well, they help protect the authenticity of transactions over the internet by working to verify the identity of the parties on either end.

Unfortunately, recent incidents, new vulnerabilities, and improved data indicate that serious flaws in the CA system pose critical risks to the long-term maintenance of internet security. To address the weaknesses in the CA structure, a variety of organizations in industry, academia, government, and the nonprofit world have begun actively working on solutions for rearchitecting the CA system. Recent proposals for improving the system are largely concentrated within the private sector, but there are opportunities for governments to influence activity as well. This chapter first provides an overview of the CA system, and then discusses current risks to internet security in the system today. Concluding, the chapter highlights opportunities for U.S. policy intervention and some near-term actions to support market-based changes.

THE CA SYSTEM

Before discussing some of the central risks in the CA system, this section first provides an overview of the online communications these authorities facilitate. This includes the authentication path, an overview of the structure of CAs, and additional detail on two other key players in the system: registration authorities and browser vendors.

Overview of Web Authentication

A CA is one actor in a web of trust that includes browsers, operating systems or servers, end users, and observers. There are differences between CAs and how their product—certificates—functions. CAs include companies, non-profits, governments, consortia, and other organizations that supply digital X.509 certificates to facilitate the trusted exchange of data online.[2] The fundamental concept behind a digital certificate is trust: How do you know which website's identity is valid? And by trusting that a certain website is what it claims to be, who else are you implicitly trusting? Instead of manually verifying the identity of each website, the vast majority of web users rely on CAs to do this for them. Importantly, CAs do nothing to evaluate the content of a website or its operators. A CA and its associated certificates act only to verify the identity of a site, a narrow but critical function for the internet.

When a client (such as a web browser) and a server want to communicate, the client has to first decide whether the server is who it represents to be. The client will initiate a request to the server using the Secure Sockets Layer (SSL) protocol, which Netscape devised in 1994 to encrypt the data path between a browser and a server as well as to verify the identity of the server.[3] In later years, SSL was standardized and upgraded to become Transport Layer Security (TLS), and fortunately more websites and online services are shifting to use TLS encryption as SSL vulnerabilities become widespread.[4]

SSL/TLS relies on public-key cryptography, which consists of generating a pair of keys, one public and the other private, between both parties in a communication session. Entities can share their public keys far and wide, but they keep their private keys secure as a guarantor of their identity. One party, Lisa, uses the public key of a second party, Tom, to encrypt a message that Lisa wants to send to Tom. Tom then uses his private key to decrypt the message. Public-key infrastructure (PKI) is the technology that binds a key to a specific entity. PKI also includes the actors that validate and use this structure.

Once the request is initiated between browser and server, the server provides the browser with an SSL/TLS certificate, which includes two components: (1) the server's public key, and (2) the CA's digital signature, which is a hash (or a fixed-length number generated from a string of text) of the data signed with the CA's private key. The browser authenticates the server by checking the CA's public key against its own list of "trusted root" CAs and using the CA's public key to decrypt the certificate contents. Once the trusted connection has been established, the browser generates a random number, the "session key," and sends it to the server. That shared session key, which is also secret, serves as the basis for a secure, encrypted channel for the communication session.

Overview of the Hierarchy

CAs operate within a hierarchy. At the highest level sit the "root" CAs, those that grant all the CAs in the branches extending from them the ability to sign certificates. A root certificate generally signs for intermediary certificates, which then in turn sign for others. As you go along the tree's branches (and as the power of each certificate decreases), validation requirements also decrease (see figure 13.1 for a visual representation of certificate authority hierarchy). Root CAs therefore have significant power over ever-expanding numbers of subordinate certificates and compromising a root CA can potentially impact millions of subordinate certificates, creating cascading effects throughout the trust hierarchy (see figure 8.2). At the same time, the likelihood of a compromised or bad subordinate CA increases as the number of subordinate CAs proliferate. Root CAs most commonly sign for separate intermediate CAs, allowing for easier revocation of a certificate if the keys associated with a particular intermediate CA are stolen and a degree of compartmentalization so customers can use different CAs for different functions on the web or internal networks.

Browser and operating system vendors automatically install a list of trusted root CAs in software, so that when an end user acquires a product, it comes preprogrammed to trust and allow access to a wide range of valid websites. Certificates of root CAs are automatically stored locally to verify

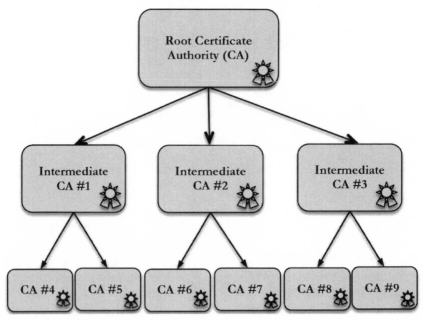

Figure 13.1   Hierarchical Certificate Authority Infrastructure

other certificates. If a root verifies and trusts a certain website, then the end
user's software will too. The onus is on the root CAs to continually audit and
verify that subordinate CAs are issuing valid certificates to legitimate website
owners. This hierarchy can become a web through a process known as cross-
certification where two root CAs each issue certificates verifying the other.
This allows intermediary and lower CAs within each of the two hierarchies
to trust each other's certificates. The result is a mesh of the two CA trees.
This provides resilience to the network as a whole; for example, if the first
root CA is removed for whatever reason the second can sign certificates in its
place.[5] It can also create problems if one of the root CAs is untrustworthy or
compromised by an attacker.

Enhancing Certificates

Not all certificates are created equal. Extended Validation (EV) certificates
provide a stronger level of authentication—High Assurance in certification
parlance—that a website belongs to its legal business owner. In order to
obtain an EV certificate, a business has to meet the EV Guidelines established by the third-party CA/Browser Forum.[6] These guidelines require CAs
to include more information about the business that requests and owns the

certificate, including the phone number, business address, and certificate requestor. The field of the certificate displays information about the business owner to the web browser and the user and EV certificates allow web browsers to display the website's name in green in the URL bar. Financial services and other high-traffic websites are the most likely to apply for and buy EV certificates to provide their customers the extra assurance that their data will be handled securely. Global growth of EV certificates has increased significantly since 2009.

The standards published for EV certs have evolved over time but are generally limited to easily supplied identity information. Part of the evaluation process for EV certs is actually confirming the existence of the company through third-party sources. The evaluation isn't independent, but it does draw on independent entities to verify some of the requirements. The EV form of a certificate is no more an attestation of a site's relative malicious or benign nature than a regular cert, adding only to the amount of detail used to verify the identity. Importantly, EV certs have somewhat spotty adherence to their data collection requirements and there are some CAs that continue to issue them even after failing public audits.[7]

Overview of the Market

The market for certificates is complex. First, there is a high barrier to entry for good quality certificates. Technical requirements for creating and managing the products, including certificates and keys, are onerous. A sample of the requirements includes secure archiving of keys, protection of certificate status (e.g., valid or revoked), and accurate tracking of certificate status. At any given point, certificate requests can be approved, rejected, or revoked.

Only a few players dominate the certificate market. According to NetCraft's 2015 SSL Server Survey, "Three certificate authorities (Symantec, Comodo, GoDaddy) account for three-quarters of all issued certificates on public-facing web servers."[8] These three CAs primarily issue the High Assurance EV certificates. Smaller CAs also abound, supplying cheaper "domain-validated" certificates that come with even fewer security features than their brand name competitors. Domain-validated certificates imply that the owner has some degree of control over the certificate, but not necessarily legal ownership over the site in question.

The CA market is also somewhat dysfunctional. The "buyers" of certificates, including companies and individuals, do not understand as much about the product—digital certificates—as the sellers do. This creates a lack of third-party visibility into what constitutes a good product and a good seller, creating conditions ripe for a market for lemons.[9] Browsers, operating systems, and users—the key actors that interact with CAs—automatically defer to the CA to determine who to trust. The burden of proof is on the CA to differentiate good from bad products and also protect itself from compromise or coercion.

THE PROBLEM: CHALLENGES IN THE SYSTEM

The CA system, which was originally the validator of identity on the internet, has revealed some widespread weaknesses. PKI and the CA system are rich fields for academic research and debate, so this chapter does not cover all weaknesses or currently proposed solutions in depth. Instead, the sections below illuminate two of the most significant problems facing the CA system: core structural vulnerabilities that could compromise the security of huge swaths of the internet and the likelihood of government abuse.

Structural Vulnerabilities in the CA System

Internet protocol programming weaknesses came to global attention after Google researchers disclosed the Heartbleed vulnerability in 2014.[10] While Heartbleed brought to light some fundamental certificate issues, it also led researchers to examine the SSL/TLS protocol, associated software libraries, and the CA system in greater depth. This section will discuss two of the major structural vulnerabilities in the CA system, the Weakest Link Problem and lack of scalability in certificate revocation.

The Weakest Link Problem

The Weakest Link Problem refers to the ability of one compromised CA to certify any domain on the web, essentially presenting a single point of failure for the entire network of trust.[11] If a rogue or compromised CA asserts that a bad website's identity is genuine, then the vast majority of web browsers will accept the CA's validation. This allows the user access to the site and potentially makes him or her vulnerable to surveillance or attacks by a malicious third party. The CA structure was originally built to allow a distributed trust model in verifying identities, but the possibility of compromise is a critical flaw. As a result, this flaw significantly decreases any advantage of buying a more expensive EV certificate over buying a cheap one, since all CAs are only as strong as the weakest link in the trust chain.

The Weakest Link Problem is significant, since it allows actors to take advantage of a security loophole. The entities that support trusted transactions are vulnerable to attacks, which undermines trust in the entire system. Some of the most compelling solutions include Accountable Key Infrastructure and DANE, discussed later in this chapter. Previous studies have also suggested instituting widely adopted rating systems to differentiate products, building on regional efforts such as WebTrust and European Telecommunications Standards Institute (ETSI) metrics.

Certificate Revocation

There are also fundamental problems with the certificate life cycle that need to be addressed. The Heartbleed Bug discovered in 2014 illustrates the time requirements and expense of certificate revocation, the process to blacklist a certificate and remove it from software's trusted list. Heartbleed is a vulnerability in the OpenSSL software library, which provides SSL/TLS protocols to websites like a sort of prefabricated software security package.[12] The OpenSSL library's implementation of TLS included a provision to maintain the same set of keys for a lengthy session, rather than renegotiating them intermittently. This means keeping the connection open, an extension called the "heartbeat," was flawed. A vulnerability in the heartbeat could allow an attacker to read data in the host server through a "leak" to find the server's private SSL encryption key. This key validates identity on the web and encrypts traffic. Possessing the private key will allow an attacker to impersonate the server and its owner without being detected. The memory leak involved could also include user names and passwords, content, and other collateral security information.

Heartbleed demonstrated the importance but also challenges behind widespread certificate revocation. The vulnerability left numerous certificates open to theft, requiring CAs to issue hundreds of thousands of replacements at a value of $100 million given the list prices of new certificates and the global scale of replacement.[13] Operating system and software makers controlled certificate removal, so as to avoid major disruption in operations. Replacing bad certificates with new ones isn't enough, however; the old ones must be blacklisted, or revoked, so they are no longer functional. This process of revocation has a much higher cost given the time it takes to identify and blacklist every affected certificate. As a result, some organizations chose to only replace their certificates. In 2014, NetCraft identified organizations as large and diverse as Yahoo and the U.S. Senate's large file transfer system that had stopped at replacing certificates but had not revoked the bad ones.[14] Any of these unrevoked certificates could still be compromised to validate undeserving websites.

Heartbleed also put strain on certificate revocation lists (CRL), the public audit trails that CAs periodically publish and organizations consult to track invalid certificates. CRLs are not comprehensive lists of bad certificates but compile the vast majority of them. Each CA provides a CRL, which browsers and companies can download at any point in time to check which certificates are valid and which are not. Widespread, systemic vulnerabilities including Heartbleed illustrate a major weakness of CRLs; with extensive revocation of certificates across the web, estimates put a revised CRL at over 100 megabytes (MB), a 35 percent increase in size after Heartbleed.[15] The bandwidth required to download the new CRL was prohibitive for many organizations and mobile users, especially when taken at a global scale. The internet security and services company CloudFlare estimated that the internet saw "40Gbps [gigabits per second] of net new traffic" from browsers downloading a CRL from CloudFlare's CA after Heartbleed, potentially adding hundreds of thousands of dollars to the CA's monthly bill for bandwidth.[16] For many CAs, this spike in demand can result in an unintentional denial of service on themselves, in addition to a steep increase in cost.

Online Certificate Status Protocol (OCSP) is an alternative or complement to CRL, allowing a client to consult an OCSP server to determine in real time whether a specific certificate is valid.[17] OCSP needs less bandwidth in order to report on certificate status, and the consulting entity needs less memory to cache the CRL.[18] OCSP is a more efficient way of checking certificate status, but some OCSP servers also rely on CRL lists and may therefore run into the same timing issues as CRLs. The cost, inconsistency, and lack of education about certificate revocation leave the internet vulnerable to the next disclosure of a systemic vulnerability.

Potential for Government Abuse

Some of the most vivid consequences of the Weakest Link Problem are seen in the potential for compromise by national governments. During the Arab Spring in 2011, a group hacked a CA called DigiNotar in order to release a bad certificate for all Google domains in an incident later dubbed "Operation Black Tulip."[19] The bad certificate allegedly allowed the Iranian government to intercept dissident communications in Gmail during August 2011. Later forensic analysis revealed that hundreds of bad certificates appeared on the web, and other services, including Mozilla and Yahoo, had been compromised as well. DigiNotar's large market presence meant that certificates all over the world were affected and had to be replaced and revoked.

In 2015, Google discovered unauthorized digital certificates for Google domains on the internet issued by the China Internet Network Information Center (CNNIC) root CA to MCS Holdings, an Egyptian intermediate CA.[20] MCS Holdings installed these certificates in software that could then impersonate Google services to intercept user communications through a man-in-the-middle attack. The certificates were ostensibly generated by accident but Google subsequently blacklisted all of CNNIC's certificates and chided the CA for "[delegating] substantial authority to an organization [MCS Holdings] that was not fit to hold it."[21] As an intermediate CA, MCS Holdings should have only been able to issue certificates for its own domains. Unfortunately, CNNIC's delegation of its root status to MCS Holdings meant that it had the full capability of a trusted root CA, which enabled it to issue certificates for external domains.[22] After conducting more research into the incident, Google announced that the blacklist would continue until CNNIC could implement better "technical and procedural controls," including Google's Certificate Transparency (CT) initiative.[23]

Immediately following Google's publication of the bad certificates, major browser makers including Mozilla and Microsoft entered into substantive deliberation about blacklisting the certificates. Mozilla blacklisted CNNIC on Firefox, but Microsoft only invalidated MCS Holdings certificates in Internet Explorer, without blacklisting CNNIC as the root CA.[24] Apple eventually whitelisted what it deemed to be trusted CNNIC certificates by creating "a mechanism to partially trust a CA by trusting only a set of certificates."[25] The whitelist enabled customers to revoke certain CNNIC certificates not on the list. The diversity in browser manufacturer responses may indicate different perspectives on CNNIC's responsibility and intentions with the crisis. All of these actions have a tremendous impact on web service, as any blacklist will prevent users from accessing numerous sites normally enabled by the CA.

One of the major problems with this scenario is that CNNIC was listed as a trusted root in major browsers and operating systems at the time, meaning the certificates it issued to MCS Holdings effectively acted as a proxy of this root authority and were automatically trusted. Roots like CNNIC enable other subordinate certificates to operate so if a root is compromised or in this case, if root status is granted to a proxy, then the subordinate certificates are vulnerable to compromise and manipulation. The consequences of this scenario were far less severe than the DigiNotar fallout, but show how easily an unintentional incident can pave the way for deliberate attacks.

Sensitivity toward national governments operating or authorizing bad certificates has heightened in the wake of the Arab Spring as well as the revelations of Edward Snowden. Governments are not consistently trustworthy as CAs, and countries may have the capability to put pressure on commercial CAs to sign for certain domains. Multiple discoveries of governments accidentally enabling or sponsoring compromises of CAs or certificates, such as in the Iran, Egypt, and China examples, are eroding trust in a government's ability to function as a CA.

PROPOSED SOLUTIONS

A variety of technical revisions have been proposed as a means to alleviate some of the core vulnerabilities of the CA system and potential for manipulation. While these each suggest changes in technology, the process of modifying and implementing each represents a complicated balance of public policy, business, and consumer interests.

Certificate Transparency

One public solution includes Google's Certificate Transparency, a "public, verifiable, append-only log."[26] CT "requires early disclosure and logging of publicly trusted SSL/TLS certificates," which in theory should alert the community to inappropriately issued certificates as each action to issue or change a certificate is publicly recorded.[27] In the China and Egypt examples discussed in the previous section, the use of CT could have helped to broadly communicate misuse of the fraudulent certificates.

CT can provide better visibility into CA operations, but doesn't directly prevent a compromise from taking place. Adoption has also proven difficult.[28] Google wants to enforce transparency requirements across all types of certificates and has taken steps to encourage use of CT. Websites that have not participated in CT—meaning they have not yet publicly logged new certificates or included a signed time stamp—are no longer able to ensure their user's URL bar appears green. Usually, having a green URL bar indicates a High Assurance EV certificate, in that the website owner has invested additional funds to prove their identity. Without the green bar, these owners are not seeing the return on their investment in more expensive certificates and security processes.

Domain Name System (DNS) Authentication for Named Entities

Domain Name System (DNS) Authentication for Named Entities (DANE) is a new internet protocol that would perform authentication and fix some of the flaws with CAs.[29] With DANE, the owner of a domain name could securely bind part of a TLS certificate to a DNS name, using a security protocol called Domain Name System Security Extensions (DNSSEC) to sign the record and prevent forgery, all without consulting a CA.[30] In this scenario, a client could ask a DNS zone operator which certificates are valid for a specific domain; the DNS operator could specify conditions around certificate use as well as around trusted root activity. DNS operators could also maintain a more dynamic status of trusted roots instead of the static CA lists currently baked into browsers and operating systems.

However, DANE would not avoid the single point of failure risk also inherent in CAs. DNS operators could be vulnerable to the same compromises that plague CAs, though the possible impact of a compromised operator would arguably be less than that of a compromised CA. In addition, the domain holder, who controls content in a given domain, differs from the domain operator, a third party that has administrative function for the domain. A domain operator could pose a vulnerability as the middleman between the domain holder and the client.[31] DANE implementation would further require widespread, consistent definition of conduct for domain operators as well as oversight by domain holders.

Let's Encrypt

In addition to changes which address transparency, alternative products are being developed that can supplement the small handful of large firms in the certificate marketplace. Let's Encrypt is a new CA, first made operational in 2015, developed by a consortium of industry partners through the Internet Security Research Group (ISRG), and now hosted by the Linux Foundation.[32] Created to facilitate the spread of TLS-protected communications, Let's Encrypt offers any organization the opportunity to set up a free server certificate for its domain.

Some of the Let's Encrypt features include publicly available records of all certificates ever issued, to address transparency concerns, as well as a new and open "protocol for automating the management of domain-validation certificates" currently in development with the Internet Engineering Task Force (IETF).[33] Given that Let's Encrypt only provides domain-validated certificates, it is not in direct competition with the CAs that issue the High Assurance EV certificates. Shortly after the public beta of Let's Encrypt, Amazon also announced it would be releasing free SSL certificates to Amazon Web Services users.[34] The launches of both Let's Encrypt and Amazon's new product signal that there will be growing pains but that the market is changing as web sites start to adopt the more secure TLS protocol.

OPPORTUNITIES FOR THE UNITED STATES

The critical focus for U.S. policymakers should be to encourage maximally pervasive and effective use of encryption on the internet. In response to the structural vulnerabilities in the authentication ecosystem and the potential impact of government activity, there are opportunities for the policy community to contribute to constructive change. Central concerns with the CA system include the potential abuse of CAs by governments, as well as the systemic lack of accountability and visibility into this activity. Ultimately, the ability to identify and isolate a bad actor to protect the rest of the system without causing significant collateral harm will increase overall resiliency. The goals for any policymaker, therefore, are to collaborate with civil society and private sector organizations to implement secure technical changes, decrease the required trust of any one node, and improve accountability for and visibility into those nodes. This section outlines three policy proposals that would support these goals.

Define a Global Norm for Government CA Behavior

First, the United States has an opportunity to define a new global norm regarding governments that operate as CAs (the United States included). Many agencies in the U.S. government currently sign for their own domains, and have requested inclusion in list of trusted root CAs maintained by groups such as Mozilla.[35] Given the fear that governments will abuse this power, based on past countries' action compromising certificates and intensified by the recent Snowden revelations, governments should not have the ability to sign for any domain aside from the domains they already own.[36] This behavior is detrimental to the new pyramid of influence discussed in the beginning of this chapter, and consequently, the new form of trust. Creating a new global norm for restrained government behavior among and with CAs is overdue.

The United States has the opportunity to recommend this new norm in international forums such as the IETF, International Corporation for Assigned Names and Numbers (ICANN), and other international bodies which administer internet functions. A new norm would establish limits for government action while performing the functions of a CA. Surveillance by nation-states is a timeless, permanent function of intelligence services; however, when governments sign for unauthorized domains, they weaken the system of trust as a whole. Even strategic intelligence gains would come at the prohibitive cost of prompting other actors to sign for unauthorized domains, and promoting more general insecurity in internet security governance around the globe.

Like many other global internet norms, the United States is caught between proposing changes that improve security and maintaining flexibility. However, while there is little direct benefit to the majority of U.S. agencies in expanding their roles as CAs, there is the potential for substantial gains in recommending a limited role for governments worldwide. A norm limiting a government's ability to sign certificates to only their own domains would have positive benefits for the larger information security governance community as it would define expected behaviors and help limit attacks on this core trust infrastructure. Browser vendors would be able to enforce this policy by rejecting government requests to serve as root CAs, and both governments and browser vendors would have additional clarity about their roles and boundaries of behavior.

Advocate for a Network of Validators

Another opportunity for U.S. policymakers is to enable the network of validators in the CA system and to define global metrics as part of a holistic policy to strengthen internet checks and balances. The role of third-party validators and observers is key to identifying suspicious activity online and drawing attention to encroachments on civil liberties.[37] Validators act to monitor and report on the reputation of CAs, allowing actors in the marketplace to choose between high- and low-performing companies. For example, the Electronic Frontier Foundation (EFF) collects certificates across the internet and monitors CA behavior through its SSL Observatory. EFF serves as a third-party or independent validator of certificate behavior, because of its routine reviews of certificates, CA market analysis, and research to propose improvements to the current CA system.[38] EFF observations are often after the fact or highlight ongoing threats, but its function of independently identifying risks and issues is key to the checks and balances that keep CAs trustworthy and effective.

The United States can make validators part of its strategy by establishing or encouraging grants for civil society organizations interested in pursuing this role, as well as encouraging private sector partners and third-party organizations in international forums to do the same. Establishing a position in favor of increasing the number and quality of validators can help bolster visibility into authentication, including certificate operations. As each validator grows in maturity, there will also be an opportunity to suggest metrics for CA behavior, possibly building off of those maintained by current evaluation companies like WebTrust, or developed anew such as Duration of Compromise (DoC), which would quantify how long a key has been compromised, and Duration of Unavailability (DoU), which would quantify impact to availability.[39] The United States can call for international partners to jointly evaluate and enforce metrics for CAs, incorporate them into grant programs, and encourage internal and external organizations including third-party validators to evaluate CAs based on the metrics and propose new metrics when needed.

Successful use of metrics would include CAs (both government and commercial) and alternatives to CAs, such as DNS zone operators, agreeing to hold themselves to these metrics and publishing information about their performance. Public log-based solutions should disseminate the metrics' taxonomy for organizations to use when identifying breaches of conduct and alerting the information security community to bad behavior. Relying on a common set of metrics, such as DoC, can also equip CAs and observers to assess and communicate the severity of risk from a particular compromise. Taken alone, validator's effectiveness is premised on the expectation that customers will respond to publicly available information on their CA's reputation but this is not always the case.[40] Supporting third parties and community-supported metrics would strengthen a peer-networked approach to trust in the internet and create additional levers for pressure on bad actors.

Commission a National Strategy

In recent years, the National Strategy for Trusted Identities in Cyberspace (NSTIC) under NIST has focused on building a new framework for identity management online to usher the United States into a post-password world. The NSTIC began through a public-private partnership focused on developing interoperable standards for identity and is a related trust-focused issue that has implications for the internet. The NSTIC pursued a long-term strategy of partnering with specialized industry groups and customers to pilot various forms of adoption. NSTIC outcomes include defining core principles for an Identity Ecosystem, issuing grants for companies working on innovative, pilot identity solutions, and building a foundation framework for companies to adopt and self-certify through displaying a trust icon.[41] One of the key principles of NSTIC is that change must be led and managed by the private sector and that the most effective role for government in this context is as a convener to call on stakeholders, define guiding principles, and strengthen the market as a consumer.

To facilitate similar change in the CA system, the government could sponsor a national strategy for digital authentication, where a joint public-private partnership would focus specifically on evaluating and extending an ecosystem to support current and future proposals. With a bevy of technical solutions but weaknesses to each and a requirement for global change, convening all technical proposals in the same community could help define guiding principles to simplify concurrent efforts and accelerate development through pilot projects. Given that CAs are a global market, the U.S. government can focus primarily on supporting economic change through a coherent national strategy for digital authentication. The market for certificates is already changing with innovative efforts like Let's Encrypt, which suggests there are opportunities to spur still-nascent competition. Thus far, industry bodies and organizations have independently created technical possibilities, but widespread adoption will require significant change management and education. The U.S. government can play a key role to manage the politics of policy change, helping to cement defining principles and convene a focused multistakeholder group.

CONCLUSION

The trusted network of CAs is critical to the health of cryptographically secure communication and authentication on the internet. However, this global system currently has several core vulnerabilities and potential for abuse which pose major challenges to long-term internet security. Whether accidental or deliberate, national governments are showing up ever more frequently in certificate compromises and the possibility for intentional surveillance on web communications undermines trust in the certificate system. To preserve, and future-proof, internet functionality the United States and the international community must invest in securing authentication mechanisms, despite whatever short-term gains for intelligence gathering might be lost. A spate of solutions developed by the private sector is changing the market for certificates, which is itself slowly expanding to cover nearly 2 percent of websites including all major retail, banking, and e-commerce portals.[42] This shift offers policymakers an opportunity to support the growing market by establishing a global norm for government CA operation, providing resources to validators to observe CA behaviors, thereby improving transparency, and developing a national strategy for digital authentication. As communications and influence become more distributed, policymakers should focus on stabilizing this new trust model; each node in the system should be trusted less, and supported more, to form a stronger system of distributed checks and balances and help ensure a more secure future for the internet.

CHAPTER HIGHLIGHTS

Internet Trust. Trust is the "psychological state comparing the intention to accept vulnerability based upon positive expectation of the intentions or behavior of another." On the internet, trust takes the form of individual entities accepting vulnerability by entering into a variety of relationships to provide or consume goods and services.

Certificate Authorities. One of the central mechanisms to the internet's system of trust is the digital certificate and the network of certificate authorities (CA) that validate them. Users worldwide rely on this system every day to decide whether or not they trust the identity of a certain website, to complete a secure transaction with their bank, file online taxes, or buy goods and services. When CAs function well, they help protect the authenticity and confidentiality of data transmitted through the internet.

CA Root Hierarchy. A root certificate can sign for intermediary certificates, which then in turn sign for others. As you go down the CA hierarchy (and as the power of each certificate decreases), validation requirements also decrease. If a root verifies and trusts a certain website, then the end user's software will too. The onus is on the root CAs to continually audit and verify that subordinate CAs are issuing valid certificates to legitimate website owners.

Replacing Compromised CAs. Replacing bad certificates with new ones isn't enough; the old ones must be blacklisted, or revoked. This process of revocation has a much higher cost, given the time it takes to identify and blacklist every affected certificate. The cost, inconsistency, and lack of education about certificate revocation leave the internet vulnerable.

Protecting Against Government Abuse. Sensitivity toward national governments operating or authorizing bad certificates has heightened. Governments are not consistently trustworthy as CAs, and countries may have the capability to put pressure on commercial CAs to sign for certain domains. Multiple discoveries of governments accidentally enabling or sponsoring compromises of CAs or certificates are eroding trust in a government's ability to function as a CA.

Bolster Network of Validators. The U.S. government should enable the network of validators in the CA system and define global metrics as part of a holistic policy to strengthen internet checks and balances. The role of third-party validators and observers is key to identifying suspicious activity online and drawing attention to encroachments on civil liberties. The United States can call for international partners to jointly evaluate and enforce metrics for CAs, incorporate them into grant programs, and encourage internal and external organizations, including third-party validators, to evaluate CAs on the basis of the metrics and propose new metrics when needed.

NOTES

1. Shu-Hua Chien, Ying-Hueih Chien, and Jyh-Jeng Wu, "Building Online Transaction Trust through a Two-Step Flow of Information Communication," *Journal of Global Information Technology Management* 16, no. 4 (2013): 8.

2. The X.509 is an ITU-T standard that "defines a standard certificate format" for public-key infrastructure. The IETF defines certificates as "data structures that bind

public key values to subjects." See IETF's *Internet X.509 Public Key Infrastructure Certificate and Certificate Revocation List (CRL) Profile:* https://tools.ietf.org/html/ rfc5280#page-10.

3. "History of SSL Certificate," *Extended Validation SSL Certificate*, Comodo CA Ltd.

4. Ilya Grigorik, "Chapter 4: Transport Layer Security," in *High Performance Browser Networking* (Sebastopol: O'Reilly Media, 2013), http://chimera.labs.oreilly. com/books/1230000000545/ch04.html.

5. Michael Alan Specter, "The Economics of Cryptographic Trust: Understanding Certificate Authorities" (Masters, MIT, 2016), http://www.mit.edu/~specter/ thesis.pdf.

6. "About EV SSL," *CA/Browser Forum*, https://cabforum.org/about-ev-ssl/.

7. "Netcraft BR, EV and CT Compliance Checking for Certificate Authorities," *Netcraft*, accessed April 26, 2016, http://www.netcraft.com/internet-data-mining/ netcraft-br-ev-and-ct-compliance-checking-for-certificate-authorities/; J. Clark and P. C. van Oorschot, "SoK: SSL and HTTPS: Revisiting Past Challenges and Evaluating Certificate Trust Model Enhancements," in *2013 IEEE Symposium on Security and Privacy (SP)*, 2013, 522, doi:10.1109/SP.2013.41.

8 "Counting SSL certificates," *Netcraft*, http://news.netcraft.com/archives/ 2015/05/13/counting-ssl-certificates.html (May 13, 2015).

9. George Akerlof, "The Market for 'Lemons': Quality Uncertainty and the Market Mechanism," *Quarterly Journal of Economics*, 89 pp. 488–500; James Backhouse, John Baptista, and Carol Hsu, "Rating Certificate Authorities: A Market Approach to the Lemons Problem," in *AMCIS 2004 Proceedings*, Paper 173, 1372, 2004, http://aisel.aisnet.org/amcis2004/173.

10. "The Heartbleed Bug," *Codenomicon*, http://heartbleed.com (April, 2014).

11. Nico Van Eijk and Axel Arnbak. "Certificate Authority Collapse: Regulating Systemic Vulnerabilities in the HTTPS Value Chain," *TRPC*, http://cyber.law.harvard. edu/events/2012/09/vaneijk_arnbak (2012).

12. "The Heartbleed Bug," *Codenomicon*, http://heartbleed.com (April, 2014).

13. "Heartbleed: Revoke! The Time Is Nigh!" *Netcraft*, http://news.netcraft.com/ archives/2014/04/15/revoke-the-time-is-nigh.html. (April 15, 2014).

14. Ibid.

15. Ibid.

16. Matthew Prince, "The Hidden Costs of Heartbleed," *CloudFlare*, https://blog. cloudflare.com/the-hard-costs-of-heartbleed/ (April 17, 2014).

17. Ilya Grigorik, "Chapter 4: Transport Layer Security," in *High Performance Browser Networking* (Sebastopol, CA: O'Reilly Media, 2013), http://chimera.labs. oreilly.com/books/1230000000545/ch04.html.

18. "Public Key Infrastructure Certificate Revocation List vs. Online Certificate Status Protocol," *Cisco Systems, Inc.,* http://www.cisco.com/c/dam/en/us/prod-ucts/collateral/ios-nx-os-software/public-key-infrastructure-pki/product_data_shee-t0900aecd80313df4.pdf.

19. "Final Report on DigiNotar Hack Shows Total Compromise of CA Servers,"*Threatpost*, https://threatpost.com/final-report-diginotar-hack-shows-total-compromise-ca-servers-103112/77170/ (October 31, 2012).

20. Adam Langley, "Maintaining Digital Certificate Security," *Google Online Security Blog*, https://googleonlinesecurity.blogspot.com.au/2015/03/maintaining-digital-certificate-security.html (March 23, 2015).

21. Ibid.

22. Liam Tung, "Google boots China's main digital certificate authority CNNIC," *ZDNet*, http://www.zdnet.com/article/google-banishes-chinas-main-digital-certificate-authority-cnnic/ (April 2, 2015).

23 Adam Langley, "Maintaining Digital Certificate Security," *Google Online Security Blog*, https://googleonlinesecurity.blogspot.com.au/2015/03/maintaining-digital-certificate-security.html (March 23, 2015); Google also noted that pinning would have mitigated the incident. Pinning refers to the practice where each website features a "pin" that lists which certificates are correct for that site. Each pin has an expiration date to prevent development of fraudulent pins. The browser must reject any certificate not included in the website's list. Critics of pinning contend that pins are mostly just transference of risk from CAs to an equally centralized solution (the browser).

24. Dan Goodin, "Google Chrome will banish Chinese certificate authority for breach of trust" [Updated], *Ars Technica*, http://arstechnica.com/security/2015/04/google-chrome-will-banish-chinese-certificate-authority-for-breach-of-trust/ (April 1, 2015); Joel Hruska, "Apple, Microsoft buck trend, refuse to block unauthorized Chinese root certificates," *Extreme Tech*, http://www.extremetech.com/computing/203049-apple-microsoft-buck-trend-refuse-to-block-unauthorized-chinese-root-certificates (April 9, 2015).

25. "About the security partial trust allow list,"
https://support.apple.com/en-gb/HT204938.

26. Ben Laurie, "Certificate Transparency," *ACM Queue*, https://queue.acm.org/detail.cfm?id=2668154 (September 8, 2014).

27. Ben Wilson, "In the Wake of Unauthorized Certificate Issuance by the Indian CA NIC, Can Government Still Be Considered 'Trusted Third Parties?'" *CA Security Council RSS*, https://casecurity.org/2014/07/24/unauthorized-certificate-issuance/ (July 24, 2014).

28. British cybersecurity firm Netcraft finds a lot of major certificate issuers aren't bothering. No transparency, no green bar. No green bar, and websites may well have not shelled out for their expensive (around $1,000 a year) certificates, as far as Chrome is concerned. Consumers are affected too, since the identity validation for a lock-icon-only certificate is minimal. Even hackers have obtained them for their fake-looking sites. Google wants to eventually make transparency a requirement for all types of digital certificates. Netcraft: http://bit.ly/1NFFnCx.

29. "The DNS-Based Authentication of Named Entities (DANE) Transport Layer Security (TLS) Protocol: TLSA," RFC 6698, https://tools.ietf.org/html/rfc6698.

30. Richard L. Barnes, "DANE: Taking TLS Authentication to the Next Level Using DNSSEC," *IETF Journal*, http://www.internetsociety.org/articles/dane-taking-tls-authentication-next-level-using-dnssec (October, 2011).

31 Ibid.

32. "Let's Encrypt: Delivering SSL/TLS Everywhere!," *Lets Encrypt Blog*, https://letsencrypt.org/2014/11/18/announcing-lets-encrypt.html (November 18, 2014).

33. "Let's encrypt/acme-spec," *GitHub*, https://github.com/letsencrypt/acme-spec.

34. Chris Brook, "Amazon Certificate Manager Brings Free SSL Certificates to AWS Users," *Threatpost*, https://threatpost.com/amazon-certificate-manager-brings-free-ssl-certs-to-aws-users/116025/ (January 26, 2016).

35. Glenn Fleishman, "The Huge Web Security Loophole that Most People Don't Know About and How It's Being Fixed," *Fast Company*, http://www.fastcompany.com/3042030/tech-forecast/the-huge-web-security-loophole-that-most-people-dont-know-about-and-how-its-be (February 19, 2015).

36. Ben Wilson, "In the Wake of Unauthorized Certificate Issuance by the Indian CA NIC, Can Government Still Be Considered 'Trusted Third Parties?'" *CA Security Council RSS*, https://casecurity.org/2014/07/24/unauthorized-certificate-issuance/ (July 24, 2014).

37. Joseph Bonneau, "What Happened with Crypto This Year? 2015 in Review," *Electronic Frontier Foundation*, https://www.eff.org/deeplinks/2015/12/technical-crypto-2015-review (December 27, 2015); Tiffany Kim, Hyun-Jin et al., "Accountable Key Infrastructure (AKI): A Proposal for a Public-Key Validation Infrastructure," *CyLab / Carnegie Mellon University*, May 13–17, 2013, Rio de Janeiro, Brazil.

38. EFF SSL Observatory, *Electronic Frontier Foundation*, https://www.eff.org/observatory; "Sovereign Keys: A Proposal to Make HTTPS and Email More Secure," *Electronic Frontier Foundation*, https://www.eff.org/deeplinks/2011/11/sovereign-keys-proposal-make-https-and-email-more-secure (November 28, 2011).

39. Tiffany Kim, Hyun-Jin et al., "Accountable Key Infrastructure (AKI): A Proposal for a Public-Key Validation Infrastructure," *CyLab/Carnegie Mellon University*, May 13–17, 2013, Rio de Janeiro, Brazil.

40. Michael Alan Specter, "The Economics of Cryptographic Trust: Understanding Certificate Authorities"

41. "FAQ's," *National Strategy for Trusted Identities in Cyberspace*, http://www.nist.gov/nstic/faqs.html.

42. Zakir Durumeric et al., "Analysis of the HTTPS Certificate Ecosystem," in *Proceedings of the 2013 Conference on Internet Measurement Conference* (ACM, 2013), 291–304, http://dl.acm.org/citation.cfm?id=2504755.

Chapter 14

Multistakeholder Approaches to Cybersecurity Challenges

Allan Friedman and Jonah F. Hill*

The internet† presents one of the most unique and dynamic environments for public policy and governance. By design, the internet contains few centralized points of control. The few centralized points that do exist historically have been managed not by governments, but through the voluntary engagement by and contributions of companies, organizations, and individual users with a stake in the evolution of the network. This decentralized governance model has proven itself to be an amazingly effective—if at times imperfect—enabler of innovation and growth. By leaving such a wide array of governance decisions to the community of internet stakeholders, and not to national governments or other centralized authorities, the so-called "multistakeholder" model of internet governance has allowed for a degree of coordination and adaptiveness unimaginable in a system with greater top-down control. Given the successes of the "multistakeholder" approach in the global internet governance space, the question before us is this: What lessons might be drawn from the structures and features of global multistakeholder internet governance and applied to cybersecurity?

As the volume of digital commerce and social interaction has grown exponentially, the potential consequences of malicious activity have made security

---

* The views expressed in this chapter are solely the views of the authors, in their private capacity and based on their extensive experience in internet policy and cybersecurity, and do not represent the views of any government agency.

† Both the authors, as a general matter, advocate for the capitalization of the word, "Internet," but deferred to the editors per their preference. We note, however, that while it may seem trivial to some, capitalization of the word does carry some significance. We believe that the Internet is a proper noun, a single coordinated network system, one unified by shared technical protocols and standards and coordinated through the group of global multistakeholder governance organizations. To leave it lower case, we believe, contradicts the fact that there is only one Internet and empowers those who might wish to fracture the existing Internet into multiple, smaller, "internets."

a priority to a wide range of responsible parties, from governments protecting their citizens to companies safeguarding customers. These interests continue to multiply, and sometimes compete. The challenge of coordinating and reaching agreement on these policy approaches and solutions resembles the hurdles of governing the internet itself, and thus presents a promising test case for the kind of multistakeholder approaches developed in the world of internet security governance. This chapter summarizes the history and key concepts of the multistakeholder approach, highlighting both domestic and international dimensions through the lens of a U.S. government agency which has utilized the practice of multistakeholder governance for technology to help further technology policy. We offer several examples of security challenges being addressed by bringing stakeholders together.

The Internet and Multistakeholder Governance

The internet famously has no central government. From its earliest days as a university research project, up to the present day, the internet has been "governed" by a diverse assortment of actors, institutions, and processes. Academics and engineers, telecommunications companies and software developers, hackers, government agencies, and international organizations have all played a role in developing and expanding the network.[1] No single actor has the authority to dictate how the internet will develop; no one party decides what rules will govern it.

But at a deeper, and perhaps more philosophical, level the internet has also been shaped by a core set of underlying principles, norms, and values that have acted as guideposts for the internet's evolution and maturation. These principles are not enshrined in any single document or rulebook; there is no "constitution" for the internet.[2] Yet from the earliest days of the network there have been broadly agreed-upon values that have formed the normative basis of both the internet's technical architecture and the institutions, processes, and rules that manage its standards and critical resources.

The principles vary according to particular organizations or individuals, but broadly they include:[3]

- *Decentralization* (the network topology should be flat and peer-to-peer, and resistant to centralized control);
- *Interoperability* (the widest range of systems, technologies, and services should be able to send information to, and accept information from, the widest range of other systems, technologies, and services);
- *Heterogeneity* (a diversity of hardware, software, protocols, applications, information, and individuals should be able to access and benefit from the network);

- *Freedom* (users should have the greatest possible choice about the applications and services they use and which lawful content they can access, create, or share with others);
- *Inclusiveness* (the network should be available to all applications, services, technologies, and users without the permission of "gatekeepers" or intermediaries); and
- *Resilience* (the network should provide and maintain service in the face of faults and challenges to normal operation). [4]

Accepting the premise that adherence to these underlying values and principles has been responsible for the internet's great success and growth over the past decades, the question becomes: *What governance mechanisms are best suited to encourage and reinforce these values?*

Clearly the answer to that question will depend upon the nature of the governance issue under consideration. There can be no one-size-fits-all answer to the wide range of technical, social, and administrative challenges that arise in the internet context. The management of critical internet resources, the standardization of the internet's protocols, and the development of online behavioral norms, all require specifically tailored governance solutions. Unique problems require correspondingly unique responses.

Yet it is also clear that policymaking processes incorporating and reflecting the values that have led to the success of the internet are the kinds of processes most likely to generate outcomes consistent with those values. To put it another way, just as democratic systems of governance are the systems most likely to produce democratic outcomes, so too are open and inclusive internet governance processes the approach most likely to produce open and inclusive outcomes.

The Multistakeholder Approach

It is with this commitment to inclusiveness that the United States—alongside like-minded governments, civil society groups, technologists, and industry leaders—has turned to "multistakeholder models, approaches, or processes" as the preferred mode of internet governance. The reasons are many and largely self-evident: similar to the internet itself, multistakeholder approaches are characterized by open participation and decentralized structures. They enable a wide range of stakeholders to participate in the governance process, fostering a free market of opinions and ideas. They are systems best suited to foster an open, inclusive, and innovative network environment, precisely because they themselves are open, inclusive, and innovative.

This is not merely a theoretical exercise. Multistakeholder approaches have repeatedly proven themselves to be better suited to rapidly changing technologies, business practices, and markets than traditional regulatory or legislative models. Complex policy issues often take years to make their way over the regulatory and legislative hurdles found in Washington, Brussels, or Geneva. Many efforts at traditional policymaking end in failure. The few that do reach a conclusion commonly aim to solve a problem that no longer exists, or has been overtaken by newer issues, which need urgently to be addressed.

For this reason, members of the U.S. executive and legislative branches have been resolute in their advocacy for the multistakeholder approach for internet governance. The Obama administration has made support for multistakeholder internet governance a cornerstone of its 2011 International Strategy for Cyberspace, and the U.S. Congress in 2012 declared its unanimous, bipartisan, commitment to "preserve and advance the successful multistakeholder model that governs the internet."[5]

But what specifically does the term "multistakeholder model" imply? There is no one single conceptualization of what is appropriately viewed as a "multistakeholder model." There are instead numerous models currently in use today, each with its own unique contours. Few if any of the models currently in use are static. They are constantly evolving to meet the new and yet uncharted governance challenges.[6]

Accordingly the term "multistakeholder model," which may imply that there is solely one exclusive model, has fallen out of favor in some circles. Instead, the term, "multistakeholder approach," or "multistakeholder process" may be better suited to describe the reality that there are multiple ways of conducting a multistakeholder engagement (although, for practicality's sake, the terms are often used interchangeably). Multistakeholder approaches encompass a range of procedures, formats, resolution mechanisms, communication strategies, and outcomes. In the same way that democratic governments may follow a parliamentary or a presidential system of governance, so too do multistakeholder approaches vary and must be adapted to fit a particular governance question. Certain models lead to decisions, others are merely deliberative; some have established membership criteria, others allow anyone to participate; some models are intended to last decades, others are one-off processes designed to address a specific challenge of the day.

The diversity of multistakeholder approaches is revealed perhaps most comprehensively in a study by the Global Network of Internet and Society Research Centers and the Berkman Center for Internet and Society at Harvard University, entitled "Multistakeholder as Governance Groups: Observations from Case Studies."[7] The report analyzes twelve geographically and topically diverse case studies of internet, as well as non-internet, multistakeholder governance processes, ranging from water resource management in the Volta River Basin in West Africa, to arbitration of disputes within the Bitcoin community. Their research was conducted with an eye toward describing the formation, operation, and critical success factors for multistakeholder governance. Based on their research, the study's authors unambiguously conclude that "there is no single best-fit model for multistakeholder governance groups that can be applied in all instances."

Yet despite the efforts to highlight the range of multistakeholder approaches (or even perhaps because of them), there is no agreed-upon definition of "multistakeholder governance." Laura DeNardis and Mark Raymond have constructed a taxonomy of multistakeholder processes in which different approaches are defined by types of actors involved and the nature of the authority relations between those actors.[8] They argue that in order for a process or organization to qualify as multistakeholder, at least two broad categories of actors, such as states, civil society, firms, and intergovernmental organizations, must be involved.

Ultimately, arriving at an agreed-upon definition of multistakeholder governance may be unnecessary. Indeed, it may even be detrimental in that an agreed-upon definition could ossify thinking on how multistakeholder processes can and should function, and thus hamper their evolution and capacity for adaptation to new settings. The advantages of multistakeholder model are found in its flexibility and adaptability, so it benefits the approach to keep it loosely defined, yet sufficiently rooted in key principles to allow it to serve its purposes.

Still, there are undeniably benefits in providing at least a rough outline of a definition. The fact of the matter is that the term "multistakeholder" is often used haphazardly. It has become a bit of a buzzword in governance circles. It may be useful to articulate an outline of a definition that serves both to reinforce the internet's core values and to protect the term "multistakeholder" from becoming little more than a marketing meme for governance schemes. Toward that end, NTIA might view an "authentic" multistakeholder process as one that,

- Stakeholder-driven: Stakeholders determine the process and decisions, from agenda setting to workflow, rather than simply fulfilling advisory role;
- Openness: Includes and integrates the viewpoints of a diverse range of stakeholders, importantly the viewpoints of those stakeholders who hold specialized expertise applicable to the governance challenge at hand;
- Transparency: Creates an environment of trust, legitimacy, and accountability, most importantly by maintaining a high degree of transparency; and
- Consensus: Produces outcomes (when outcomes are desirable) that are consensus-based, arrived at by compromise, and are a win-win for the greatest number or diversity of stakeholders.

Once again, just as this chapter cautions against treating the principles that have defined the internet's growth as fixed doctrine, likewise it would be advisable not to view these distinguishing characteristics of multistakeholder process as anything more than current thinking of the day. They are not written in stone but they are reflective of the actual practice of multistake-holder governance, and of the views of various multistakeholder community. We would argue that they represent at least the contours of an ideal multi-stakeholder process.

Viewing these five characteristics together, it becomes clear why multistakeholder models are so advantageous and how they serve to promote an internet environment consistent with the core internet values listed above (i.e., decentralization, interoperability, heterogeneity, freedom, inclusiveness, and resilience). When utilized well, the multistakeholder approach creates practices and outcomes that are effective, accountable, transparent, expert-driven, and viewed as legitimate by a majority of stakeholders.

Domestic Applications of the Multistakeholder Approach

Multistakeholder governance approaches have historically been employed for the global internet governance functions, such as the management of the Domain Name System and standardization of internet technical protocols. Given its confidence in the multistakeholder approach, the U.S. government in recent years has begun applying it to domestic internet policymaking. One particular champion of this policy approach is the National Telecommunica-tions and Information Administration (NTIA), part of the U.S. Department of Commerce. NTIA has made use of multistakeholder processes to address a range of internet and technology policy questions, from copyright protec-tion, to privacy, and, most recently, to cybersecurity. The agency has found that these processes have successfully brought diverse stakeholders together to identify and promulgate industry best practices and codes of conduct for commercial activity. They have proven themselves an effective means to advance the public interest without the need for conventional regulatory rulemaking, thus sidestepping the risks top-down governance systems often pose to innovation. They help advance domestic technology policy by allow-ing stakeholders themselves to develop solutions, to agree to the best way forward without the need for a government mandate that will likely be less flexible and slower to evolve.

Indeed, the focus of these domestic multistakeholder initiatives is on fos-tering shared solutions. Their success rests on the belief of the participants that a shared solution is better than no solution. This follows from the net-worked world of global internet governance, where a common resolution is vital for interoperativity. In these situations, no single actor can unilaterally determine effective standards or practices for the broader ecosystem, but a large enough determined minority can disrupt gains from collective action by refusing to participate in the community to work for a shared solution. For the internet to function as a global network, all stakeholders must use the same suite of protocols and naming conventions. To ensure that these standards and protocols favor the greatest number of stakeholders it is crucial that decisions are made by consensus and in an open and transparent way so that as many stakeholders are "bought into" the system as possible.

In domestic technology policy, the multistakeholder approach fits similarly well in situations where disparate players can find room to work together better. In game theory terms, these are "coordination games," where each player would like to work together, but no one wants to take on the full risks of moving toward a collaborative posture, without an understanding that they will have some potential reward for these costs.[9] One simple analogy might be a bunch of kids who all want to be in a swimming pool, but no one wants to be the first to jump in. The multistakeholder model allows them to coordinate the count in a fair and open environment. In the policy world, this approach has been applied to questions of copyright, privacy, and cybersecurity.

In the area of copyright, for instance, NTIA has, together with the U.S. Patent and Trademark Office (USPTO), convened a multistakeholder process to improve the operation of Digital Millennium Copyright Act (DMCA). The DMCA has a provision that allows copyright owners to notify web publishers that they are hosting copyrighted content. In exchange for responding to these notices, the law protects publishers from the liability of infringement. As a result, the DMCA forces web publishers and copyright owners to work together, despite the fact that they often see each other as natural adversaries in their business models.

The goal of the DMCA multistakeholder process was to enable better, more efficient, and more productive interactions between these two rival camps in the copyright world. Stakeholders set out to identify best practices and/or to produce voluntary agreements for improving the operation of the notice-and-takedown system, without the need for legislative or regulatory action. Launched in March 2014, the process brought together participants across a wide range of stakeholder communities, from rights holders to individual creators, service providers of different sizes, and consumer and public interest representatives. The meetings considered a broad range of issues, and, in April 2015, adopted a nonbinding set of principles entitled, "Good, Bad and Situational Practices for the DMCA Notice-and-Takedowns," as well as a standardized copyright infringement notice submission process.[10] It was an important step toward improving the operation of the DMCA, which for years had been hampered by ineffective coordination and persistent disagreement between rights-holders and hosting providers.

This approach is useful for privacy as well. NTIA has also organized a series of multistakeholder processes to develop codes of conduct that specify how the White House's *Consumer Privacy Bill of Rights* applies in specific business contexts.[11] The first of these forums focused on the development of a code of conduct for the commercial use of personal data for applications on mobile devices, such as smartphones.[12] Mobile applications pose distinct consumer privacy challenges and the practices surrounding disclosure of consumer data privacy policies for mobile apps had not kept pace with rapid developments in technology and business models. Hundreds of stakeholders participated, including developers of mobile apps, providers of sophisticated interactive services for mobile devices (such as those utilizing HTML5 to access mobile application programming interfaces [APIs]), as well as consumer protection and civil liberties groups. The code of conduct took a year of meetings to draft and not every participant were pleased with the final outcome, but the process enabled industry and civil society groups to make significant progress on an emerging privacy issue for which traditional policymaking and regulatory approaches had been unable to effectively address.

Across all of these various efforts, from copyright, to privacy, to cybersecurity, NTIA has stressed the values behind the multistakeholder approach, working to ensure the processes are stakeholder driven, reflective of input from the broadest array of stakeholders possible, and open to any participant. Critically, all of NTIA's processes have been highly transparent—with meetings webcast and minutes readily available online—and the outcomes consensus-based and voluntary (i.e., non-binding and non-mandated.).

At the same time, any such process, consistent with the essential characteristics of the multistakeholder model, to remain flexible and to allow each process to adapt to fit the requirements of each unique governance challenge. No two processes have been the same. In the case of the mobile apps, for instance, the code of conduct, while voluntary, can become binding on companies that clearly adopt the code (a commitment that is then enforceable by the Federal Trade Commission). The DMCA process, in contrast, developed a set of principles and a standardized format for notice-and-takedown submissions. These principles were merely meant to provide industry with guidance and best practices. This flexibility of approach, bounded within the core tenets of an "authentic" multistakeholder model, has paid tremendous dividends, helping to create a more innovative, productive, and civically focused technology environment today and into the future.

The Multistakeholder Approach in Security: The Vulnerability Disclosure Example

Just as the multistakeholder approach can be applied to questions of intellectual property protection and digital privacy, there is good reason to believe that it can help address contentious security challenges as well. The cybersecurity challenge is one often characterized by market failures, where potential solutions are available but stakeholders have yet to coalesce around them. Again, the goal is not to dictate a particular solution, but to help stakeholders identify and build a shared vision. When the status quo is increasingly unsustainable, this approach can help identify potential directions and allow stakeholders to crystalize around potential solutions.

A clear example of this is in the disagreements between software vendors and researchers on vulnerability disclosure. There is widespread recognition that information technology systems—from traditional software to popular websites and cloud platforms to embedded devices—will never be completely secure. It is inevitable that vulnerabilities will be discovered, as a key aspect of security research as well as an integral part of the burgeoning security industry. By reporting flaws to the vendors, the bug can be fixed and the software will be more secure as a result.

Unfortunately, this issue of vulnerability disclosure has traditionally been a source of controversy and debate. On one side, many argue that vendors and other organizations responsible for maintaining software don't always respond quickly, or even at all, to the concerns raised by these discoveries. In some instances, companies have even sued researchers for violating the terms of service and copyright of their products by working to discover the vulnerability.[13] This creates a conflict for the researchers who discover a vulnerability. Do they tell no one and hope for the best, or tell the world and expect the company to respond to public pressure to create and issue a patch?

For their part, vendors may not know the best way to respond. Understanding the vulnerability, and developing a fix may be simple, or it may take months. The firm may not feel comfortable explaining the delay to the researcher, especially when the researcher is not aware of just how critical the bug might be. Yet the risks of "full disclosure," where researchers make the bug information available to the public and the vendor simultaneously, are also significant. This approach can expose countless users to attacks if the vendor is unable to develop, test, and deploy protections or mitigations in time.

This debate has gone on for two decades, and often rests on assumptions each side makes about the other. Vendors can use laws such as the DMCA or the Computer Fraud and Abuse Act (CFAA) to deter researchers who may, in the course of finding a vulnerability, damage other interests, reducing trust across the entire community. Similarly, a small cohort of researchers who flagrantly ignore the interests of vendors can sow distrust, even with those eager to collaborate. All the while, the stakes have been growing. Vulnerabilities are no longer just the domain of advanced software companies. We are heading toward a world where everyone is a software provider or manager: banks run complex websites; retail firms have elaborate back-end systems; the very cars we drive are computers on wheels.

Where can this debate go from here? A precarious, often adversarial relationship could continue—as some firms embrace bug bounties (open calls for researchers to find and receive compensation for discovered software vulnerabilities) as a means of improving their product's security while others resist and ignore or even seek to prosecute disclosure. Some researchers will try to improve security through collaboration, while others will continue to push for change by publicly naming and shaming bad security practices, even at the risk of collateral damage. Alternatively, if the collateral damage grows too high, one can imagine a crackdown on freelance security research and vulnerability discovery outside of direct vendor control. This move to punish discovery and disclosure would drive the activity underground and may well result in a surge of vulnerabilities available on the malware market.[14] Some might argue for a mandate that companies of all shapes and sizes employ a bug bounty program, regardless of whether these organizations are ready or if such a security process would fit. Clearly none of these forced outcomes is desirable.

Hoping to bridge the divide between stakeholders, NTIA has engaged researchers, vendors, and civil society in an ongoing discussion about the core values and virtues of a vulnerability disclosure policy. This process is helping stakeholders to identify what their common challenges are and works with them to address each in turn, instead of establishing a single overarching solution. By bringing different parts of the community together, the multi-stakeholder initiative seeks to foster empathy, to help different stakeholders understand the motivations and assumptions of each party. This, in turn, fosters trust as a foundational step for collaboration. For vulnerability disclosure, the process' outcome may take the form of guidance to firms and researchers, helping to diffuse good practices and solutions throughout the security eco-system. The structure of the process itself helps determine both the outcome and the merits of the outcome.

The keys to generating a positive outcome, and the success of that outcome are, in part, a function of the process itself. As was noted above, the most effective processes rest on the principles of multistakeholder governance developed in the expansion of the internet writ large: *openness, consensus, and transparency.*

Openness is more than having an open door to the room where conversation is taking place. Facilitators, NTIA in this case, have to take on the burden to seek out participants, particularly from traditionally underrepresented communities. Particular challenges include insufficient awareness of the process, lack of trust in the process or other stakeholders, and a paucity of funds to set up vulnerability management and disclosure programs. For the vulnerability disclosure process, NTIA worked hard to find security researchers, especially those who were independent. It is easier for a government process to attract senior staff from large companies who work well with government officials. Fostering participation from security researchers distrustful of the motives of both government and large corporations requires a dedicated effort to build personal relationships with potential participants.

Consensus is a decision-making tool but also key to moving from discussion to outcome in the multistakeholder approach. Anyone can participate so using basic majority-voting to determine outcomes doesn't necessarily take into account all interests or the content of previous debate. Rather, consensus can help balance between the dangers of a group being held captive by a particular individual or organization and strict majoritarianism. If a major set of stakeholders objects to a proposal, then the group cannot claim to have consensus.

Transparency forms the foundation of the process by establishing legitimacy through accessible dialogue. Smoke-filled rooms are a recipe for mistrust and discord but being able to point to concerns of different participants that have been addressed helps to bridge different value systems. In practice, this is contingent upon ensuring every stakeholder is able to engage with each other and tracking progress over time as participants weigh-in. NTIA webcasts its meetings, allows remote participation, and publishes working documents, so that those who cannot attend in person because of time or resource constraints can still engage.

One challenge in the vulnerability disclosure process is that the topic covers a wide swath of issues, all of which interact, making conversations difficult to scope. The stakeholders in the on-going process addressed this by forming three subject-specific working groups within the larger multistakeholder process, allowing participants with strong concerns to focus on those particular issues before sharing them out with the broader community. This also helped overcome the sensitivity of regulated companies in an atmosphere where security researchers and policymakers comingled, as working groups could have discussion in smaller, trusted environments. Transparency creates trust and accessibility thereby helping to drive openness and create conditions for consensus.

Security and the Multistakeholder Approach

NTIA by no means has a monopoly on the use of the multistakeholder process to promote security. There are other areas where different stakeholders have been brought together to identify and address security issues. Perhaps the largest process thus far is the Cybersecurity Framework, developed by NTIA's sister agency in the Department of Commerce, the National Institute for Standards and Technology (NIST).[15] In 2013, recognizing the importance of securing U.S. critical infrastructure, President Obama issued Executive Order 13636, "Improving Critical Infrastructure Cybersecurity."[16] This Order directed NIST to work with stakeholders to develop a voluntary framework of "standards, methodologies, procedures, and processes that align policy, business, and technological approaches to address cyber risks."

This process yielded one of the foundational documents for cybersecurity from the Administration. It was a massive undertaking, with a public review and comment period, and six public workshops. These workshops were held across the country to maximize participation and input. It was large enough that NIST itself held the pen, in contrast to the NTIA approach where stakeholders themselves do all drafting. Still, NIST worked hard to build the legitimacy of the outcome through the process. It gathered feedback, shared drafts and iterated versions for transparency, and traveled and used web tools to ensure openness. The final document, the Cybersecurity Framework, has been used by actors across industries, and was designed to be adapted to a wide range of situations. In 2016, NIST used public comments and more public meetings to ask stakeholders from government, business, and the research community whether and how the Framework should evolve over time.

The use of the multistakeholder approach is not limited to governments. The Online Trust Alliance is an industry membership group of over fifty internet-oriented firms ranging from some of the largest online firms to small start-ups. The organization focuses on fostering trust online through improving privacy and security through developing and fostering best practices in a range of issues. Using collaborative tools, and bringing together their own members from across a range of business interests and technical capabilities, OTA developed an Internet of Things (IoT) Trust Framework for security, privacy, and sustainability in IoT.[17] While participants in a membership-driven trade organization developed the document, it still has multiple features of a multistakeholder process. Internally, the OTA working group that developed comprised a broad and diverse set of interests. After its development, OTA has been committed to sharing the Trust Framework, and seeking feedback from stakeholders outside the membership, including other firms, trade groups, and government agencies.

More generally, there are a host of security issues that cannot be resolved through technical innovation alone, and span across multiple organizations, sectors, and stakeholder groups. These issues can benefit from a shared understanding, best practices, or sometimes even just a common, universal definition. With the right language or framework, industry can collaborate across traditional barriers, using the power of the free market to actually resolve the issue at hand. In these instances, the role of the convener is to act as a catalyst.

CONCLUSION

There are limitations and challenges in the multistakeholder approach. The approach doesn't apply well to every security challenge. Where the problem at hand takes the form of a zero-sum game, the losses of one party translate directly to the gains of another. In these situations, consensus and transparency can only overcome so much embedded self-interest. Engaging a wide array of stakeholders is also less useful when there is a clearly identified set of participants with strong interest in preserving the status quo, or little interest in any outcome that doesn't wholly conform to their vision. In these instances, not only is consensus difficult, but the initial engagement might even fail.

There are also some policy questions that simply don't lend themselves to voluntary collective action. While the multistakeholder approach can be more efficient than administrative rulemaking or the legislative process it requires a steady experienced hand in managing personalities and competing agendas. It won't replace all forms of policymaking, It won't replace all forms of policymaking, but it has proved itself to be valuable in a diversity of contexts.

Still, given a wide range of security policy challenges, the multistakeholder approach can be a valuable tool in the policymaker's toolkit. The foundational informality of existing governance mechanisms leaves open the opportunity for a multistakeholder engagement model to overcome resistance to new and more effective security practices and encourage dialogue.

The technical standards community has found ways to work together to develop the technical underpinnings of the digital ecosystem. Further up the stack, policy issues appear to pose a very different kind of problem. While the habitual organization into industry consortia can solve specific challenges, these types of organizations limit the number of participating parties. The history of the internet is one that impacts a broad group of stakeholders and users and so the manner in which a decision is made matters as well as the outcome. For policymaking regarding internet security governance, stakeholders are diffuse enough that existing regulatory and legislative structures may not work. Security is about responding to challenges, and governance of security requires coordinating that response over a wide swath of participants. In specific circumstances, a multistakeholder approach can offer the opportunity for constructive policy development and greater security for all.

CHAPTER HIGHLIGHTS

The Need for Governance. The internet famously has no central government. From its earliest days as university research project, up to the present day, the internet has been "governed" by a diverse assortment of actors, institutions, and processes. Academics and engineers, telecommunications companies and software developers, hackers, government agencies, and international organizations have all played a role in developing and expanding the network. No single authority has the authority to dictate how the internet will develop; no one party decides what rules will govern the net. But at a deeper, and perhaps more philosophical, level, the internet has also been shaped by what might be described as a core set of underlying principles, norms, and values that have acted as guideposts for the internet's evolution and maturation.

Multistakeholder Approaches encompass a range of procedures, formats, resolution mechanisms, communication strategies, and outcomes. In the same way that democratic governments may follow a parliamentary or a presidential system of governance, so too do multistakeholder approaches vary and must be adapted to fit a particular governance question. They have repeatedly proven themselves to be better suited to rapidly changing technologies, business practices, and markets than traditional regulatory or legislative models.

Vulnerability Disclosure Debate Example. Some firms embrace bug bounties as a means of improving their product's security, while others resist and ignore or prosecute disclosure. Some researchers will try to improve security through collaboration, while others will continue to push for change by publicly naming and shaming bad security practices, even at the risk of collateral damage. Alternatively, if the collateral damage grows too high, one can imagine a crackdown on freelance security research and vulnerability discovery outside of direct vendor control. This move to punish discovery and disclosure would drive the activity underground and may well result in a surge of vulnerabilities available on the malware market. Utilizing the multistakeholder approach of engaging researchers, vendors, and civil society in an ongoing discussion about the core values and virtues of a vulnerability disclosure policy is crucial.

Keys to Multistakeholder Success. Consensus is a decision-making tool but also key to moving from discussion to outcome in the multistakeholder approach. Anyone can participate so voting such as a direct democracy doesn't necessarily take into account all interests or the content of previous debate. Rather, consensus can help balance between the dangers of a group being held captive by a particular individual or organization and strict majoritarianism. If a major set of stakeholders objects to a proposal, then the group cannot claim to have consensus. Transparency is another key to the multistakeholder approach for internet security governance, establishing legitimacy through accessible dialogue. Smoke-filled rooms are a recipe for mistrust and discord but being able to point to concerns of different participants that have been addressed helps to bridge different value systems.

NOTES

1. Miles Townes, "The Spread of TCP/IP: How the Internet Became the Internet," *Millennium—Journal of International Studies* 41, no. 1 (September 2012): 43–64, http://mil.sagepub.com/content/41/1/43.short.

2. B. Carpenter, June 1996, Network Working Group, Architectural Principles of the Internet, https://www.ietf.org/rfc/rfc1958.txt.

3. The Internet standards organizations have put forward a list of principles they have dubbed OpenStand, which includes such values as: *Cooperation* among standards organizations; *Adherence* to due process, broad consensus, transparency, balance and openness in standards development; *Commitment* to technical merit, interoperability, competition, innovation and benefit to humanity; *Availability* of standards to all; *Voluntary* adoption—https://open-stand.org/about-us/principles/.

4. Jeremy Malcolm, *Multi-Stakeholder Governance and the Internet Governance Forum* (Australia: Terminus Press, 2008), http://library.uniteddiversity.coop/Cooperatives/Multi-Stakeholder_Co-ops/Multi-Stakeholder_Governance_And_The_Internet_Governance_Forum.pdf; the IETF H. Alvestrand, October 2004, Network Working Group, A Mission Statement For the IETF, http://www.ietf.org/rfc/rfc3935.txt.; The Internet Society, "The Value of Openness for a Sustainable Internet," October 2013, https://www.internetsociety.org/sites/default/files/Internet_Society_openness_and_susstainability-en.pdf.

5. The White House, *International Strategy for Cyberspace: Prosperity, Security, and Openness in a Networked World* (Washington, DC, May 2011), https://www.whitehouse.gov/sites/default/files/rss_viewer/international_strategy_for_cyberspace.pdf.

6. H.Con.Res. 127 (2012) and S.Con.Res. 50 (2012).

7. Urs Gasser, Ryan Budish, and Sarah Myers West, *Multistakeholder as Governance Groups: Observations from Case Studies,* Berkman Center for Internet and Society, January 15, 2015, https://cyber.law.harvard.edu/publications/2014/internet_governance.

8. Dr. Laura DeNardis and Dr. Mark Raymond, "Thinking Clearly About Multistakeholder Internet Governance" (paper presented at the eighth annual GigaNet Symposium, Bali, Indonesia, October 21, 2013), http://www.phibetaiota.net/wp-content/uploads/2013/11/Multistakeholder-Internet-Governance.pdf.

9. Fritz W. Scharpf, "Games Real Actors Could Play: Positive and Negative Coordination in Embedded Negotiations," *Journal of Theoretical Politics* 6, no. 1 (January 1994): 27–53, http://jtp.sagepub.com/content/6/1/27.short.

10. "DMCA Notice-and-Takedown Processes: List of Good, Bad, and Situational Practices," http://www.uspto.gov/sites/default/files/documents/DMCA_Good_Bad_and_Situational_Practices_Document-FINAL.pdf.

11. The White House, *Consumer Data Privacy in a Networked World* (Washington, DC, February 2012), https://www.whitehouse.gov/sites/default/files/privacy-final.pdf.

12. National Telecommunications and Information Administration, "Big Data and Consumer Privacy in the Internet Economy," *Federal Register* 79, no. 109 (June, 2014): 32714–32716, https://www.ntia.doc.gov/files/ntia/publications/big_data_rfc.pdf.

13. Stephen Lynch, "Full Disclosure: Infosec Industry Still Fighting Over Vulnerability Reporting," *OpenDNS Blog,* October 16, 2015, https://blog.opendns.com/2015/10/16/full-disclosure-infosec-industry-still-fighting/.

14. For more see chapter 7—"Disrupting Malware Markets."

15. National Institute of Standards and Technology, *Framework for Improving Critical Infrastructure Cybersecurity,* February 12, 2014, http://www.nist.gov/cyber-framework/upload/cybersecurity-framework-021214.pdf.

16. Executive Order 13636 of February 12, 2013, Improving Critical Infrastructure Cybersecurity, *Code of Federal Regulations,* (2013) https://www.whitehouse.gov/the-press-office/2013/02/12/executive-order-improving-critical-infrastructure-cybersecurity.

17. *IoT Trust Framework (Discussion Draft),* Online Trust Alliance, August 13, 2015, https://otalliance.org/system/files/files/resource/documents/iot_trust_frameworkv1.pdf.

Chapter 15

Countering the Proliferation of Malware

Trey Herr and Paul Rosenzweig

International cooperation targeting malicious actors and their tools has so far seen limited success.[1] Existing institutional arrangements like the Budapest Convention and Wassenaar Arrangement suffer from the design limitations inherent to harmonization accords but also suffer from the deficit of policy discussion about the explicit goals of what these institutions should hope to achieve. Counter-proliferation of malware, attempting to limit the scale of infections and the sophistication of code, presents the dual challenge of restricting both state and nonstate behavior. Unfortunately, the malware counter-proliferation debate has been improperly framed for an extended period of time, which helps to explain the lack of progress in international cooperation. A broader debate about policy goals was largely short-circuited by the rise of export controls as a flashpoint between policy and technology communities.

Critiquing the limitations of export control could fill a much longer volume so we will only address the most salient points here. This chapter evaluates the most recent attempt at imposing limits on malware, through export controls in the Wassenaar Arrangement, and suggests that there are several common features of the counter-proliferation problem that would be better addressed by a different path forward—supporting vulnerability research and organizing a coherent set of objectives focusing on state or nonstate groups. In addition to highlighting the shortcoming of recent export control-focused efforts, the chapter proposes a framework for discussion of the broader policy goals and suggests a more effective initial approach to target proliferation of malware. It also suggests creating a functional definition of secure software that leads toward a consideration of a better definition of malware.

Background

What Is Malware?

There are a host of different ways to talk about malicious code and categorize their various functions and features—perhaps too many—as competing definitions and naming schemes abound. To focus the discussion, this chapter employs the PrEP framework, which describes all malicious software as a combination of three components: a Propagation method, Exploits, and a Payload.[2] Propagation moves malware from its origin to a target, exploits support gaining access to computers and networks, while the payload accomplishes a particular goal like pilfering intellectual property or causing physical damage. A more complete description of malware can be found in Chapter 7 of this book. This PrEP framework is an abstraction from commonly observed features in malicious software and should serve as a conceptual tool rather than a simple definition for direct use by regulatory authorities.

A Market for Malware

The existence of a market-like apparatus for the exchange, purchase, and sale of malware components is not a novel idea.[3] Previous work has focused on aspects of the pricing and commoditization process as well as larger economic structure.[4] The buyers and sellers are individuals, firms, and even governments.[5] Understanding the function of this market is important to evaluating the application of export controls to limit the type of goods offered and the behavior of participants.[6] Buyers look across a variety of sources to find commodities and services, and sellers will concentrate expertise into particular products to improve economies of scale.

Specialization has become nearly a de facto standard among sellers, with groups focusing on developing exploits and combining tools for sale to others. One example of this effort is the venerable exploit kit, which combines a propagation method and exploits to allow customers to add their selected payload and begin infecting users quickly.[7] The price a state is willing to pay for a certain vulnerability, for example, may set the market for other players, thereby encouraging new suppliers to develop exploits for the vulnerability and potentially price out relatively "friendly" actors like the vendor responsible for the affected software.

The source of many vulnerabilities, and even some associated patches, is a large community of hackers labeled "white hats," a collective moniker for actors who seek out security flaws for the purpose of fixing them. The white-hat community is composed of researchers who endeavor to find and propose patches for vulnerabilities in proprietary and open source software. Operating in parallel are so-called "black hats" who employ the same skills and techniques to seek out the same vulnerabilities, intending to develop exploits for use in malicious software.

The term hacker has a long history but its original and most widely used form encompasses anyone who modifies or tinkers with hardware and software systems.[8] The role of first-generation security collectives, such as the Cambridge based *L0pht*, in developing a rudimentary code of ethics and norms for hard- and software researchers helps provide a counternarrative to the more freewheeling black and gray hat communities that emerged out of the phone-phreakers like Kevin Mitnick.[9] Originally associated with some of the most respected computer engineers and technical entrepreneurs of the twentieth century, the term hacker's modern usage often inaccurately imparts a purely malicious connotation. Malicious hackers, or "black hats," are in the minority of a much larger community of developers, tinkerers, and engineers that includes luminaries such as Steve Wozniak and Bill Gates.

White Hat has thus become a common turn of phrase to delineate well-intentioned hackers from the more malign. The good/bad and white/black hat dichotomy can only carry so far; there are a range of other actors who discover vulnerabilities and may alternately choose to sell them to vendors or criminal groups. Part of this decision is motivated by reputation—firms such as HackerOne, which coordinates programs for vendors to pay for identifying vulnerabilities in their software, also maintains a leaderboard where researchers can rank their accomplishments against each other.[10] Another factor is money—some individuals may simply sell their discoveries to the highest bidder.

Sophistication

Malicious activity is the natural by-product of technologies that, by default, assume trust between user and information. Stretching back to the design choice that instructions and information be considered the same but differentiated prior to execution, information security has faced a challenge in protecting the majority of users from a malicious minority. There is a recent trend toward more capable malware samples emerging in an otherwise slowly evolving sea of code, often with exotic propagation and compromise capabilities. These more capable samples represent an aberrant spike in an otherwise slow evolution over time.[11] According to analysis from information security firms like Symantec and Kaspersky, much of this new code originates with governments. The implication for well-resourced political entities as a more common source of malicious software samples is potentially significant.

Scale

Malware's propagation has a quality of how broadly it can be distributed. Scale determines the total possible target pool, that is, how many computers and devices from the global population are accessible. Malware which propagates over the internet is likely to be found much farther afield than that spread over compromised storage media. The scale of a compromised web site may be tremendous if the site in question is Google or tiny if it is a GeoCities page. Conventional botnets (a large contingent of compromised computers unbeknownst to their owners) like Kelihos have up to tens of millions of slave machines and present an excellent means of propagating to targets indiscriminately.[12] A propagation method that targets all internet-connected computers is thus different from one that targets only users connected to a single university network.

The breadth of malware's use is also a function of the originating actor's intent. Criminal groups often target hundreds of thousands of users at once, compensating for a low rate of infection by expanding the size of the total target pool. Intelligence agencies and other state actors have appeared more interested in small set of targets, both to limit the chance of discovery by other parties and to concentrate resources on successful infection of their selected victims. Countering malware built and deployed by these different groups, which represent opposing poles of a continuum rather than distinct categories, requires different responses. So far, efforts have been focused on export controls but lacked the discussion of desired ends and policy tools to achieve them.

A Need to Shape the Debate

Problematically, there has been no evaluation of the efficacy and trade-offs inherent in variously targeting the supply, demand, or use of malicious software. It may be that achieving a reduction in the scale of malware use or restricting its average sophistication may be possible through international coordination of a different sort than legal restrictions on transmission. Indeed, a more complete consideration of the policy tools available to target supply, demand, and use as well as their underlying causes could provide a much healthier array of options for policymakers without the implementation difficulty and costly consequences of export controls.

International Coordination

The rapid digitalization of commerce and other traditionally real-world interactions has given rise to a plethora of new opportunities for crime and fraud. Most malicious groups operate across borders, posing a challenge to existing U.S. law enforcement both for prosecution and for coordination across a wide array of domestic legal arrangements. In Russia there are greater controls on the provision of internet-related services, so fraud presents a more significant challenge for criminal groups owing to the involvement of state firms in some aspects of payment processing and financial transactions. Germany still remains scarred by the legacy of the Stasi, which ran one of the most extensive counterintelligence and surveillance programs in history during the Cold War, and thus yielded more circumspect lingering sensitivities to unbridled state power and strict criminal penalties.[13]

Budapest

The Budapest Convention on Cybercrime stood as the first international agreement to address internet and computer crime by bringing domestic laws closer into coordination, providing enhanced investigative authorities for international efforts, and building a foundation for policy coordination and cooperation between states. The harmonization object of Budapest centered on investigative powers and enforcement, attempting to reinforce the ability for national law enforcement agencies to target crimes in which the perpetrators, their tools, or ill-gotten gains are located outside of the country originating the legal action. The Convention doesn't provide particular definitions but does require that signatory states pass laws which criminalize illegal access, illegal interception, system interference, and misuse-of-devices among others. Budapest suffered from inconsistent implementation however and was focused on prosecution of criminal behavior, rather than the interdiction of the malicious tools themselves.

Wassenaar

The Wassenaar Arrangement was born in 1996, out of a desire to revise a Cold War era export control process (CoCom) and integrate former Soviet bloc states.[14] The Arrangement is not an enforceable legal regime but rather a harmonization device for member states to coordinate their respective domestic policies and prevent the sort of regulatory arbitrage, relocating business activities to the least restrictive jurisdiction, which can undermine an export control, a particular challenge for information security.[15] In December 2013, the UK and French governments successfully instigated a change to include tools and technology associated with malicious software.[16] One goal for the new controls was to restrict sales of malware to repressive governments used to monitor journalists and political dissidents. Over years prior, Citizen Lab and Reporters Without Borders had uncovered evidence of products like Gamma Group's FinSpy and Hacking Team's Galileo surveillance tools being sold to or used by a variety of states including Egypt, Bahrain, and Pakistan.[17]

These changes to Wassenaar created a new restricted product, "intrusion software" which referred to tools designed for (1) "the extraction of data or information, from a computer or network capable device, or the modification of system or user data"; or (2) "modification of the standard execution path of a program or process in order to allow the execution of externally provided instructions." Rather than target these products directly, Wassenaar provided for controls on the software, systems, equipment, components, or technology (specific information including technical data or assistance) used to generate, operate, deliver, or communicate with this "intrusion software."[18] The controls discussed here are a subset of the larger Wassenaar changes which include separate restrictions on IP network surveillance tools intended for the collection and analysis of large volumes of network traffic.

Challenges with Export Controls Used for Counter-proliferation

Neither Budapest nor Wassenaar substantially restricts the diffusion of malicious software. Looking particularly at export controls, Wassenaar also fails to restrict the activities of state organizations responsible for some of the latest malware components, especially exploits.[19] One of the major espionage platforms discovered in the past several years, Duqu (malware ostensibly created by the United States and Israel) utilized an exploit in the Windows operating system to escalate privileges on a target machine and enable payload execution.[20] Less than a year after the announcement of its discovery, the same exploit was integrated into two major exploit kits and used in attacks against a range of targets.[21] This reuse of the originally state-authored package drove renewed interest in sophisticated exploits to the point where Microsoft was forced to include patches relevant to this and related vulnerabilities for more than a year afterward.[22]

Wassenaar's controls are written in such a blunt manner as to cover common software engineering and security tools, leading to potential for the same negative effects restrictions on cryptographic tools had on American researchers and companies in the 1980s and 1990s. It isn't that this definition of "intrusion software" won't encompass malware but that so much more is swept up at the same time. In the language of the controls, one definition of intrusion software covers any code which is capable of performing a "modification of a standard execution path." Perhaps intended to cover exploits, this definition would also include patches from a software vendor to improve a user's security or software plug-ins like Firefox's Add-ons, which, "interleave externally provided instructions with the main Firefox code logic."[23]

As with restrictions on cryptography, export controls on malware not only struggle to achieve their goal of restricting the flow of tools around the world but also create challenges to legitimate users and security research. In security research communities and industry, much of the concern has arisen around the restrictions placed on any "technology" used to create or control intrusion software, which would cover exploits developed to demonstrate a vulnerability and communicate it to a vendor.[24] Demonstrated in figure 15.1, this has the effect of truncating the flow of vulnerability information to patches far more than to malware, a substantial chilling effect for the defensive community.

Wassenaar's language poses the risk of considerable collateral damage in being most effective targeting organizations contributing to software security and standard software development practices. A vulnerability can be used for ill, by malicious actors, or for good to patch and improve software security.[25] There are a variety of actors searching daily for new vulnerabilities, contributing to what has become an arms race of sorts between these many researchers and vendors trying to secure their software. Many vulnerabilities are found and resolved by teams housed within giant software vendors like Google, Microsoft, and Adobe. Smaller security firms, academic groups, and independent security researchers play crucial roles however, bringing new vulnerabilities to light through independent audits, hacking competitions, and bug bounty programs.[26]

International Coordination Can Be Difficult

The use of export controls for counter-proliferation of information products has substantial limitations.[27] For both cryptographic tools and malware, one of the key obstacles to successful regulation is the necessity of harmonizing all member states' restrictions to prevent regulatory arbitrage. The lack of a

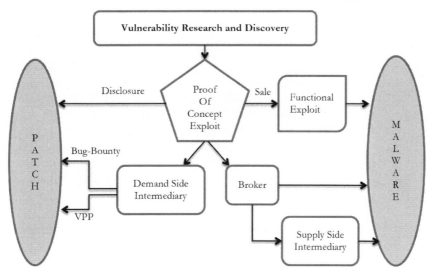

Figure 15.1 Vulnerability Research and Discovery

standard enforcement mechanism as part of Wassenaar reduces the likelihood of overcoming resistance from domestic constituencies.[28] The international framework also lacks a rule forbidding undercutting, where one state grants export licenses for a product denied by another.[29] There is a provision for notification in these instances but it does not compel corrective action. In addition, while Wassenaar's membership is greater than that of its predecessors, it still excludes the majority of countries, including information security hubs like Israel.[30]

Stepping back from the Arrangement, any successor multilateral approach has to consider reporting requirements in specific controls, licensing activity, and violations; must include some means of maintaining compliance; and needs to cover all states with current or potential information security research programs. The difficulty in designing an institution along these lines is daunting, from the particular challenges of crafting an agreement with the necessary reporting and compliance mechanisms states will conform with to identifying countries currently or likely to be home to the sort of research and criminal activity of interest. Moreover, even *if* such an agreement were in place, the internet has provided more than enough capability for individuals involved in producing, reselling, or brokering malware components to live and work almost anywhere, thereby evading the agreement's controls to some degree.

Moving Forward

Export controls ineffectively focus on the restriction of transmission and distribution but selecting approaches that target one of these different aspects of the malicious software life cycle implies an understanding of the desired outcome to which a policy might be crafted. The first and most important means of moving the debate forward would be to explicitly have a discussion, in the public sphere, about how to limit the sophistication and scale of both state- and nonstate-authored malicious software. Clarifying policymaker's goals as they relate to these different groups would help winnow the list of possible policy interventions reasonable to achieve them.

Furthermore, different goals including targeting the behavior of states versus criminal organizations, for example, imply different institutional arrangements to drive international cooperation or coordination. Cooperative legal frameworks to prosecute criminal groups or exchange information on their activities would necessitate clarification of domestic cyber crime law and provision for information sharing mechanisms. Targeting the activities of states will require greater buy-in from these groups and a strong means of enforcing whatever restrictions are put in place. Designing these institutions will require a longer conversation about ends and means. Crafting a more particular set of policy priorities for countering malware proliferation would be a valuable process. In the meantime, there are at least two other actions which could help address the scale and sophistication of malware.

Attack the Exploit Pool—Supporting Vulnerability Research

Exploits are not intrinsically malicious and so have limited use as a signal of intent; they have an array of potential applications in the security industry and are a principal means by which software vendors are made aware of holes in their products to be patched. For the majority of criminal groups, it is not necessary to exploit a "zero-day" vulnerability (one that is unknown to the vendor prior to exploitation) to be effective. The majority of incidents reported in 2015 for example were the result of malware leveraging vulnerabilities that were publicly reported and had a patch developed.[31] In each case, however, exploits served as a critical enabling component. How best then to limit the sophistication and scale of malicious software?

An alternative to direct restriction of the demand for or use of malware is to target exploits and shrink the supply available for use by criminal organizations and states. The community of information security firms and independent researchers responsible for discovering and disclosing a large portion of vulnerabilities every year labor under uncertain legal frameworks that vary between countries. Provisions of the Digital Millennium Copyright Act (DMCA), for example, can restrict the analysis of vendor's products required to find and prove the existence of bugs, enabling lawsuits to prevent this discovery and discouraging security research.[32] In Belgium, similar laws protecting digital rights management (DRM) systems provide restrictions on the form and content of information that can be disclosed about software systems.[33] A temporary exemption to the DMCA was passed in 2015 though it will not come into effect for a period of twelve months.[34]

While limited changes to existing law are a positive step, potentially more useful would be an effort to further revise these protections for research and, importantly, harmonize their application and interpretation across the international community. Coordination vehicles, like the multistakeholder process run by the Department of Commerce on vulnerability disclosure policies, can drive the development of common standards and syntax. This in turn can help encourage clarity and specificity in new laws protecting positive security research.

Vulnerability research is an international enterprise with a bevy of conferences, academic outlets, and competitions taking place across the world. Encouraging security research, growing the pool of individuals looking to discover and disclose vulnerabilities to vendors, would help shrink the pool of these flaws available to states and criminal groups engaged in malicious activity. Enabling this research through a clear legal framework across states would encourage broader participation and make it easier for vulnerabilities to be disclosed rather than sold on the malicious software market. This in turn will help limit the supply of vulnerabilities available to threat groups.

Defining the Exploit Pool

As our discussion has made clear, the very definition of malware is subject to ambiguities that are incapable of ready resolution. Malware, in the end, is often not recognized until implementation, a circumstance that challenges efforts to control or regulate it directly.

An alternative possibility for consideration is the prospect of taking the contrapositive approach of defining software that is not (or, less ambitiously, is unlikely to be) malicious in nature. This effort focuses not on control of the adverse market but in international cooperation to channel commerce into markets where we can have a higher confidence in the security of the systems components that form part of a supply chain. One further area for exploration would be an effort to define the processes that would be evident in the provision of software within such a chain. While we have not explored the question fully, here are some initial thoughts on characteristics of secure software. Secure software would come with:[35]

- A published attestation as to the security of its development, including documentation of the design, development, and adversarial resilience testing;
- a coordinated disclosure policy that welcomes outside vulnerability research;
- a tamper-evident, forensically sound logging and evidence capture system to facilitate investigations of failures;
- a capability for prompt and agile repair through updates and patching; and
- a design that segments and isolates, physically and logically, critical functionality from noncritical functionality.

It may well be possible to devise an affirmative method of assessment and certification as to some, or all, of these characteristics. If so, then rather than efforts that are unlikely to succeed in eradicating a market for malware, one could consider the creation of a market in safer software. While this would not directly address the proliferation of malicious tools, it would help combat the hijacking of legitimate vendor's update pathways or trademarks for the distribution of malware. This approach to reinforce trusted software distribution could further provide a foundation for future efforts focused less on constraining adversaries and more on reducing the value of proliferation by hardening defenses.

CONCLUSION

International cooperation to reduce the spread and sophistication of malware has so far focused on developing cooperative legal tools to target malicious actors and harmonizing export controls to restrict their sale and transmission. Neither of these approaches, through the Budapest Convention and the Wassenaar Arrangement respectively, have seen substantial success. This is due in part to the incomplete attention paid to the incentives for criminal groups to target public and private sector organizations. International agreements have focused on the most difficult challenge of cross-jurisdictional law enforcement activity and restricting the diffusion of malicious tools. This chapter proposes to enhance the legal framework for vulnerability research to encourage growth in the white-hat community, improving the market for their efforts, and for defensive efforts to reinforce the network of verifiably trusted software development and distribution pathways. The counter-proliferation debate envelops an array of issues across U.S. foreign and national security policy. Of equal importance to the recommendations listed here is for the United States to develop a more coherent set of objectives within malware counter-proliferation, rather than continuing to risk different agencies working at cross purposes to little, or even harmful, effect. Differing incentives is an inevitable by-product of coordination across a complex security environment but existing efforts would be measurably improved by a concerted interagency effort to identify and attempt to reconcile clearly divergent priorities. Malware is not developed in a vacuum and restricting its capability or diffusion throughout the world forces us to recognize the humans behind the keyboard and their various incentives. Clarifying policy goals and supporting a vibrant security research community is only the start.

CHAPTER HIGHLIGHTS

Wassenaar Arrangement (1996). The arrangement is not an enforceable legal regime but rather a harmonization device for member states to coordinate their respective domestic export control policies and prevent the sort of regulatory arbitrage, relocating business activities to the least restrictive jurisdiction, which can undermine an export control, a particular challenge for information security.

Wassenaar's Limitations. Wassenaar's language poses the risk of considerable collateral damage in being most effective targeting organizations contributing to software security and standard software development practices. A vulnerability can be used for ill, by malicious actors, or for good to patch and improve software security. There are a variety of actors searching daily for new vulnerabilities, contributing to what has become an arms race of sorts between these many researchers and vendors trying to secure their software. Additionally, the lack of a standard enforcement mechanism as part of Wassenaar reduces the likelihood of overcoming resistance from domestic constituencies. The international framework also lacks a rule forbidding undercutting, where one state grants export licenses for a product denied by another. Finally, Wassenaar excludes the majority of countries, including information security hubs like Israel.

Encouraging Public Debate. The most important means of moving the debate on countering malware proliferation forward would be to explicitly have one; to organize a discussion in the public sphere about how to limit the sophistication and scale of both state and nonstate-authored malware.

Improved International Cooperation. Cooperative legal frameworks to prosecute criminal groups or exchange information on their activities would necessitate clarification of domestic cyber crime law and provision for information sharing mechanisms. Targeting the activities of states will require greater buy-in from these groups and a strong means of enforcing whatever restrictions are put in place.

Promoting Security Research. Growing the community of individuals looking to discover and disclose vulnerabilities to vendors would help shrink the pool available to states and criminal groups engaged in compromising computer systems. Enabling this research through a clear legal framework across states would encourage broader participation and make it easier for vulnerabilities to be disclosed rather than sold on the malicious software market.

NOTES

1. Selected portions of this chapter have previously appeared in Trey Herr, "Malware Counter-Proliferation and the Wassenaar Arrangement," in 2016 8th International Conference on Cyber Conflict: Cyber Power (CyCon, Tallinn, Estonia: IEEE, 2016). http://dx.doi.org/10.2139/ssrn.2711070.

2. Trey Herr, "PrEP: A Framework for Malware & Cyber Weapons," *The Journal of Information Warfare* 13, iss. 1, February 2014, 87–106.

3. For more, see chapter 7—"Disrupting Malware Markets."

4. Lillian Ablon, Martin C. Libicki, and Andrea A. Golay, "Markets for Cybercrime Tools and Stolen Data: Hackers' Bazaar," *Rand Corporation*, 2014, http://www.rand.org/content/dam/rand/pubs/research_reports/RR600/RR610/RAND_RR610.

pdf; Chris Grier et al., "Manufacturing Compromise: The Emergence of Exploit-as-a-Service," in *Proceedings of the 2012 ACM Conference on Computer and Communications Security*, 2012, 821–32, http://dl.acm.org/citation.cfm?id=2382283; Kurt Thomas, Danny, Huang, David Wang, Elie Bursztein, Chris Grier, Thomas Holt, Christopher Kruegel, Damon McCoy, Stefan Savage, Giovanni Vigna, "Framing Dependencies Introduced by Underground Commoditization," 2015, http://damonmccoy.com/papers/WEIS15.pdf.

5. Brian Fung, "The NSA Hacks Other Countries by Buying Millions of Dollars' Worth of Computer Vulnerabilities," *The Washington Post*, August 31, 2013, https://www.washingtonpost.com/news/the-switch/wp/2013/08/31/the-nsa-hacks-other-countries-by-buying-millions-of-dollars-worth-of-computer-vulnerabilities/.

6. Marti Motoyama et al., "An Analysis of Underground Forums," in *Proceedings of the 2011 ACM SIGCOMM Conference on Internet Measurement Conference*, 2011, 71–80, http://dl.acm.org/citation.cfm?id=2068824.

7. Team Cymru, "A Criminal Perspective on Exploit Packs," May 2011, https://blog.qualys.com/wp-content/uploads/2011/05/team_cymru_exploitkits.pdf.

8. John Markoff, *What the Dormouse Said: How the Sixties Counterculture Shaped the Personal Computer Industry* (New York: Penguin Books, 2005); Steven Levy, *Hackers: Heroes of the Computer Revolution—25th Anniversary Edition* (Sebastopol: O'Reilly Media, Inc., 2010).

9. Tom Bearden, "L0pht on Hackers," *Online NewsHour*, June 8, 1998, http://mail.blockyourid.com/~gbpprorg/l0pht_hackers.txt; Mitnick was an early black hat who leveraged a form of social engineering called phone-phreaking which allowed him and others to map out and manipulate telephone networks by targeting company employees and analog signaling and control equipment. Eventually arrested, Mitnick was charged with the compromise of systems at a number of companies including Pacific Bell and Digital Equipment Corporation (DEC). He later wrote a book.

10. Sean Martin, "Bug Bounty Programs Narrow the Crowd," *SearchSecurity*, March 2016, http://searchsecurity.techtarget.com/feature/Bug-bounty-programs-narrow-the-crowd.

11. Trey Herr and Eric Armbrust, "Milware: Identification and Implications of State Authored Malicious Software," in *NSPW '15 Proceedings of the 2015 New Security Paradigms Workshop* (Twente, Netherlands: ACM, 2015), 29–43, doi:10.1145/2841113.2841116.

12. Brian Krebs, "Researchers Clobber Khelios Spam Botnet," *Krebs on Security*, March 28, 2012, http://krebsonsecurity.com/2012/03/researchers-clobber-khelios-spam-botnet/.

13. Avner Levin and Daria Ilkina, "International Comparison of Cyber Crime" (Ryerson University: Privacy and Cyber Crime Institute, March 2013), http://www.ryerson.ca/tedrogersschool/privacy/documents/Ryerson_International_Comparison_ofCyber_Crime_-March2013.pdf.

14. Kenneth A. Dursht, "From Containment to Cooperation: Collective Action and the Wassenaar Arrangement," *Cardozo L. Rev.* 19, 1997, 1079.

15. Henry Farrell, "Regulation Information Flows: States, Private Actors, and E-Commerce," *Annual Review of Political Science* 9, iss. 1, June 2006, 353–74, doi:10.1146/annurev.polisci.9.060804.162744.

16. CDT, EFF, HRW, & OTI, "Comments to the U.S. Department of Commerce on Implementation of 2013 Wassenaar Arrangement Plenary Agreements," July 20, 2015, https://cdt.org/files/2015/07/JointWassenaarComments-FINAL.pdf.

17. Morgan Marquis-Boire et al., "For Their Eyes Only: The Commercialization of Digital Spying" (Citizen Lab, April 30, 2013), https://citizenlab.org/storage/finfisher/final/fortheireyesonly.pdf; "Gamma International" (Reporters Without Borders, 2013), http://surveillance.rsf.org/en/gamma-international/; Mikko Hypponen, "Egypt, FinFisher Intrusion Tools and Ethics," *F-Secure Labs*, March 8, 2011, https://www.f-secure.com/weblog/archives/00002114.html.

18. The Wassenaar Arrangement, "THE WASSENAAR ARRANGEMENT ON EXPORT CONTROLS FOR CONVENTIONAL ARMS AND DUAL-USE GOODS AND TECHNOLOGIES LIST OF DUAL-USE GOODS AND TECHNOLOGIES AND MUNITIONS LIST," March 12, 2015, http://www.wassenaar.org/wp-content/uploads/2015/08/WA-LIST-15-1-2015-List-of-DU-Goods-and-Technologies-and-Munitions-List.pdf.

19. Trey Herr, "Malware Counter-Proliferation and the Wassenaar Arrangement."

20. Guillaume Bonfante et al., "Analysis and Diversion of Duqu's Driver," in *Malicious and Unwanted Software: "The Americas" (MALWARE), 2013 8th International Conference,* 2013, 109–15, http://ieeexplore.ieee.org/xpls/abs_all.jsp?arnumber=6703692.

21. Julia Wolf, "CVE-2011-3402—Windows Kernel TrueType Font Engine Vulnerability (MS11-087)," March 8, 2013, https://cansecwest.com/slides/2013/Analysis%20of%20a%20Windows%20Kernel%20Vuln.pdf.

22. Michael Mimoso, "Of TrueType Font Vulnerabilities and the Windows Kernel," *Threat Post*, July 11, 2013, https://threatpost.com/of-truetype-font-vulnerabilities-and-the-windows-kernel/101263/.

23. Sergey Bratus et al., "Why Wassenaar Arrangement's Definitions of Intrusion Software and Controlled Items Put Security Research and Defense At Risk—And How To Fix It" (Public Comment, October 9, 2014), http://www.cs.dartmouth.edu/~sergey/drafts/wassenaar-public-comment.pdf.

24. Thomas Dullien, Vincenzo Iozzo, and Mara Tam, "Surveillance, Software, Security, and Export Controls" (Public Comment, February 10, 2015), https://tac.bis.doc.gov/index.php/component/docman/doc_view/299-surveillance-software-security-and-export-controls-mara-tam?Itemid=.

25. S. Shepherd, "Vulnerability Disclosure: How Do We Define Responsible Disclosure?" *GIAC SEC Practical Repository, SANS Inst* 9, 2003, https://www.sans.org/reading-room/whitepapers/threats/define-responsible-disclosure-932.

26. Gregg Keizer, "Single Code Typo Triggers Massive Internet Explorer Hack Attacks," *IT Business*, August 4, 2009, http://www.itbusiness.ca/news/single-code-typo-triggers-massive-internet-explorer-hack-attacks/13806; Dan Goodin, "All Four Major Browsers Take a Stomping at Pwn2Own Hacking Competition," *Ars Technica*, March 20, 2015, http://arstechnica.com/security/2015/03/all-four-major-browsers-take-a-stomping-at-pwn2own-hacking-competition/; Matthew Finifter, Devdatta Akhawe, and David Wagner, "An Empirical Study of Vulnerability Rewards

Programs," in *USENIX Security*, 2013, https://www.usenix.org/system/files/conference/usenixsecurity13/sec13-paper_finifter.pdf.

27. Trey Herr and Paul Rosenzweig, "Cyber Weapons & Export Control: Incorporating Dual Use with the PrEP Model | Journal of National Security Law & Policy," *Journal of National Security Law and Policy* 8, iss. 2, October 23, 2015, http://jnslp.com/2015/10/23/cyber-weapons-export-control-incorporating-dual-use-with-the-prep-model/.

28. Karim K. Shehadeh, "Wassenaar Arrangement and Encryption Exports: An Ineffective Export Control Regime That Compromises United States Economic Interests, The," *Am. U. Int'l L. Rev.* 15, 1999, 271.

29. Innokenty Pyetranker, "Umbrella in a Hurricane: Cyber Technology and the December 2013 Amendment to the Wassenaar Arrangement, An," *Nw. J. Tech. & Intell. Prop.* 13, 2015, 168.

30. Andrea Little Limbago and Cody Pierce, "Much Ado About Wassenaar: The Overlooked Strategic Challenges to the Wassenaar Arrangement's Implementation," *Endgame*, 2015, https://www.endgame.com/blog/much-ado-about-wassenaar-overlooked-strategic-challenges-wassenaar-arrangement%E2%80%99s-implementation.

31. "2015 Data Breach Investigations Report (DBIR)," *Verizon Enterprise Solutions,* 2015, http://www.verizonenterprise.com/DBIR/2015/.

32. Pamela Samuelson, "Anticircumvention Rules: Threat to Science," *Science* 293, iss. 5537, September 14, 2001, 2028–31, doi:10.1126/science.1063764; Stan Adams, "Security Research under the DMCA: A Quest for Flexibility and Certainty," *Center for Democracy & Technology*, July 1, 2015, https://cdt.org/blog/security-research-under-the-dmca-a-quest-for-flexibility-and-certainty/.

33. Federico Biancuzzi, "The Laws of Full Disclosure," *Security Focus*, February 26, 2008, http://www.securityfocus.com/columnists/466.

34. Jen Ellis, "New DMCA Exemption Is a Positive Step for Security Researchers," *Rapid7—Information Security*, October 28, 2015, https://community.rapid7.com/community/infosec/blog/2015/10/28/new-dmca-exemption-is-a-positive-step-for-security-researchers.

35. Derived from a proposal by the security and vulnerability research consortium known as "I Am The Cavalry," www.iamthecavalry.org.

Section IV

MILITARY CYBER OPERATIONS

Chapter 16

Understanding Military Cyber Operations

Trey Herr and Drew Herrick

Today, more than 100 of the world's militaries have some sort of organiza-
tion in place for cyber warfare. These organizations' size, scale, training and
budgets all differ, but they all share the same goals: In the words of the U.S.
Air Force, the purpose of cyber warfare is "to destroy, deny, degrade, dis-
rupt, [and] deceive," while at the same time "defending" against the enemy's
use of cyberspace for the very same purpose. Among military planners, it's
known as the "Five D's plus One."

Interest in these kinds of operations is exploding within the U.S. military.
There is also a broader debate beginning in various militaries as to how such
units should be organized. This very shift is underway in China. Spending on
cyber warfare became a "top funding priority," up a reported 20 percent
in 2015 alone as a host of new units were created with the responsibility of
"preparing attacks on enemy computer networks."

We won't just see the stealing or revealing information, but the blocking or
changing of information. And, as such, we will see cyber operations shift from
the field of espionage to having actual direct effects on the flow of battle. For
example, one of the key advantages of the U.S. military has been its global
network of command and control, with the Global Positioning System being
a key part of the architecture that allows forces to operate with incredible
precision. But that dependence points to a key aspect to target. In 2010, a
software glitch knocked 10,000 military GPS receivers offline for more than
two weeks.

Maybe worse is gaining access to a system not to steal or block informa-
tion, but to change it. In 2007, through a mix of cyber and electronic means,
Israel was able to deceive Syrian air defenses into thinking that their skies
were secure, when in fact seven Israeli F-15s were flying overhead on their
way to drop bombs on a suspected nuclear site.

Changing information might not just allow physical damage to happen through other means, but even directly cause it. Stuxnet was a piece of software code, allegedly created by U.S. and Israeli intelligence that was used to sabotage Iranian nuclear research facilities. It did so by instructing the industrial control systems to literally damage themselves, all the while telling their human operators that everything was functioning well. Or, we might see "battles of persuasion," where one's own weapons are instructed to do something contrary to the owner's intent. Such changes are not just something that can be caused by outside software sneaking in, but they also come through a hardware hack, where the flaws are literally baked into the systems themselves. The result for the targets would be an experience akin to the first episode of Battlestar Galactica, where the good guys' aircraft stopped working all at the same moment, opening them up to a devastating attack.

—Dr. Peter Singer, November 2015
Coauthor of *Cybersecurity and Cyberwar: What Everyone Needs to Know*

EXPLAINING MILITARY CYBER OPERATIONS

What are the role of cybersecurity capabilities in the conduct of war and ongoing security operations? Policymakers, academics, and journalists often think of cybersecurity as a single domain problem—that cyber operations take place solely within their own domain and separate from land, sea, air, or space.[1] However, this overlooks the fact that computer systems and networks pervade society and the physical environment, and are present to some degree in all physical environs and across the three levels of war (strategic, operational, and tactical). Modern militaries employ forces in a "joint" manner, combining the specific platforms and technologies of different services to achieve a more effective force. Similarly, kinetic and cyber capabilities can be conceived as part of a broad set of tools available to achieve national security objectives. Thinking of cybersecurity as a limited or separate space, wholly distinct from the other domains of conflict, limits the potential for understanding its strategic utility.[2]

The term "Military Cyber Operations" covers the acquisition and use of cyber capabilities in the strategic, operational, and tactical realms by states and nonstate actors. It encompasses a broad array of defensive efforts and offensive missions, both on and off the battlefield. This chapter, and larger section, focuses on the development of cyber capabilities, their deployment to defend the United States and allied forces, their use in targeting hostile networks, key relevant legal and diplomatic issues, the budgeting and procurement process involved in each of these areas, and, importantly, the recruitment and training of uniformed personnel to carry out these missions across all five services in the U.S. military. Notably, only a small percentage of cyber operations are offensive and destructive in nature. While incidents like Stuxnet (the malicious software deployed against Iran's nuclear program) certainly grab headlines, the ongoing challenge of securing organizations against attack is a far more frequent activity.

Military Cyber Operation (MCO) is an umbrella term for the acquisition and use of cyber capabilities at the strategic, operational, and tactical levels of conflict. MCO is *not* the same as "cyber war." Cyber war, as usually articulated, focuses on two (or more) combatants exclusively deploying malicious cyber capabilities against the other side's systems, resulting in death and destruction, in order to achieve a set of explicit political goals.[3] This formulation, however, ignores both existing U.S. military doctrine and the manner in which modern forces actually deploy these capabilities.[4] In fact, there are potentially good reasons to think that cyber war, when properly defined, won't actually take place or may constitute an ineffective policy tool.[5]

Instead of "cyber war," MCO focuses on cyber conflict or "cyber-enabled warfare," where capabilities are deployed in conjunction with conventional forces. MCO is further broken up into three categories (see figure 16.1): Department of Defense (DoD) information network operations (DoDIN), defensive cyberspace operations (DCO), and offensive cyberspace operations (OCO).[6] DoDIN deals with routine information assurance, such as securing networks, systems administration, patching, and educating individual users.[7] DCO focuses on both passive and active defense measures, and usually entails a higher degree of expertise than DoDIN activities (including detecting, analyzing, and mitigating active threats). OCO, although involving a comparatively small sliver of both personnel and resources, is perhaps the most technically challenging aspect of MCO, and involves deploying cyber capabilities to disrupt, deny, degrade, or destroy another actor's systems. Here, the difference usually focuses on whether the operation is taking place on friendly systems, neutral systems, or on an adversary's systems.

MCO also includes Intelligence, Surveillance and Reconnaissance (Cyber ISR) activities and Operational Preparation of the Environment (Cyber OPE).[8] Cyber-enabled ISR focuses on gathering information on a specific adversary's systems, including their hard/software configurations, personnel, and operational security. This information is critical for effective targeting, operational planning, and "weaponeering" or preparing capabilities to achieve their desired effects. Cyber OPE, for its part, focuses on access to a target system, and on the means of preparing it for the specific operation. Up-to-date working knowledge of a target system is generally considered a prerequisite for ensuring access for further reconnaissance and follow-on operations.[9]

Previously in the United States, MCO has been considered distinct from Information Operations (IO), Information War (IW), and Military Information Support Operations (MISO) (formerly known as PSYOP).[10] However, the line between these operational forms could well be blurring as the United States engages with opponents wielding information and social media as tools of conflict.[11] In fact, recent operations against ISIS seem to bear this out.[12] IOs focus on attacking an adversary's human or automated decision-making, as

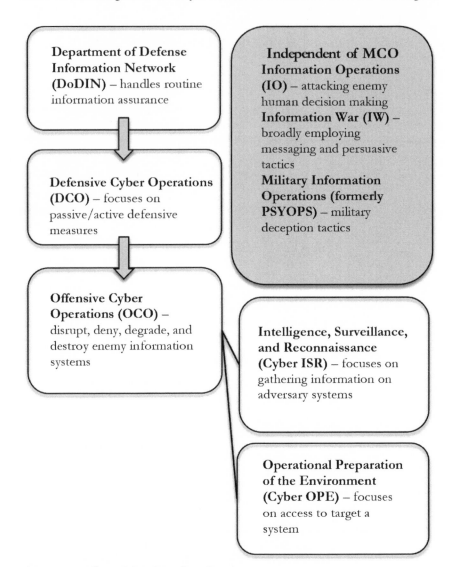

Figure 16.1 Military Cyber Operations Overview

well as on bolstering that of friendly forces. They focus on diverse areas such as military deception, operations security, and public affairs. In practice, IOs often include elements of cyber operations, but can be broader, encompassing messaging and persuasive efforts governed by separate doctrine and employing a different set of personnel.[13] The degree of integration between Cyber, Electronic Warfare (EW), and IO varies among the different U.S. military services. There is an ongoing set of policy discussions that focus on whether there should be deeper doctrinal and organizational integration between Cyber, EW, and IO to facilitate better asset coordination and improve military effectiveness.[14] Importantly, in other countries, such as Russia and China, IOs are significantly more integrated with MCO and EW.[15]

There is an array of issues that affect the military's ability to train, equip, and employ cyber capabilities within both offensive and defensive missions alongside conventional forces. MCO demands newly capable talent in uniform, trained to use the same targeting and planning tools as their kinetic counterparts but with an understanding of both wired and wireless networks. Doctrine on everything from the use of force to passive reconnaissance has to be developed in line with the needs and capabilities of individual services and bounded by a coherent legal framework. In addition to understanding how to properly deploy these capabilities, policymakers must also grapple with how to oversee technology procurement and maintenance as part of a range of joint capabilities.

Buy and Build

How does the military build, buy, and train for these sorts of operations? Part of the challenge in acquiring a capability is integrating it into an existing concept of operations. Simply put, how a service wants to fight will shape the way it buys equipment and trains personnel.

Developing Capabilities

Development is the process of writing code to create capabilities. A useful way of thinking about these software tools is the PrEP framework, which defines malicious software as the combination of a propagation method, exploits, and a payload designed to create effects.[16] Malware's three components work in concert, but have substantially different roles. Exploits are critically important; these open the door for a payload but without doing anything directly malicious. Stuxnet, perhaps the most famous piece of malware ever built, was developed by the United States and Israel to damage Iran's nuclear enrichment program.[17] Stuxnet was able to move across the Iranian network because of a vulnerability in the Windows operating system's print service, sliding from computer to computer until it located those controlling the centrifuges.[18] The propagation method spreads the malicious tool, while the payload is written to create some effect on a computer system.

Stuxnet's payload was a substantial feat of engineering, targeting centrifuges being used to separate different isotopes of uranium in order to obtain pure fissile material. The code was designed to hide in the centrifuge's programmed logic and carry out the attack without alerting Iranian staff. Building a destructive payload, like the one in Stuxnet, takes time and a fair degree of expertise. The attacker has to know a great deal about the hardware systems in use at a potential target, the software and its version in use, and a great deal about the programming language the targeted software is written in. Once a payload is written, it then has to be tested for reliability under a number of different conditions to ensure that it will properly function.[19] Over months, Stuxnet worked to change rotor speeds and valve sequences to slowly degrade the centrifuges, weakening the metal, and causing them to fail much faster than designed.

Vulnerability Acquisition

Acquiring and integrating vulnerabilities into these cyber tools plays a central role in their development. It also creates a serious quandary for the policymaker. On the one hand, many of the targets for offensive action are foreign hard- and software systems. As a result, locating a vulnerability and building an exploit for them will be far less likely to directly impact U.S. citizens. Attacking some of these targets, however, requires compromising common commercial software and less specialized civilian hardware, like routers.[20] Finding vulnerabilities in software made by American vendors like Google or Microsoft requires locating security holes in this software and keeping the information secret from these same firms, thus denying them the opportunity to fix the bugs and improve security for average users. This secrecy is necessary; a target's vulnerability, once patched, is no longer useful. However, this state of affairs engenders a debate about the cost of preserving a capability versus allowing vendors to improve the security of software commonly used by U.S. citizens.

Exploits are a commodity-like component, actively bought and sold on underground markets around the web as well as between private companies, defense contractors, and governments.[21] Because an exploit targets a vulnerability in a particular piece of software—for example, Internet Explorer as opposed to Google's Chrome browser—developing a good one can yield tremendous value, with quoted prices ranging into the hundreds of thousands of dollars.[22] Increasingly, companies such as VUPEN and a sizable collection of freelancers are selling newly discovered vulnerabilities and exploits to governments and nonstate actors rather than the original software vendors themselves.

This presents a problem because building and maintaining secure software is critical to cybersecurity. The ability for vendors to discover vulnerabilities and patch them is an important part of building software without bugs potentially of use to attackers. Hidden vulnerabilities retain value for future military use, but also risk discovery by malicious parties who may deploy them against the United States. Vendors are left unaware of the flaws, and thus are unable to secure their code. This also impacts military and government users, because the use of commercial off-the-shelf (COTS) solutions like Amazon Web Services and the Microsoft operating system mean those same unpatched vulnerabilities leave .mil and .gov networks open to attack.

Creating a legal framework for the acquisition of these capabilities requires balancing security against capability. So far, this debate has taken place largely in the classified realm, with interagency wrangling overseen initially by the National Security Agency and now the National Security Council.[23] Problematically, this approach emphasizes selective disclosure on a case-by-case basis, rather than the establishment of broad and consistent standards that can build in existing research, procurement law, and oversight mechanisms.[24] Part of this ad-hoc arrangement comes from previous trends in recruiting talented information security specialists without a larger education and retention pipeline.

Personnel

The individual military services have the responsibility to organize, train, and equip forces for operational use by the unified-combatant commands.[25] This distribution of responsibility is intended to centralize the personnel training and retention pipeline in the services while seating operational control with the unified-combatant commanders.[26] How each of the services defines their missions, however, can have a sizable impact on the type of roles they organize for and capabilities they seek to develop. While there are common challenges—assuring the integrity of information systems and conducting defensive cyber operations—the offensive missions and concept of operations each service organizes around is different. Integrating officers, warrant officers, and enlisted personnel trained in each of these respective cultures can pose a challenge to the unified-combatant commands, and to the dedicated U.S. Cyber Command (CYBERCOM), currently part of U.S. Strategic Command (STRATCOM), which is responsible for much of the MCO mission set.[27]

Another challenge is integrating existing occupational specialties across different service branches. For example, in 2014 the Army created a dedicated Cyber Branch—its first new specialized occupational area since the establishment of the Special Forces in the 1980s.[28] The goal of this effort was to integrate individuals dispersed between the Signal Corps and Intelligence branches, as well as to centralize the training and certification pipeline for cyber operations.[29] Previously, the Army had split its specialties between network defense and network offense; defensive enlisted personnel were classed as Signal Corps personnel under 25D (Cyber Network Defender), while Military Intelligence housed 35Q, the cryptologic network warfare specialty.[30] The demand for trained personnel remains high, as the service components supporting CYBERCOM's Cyber Mission Forces remain undermanned. But the relevant pipelines are coming online slowly; the Army Cyber School in Fort Gordon Georgia graduated its first class of officers only in August 2015.[31]

There is a personnel shortfall in existing units, and it will be difficult to train individuals to a high degree and then retain them against highly competitive private sector salaries. However, two mitigating factors exist. First, not all roles are created equal—many defensive and offensive personnel act in a supporting capacity, especially in managing the configuration and security maintenance of networked systems. The level of training and specialization required for these roles defending the DoDIN is different and potentially lower than for the operators developing and deploying capabilities organically within maneuver units on the battlefield or in offensive roles within the Cyber Mission Forces. The variety of skill sets and training requirements will benefit from increased standardization and clarity across the length and breadth of the Defense Department.[32] Second, and perhaps equally important, even where trained personnel return to the private sector, the skills and experience they bring with them could help firms enhance their security and potentially avoid some of the challenges facing the public sector. This crossover effect could be further enhanced with more expansive use of the reserve and National Guard components as a means to retain the ability to mobilize this talent in the event of a national security need.[33]

Spectrum of Use

As briefly discussed above, MCOs pervade all three levels of war (strategic, operational, and tactical; see table 16.1).[34] At the *strategic level*, the motivating question is how to deploy military forces to defend the homeland and support broad national objectives. The *operational level* examines how military force is able to achieve the goals of a particular military campaign. Finally, the *tactical level* focuses on the conduct of individual battles within a campaign. In practice, the difference comes down to a question of scale and what type of forces are involved at any given point. In terms of MCOs, each level of war presents a different set of relevant targets and trade-offs, and requires varying degrees of expertise. Each level also presents distinct challenges to operational planners, personnel engaged at the point of attack, and national policymakers.

Table 16.1   Military Cyber Operations—Levels of War

Level of War	Area of Focus	Example Targets
Strategic	Create effects that advance national priorities	Civilian infrastructure with national security implications as well as military hardware, creating both digital and physical destructive effects
Operational	Supports ongoing operations of a particular campaign or theater of conflict	Adversary's integrated air defense systems, logistics train, or supporting intelligence collection and analysis chain
Tactical	Focuses on individual engagements across the battlefield	Weapons platforms, systems embedded in vehicles, and command-and-control assets like communication systems

Strategic

Most of the conversations about MCOs tend to focus on the strategic level, where the national assets and capabilities of the military and associated intelligence organizations are at the fore. The primary purpose at this level is to create effects that advance national priorities, above the objectives of a particular battlefield or campaign. Targets at the strategic level may include civilian infrastructure with national security implications as well as military hardware, creating both digital and physical destructive effects. Power production and transmission facilities as well as high-value telecommunications nodes could both be deemed legitimate targets. The scope of potential targets is global, and the larger political context where defensive and offensive cyber operations (DCO and OCO, respectively) take place could impact all countries, either directly or by implication. An important consideration is the role of precedent, where the use of novel techniques, especially in offense, can establish a new baseline for permissible (or tolerable) behavior among allies and opponents.

At this level, capabilities and the chain of command associated with their employment in the United States are closely interlinked by virtue of physical proximity—major headquarters for CYBERCOM and the National Security Agency are just up the road from Washington, D.C. However, there are some important legal separations, based largely on the types of organization involved. The military typically distinguishes between main and supporting elements, that is, the force intended to execute an operation on the target, and another providing additional capabilities or reinforcements. Operational responsibilities can thus end up split between multiple organizations over these main and supporting forces. This can lead to resource imbalance, where the group that owns the expertise dictates the terms and focus of an operation.[35] It also creates a complicated set of turf wars which have evolved from "the DoD's communications and intelligence 'tribes,' each [of whom] has developed legacy capabilities and counter-capabilities largely independent of other tribes' efforts."[36]

There are legal distinctions as well. Title 10 of the U.S. Code covers all three military departments (as well as the associated services) and their overt operations, both in peacetime and war. The intelligence community by contrast, including their collection activities, and all covert action, fall under Title 50. This segmentation poses a challenge, because tools used on hostile networks for intelligence gathering can also be employed as a platform to support or even conduct offensive operations. Similarly, espionage activities may also be used to support ongoing defensive and offensive operations, including providing information to attribute the source of compromise or target a response.

At one point, cyber operations may have been considered the domain of the intelligence community, where Title 50 requires a presidential finding prior to the initiation of a covert action.[37] The 2011 *National Defense Authorization Act* (NDAA), however, included a provision (Section 954) which granted the Defense Department authority to conduct offensive operations, "to defend our Nation, Allies and interests" upon the direction of the president.[38] Several scholars have interpreted this change as providing authorization for offensive activities by the Defense Department without the explicit acknowledgment of U.S. involvement—a definition verging close to that of covert action. The scope of authorization for these operations may have shifted as well, allowing broader execution orders (EXORDs) that encompass a range of potential responses and obviate the need to obtain a presidential authorization for every particular operation.[39]

Operational

At the operational level, military forces may focus on an adversary's integrated air defense systems, logistics networks, or intelligence collection and analysis chain.[40] In practice, much of the deployment of capabilities happens at higher echelons that are not in the direct area of the campaign. Relevant parties are able to communicate easily, and friendly systems can be properly secured and supported. This stands in contrast to activities at the tactical level, where operators are often forward deployed and require more mobile capability and flexible deployment options.

The importance of joint operations becomes clear at the operational level. For example, in the case of air defenses, offensive cyber capabilities may be deployed to temporarily disrupt an adversary's systems in order to allow friendly sorties in the area in support of ground forces, humanitarian supply drops, or even for longer-range cruise missile strikes. Conversely, a cyber capability can be used to temporarily disrupt an adversary's air defenses so more conventional airstrikes can be conducted on the relevant facilities without concern of retaliatory fire. In 2007, Israeli fighter aircraft struck a half-built nuclear facility in the Syrian desert. The seven planes, a mix of modified F-15 and F-16s, were decidedly unstealthy but were able to slip into and out of Syrian airspace without retaliatory fire or, apparently, detection. The attack, part of Operation Orchard, was likely made possible by Israeli success disabling Syrian air defense networks with a piece of malicious software to blind the systems or display false targets.[41]

These same tools can help provide information to friendly forces like using Wi-Fi networks in an urban environment to search for the connected devices of insurgents communicating over computers or mobile phones. In 2016, Secretary of Defense Ash Carter testified before Congress that CYBERCOM was planning to launch sustained operations against ISIS' computer networks and mobile phones.[42] Software tools, developed by CYBERCOM, could be used to disable devices and disrupt their operations or to spy on their users and provide their location for air strikes or capture.[43]

A key policy consideration in structuring the acquisition and use of cyber capabilities is the extent of cooperation with allied forces who may possess different organizational structures and technical or policy capacity. As has been reported, the U.S. military does not habitually share offensive capabilities with military allies.[44] In some cases, however, sharing agreements could entail a limited exchange of threat detection or intelligence information.[45] On average, offensive cyber interoperability with allies is unlikely to be a high priority, due to obvious concerns over information sensitivity and the high stakes that are involved while defensive missions will likely take precedence. Alliance cooperation can also take place within the larger joint operations framework. For example, U.S. cyber operators may unilaterally deploy a specific capability while allies either separately deploy their own or use conventional forces in a supporting role.

Tactical

At the tactical level, military forces are focusing on smaller units and must consider immediate environmental variables, like the organization of a city's physical layout and its associated electrical grid or civilian wireless networks. Vulnerabilities exist in potentially new targets like weapon systems and the larger Internet of Things, like vehicles,[46] as well as in traditional assets like communications systems.[47] On the battlefield, malicious software deployed by a combat unit could be used to target opponent radio networks, disabling receivers or deleting the codes used to encrypt transmissions.

The degree of mobility involved at the tactical level, combined with the smaller target area, presents several different challenges. First, since operators are working in an active combat zone, they are vulnerable to counter fire. Second, there are likely to be more substantial time constraints in combat, with military forces attempting to deliver capabilities in real time during an ongoing engagement. Combined with moving targets and varying distances, this may shrink the window in which a particular vulnerability is effective. Finally, the particular nature of the environment may also make tailoring and testing cyber capabilities more difficult.

On the other hand, tactical cyber mission may have a few important advantages over those at the operational or strategic level. Adversaries may not be attuned to their poor security and hardware vulnerabilities for common devices like radios or command-and-control equipment. Consequently, opponents may mistakenly believe that the tactical level is comparatively less vulnerable than the operational or strategic environment. At the tactical level, close proximity to the target also opens up the opportunity for not just network but also spectrum attacks. Traditionally, cyber capabilities are thought of as network-centric only, accessing an adversary's system and causing an effect through networked information systems. However, at the tactical level, operators can exploit the electromagnetic spectrum as a means to access, disrupt, or degrade a target's systems like radios or power generation equipment.[48] Friendly forces can even use the electronic spectrum as a delivery mechanism for a cyber capability.[49] Finally, close proximity to the battlefield enables forces to more reliably gauge the effectiveness of a capability on a target.

Setting the Rules

MCO is a relatively new strategic arena, and therefore the rules and norms that exist are less developed than in other military and technological contexts, and are subject to greater debate between domestic and international actors. However, as more and more countries formally set up unified cyber commands there will be opportunities to promote domestic norms, at least at the operational and tactical levels. This final section addresses several norms that may potentially govern the strategic, operational, and tactical use of offensive cyber capabilities. The problem of MCO's "newness" is made even more difficult by the lack of large-scale use of cyber capabilities in conflict—at least to date. This is certainly a positive historical development, but one that exacerbates the lack of precedent, since militaries are reluctant to either promote or contest any particular rule or norm absent an understanding of its operational impact. A separate but related issue is the enforcement question:

if international rules and norms are adopted, how can countries ensure that signatories are properly following the agreements? Nevertheless, there are a few areas where ideas have begun to converge.

The UN Group of Governmental Experts

The United Nations Group of Governmental Experts on Information Security (GGE) agreed in July 2015 to a consensus document laying out recommendations for state activity in cyberspace.[50] The 2015 document reiterates the importance of confidence building measures but went farther than previous drafts by outlining guidelines for MCOs and critical infrastructure protection.[51] It stated specifically that countries should respond to requests for support and refrain from engaging in activity that intentionally damages or impairs critical infrastructure or computer emergency response teams (CERTs). The report goes even further toward applying international legal principles (such as necessity and proportionality) to cyber activity. A slightly expanded successor group has been formed to run through 2016–2017.

The U.S. Department of Defense (DoD) Law of War Manual

The DoD's Law of War Manual reinforces previous claims that existing laws of war are generally applicable to cyber operations, but leaves open the possibility of changes in the future, by redefining the types of tools classified as weapons for example.[52] On the issue of a cyber "act of war," the manual argues that cyber incidents are not necessarily armed attacks for the purposes of triggering a country's right to self-defense. Cyber incidents are also "not necessarily 'attacks' for the purposes of applying rules on the conduct of operations during hostilities."[53] As well, the manual does not create an obligation for neutral parties to refrain from relaying an actor's information or data through their own cybersecurity infrastructure. Through these and related claims, the manual largely codifies existing U.S. positions and, importantly, does not create a definition for the use of force.

The Tallinn Manual, Tallinn 2.0, and The Laws of Armed Conflict

The Tallinn Manual on the International Law Applicable to Cyber Warfare[54] is the product of a three-year NATO Cooperative Cyber Defense Center of Excellence effort to offer a summary of international law as it applies to ongoing cyber conflict. This manual outlines ninety-five rules that govern international cyber conflict, addressing issues such as sovereignty, state responsibility, the conditions for the onset of war, international humanitarian law, and the law of neutrality. Importantly, the Tallinn Manual focuses on incidents that occur as the use of force and therefore does not directly address issues of cyber crime or espionage. The Tallinn Manual's key point is that cyber conflict or "cyber warfare" is governed by existing international law, the same international rules that concern other forms of conflict including relevant portions of the UN charter, The Hague Convention of 1899, and the Geneva Convention of 1949.[55] Launched in June 2016, Tallinn 2.0 acts as a set of legal definitions and framework to deal with issues below the level of ongoing conflict. This document covers incidents without destructive effect, issues of attribution, and the assignment of responsibility for proxies (groups acting on behalf of countries).[56]

CONCLUSION

Military Cyber Operations cover the acquisition and use of cyber capabilities at the strategic, operational, and tactical levels of conflict. MCO is properly understood as part of a combined arms approach to warfighting codified in the military doctrines of several countries, including the United States. This casts doubt on the notion of cybersecurity as a single domain issue and militates against the likelihood of a domain-specific "cyber war." While offensive issues dominate doctrinal and legal discussions, defensive missions have proven to be more frequent and resource-intensive challenges for the military and related organizations. There is also an unresolved set of procurement, personnel, and strategic questions that impact the day-to-day activities of CYBERCOM and the military service—a fact which may undermine U.S. operational effectiveness over time. While the norms of behavior governing MCO are still far from settled, there is at least some consensus over the application of existing international law, rules like proportionality and restraint, especially in reference to civilian targets. The pace of technological change is rapid, but the selection of organizational, planning, and oversight challenges discussed in the following chapters remain persistent. How policy adapts to fit and fulfill the needs of soldiers employing these capabilities on and off the battlefield will help shape the future of the force and impact national security decision-making for decades to come.

CHAPTER HIGHLIGHTS

Military Cyber Operations. Instead of "cyber war," MCO focuses on cyber conflict, or "cyber-enabled warfare," in which cyber capabilities are deployed in conjunction with conventional forces as well as independently.

Commercial Software Vulnerabilities. Hidden vulnerabilities in commercial off-the-shelf (COTS) software retain value for future military use, but also risk discovery by malicious parties. This impacts military and government agencies using COTS solutions as those same unpatched vulnerabilities leave .mil and .gov networks open to attack.

Behavior Shapes Precedent. An important consideration is the role of precedent, where the use of novel techniques, especially in offense, can establish a new baseline for permissible (or tolerable) behavior among allies and opponents.

Cyber Interoperability. On average, cyber interoperability with allies will be a challenge for offensive and secretive reconnaissance activities but are ongoing for defensive operations. Alliance cooperation can still take place within the larger joint operations framework.

Understanding and Enforcing Norms. Militaries are reluctant to either promote or contest any particular rule or norm absent an understanding of its operational impact. If international rules and norms are adopted, how can countries ensure that signatories are properly following the agreements?

NOTES

1. "War in the Fifth Domain," *The Economist*, July 1, 2010, http://www.economist.com/node/16478792.

2. For more, see Drew Herrick and Trey Herr, "Combating Complexity: Offensive Cyber Capabilities and Integrated Warfighting" (International Studies Association, Atlanta, GA, 2016).

3. Herrick and Herr, "Combating Complexity."

4. For example, consider Russian forces in Georgia or Ukraine. Similarly, consider U.S. cyber operations in Iraq or plans for their use in Libya. Eric Schmitt and Thom Shanker, "U.S. Debated Cyberwarfare Against Libya," *New York Times*, October 17, 2011, http://www.nytimes.com/2011/10/18/world/africa/cyber-warfare-against-libya-was-debated-by-us.html.

5. Thomas Rid, *Cyber War Will Not Take Place*, first edition, New York: Oxford University Press, 2013; Erik Gartzke, "The Myth of Cyberwar: Bringing War in Cyberspace Back Down to Earth," *International Security* 38, no. 2 (October 1, 2013), 41–73.

6. Chris Demchak, "Cybered Conflict vs. Cyber War," *New Atlanticist*, October 20, 2015, http://www.atlanticcouncil.org/blogs/new-atlanticist/cybered-conflict-vs-cyber-war; Joint Publication 3–12, "USCYBERCOMMAND Cyber Mission Force,"

Headquarters U.S. Air Force, February 5, 2013, accessed March 8, 2016, http://www.
safcioa6.af.mil/shared/media/document/AFD-140512-039.pdf.

7. For more, see chapter 1—"Understanding Information Assurance."

8. Joint Publication 3–12, "USCYBERCOMMAND Cyber Mission Force,"
Headquarters U.S. Air Force, February 5, 2013, accessed March 8, 2016, http://www.
safcioa6.af.mil/shared/media/document/AFD-140512-039.pdf.

9. Maren Leed, "Offensive Cyber Capabilities at the Operational Level," *CSIS,*
September 2013, http://csis.org/files/publication/130916_Leed_OffensiveCyberCa-
pabilities_Web.pdf.

10. Chris Paul, *Information Operations—Doctrine and Practice: A Reference
Handbook*, (Westport, Conn: Praeger, 2008).

11. For more, see chapter 20—"Creating Influence through Information."

12. David Sanger, "U.S. Cyberattacks Target ISIS in a New Line of Combat," *The
New York Times,* April 24, 2016 http://www.nytimes.com/2016/04/25/us/politics/us-
directs-cyberweapons-at-isis-for-first-time.html?_r=0.

13. Chris Paul, *Information Operations—Doctrine and Practice: A Reference
Handbook* (Westport, CT: Praeger, 2008).

14. Kristen Kushiyama, "Army Looks to Blend Cyber, Electronic Warfare Capabilities on Battlefield," U.S. Army, October 29, 2013, accessed March 7, 2016, http://
www.cerdec.army.mil/news_and_media/Army_looks_to_blend_cyber__electronic_
warfare_capabilities_on_battlefield/.

15. Richard Bejtlich, "TaoSecurity: More Russian Information Warfare,"
TaoSecurity, February 6, 2014, http://taosecurity.blogspot.com/2014/02/more-russian-
information-warfare.html; Oscar Jonnson and Robert Seely, "Russian Full-Spectrum
Conflict: An Appraisal After Ukraine," *The Journal of Slavic Military Studies* 28,
no. 1 (January 2, 2015): 1–22. doi:10.1080/13518046.2015.998118; Vinod Anand,
"Chinese Concepts and Capabilities of Information Warfare," *Strategic Analysis* 30,
no. 4 (2006): 781–97.

16. For more on malware, see chapter 7—"Disrupting Malware Markets."

17. Kim Zetter, *Countdown to zero day: Stuxnet and the launch of the world's first
digital weapon* (Crown/Archetype, 2014).

18. Ralph Langner, "Langner—To Kill a Centrifuge.pdf," The Langner Group,
November 2013, http://www.langner.com/en/wp-content/uploads/2013/11/To-kill-a-
centrifuge.pdf.

19. William J. Broad, John Markoff, and David E. Sanger, "Stuxnet Worm Used
Against Iran Was Tested in Israel," *The New York Times*, January 15, 2011, http://www.
nytimes.com/2011/01/16/world/middleeast/16stuxnet.html; Nicolas Falliere, Liam O.
Murchu, and Eric Chien, "W32. Stuxnet Dossier" (Symantec, 2011), http://www.h4ckr.
us/library/Documents/ICS_Events/Stuxnet%20Dossier%20(Symantec)%20v1.4.pdf.

20. Michael Mimoso, "Disclosed Netgear Router Vulnerability Under Attack,"
Threatpost: The First Stop for Security News, October 8, 2015, https://threatpost.com/
disclosed-netgear-router-vulnerability-under-attack/114960/.

21. For more, see chapter 7—"Disrupting Malware Markets."

22. Andy Greenberg, "Here's a Spy Firm's Price List for Secret Hacker
Techniques," *Wired.com,* November 18, 2015, http://www.wired.com/2015/11/
heres-a-spy-firms-price-list-for-secret-hacker-techniques/.

23. Kim Zetter, "Turns Out the US Launched Its Zero-Day Policy in Feb 2010," *Wired.com,* June 26, 2015, http://www.wired.com/2015/06/turns-us-launched-zero-day-policy-feb-2010/.

24. For more, see chapter 17—"Government Acquisition and Use of Zero-Day Software Vulnerabilities."

25. JP-1, "Doctrine for the Armed Forces of the United States," March 23, 2013, 1-172, accessed March 8, 2016, http://www.dtic.mil/doctrine/new_pubs/jp1.pdf.

26. James R. Locher III, "Has It Worked? The Goldwater-Nichols Reorganization Act," *Naval War College Review* 54, no. 4 (Autumn 2001): 95–115, https://www.usnwc.edu/getattachment/744b0f7d-4a3f-4473-8a27-c5b444c2ea27/Has-It-Worked--The-Goldwater-Nichols-Reorganization.

27. Joint Publication 3–12, "USCYBERCOMMAND Cyber Mission Force," Headquarters U.S. Air Force, February 5, 2013, http://www.safcioa6.af.mil/shared/media/document/AFD-140512-039.pdf.

28. Kevin McCaney, "Army's New Cyber Branch Looking to Recruit Talent—Defense Systems," *Defense Systems,* December 11, 2014, https://defensesystems.com/articles/2014/12/11/army-cyber-branch-new-career-field.aspx.

29. Jim Tice, "Staffing Goal for Cyber Branch Totals Nearly 1,300 Officers, Enlisted Soldiers," *Army Times,* June 15, 2015, http://www.armytimes.com/story/military/2015/06/15/cyber-transfer-panels-and-reclassification-actions/71060716/.

30. Wilson A. Rivera, "Cyberspace Warriors Graduate with Army's Newest Military Occupational Specialty," ARMY.MIL, The Official Homepage of the United States Army, December 6, 2013, http://www.army.mil/article/116564/ and 35Q - http://www.army.mil/article/92099/Army_opens_new_intelligence_MOS/.

31. Laura Levering, "Cyber School Marks Major Milestone," *Fort Gordon Globe,* August 8, 2014, http://www.fortgordonglobe.com/news/2015-08-14/Front_Page/Cyber_School_marks_major_milestone.html.

32. United States Accountability Office, "More Detailed Guidance Needed to Ensure Military Services Develop Appropriate Cyberspace Capabilities," *Defense Department Cyber Efforts,* May 2011, http://www.gao.gov/assets/320/318612.pdf.

33. For more, see chapter 18—"The Joint Cyber Force: Challenges and Opportunities."

34. Stephen Biddle, "Strategy in War," *PS. Political Science & Politics* 40, no. 3 (July 2007): 461.

35. Admiral Stavridis, "Divide and Conquer: Why Dual Authority at the NSA and Cyber Command Hurts U.S. Cybersecurity," *The Fletcher School Dean Stavridis Blog,* October 24, 2013, http://sites.tufts.edu/fletcherdean/divide-and-conquer-why-dual-authority-at-the-nsa-and-cyber-command-hurts-u-s-cybersecurity/.

36. Lt. Col. Charles W. Douglas, "21st-Century Cyber Security: Legal Authorities and Requirements," strategy research project, US Army War College, 2012, http://handle.dtic.mil/100.2/ADA561641.

37. Aaron P. Brecher, "Cyberattacks and the Covert Action Statute: Toward a Domestic Legal Framework for Offensive Cyberoperations," *Michigan Law Review* 111 (2012): 423, http://repository.law.umich.edu/mlr/vol111/iss3/3.

38. Ryan Singel, "Congress Authorizes Pentagon to Wage Internet War," *Wired.com,* December 14, 2011, http://www.wired.com/2011/12/internet-war-2/.

39. Joint Publication 5-0. JOPES, *Joint Operation Planning and Execution System*, Washington, DC: Chairman, Joint Chiefs of Staff, 2011, http://www.dtic.mil/doctrine/new_pubs/jp5_0.pdf.

40. Stephen Biddle, "Strategy in War," *PS, Political Science & Politics* 40, no. 3 (July 2007): 461.

41. John Leyden, "Israel Suspected of 'hacking' Syrian Air Defences," *The Register,* October 4, 2007, http://www.theregister.co.uk/2007/10/04/radar_hack_raid/.

42. Mark Pomerleau, "US Prepares to Take the Cyber Fight to ISIS," *Defense Systems,* December 23, 2015, https://defensesystems.com/articles/2015/12/23/us-cyber-fight-against-isis.aspx.

43. Sean Lyngaas, "Carter Calls on Cybercom to Intensify Online Push against ISIS," *FCW,* January 29, 2016, https://fcw.com/articles/2016/01/29/daesh-cyber-lyngaas.aspx.

44. James A. Lewis, "The Role of Offensive Cyber Operations in NATO's Collective Defense," *Atlantic Council,* accessed October 30, 2015, http://www.atlanticcouncil.org/blogs/natosource/the-role-of-offensive-cyber-operations-in-natos-collective-defense; Lt. Col. Jason B Nicholson, and Lt. Col. David A. Pokrifchak, "Cyber sharing," *Armed Forces Journal,* December 16, 2013.

45. Ibid.

46. Michael Hardy, "Demo Jeep Hack Could Have Military Implications," *C4ISR & Networks*, accessed October 30, 2015, http://www.c4isrnet.com/story/military-tech/cyber/2015/07/24/vehicle-hack-could-have-military-implications/30628191/.

47. James J. Coyle, "Russia Has Complete Information Dominance in Ukraine," *Atlantic Council,* accessed October 30, 2015, http://www.atlanticcouncil.org/blogs/new-atlanticist/russia-has-complete-informational-dominance-in-ukraine.

48. Kristen Kushiyama, "Army Looks to Blend Cyber, Electronic Warfare Capabilities on Battlefield," U.S. Army, October 29, 2013, http://www.cerdec.army.mil/news_and_media/Army_looks_to_blend_cyber__electronic_warfare_capabilities_on_battlefield/.

49. Ibid.

50. United Nations, "Group of Governmental Experts on Developments in the Field of Information and Telecommunications in the Context of International Security," July 22 2015, http://www.un.org/ga/search/view_doc.asp?symbol=A/70/174; "Net Politics: The UN GGE on Cybersecurity: What Is the UN's Role?" *Council on Foreign Relations,* accessed October 30, 2015, http://blogs.cfr.org/cyber/2015/04/15/the-un-gge-on-cybersecurity-what-is-the-uns-role/.

51. Ibid.

52. U. S. Department of Defense, *U.S. Department of Defense Law of War Manual,* 2015.

53. Ibid.

54. Michael N. Schmitt, ed., *Tallinn Manual on the International Law Applicable to Cyber Warfare* (New York: Cambridge University Press, 2013).

55. Ibid.

56. Tim Maurer, "Proxies and Cyberspace," *Journal for Conflict and Security Law* 21, no. 3 (Forthcoming), http://jcsl.oxfordjournals.org/.

Chapter 17

Government Acquisition and Use of Zero-Day Software Vulnerabilities

Mailyn Fidler

The American public started worrying about "zero-day" vulnerabilities—unpatched flaws in software that remain unknown to software vendors and leave users at risk—in April 2014, when computer security experts discovered the dramatically named "Heartbleed" vulnerability. "Heartbleed" was a flaw in software encrypting information transmitted over the internet.[1] The bug existed in OpenSSL, an open source cryptographic library used by up to two-thirds of websites to encrypt internet traffic.[2] Heartbleed exposed large swaths of data to interception and exploitation. Initially, news stories speculated the U.S. government knew about Heartbleed, and purposely avoided disclosing the vulnerability so it could kept secret for intelligence gathering or other government activities, leaving internet users at risk.[3]

Although speculation about the U.S. government's role in the Heartbleed incident seems to have been unfounded, concerns about the U.S. government's role in discovering, purchasing, and using such software vulnerabilities are real. Edward Snowden's disclosures indicated the National Security Agency (NSA) uses and purchases zero-days, and the FBI has since revealed its own use and purchase of zero-days.[4] The Heartbleed controversy and Snowden's disclosures about the NSA spurred the U.S. government to detail its oversight process for its use of vulnerabilities.[5] These revelations and the U.S. government's responses have raised further questions about U.S. policy on zero-days. What other agencies—federal or state—use software vulnerabilities, including zero-days? Is oversight of agency discovery, use, purchasing, and disclosure of vulnerabilities adequate? Should the U.S. government take action to stem international availability of zero-days to bad actors, such as repressive regimes? This chapter explores the mechanics of U.S. government purchase and use of software vulnerabilities, discusses current government oversight mechanisms and how they might be improved, and looks at debates about controlling zero-days internationally.

What's the Problem?

Conflicts Between National Security and Citizen Cybersecurity

The U.S. government's participation in this market raises concerns because keeping zero-days secret to preserve military, intelligence, or law enforcement capabilities may present conflicts between national security and citizen cybersecurity. According to post-Heartbleed statements by U.S. officials, if the government discovers a zero-day, it has a "bias" toward disclosure.[6] Exceptions to this policy exist, providing opportunities for the government to keep vulnerabilities without notifying software vendors. Keeping vulnerabilities secret means other governments or cyber criminals may independently discover or purchase the vulnerability and use it to the detriment of U.S. cybersecurity.[7] Furthermore, U.S. nondisclosure of zero-days leaves global users at risk, because undisclosed vulnerabilities affect anyone using widely disseminated software. The use of zero-days is also tied up with larger debates about civil liberties: what tools are appropriate for the government to possess and use in pursuit of security aims?

International Security Ramifications

U.S. government acquisition and use of zero-day vulnerabilities has contributed to the growth of a market that also allows less cyber-capable nations and nonstate actors unfriendly to U.S. interests to improve their cyber capabilities.[8] The global nature of this market means that other governments, as well as nonstate actors and criminals, can gain cyber capabilities that could be used against U.S. interests or to violate human rights and civil liberties within their borders.[9] Before these vulnerabilities were available on the market, the ability to discover zero-days in-house was largely a boutique capability, the privilege of a few competent governments or those who could hire skilled hackers.[10] Nonstate actor access to zero-days is also a national security concern, keeping Eric Rosenbach, Deputy Assistant Secretary of Defense for Cyber Policy, "awake at night."[11] U.S. involvement in purchasing vulnerabilities may also build the vulnerabilities market.[12]

Concerns that zero-days can contribute to human rights abuses have also emerged. For instance, in April 2014, computer security researchers revealed that a vulnerability in Adobe Flash had been used to target Syrians who visited a government "complaints" website since September 2013.[13] This effort appears to have been professionally planned and executed.[14] This situation demonstrates that concerns about connections between human rights abuses and zero-days are real. European Union politician Marietje Schaake has advocated regulating trade in such cyber technologies that could be used to abuse human rights.[15]

The Basics of Vulnerabilities, Exploits, and Zero-Days

What are Vulnerabilities and Exploits?

Software is largely written by people, and people rarely write perfectly secure code. As a result, mistakes are often present in software. A software vulnerability is a flaw in a software program that exposes the program or computer to external manipulation.[16] Some flaws are simple mistakes, such as typos or poor and incomplete designs. Other vulnerabilities come from failing to foresee interactions among components of a larger system of software. Still others are failures to protect programs from creative misuse or abuse. The presence of vulnerabilities usually does not affect the normal operation of a software program, but instead provides a narrow window through which the program can be exploited.

A new piece of software written to take advantage of vulnerabilities in software is called an exploit. Exploits take advantage of vulnerabilities to manipulate the target system. One common use of exploits is to grant an outsider access and administrative privileges to the target system. For instance, an exploit may be a very short section of code that would allow an outsider access to a program he or she shouldn't have, perhaps to a common browser such as Internet Explorer. Once an outsider has access to a system, they can execute other code—for instance, installing a keystroke logger—to accomplish their aims.

Zero-Day Vulnerabilities and N-Day Vulnerabilities

A zero-day vulnerability is a certain kind of software vulnerability—a previously unknown flaw in a computer program. What differentiates a zero-day from other computer vulnerabilities, and what makes it valuable, is that it is unknown to the software's developers and users. Whomever has knowledge of a zero-day can exploit it from the "zero-th" day of its discovery, until the software vendor or users learn of it and fix it by issuing a patch. The secrecy of zero-days makes them valuable, which adds to the opacity of the market for zero-days and makes them difficult to regulate. Zero-day vulnerabilities are a natural by-product of the coding process and have been found in many programs, including Microsoft, Internet Explorer, Adobe, and Apple products.[17] Zero-day vulnerabilities also appear in software running critical infrastructure, such as power plants. For instance, the Stuxnet program allegedly used by the United States to damage Iranian uranium-enrichment centrifuges used four zero-day vulnerabilities.[18]

A zero-day vulnerability is simply information, making it different from other cyber tools: a zero-day encapsulates the knowledge that X could happen if you do Y. As ReVuln, a zero-day seller, argues, "we don't sell weapons, we sell information."[19] Other companies sell exploits, new software code, written to take advantage of zero-day vulnerabilities—a zero-day exploit. Although turning a vulnerability into an exploit can be relatively easy, motivations for finding and exploiting them often differ. For instance, cybersecurity researchers have less motivation to turn vulnerabilities into reliable exploits than someone selling or buying zero-days. If someone is only attempting to demonstrate that a vulnerability exists, the 'proof-of-concept' exploit necessary to do so can be extremely limited. This distinction between tools and motivations is important to make when analyzing regulatory options for the zero-day vulnerability trade, to ensure regulations target the right actors and actions.[20]

Once a zero-day is revealed to the public or its maker, it can be called an "N-day," in reference to it being known and exploitable for "N" number of days before getting fixed, or before most people adopt an available fix. N-days are generally less valuable than zero-days, because some systems may be updated or fixed to prevent the N-day from being used, but they can still be beneficial, especially if a user or system does not update their software frequently or if a solution to the flaw is difficult to create.

The Stuxnet Example: Zero-Day Vulnerabilities and Exploits Working in Tandem

Vulnerabilities and exploits are inextricably linked. Stuxnet, software allegedly built by the U.S. and Israel, took advantage of four zero-day vulnerabilities to spread itself across computer networks, searching for equipment associated with the Iranian nuclear enrichment processes.[21] One of the vulnerabilities used in Stuxnet involved a part of the Windows operating system that handles printing. A Stuxnet exploit took advantage of this flaw to spread the malware across the Iranian network by sending these specially formatted printing requests to noninfected machines, which would then infect a new machine with Stuxnet instead of printing something.[22] Both the underlying vulnerability and new code written to take advantage of that vulnerability (the exploit) were necessary to propagate Stuxnet across its targets. The use of zero-days in Stuxnet demonstrates their high value to the U.S. government for offensive cyber operations.

The Market for Zero-Day Vulnerabilities

The NSA likely possesses in-house capabilities for discovering new zero-day vulnerabilities. However, the NSA also purchases zero-day vulnerabilities.[23] It is useful to think of zero-day vulnerabilities as being purchased on three different kinds of markets. This "three-market" approach is not the only way of conceptualizing zero-day markets, but it provides a useful simple heuristic for thinking about the market. Other chapters in this volume introduce alternative ways of thinking about the market, including a binary offensive and defensive distinction between actors and their purchasing mechanisms.[24]

The "white market" encompasses sales of vulnerabilities between zero-day vulnerability hunters and software vendors or third-party clearinghouses.[25] Many software companies also offer their own bug bounties, including Facebook, Google, and Microsoft. [26]An example of a new third-party clearinghouse is HackerOne, which operates as a middleman between software companies and flaw-finders, orchestrating paid deals.[27]

The "black market" describes interactions where at least one party has criminal intent, and sales are often conducted freely online or on restricted-access marketplaces.[28] Sellers include freelance hackers and organizations.[29] Black-market buyers include individual criminals and criminal organizations.[30] Some governments may turn to the black market if legitimate sellers refuse them. Interviews with black-market participants reveal that prices are generally elevated on the black market.[31]

The "gray market" refers to legal trade between vulnerability sellers and government agencies or other noncriminal clients. This set of transactions is designated "gray" because of the controversial but legal aspects of this trade. Potential buyers of gray-market zero-days include private sector clients, brokers reselling vulnerabilities, and governments.[32] Private sector clients typically include high-end penetration testing firms, but this customer base is considered much smaller than the government base.[33]

NSS Labs concluded that "half a dozen boutique [gray-market] exploit providers have the capacity to offer more than 100 exploits per year, resulting in 85 privately known exploits being available on any given day," at minimum.[34] Based on this author's estimates, total U.S. revenues of publically identifiable zero-day gray-market sellers would be about $10 million.[35] The Grugq, a well-known zero-day seller, responded to this author's estimates. He sized the market at less than $5 million but calls this author's individual revenue figures for the companies "probably about right."[36] A considerable gap exists between known government purchasing figures and the revenues of identifiable companies, a gap likely attributable to the secret nature of many companies and the opaque role of government contractors as sellers. Although the gray market is the focus of this chapter because it involves government purchasing, it is not necessarily the largest. It is hard to directly compare the size and volume of the three zero-day markets as presented here using publically available data.

Which Government Agencies Use and Purchase Zero-Day Vulnerabilities?

Governments can use zero-days for law enforcement investigations, improving cyber defenses, conducting cyber espionage, and conducting offensive military cyber operations. Internationally, government purchasers of zero-days include at least the following countries: the United States, Israel, Britain, Russia, India, Brazil, Malaysia, Singapore, North Korea, Iran and possibly Canada.[37]

In the United States, the NSA devoted $25.1 million to "covert purchases of software vulnerabilities" from private vendors during the fiscal year 2013, corresponding to an estimate of 100 to 625 vulnerabilities annually.[38] The NSA also likely conducts in-house research and discovery of zero-days. The NSA is tasked with foreign and covert intelligence collection, often from sophisticated targets, and sometimes relies on vulnerabilities and exploits that are comparatively advanced.[39]

The FBI uses zero-day vulnerabilities, and recent events indicated the FBI has purchased at least one vulnerability—the agency spent up to $1.3 million to acquire a reputed zero-day to access the phone associated with the San Bernadino attacks.[40] Beyond this single purchase, the FBI likely lacks sufficient in-house capabilities and probably purchases other vulnerabilities, too.[41] The FBI's budget request for the fiscal year 2017 requests an additional $38.1 million (adding to an existing $31 million) to counter encryption technologies, and experts speculate that some of this budget will be used to purchase zero-day vulnerabilities and exploits.[42] The FBI also included a request for an increase of $85.1 million (over a $541.4 million budget) for offensive and defensive cybersecurity measures.[43] *Reuters* reported that the Department of Defense (DoD) and other intelligence agencies participate in the gray market but provided no specifics.[44] The Central Intelligence Agency (CIA) is another possible purchaser based on zero-day usefulness to intelligence and the recent creation of a CIA digital directorate.[45] Government contractors such as Northrop Grumman, Lockheed Martin, Harris Corporation, and Raytheon are likely buyers, resellers, and discoverers.[46]

U.S. Zero-Day Policy Debates

Pre-2014 Policy

Little information exists about U.S. government policy toward zero-days pre-2014. Recent documents obtained through Freedom of Information Act (FOIA) requests reveal a 2008 task force discussed the topic and indicate the establishment of a review process in 2010, but the robustness of this process, and the degree to which it was implemented, remain uncertain.[47] For instance, Richard Clarke, who advised President Bush on cybersecurity, indicated there was little actual implementation as of 2013: "[t]here is supposed to be some mechanism for deciding how they use the [vulnerability] information, for offense or defense. But there isn't."[48]

The first high-profile recommendations for reform of government use of zero-days came in December 2013, from the presidential panel tasked with proposing reforms in light of the Snowden revelations, the President's Review Group on Intelligence and Communications Technologies. The panel had access to classified information, and their recommendations suggest that, before 2014, the government probably maintained a default policy of not disclosing discovered or purchased vulnerabilities, stockpiling them instead.[49] These decisions, by default, prioritized national security and intelligence needs over broader cybersecurity. The panel recommended instating an interagency process managed by the National Security Council to review zero-day vulnerability use.[50] The panel suggested instituting a default policy of disclosing or patching zero-day vulnerabilities, rather than stockpiling them.[51] In rare instances, brief authorization could be granted for high priority intelligence use of zero-days following an interagency review process.[52] In his March 2014 confirmation hearings for the position of Director of the NSA and Commander of the U.S. Cyber Command, Vice Admiral Michael Rogers echoed the review group's language, indicating work was potentially underway to increase disclosure and establish an interagency review process.[53]

After Heartbleed, Senior Officials Detail U.S. Government Policy

After the Heartbleed controversy, senior Obama administration officials provided more details on U.S. government policy toward vulnerability disclosure. In April 2014, officials indicated that the zero-day review process is "biased toward responsibly disclosing such vulnerabilities."[54] This statement contains ambiguities—what percentage of vulnerabilities does this "bias" indicate? In what circumstances does the government decide not to disclose? The officials further indicated that, "when the National Security Agency discovers major flaws in Internet security" the NSA "should—in most circumstances—reveal them . . . rather than keep them mum so that the flaws can be used."[55] The officials noted President Obama created "a broad exception for 'a clear national security or law enforcement need,'" a loophole which Sanger indicates will "likely allow the NSA to continue to exploit security flaws both to crack encryption on the Internet and to design cyberweapons."[56]

The White House also released a blog post, authored by Michael Daniel, special assistant to the president and cybersecurity coordinator.[57] Daniel asserted the Obama administration "re-invigorated our efforts to implement existing policy with respect to disclosing vulnerabilities."[58] Is Daniel suggesting that, previously, existing policy was not implemented with sufficient vigor? Daniel also listed several questions the administration uses when deciding to disclose or stockpile a vulnerability. These considerations included:

- how much risk the vulnerability imposes if unpatched,
- how critical the system in which the vulnerability resides is to internet infrastructure,
- and how likely it is that another party would discover the vulnerability.[59]

The Vulnerability Equities Process—Information as of January 2016

After the Heartbleed controversy, the Electronic Frontier Foundation (EFF) filed a FOIA request for documents relating to the procedures Daniel mentioned. The second redacted version of the resulting document, released in January 2016, demonstrates the existence of an interagency "vulnerabilities equities process" finalized in 2010 but little else. The full list of agencies participating in the discussions is withheld, although the document indicates that both intelligence and law enforcement agencies participate. The criteria used to decide whether vulnerabilities should be disclosed or stockpiled are also redacted. One of the blacked-out sections contains the process for dealing with vulnerabilities in cryptographic software, a particularly valuable form of vulnerabilities, especially in light of the "Going Dark" debate.[60] The review process does not apply retroactively, potentially leaving previously stockpiled vulnerabilities exempt.

In October 2015, the NSA claimed that 91 percent of vulnerabilities sent through this review process have been disclosed, but this statement carries important qualifications.[61] The statement only applies to the NSA, to vulnerabilities in products made or used in the United States, and only to vulnerabilities not somehow otherwise exempted from the review process.

U.S. Policy Next Steps

Improved Transparency

Although dating from 2010, the vulnerability equities process has generally "not been implemented to the full degree that it should have been."[62] Few opportunities exist for outside experts or the public to assess (1) the robustness of current policy and (2) the degree to which it has been implemented. Gaining further knowledge about the zero-day review process is a first step toward these aims, and the EFF is currently challenging remaining redactions to the vulnerabilities equities process document. Transparency is an important underlying condition in the public's ability to ascertain whether the government's weighing of citizen security and national security is acceptable. Even regular disclosure of aggregate statistics relating to vulnerabilities discovered or purchased and disclosed would be a welcome addition to the public debate.

Questions about the Extent of Oversight

Several aspects of U.S. government policy, as publicly known, deserve improvement. Questions remain about the sufficiency of oversight guidelines. Officials describing current policy indicate the government should, "in most circumstances," disclose a major flaw in "Internet security."[63] This statement raises two questions. Are vulnerabilities in non-internet software programs, such as the Microsoft programs targeted by Stuxnet, covered by this policy? Questions also exist about whether oversight extends to purchased vulnerabilities as well as vulnerabilities discovered in-house. This possibility is discussed in its own section below. In addition, the process for resolving competing opinions between government agencies about whether to disclose a vulnerability or how to use vulnerabilities deserves further clarification.

Clarity on Vulnerability Disclosure Policies

The criteria used to assess when the U.S. government is allowed to keep vulnerabilities secret should be released in greater detail for public scrutiny. Specifically, experts disagree as to whether the review group's recommendations have been implemented. Jack Goldsmith, a Harvard Law professor and former government official, argues that the exceptions indicated by the government, "taken together, appear to be quite a lot broader than Recommendation 30 [of the review group]."[64] Specifically, current policy does not seem to presume disclosure by default except in instances of severe national security needs (it notes, for instance, law enforcement needs).[65] Peter Swire, a member of the review group, discounts these criticisms, perceiving instead that Recommendation 30 was generally adopted.[66] Summing up the confusion, Microsoft's Scott Charney summarizes U.S. government practice as a policy of "we'll share [zero-days] unless we don't."[67] This ambiguity contributes to uncertainty over the adequacy and potential harms of the equities process as currently structured.

Clarity on Oversight of Purchased Vulnerabilities

Existing U.S. government policy may not address government purchase of vulnerabilities, a problematic and inseparable aspect of the zero-day problem. When "the National Security Agency *discovers*" a vulnerability, its bias should be toward disclosure (emphasis added).[68] Does the disclosure bias extend to *purchased* vulnerabilities? If not, this gap represents a significant loophole. If current disclosure policy only extends to vulnerabilities

discovered in-house by government agencies, the U.S. government's participation in the gray market remains without evident oversight.

However, some argue that government purchasing of vulnerabilities is
actually advantageous to cybersecurity, and, as such, should not be regulated—given appropriate oversight, government purchase of vulnerabilities
could get vulnerabilities off the market and (mostly) patched.[69] Alternatively,
purchased vulnerabilities could be more valuable, dangerous, or discoverable
by third parties, making lack of oversight even more dangerous to ordinary
computer users.[70]

In addition to ensuring that oversight practices extend to purchased zero-
days, the government could also boost transparency of gray-market zero-day
prices, improving the balance between white and gray-market incentives.
[71] Currently, U.S. government agencies seem to make zero-day purchases
without coordination, potentially bidding prices up.[72] To address this issue,
government agencies could participate in a shared registry of prices. The
resulting transparency would hopefully lower prices, benefiting agency budgets and equalizing incentives between white and gray markets.[73]

Special Considerations for Law Enforcement Use

The presidential review group suggested the government should only keep
zero-days secret for "rare instances" of "high priority intelligence collection."[74] With the FBI's recent admission of its use and purchase of zero-days,
questions remain about the appropriateness of zero-day use in law enforcement contexts:

- What systems of oversight exist for law enforcement use of zero-days?
- Does the FBI participate in the interagency vulnerability equities review
  process?
- What internal controls does the FBI put in place?
- Is the FBI a significant gray-market purchaser?
- Should law enforcement use be subject to the same review process as intel-
  ligence vulnerabilities, or should it be subjected to even higher scrutiny?
- What other law enforcement agencies use zero-days?
- Should law enforcement use zero-days at all—indeed, should law enforce-
  ment agencies possess hacking powers?

These questions deserve clear policy answers. These questions could also
apply to other federal agencies bridging the law enforcement/intelligence
divide, such as the Drug Enforcement Agency, which already uses other
surveillance software systems, including stingray cellphone tracking
devices.[75] Last, given the presidential review group's endorsement of use of

vulnerabilities in limited national security instances, law enforcement purchase and use of vulnerabilities may introduce competition between agencies for vulnerability access with a range of effects, including potentially further driving up gray-market prices.

Federal law enforcement use of vulnerabilities may also establish a precedent for vulnerability use by state and local authorities. Historically, what the FBI uses, local sheriffs often end up using. The trickle-down of stingray cellphone interception tools to local and state police exemplifies this phenomenon and has raised concerns about "street-level" surveillance, especially of minority communities.[76] Although this question may seem far-fetched at present, the eventual possibility that state (and less likely, local) law enforcement agencies might use zero-days is worth considering. Particularly as law enforcement agencies request hacking powers to counter increased use of encryption, nonfederal law enforcement agencies may feel drawn to these tools. Should these agencies be permitted to use zero-days, or software supporting zero days? How can effective oversight of zero-day use be designed for such agencies, when state and local agencies are varied and decentralized? Should the federal government design codes of conduct for state and local use or regulate their access to zero-days?

International Zero-Day Policy Debates

The zero-day market and its downsides are global, which has resulted in debate about whether, and how, cross-border trade in zero-days should be controlled to prevent bad state or nonstate actors from accessing them. Concerns exist that these actors would use zero-days to violate human rights or threaten U.S. interests. Although no international agreement currently mandates controls on the trade in zero-days, zero-days are often discussed in conjunction with an international agreement controlling the export of dual-use technologies, the Wassenaar Arrangement. In December 2013, the Wassenaar Arrangement, an agreement among forty-one states establishing nonbinding regulations on export of certain dual-use technologies, was revised to include new controls on "intrusion software," systems of software that could be used for large-scale monitoring and surveillance.[77] The Wassenaar Arrangement definition of intrusion software did not explicitly include zero-day vulnerabilities, but the language was dense and caused confusion about the scope of the controls.[78]

States participating in the Wassenaar Arrangement promise to transpose the arrangement's controls into national law. The United States issued its draft implementation of the 2013 intrusion software controls in the summer of 2015, after many other states had already implemented the controls. The initial U.S. proposal deviated from the Wassenaar text. Its introduction defined intrusion software explicitly to include some zero-days, and the text of the proposed rule indicated a policy of presumptive denial for products having or supporting zero-day capabilities.[79] Civil society and industry quickly voiced concerns that such controls would thwart important computer security research, especially across borders.[80] A coalition of software companies and allies formed in response to the U.S. draft rule, arguing that the main Wassenaar intrusion software controls also needed to be renegotiated.[81] Experts have offered many suggestions for how the U.S. language could be rewritten to avoid unintended effects on legitimate computer security research.[82] Faced with this opposition, the U.S. government indicated in early 2016 that it would seek to renegotiate the relevant language in the Wassenaar Arrangement. Specifically, the U.S. government indicated it would seek to remove language controlling "technology" supporting intrusion software—many argue "technology" is defined too broadly in export control regulations—but maintain controls on the software itself.[83] The relevant negotiations will take place in December 2016.[84]

Regardless of what happens with the Wassenaar Arrangement, U.S. zero-day policy still has international implications. U.S. stockpiling, purchasing, and opaque oversight of zero-day use will encourage other countries to continue to follow suit, worsening existing security concerns about access and use of zero-days by state and nonstate actors. What role do international security concerns play in decisions to disclose or stockpile vulnerabilities during the U.S. vulnerability equities process? Although these vulnerability markets will exist with or without U.S. government participation, American resources and behavior can have a substantial impact on their size and potential for wider harm. If the U.S. is seriously concerned about the international security ramifications of the zero-day trade, it is possible that collective international action to control zero-days, while difficult, may eventually be necessary.[85]

CONCLUSION

U.S. intelligence and law enforcement agencies discover, use, and purchase zero-days to conduct investigations, improve cyber defense, gather intelligence, and carry out offensive cyber operations. These practices place national security and law enforcement aims above citizen and business cybersecurity and encourage other countries to join a vulnerability race-to-the-bottom. Concerns about the current oversight regime's robustness and transparency exist, particularly about whether such policies extend to all government agencies, all types of vulnerabilities, and to purchased vulnerabilities. Questions also exist about the appropriateness of and extent of federal and other law enforcement use of zero-days. As countries increasingly consider restricting the cross-border exchange of software that could have negative human rights or security affects, questions and confusion about regulating zero-days have emerged. U.S. domestic practices and policies will likely influence international practices and should be made with an eye toward both the consequences at home and the echoes abroad.

CHAPTER HIGHLIGHTS

Zero-Day Vulnerabilities. A software vulnerability is a flaw in a software program that exposes the program or computer to external manipulation. A zero-day is a vulnerability, which is unknown to the software vendor at the time of use. These unpatched flaws leave users at risk. It is common practice for governments, intelligence agencies, and militaries across the globe to find and keep zero-day vulnerabilities in commonly used software a secret from the respective software vendors so they can exploit the software for espionage, intelligence gathering, or other purposes.

Exploiting Vulnerabilities. A new piece of software written to take advantage of vulnerabilities in other software is called an "exploit." One common use of exploits is to grant an outsider access and administrative privileges to the target system.

Nondisclosure Disadvantages. Keeping vulnerabilities secret means other governments or cyber criminals may independently discover or purchase the vulnerability and use it to the detriment of U.S. cybersecurity. Furthermore, U.S. nondisclosure of zero-days leaves global users at risk, because undisclosed vulnerabilities affect anyone using globally disseminated software.

Vulnerability Markets. The global nature of the zero-day market means that other governments, as well as nonstate actors and criminals, can easily gain cyber capabilities that could be used against U.S. interests or to violate human rights and civil liberties within their borders. The "white market" encompasses vulnerability sales to help software vendors patch vulnerabilities. The "black market" describes vulnerability sales with criminal intent and the "gray market" describes legal trade between vulnerability sellers and government/noncriminal entities.

Purchasing Pros/Cons. Some argue that government purchasing of vulnerabilities is actually advantageous to cybersecurity, and, as such, should not be regulated—given appropriate oversight, government purchase of vulnerabilities could get vulnerabilities off the market and (mostly) patched. Alternatively, purchased vulnerabilities could be more valuable, dangerous, or discoverable by third parties, making lack of oversight even more dangerous to ordinary computer users.

NOTES

1. Marshall Scholar, Department of Politics and International Relations, University of Oxford. I would like to thank the following people for their advice, input, and support during my work on this research: Lily Ablon, Richard Bejtlich, Fred Cate, Scott Charney, Jack Goldsmith, Jennifer Granick, Herb Lin, Jonathan Mayer, Chris Soghoian, Michael Sulmeyer, and Peter Swire. This chapter updates the analysis in Mailyn Fidler, *Regulating the Zero-Day Vulnerability Trade: A Preliminary Analysis* 11.2 ISJLP (2015), http://moritzlaw.osu.edu/students/groups/is/files/2016/02/9-Fidler. pdf.

Nicole Perlroth, "Experts Find a Door Ajar in an Internet Security Method Thought Safe," *N.Y. Times,* April 8, 2014, http://bits.blogs.nytimes.com/2014/04/08/ flaw-found-in-key-method-for-protecting-data-on-the-internet/.

2. "The Heartbleed Bug," *Codenomicon,* accessed April 2014, http://heartbleed. com/.

3. Michael Riley, "NSA Said to Exploit Heartbleed Bug for Intelligence for Years," *Bloomberg,* April 11, 2014, http://www.bloomberg.com/news/2014-04-11/ nsa-said-.

4. Ellen Nakashima, "Meet the Woman in Charge of the FBI's Most Controversial High-Tech Tools," *Washington Post,* December 8 2015, https://www.washingtonpost. com/world/national-security/meet-the-woman-in-charge-of-the-fbis-most-conten- tious-high-tech-tools/2015/12/08/15adb35e-9860-11e5-8917-653b65c809eb_story. html; Ellen Nakashima, "FBI Paid Professional Hackers One-Time Fee to Crack San Bernardino iPhone," *Washington Post,* April 12, 2016, https://www.washingtonpost. com/world/national-security/fbi-paid-professional-hackers-one-time-fee-to-crack- san-bernardino-iphone/2016/04/12/5397814a-00de-11e6-9d36-33d198ea26c5_story. html.

5. Michael Daniel, "Heartbleed: Understanding When We Disclose Cyber Vulnerabilities," *White House Blog,* April 28, 2014, http://www.whitehouse.gov/ blog/2014/04/28/heartbleed-understanding-when-we-disclose-cyber-vulnerabilities.

6. Daniel, "Heartbleed."

7. Joseph Menn, "Special Report: U.S. Cyberwar Strategy Stokes Fear of Blowback," *Reuters,* May 10, 2013, http://www.reuters.com/article/2013/05/10/ us-usa-cyberweapons-specialreport-idUSBRE9490EL20130510; "In Cyberwar, Soft- ware Flaws Are a Hot Commodity," *NPR,* February 12, 2013, http://www.npr. org/2013/02/12/171737191/in-cyberwar-software-flaws-are-a-hot-commodity.

8. Julia Wolf, "CVE-2011-3402—Windows Kernel TrueType Font Engine Vulnerability (MS11-087)," March 8, 2013, https://cansecwest.com/slides/2013/Analysis%20of%20a%20Windows%20Kernel%20Vuln.pdf.

9. Erin Rosenbach, "Keynote Address at the Armed Forces Communications and Electronics," *Cyber Con 2013* video, 8:14, March 18, 2013, http://www.c-span.org/video/?c4390789/keynote-address-eric-rosenbach, at 3:24.

10. Morgan Marquis-Boire, "For Their Eyes Only: The Commercialization of Digital Spying," *Citizen Lab,* May 1, 2013, https://citizenlab.org/2013/04/for-their-eyes-only-2/; "Colonel John Adams, head of the Marine Corps' Intelligence Integration Division, states that vulnerability sellers, 'provide cyber-power to hostile governments that would otherwise lack the expertise to attack an advanced country's computer systems,' in the Digital Arms Trade," *Economist*, March 30, 2013, http://www.economist.com/news/business/21574478-market-software-helps-hackers-penetrate-computer-systems-digital-arms-trade.

11. Rosenbach, Keynote Address.

12. Marquis-Boire in "The Digital Arms Trade."

13. Dennis Fisher, "Flash Zero-Day Used to Target Victims in Syria," *Threatpost-Kaspersky Labs,* April 28, 2014, http://threatpost.com/flash-zero-day-used-to-target-victims-in-syria.

14. Recent security analyses have tied this April 2014 vulnerability to a wider surveillance operation also targeting other countries, likely originating from a Francophone country; some have implicated France. This finding complicates linking the incident directly to the Syrian government. Still, *someone* was conducting surveillance of Syrian "complainers" using a zero-day vulnerability. See Lorenzo Franceschi-Biccherai, "Meet Casper: Yet Another Malware Likely Created by France for Surveillance," *Motherboard,* March 5, 2015, http://motherboard.vice.com/read/meet-casper-yet-another-malware-likely-created-by-france-for-surveillance.

15. Ryan Gallagher, "The Secretive Hacker Market for Software Flaws," *Slate,* January 16, 2013, http://www.slate.com/articles/technology/future_tense/2013/01/zero_day_exploits_should_the_hacker_gray_market_be_regulated.html.

16. For more on vulnerabilities, see chapter 1—"Understanding Information Assurance"; for more on vulnerability's role in malware, see chapter 7—"Disrupting Malware Markets."

17. Stefan Frei, "The Known Unknowns," *NSS Labs*, December 2013, https://www.nsslabs.com/reports/known-unknowns-0/.

18. David Sanger, "Obama Order Sped Up Wave of Cyberattacks Against Iran," *N.Y. Times,* June 1, 2012, http://www.nytimes.com/2012/06/01/world/middleeast/obama-ordered-wave-of-cyberattacks-against-iran.html. The Symantec report details three zero-days in Stuxnet, while news reports have indicated four were used.

19. Menn, "Special Report."

20. The press does not always distinguish between zero-day vulnerabilities and exploits.

21. Kim Zetter, *Countdown to Zero Day: Stuxnet and the Launch of the World's First Digital Weapon* (Crown/Archetype, 2014); Ellen Nakashima and Joby Warrick, "Stuxnet Was Work of U.S. and Israeli Experts, Officials Say," *The Washington Post,*

June 2, 2012, https://www.washingtonpost.com/world/national-security/stuxnet-was-work-of-us-and-israeli-experts-officials-say/2012/06/01/gJQAlnEy6U_story.html.

22. Nicolas Falliere, Liam O. Murchu, and Eric Chien, "W32. Stuxnet Dossier," *Symantec* (2011), http://www.h4ckr.us/library/Documents/ICS_Events/Stuxnet%20 Dossier%20(Symantec)%20v1.4.pdf.

23. Barton Gellman and Ellen Nakashima, "U.S. Spy Agencies Mounted 231 Offensive Cyber-operations in 2011, Documents Show," *Washington Post,* September 3, 2013, http://www.washingtonpost.com/world/national-security/us-spy-agencies-mounted-231-offensive-cyber-operations-in-2011-documents-show/2013/08/30/ d090a6ae-119e-11e3-b4cb-fd7ce041d814_story.html.

24. For more, see chapter 7—"Disrupting Malware Markets."

25. One study reports 14 percent of all Microsoft, 10 percent of Apple, and 17 percent of Adobe vulnerabilities in the past decade came through white-market programs. See Frei, "The Known Unknowns."

26. "An Update on Our Bug Bounty Program," *Facebook,* Aug. 2, 2013, https://www.facebook.com/notes/facebook-security/an-update-on-our-bug-bounty-program/10151508163265766; "Vulnerability Reward Program," *Google* (2013), https://www.google.com/about/appsecurity/reward-program/; Microsoft Bounty Programs," *Sec. Tech. Center,* June 26, 2013, http://technet.microsoft.com/en-us/ security/dn425036; Andy Greenberg, "Meet 'Project Zero,' Google's Secret Team of Bug-Hunting Hackers," *Wired,* June 15, 2014, http://www.wired.com/2014/07/ google-project-zero/.

27. Joseph Menn, "HackerOne Gets $9 Million in Funding to Reward Spotters of Software Flaws," *Reuters,* May 28, 2014, http://www.reuters.com/article/2014/05/28/ cybersecurity-bounties-idUSL1N0OE2CI20140528?irpc=932.

28. Lily Ablon, Martin Libicki, and Andrea A. Golay, "Markets for Cybercrime Tools and Stolen Data: Hackers' Bazaar," *Rand Corporation,* March 2014, http://www. rand.org/pubs/research_reports/RR610.html; Charles Miller, "The Legitimate Vulnerability Market: Inside the Secretive World of 0-day Exploit Sales," *Workshop on the Economy of Information* (2007), http://weis2007.econinfosec.org/papers/29.pdf.

29. Ablon, Libicki, and Golay, "Markets for Cybercrime Tools."

30. Ibid.

31. Jaziar Radianti, "Eliciting Information on the Vulnerability Black Market from Interviews," *IEEE Fourth International Conference on Emerging Security Information Systems and Technology* (2010), http://ieeexplore.ieee.org/xpl/login.jsp?tp=&arn umber=5633685&url=http%3A%2F%2Fieeexplore.ieee.org%2Fiel5%2F5629472% 2F5630128%2F05633685.pdf%3Farnumber%3D5633685.

32. Ablon, Libicki and Golay, "Markets for Cybercrime Tools."

33. Interview with Richard Bejtlich in Mailyn Fidler, "Regulating the Zero-Day Vulnerability Trade: A Preliminary Analysis," 11.2 ISJLP (2015), http://moritzlaw. osu.edu/students/groups/is/files/2016/02/9-Fidler.pdf.

34. Frei, "The Known Unknowns."

35. Fidler, "Regulating the Zero-Day Vulnerability Trade."

36. The Grugq, "Only thing that was interesting was the table showing that the market is <$4m." Twitter (June 24, 2014), https://twitter.com/thegrugq/status/ 481506494416826368.

37. Nicole Perlroth and David Sanger, "Nations Buying as Hackers Sell Flaws in Computer Code," *N.Y. Times,* July 13, 2013, http://www.nytimes.com/2013/07/14/world/europe/nations-buying-as-hackers-sell-computer-flaws.html; Ben Makuch, "The 'Darth Vader' of Cyberwar Sold Services to Canada," *VICE News*, April 11, 2016, https://news.vice.com/article/the-darth-vader-of-cyberwar-sold-services-to-canada.

38. Frei, "The Known Unknowns"; Gellman and Nakashima, "U.S. Spy Agencies"; for the most recent analysis of zero-day market data as of February 2016, see Vlad Tsyrklevich, "Hacking Team: A Zero-Day Market Case Study," *Vlad Tsyrklevich's Blog,* July 22, 2015, https://tsyrklevich.net/2015/07/22/hacking-team-0day-market/.

39. Trey Herr and Eric Armbrust, "Milware: Identification and Implications of State Authored Malicious Software," in *NSPW '15 Proceedings of the 2015 New Security Paradigms Workshop* (Twente, Netherlands: ACM, 2015), 29–43, doi:10.1145/2841113.2841116.

40. Mark Hosenball, "FBI Paid under $1 Million to Unlock San Bernardino iPhone: Sources," *Reuters,* April 29, 2016, http://www.reuters.com/article/us-apple-encryption-idUSKCN0XQ032.

41. Michael Riley and Chris Strohm, "FBI Keeps Internet Flaws Secret to Defend Against Hackers," *Bloomberg,* April 29, 2014, http://www.bloomberg.com/news/2014-04-30/fbi-keeps-internet-flaws-secret-to-defend-against-hackers.html; Nakashima, "Meet the Woman in Charge"; Ahmed Ghappour, "Is the FBI Using Zero-Days in Criminal Investigations," *Just Security,* November 17, 2015, https://www.justsecurity.org/27705/law-enforcement-zero-days/.

42. FY2017 Budget Request at A Glance, Federal Bureau of Investigations, http://www.justice.gov/jmd/file/822286/download; Lorenzo Franceschi-Bicchierai, "The FBI Wants 38.1 More Million to Buy Encryption-Breaking Technology," *Motherboard,* February 10, 2016, http://motherboard.vice.com/read/the-fbi-wants-38-million-to-buy-encryption-breaking-technology.

43. FY2017 Budget.

44. Menn, "Special Report."

45. David Sanger, *Confront and Conceal: Obama's Secret Wars and Surprising Use of American Power* (New York: Random House, 2012), 200-01. Print. http://www.penguinrandomhouse.com/books/202541/confront-and-conceal-by-david-e-sanger-bestselling-author-of-the-inheritance/9780307718037/.

46. Thomas Brewster, "Words of War and Weakness: The Zero-Day Exploit Market," *Tech Week Europe,* September 10, 2012, http://www.techweekeurope.co.uk/news/zero-day-exploit-vulnerabilties-cyber-war-91964.

47. Kim Zetter, "Turns Out the US Launched its Zero-Day Policy in Feb 2010," *Wired,* June 26, 2015, http://www.wired.com/2015/06/turns-us-launched-zero-day-policy-feb-2010/.

48. Andrea Peterson, "Why Everyone is Left Less Secure When the NSA Doesn't Help Fix Security Flaws," *Washington Post,* October 4, 2013, http://www.washingtonpost.com/blogs/the-switch/wp/2013/10/04/why-everyone-is-left-less-secure-when-the-nsa-doesnt-help-fix-security-flaws/.

49. "Expert Warns of the Growing Trade in Software Security Exploits," Harvard Law Today, October 30, 2012, http://today.law.harvard.edu/expert-warns-of-the-growing-trade-in-software-security-exploits/?redirect=1.

50. "Liberty and Security in a Changing World: Report and Recommendations of the President's Review Group on Intelligence and Communications Technologies," The White House, December 12, 2013, http://www.whitehouse.gov/sites/default/files/docs/2013-12-12_rg_final_report.pdf, at 2:19.

51. Ibid.

52. Ibid.

53. Michael S. Rogers, "Advance Questions, Nominee for Commander, United States Cyber Command Before the Senate Armed Services Committee," 113th Congress (Mar. 13, 2014).

54. David Sanger, "Obama Lets N.S.A. Exploit Some Internet Flaws, Officials Say," *N.Y. Times,* April. 12, 2014, http://www.nytimes.com/2014/04/13/us/politics/obama-lets-nsa-exploit-some-internet-flaws-officials-say.html.

55. Ibid.

56. Ibid.

57. Daniel, "Heartbleed."

58. Ibid.

59. Ibid.

60. Supp. Decl. of Jennifer Hudson, *Electronic Frontier Foundation v. National Security Agency* (N.D. Cal. 2016) (14-cv-03010-RS), https://www.eff.org/document/vep-foia-second-hudson-declaration; Matt Olsen, Bruce Schneier, and Jonathan Zittrain, "Don't Panic: Progress on the "Going Dark" Debate," Berkman Center, February 1, 2016, https://cyber.law.harvard.edu/pubrelease/dont-panic/Dont_Panic_Making_Progress_on_Going_Dark_Debate.pdf.

61. The National Security Agency, "Cybersecurity Awareness Month Week 5: Building the Next Generation of Cyber Professionals," *NSA Central Security Service,* October 30, 2015, https://www.nsa.gov/public_info/news_information/2015/ncsam/discovering_solving_sharing_it_solutions.shtml.

62. Kim Zetter, "U.S. Gov Insists It Doesn't Stockpile Zero-Day Exploits to Hack Enemies," *Wired,* November 17, 2014, http://www.wired.com/2014/11/michael-daniel-no-zero-day-stockpile/.

63. Sanger, "Obama Lets N.S.A"; Jack Goldsmith, "More on USG Policy on Cyber Vulnerabilities," *Lawfare,* April 12, 2014, http://www.lawfareblog.com/2014/04/more-on-usg-policy-on-cyber-vulnerabilities/.

64. Jack Goldsmith, "Did President Obama Accept Recommendation 30?" *Lawfare*, April 19, 2014, http://www.lawfareblog.com/2014/04/did-president-obama-accept-recommendation-30/.

65. Sanger, "Obama Lets N.S.A."

66. Fidler, "Regulating the Zero-Day Vulnerability Trade."

67. Interview with Scott Charney in Fidler, "Regulating the Zero-Day Vulnerability Trade."

68. Sanger, "Obama Lets N.S.A."

69. Charney in Fidler, "Regulating the Zero-Day Vulnerability Trade"; Tim Greene, "Black Hat Keynote: U.S. Should Buy up Zero Day Attacks for 10 Times Going Rate," *Network World,* August 7, 2014, http://www.networkworld.com/article/2462706/security0/black-hat-keynote-u-s-should-buy-up-zero-day-attacks-for-10-times-going-rate.html.

70. Charney in Fidler, "Regulating the Zero-Day Vulnerability Trade."

71. D. Andrew Austin and Jane G. Gravelle, "Does Price Transparency Improve Market Efficiency? Implications of Evidence in Other Markets for the Health Sector," *Congressional Research Service*, April 29, 2008; Robert Bloomfield and Maureen O'Hara, "Market Transparency: Who Wins and Who Loses?" 12 Rev. Fin. Stud. 5 (1999). In financial and online markets, especially price comparison sites for insurance and airline tickets, transparency decreased prices (see Austin and Gravelle,). In some markets, particularly involving intermediate goods or middlemen, price transparency can make seller collusion easier, raising prices (see Austin and Gravelle).

72. Charlie Miller, "The Legitimate Vulnerability Market: Inside the Secretive World of 0-Day Exploit Sales," in *Sixth Workshop on the Economics of Information Security* (2007), http://citeseerx.ist.psu.edu/viewdoc/summary?doi=10.1.1.139.5718.

73. Credit to Chris Soghoian for inspiring this idea.

74. "Liberty and Security in a Changing World."

75. Charles Grassley, "Letter to Acting Deputy Attorney General Sally Quillian Yates," United States Senate Committee on the Judiciary, April 27, 2015, http://www.scribd.com/doc/263802691/Sen-Grassley-Letter-on-DEA-and-Hacking-Team.

76. "Stingray Tracking Devices: Who's Got Them?" *ACLU*, https://www.aclu.org/map/stingray-tracking-devices-whos-got-them; Joseph Serna, "Anti-Spying Coalition Launches Campaign Against LAPD Drones," *LA Times*, August 21, 2014, http://www.latimes.com/local/lanow/la-me-ln-anti-drone-campaign-lapd-city-hall-20140821-story.html; "Street-Level Surveillance," EFF, https://www.eff.org/sls.

77. "The Wassenaar Arrangement on Export Controls for Conventional Arms and Dual-Use Technologies: List of Dual-Use Goods and Technologies and Munitions List," December 2013, http://www.wassenaar.org/controllists/.

78. Jennifer Granick and Mailyn Fidler, "Update: Changes to Export Control Arrangement Intended to Apply to Surveillance Technology, not Exploits, but Confusion and Ambiguity Remain," *Just Security*, February 19, 2014, https://www.justsecurity.org/7276/update-export-control-arrangement-intended-apply-surveillance-technology-exploits-confusion-ambiguity-remain/.

79. Prop. Dept. Commerce Reg. §15.742, 80 FR 28853-63, July 20, 2015, https://www.federalregister.gov/articles/2015/05/20/2015-11642/wassenaar-arrangement-2013-plenary-agreements-implementation-intrusion-and-surveillance-items; Mailyn Fidler, "Proposed U.S. Export Controls: Implications for Zero-Day Vulnerabilities and Exploits," *Lawfare*, June 10, 2015, https://www.lawfareblog.com/proposed-us-export-controls-implications-zero-day-vulnerabilities-and-exploits.

80. Nate Cardozo and Eva Galperin, "What Is the U.S. Doing About Wassenaar, and Why Do We Need to Fight It?" *EFF*, May 28, 2015, https://www.eff.org/deeplinks/2015/05/we-must-fight-proposed-us-wassenaar-implementation; "Coalition for Responsible Cybersecurity," *Coalition for Responsible Cybersecurity Formed to Prevent Misguided Export Control Rule from Weakening U.S. Cybersecurity, BusinessWire,* July 14, 2015, http://www.businesswire.com/news/home/20150714006318/en/Coalition-Responsible-Cybersecurity-Formed-Prevent-Misguided-Export.

81. *White House Responds to Langevin and McCaul on Wassenaar Concerns,* Congressman Jim Langevin, February 2, 2016, https://langevin.house.gov/press-release/white-house-responds-langevin-and-mccaul-wassenaar-concerns.

82. Collin Anderson, "Considerations on Wassenaar Arrangement Control List Additions for Surveillance Technologies," *Access,* March 9, 2015, https://www.accessnow.org/cms/assets/uploads/archive/Access%20Wassenaar%20Surveillance%20Export%20Controls%202015.pdf; *Comments to the U.S. Department of Commerce on Implementation of 2013 Wassenaar Arrangement Plenary Agreements,* July 20, 2015, https://cdt.org/files/2015/07/JointWassenaarComments-FINAL.pdf; Sergey Bratus, DJ Capelis, Michael Locasto, Anna Shubina, "Why Wassenaar Arrangement's Definitions of Intrusion Software and Controlled Items Put Security Research and Defense at Risk—And How to Fix It," October 9, 2014, http://www.cs.dartmouth.edu/~sergey/drafts/wassenaar-public-comment.pdf.

83. Sean Gallagher, "US to Renegotiate Rules on Exporting 'intrusion Software,'" *Ars Technica,* March 2, 2016, http://arstechnica.com/tech-policy/2016/03/us-to-renegotiate-rules-on-exporting-intrusion-software-under-wassenaar-arrangement/.

84. Perera, "US Will Renegotiate Wassenaar Arrangement," *POLITICO Pro,* February 29, 2016, https://www.politicopro.com/cybersecurity/whiteboard/2016/02/us-will-renegotiate-wassenaar-arrangement-068170.

85. For a full discussion of the pros and cons of various collective action solutions to the zero-day problem, see Fidler, "Regulating the Zero-Day Vulnerability."

Chapter 18

The Joint Cyber Force

Challenges and Opportunities

Jason Rivera, Lauren Boas Hayes, Anastasia Mark,
Matthew Russell, and Nathaniel Tisa[1]

The rise in prominence of cyber-enabled warfare has forced militaries around the world to evolve their existing infrastructure for operations in a new environment. As demonstrated by the emergence of specialized cyber operations forces in the vast majority of significant military organizations, the ability to operate in this quickly evolving space is essential to success in modern conflict.[2] In 2009, recognizing the need for a central organization with authority over and responsibility for U.S. military action in cyberspace, the United States government formally created U.S. Cyber Command (CYBERCOM) under the existing Strategic Command (STRATCOM).[3] CYBERCOM, is the umbrella organization over the joint cyber force and has primary responsibility to execute cyber operations in defense of the United States' national security interests.

Developing and effectively deploying cyber operations forces will require continued effort and focused organization in order to mature the nation's military capacity in cyberspace. The establishment of CYBERCOM has helped to address issues pertaining to the unification of mission efforts and command and control. However, there remain unaddressed offensive and defensive challenges that hinder the ability of the United States to defend against and respond to cyber-attacks. The common theme among these challenges relate to personnel training and retention, infrastructure use, lack of doctrine and legal support, and the ability to effectively carry out cyber operations. This chapter aims to provide a clear understanding of the joint cyber force, current challenges to operational effectiveness, and policy recommendations for Executive branch and Congressional leaders in an effort to reform current military practices for cyber operations.

The Nature of the Joint Cyber Force

For the purpose of this chapter, the term "joint cyber force" should be understood as a collection of units from two or more Department of Defense (DoD) military services. For USCYBERCOM, this functionally means that a four-star general is put in charge of coordinating with senior leaders from each of the armed services to conduct military cyber operations. CYBERCOM, "plans, coordinates, integrates, synchronizes and conducts activities to: direct the operations and defense of specified Department of Defense information networks and; prepare to, and when directed, conduct full-spectrum military cyberspace operations in order to enable actions in all domains, ensure U.S./Allied freedom of action in cyberspace and deny the same to our adversaries."[4] The teams in each branch still operate independently but under the direction of a service senior leader. Their efforts are meant to dovetail with those of the other branches to further the overall objectives of the joint cyber force.

Federal law limits the role active duty military personnel can play on U.S. soil. The Posse Comitatus Act states that the Army and Air Force may not be used to enforce domestic law except in instances expressly authorized by the Constitution or Act of Congress.[5] Unlike traditional warfare, cyber-attacks rarely delineate neatly by geography and often times the targeted assets are held by private companies. Protection of private property falls initially to the governor of the state in which the property is physically located, which further serves to complicate jurisdiction within the cyber domain.[6]

The structure of CYBERCOM, currently a subunified command, is dissimilar from unified-combatant commands that are either geographic or functional in nature like the U.S. Pacific Command (PACOM) or Transportation Command (TRANSCOM). In cyberspace, where operations span across geography and different functions, areas of responsibility are less clear. The legal considerations make it such that, depending on the nature of the attack, CYBERCOM may not have clear authority to respond. In such a case, National Guard units are authorized by state governors to respond to threats to critical infrastructure.[7] Under State Active Duty (SAD), National Guard units have much broader authority to conduct incident response (IR) activities and defensive cyber operations. In this context Guard units serve at the front line of cyber defense at the behest of the state governor.[8]

Organizational Structure of the Joint Cyber Force

Comprehending the organizational structure of the joint cyber force requires understanding how CYBERCOM exercises administrative and operational control. Administrative control can best be understood as the day-to-day exercise of authority over a fighting force covering logistics and support, including provisioning resources and equipment, managing unit readiness, and individual discipline.[9] By contrast, operational control is the authority to designate military objectives, give command direction, and execute military strategy. Similar to full unified-combatant commands, CYBERCOM is led by a four-star general officer who exercises both administrative and operational control. Underneath CYBERCOM there are four service component commands, each led by a three-star general (with the exception of the Marine's two-star commanding officer). The individual service components exercise only administrative control over forces within their purview. This means that the services each independently recruit, provide specialized occupational training, and equip cyber forces with the required materials needed to accomplish the mission but then release these units to CYBERCOM for use in defensive and offensive operations. Figure 18.1 illustrates CYBERCOM's organizational structure.[10]

From the perspective of operational control, CYBERCOM executes its mission across three sets of teams: National Mission Teams (NMTs), Cyber Protection Teams (CPTs) and Combat Mission Teams (CMTs). Personnel openings are filled by the four branches and each team is assigned one of three distinct missions. National Mission Teams (NMTs) are tasked with "defending the nation's critical infrastructure and key resources," including identifying enemy forces, tracking them, and disrupting their activities against U.S. targets.[11] Cyber Protection Teams (CPTs) perform a broader

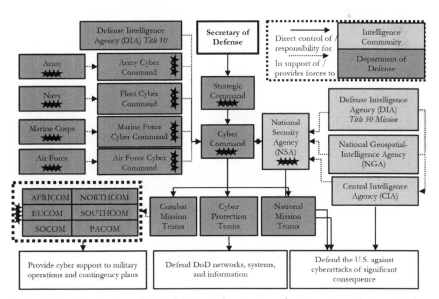

Figure 18.1 Organization of United States Cyber Command. *Source*: Special Report: Cyber Strategy," U.S. Department of Defense, http://www.defense.gov/News/Special-Reports/0415_Cyber-Strategy.

range of defensive measures, including penetration testing and hunting attackers within U.S. military networks. Combat Mission Teams (CMTs) cover offensive cyber operations to include providing "cyber support to military operational and contingency plans" that may be included in broader military campaigns.[12]

Offense-Defense Paradigm and Cyberspace

Military operations can generally be divided into offensive and defensive mission sets. Within the scope of cyber operations this strict division is often at odds with organizational practice and the unique demands of the cybersecurity environment. There are three defining aspects of cyber-enabled warfare. First, the internet provides a potentially high degree of anonymity to attackers in ways that have rarely been possible in conventional warfare. Second, effective attacks can go undetected for long periods of time. Third, attacks are made possible and can be sustained only because of information about a targeted computer system. This information, be it about human behavior or a specific software vulnerability, is key to gaining and maintaining access to targets.

The separation between offense and defense creates artificial boundaries, as does the stringent definition of what constitutes a cyber-attack. Cyberspace operations are differentiated and defined by Joint Publication 3-12 as follows:

Offensive Cyberspace Operations *["OCO"]*. *OCO are CO [cyberspace operations] intended to project power by the application of force in or through cyberspace.*
Defensive Cyberspace Operations *["DCO"]*. *DCO are CO intended to defend DoD or other friendly cyberspace. Specifically, they are passive and active cyberspace defense operations to preserve the ability to utilize friendly cyberspace capabilities and protect data, networks, net-centric capabilities, and other designated systems.*[13]

These definitions include a wide breadth of activity, requiring approval at multiple levels in the chain of command. Furthermore, these activities (particularly offensive) may affect resources crossing several geographic combatant commands, requiring further coordination and approval.

Current doctrine and approved operational guidance sometimes hinders joint cyber force operations because it was developed using kinetic operations as a precedent and often does not account for the unique physics of the cyber domain. Defining the scope of a purely offensive or defensive activity can be difficult. For example, computer network defense response actions (CND-RA) are theoretically considered a defensive cyberspace operation.

However, this defensive activity could involve the use of offensive tactics such as traversing an opponent's computer network looking for information. In the process of defending against a distributed denial of service (DDoS) attack, it may behoove a defender to take measures to disrupt their adversary's capability to perform this DDoS attack. Doing so may require offensive activities designed to disrupt the adversary's control over their own forces. Does an effective defense constitute solely measures designed to detect, prevent, and stand resilient against an attack? Or does an effective defense also consist of taking the response actions required to defeat the attacker's actions? This has historically been, and remains, a challenge in the policy world in terms of differentiating offense from defense.

Bifurcating CYBERCOM's mission and operational organization to map to offensive and defensive teams and authorities presents substantive challenges. For example, under the current team structure, the defensively oriented CPTs are limited in their ability to execute counter-attacks in defense of DoD networks.[14] Currently, prohibited activity that hinders such an approach may include disabling opponent's servers or other infrastructure outside of the United States even where it is being used to actively engage U.S. targets.

CHALLENGES FOR THE JOINT CYBER FORCE

The rise of cyber-enabled warfare has brought dramatic change to the means by which the tools of conflict are acquired and deployed as well as to how war is waged by each of the different branches of the armed services. Each of these organizations faces challenges of agility; each branch is hampered by traditional differentiation in priorities between the branches as well as by legal and regulatory requirements that do not match the quickening tempo of contemporary operations.

Standardizing Acquisition

There are differences in priority and focus between the U.S. military services because each holds a different vision of how forces should be developed and deployed. This contributes to redundant tool and personnel acquisition, and at times reduced interoperability between cyber operational personnel in each of the services. Budgetary pressures play a role in this ongoing dispute. As U.S. expenditures on defense stay steady or decline, each service has attempted to lay claim to an ever larger proportion of the budget devoted to military cyber operations. Budget applications for CYBERCOM have been notoriously vague and hard to pin down throughout the annual appropriations process in part because of these budgetary disputes.[15]

Adding Interoperability

Differentiation in conventional mission sets between the services has resulted in varied standards for training and technology in preparation for the cyber mission set; this in turn has led to impacts on service technology interoperability. Perhaps the greatest interoperability challenge comes in the form of technology implementation and employment. In the traditional kinetic space, the services are responsible to recruit, train, and equip personnel to fight the specific mission set of that branch. As such, the Army does not maintain a large fleet of ships and airplanes, and the Air Force is not equipped with many armored vehicles. This separation of roles allows for specialization as each branch develops and implements the most effective tool for their needs.

Partly a result of the Goldwater-Nichols reforms of the 1980s and agreements going back to the end of the Army Air Force after World War II, the services have traditionally had differing technology and procurement requirement along with their separate roles in the kinetic domains. This has unfortunately extended into cyberspace. Unlike the difference between an Army tank, an Air Force aircraft, or a Navy ship, cyber capabilities in use by the different services are generally much more homogenous in nature and are often designed for the same strategic purpose. Yet at the moment, the services are engaged in their own separate procurement processes, leading to redundancy and challenges with interoperability. To succeed in the future, the joint cyber force will need to have a universal toolkit that different teams leverage to defend against and defeat adversaries. Leadership of the joint force will need to ensure that these issues are addressed and equalized by creating a baseline standard for the services.

Recruiting and Retaining Personnel

The joint cyber force has challenges finding and retaining qualified personnel. The training requirements for military cyber operations differ from strictly kinetic roles and the military services are still working to adapt to these differences. The Marines and Army have historically prioritized their respective members' ability to lead and execute ground combat operations, often valuing skills like marksmanship and physical fitness over others. These services can, as a result, sometimes face challenges in finding qualified personnel for highly technical occupations like billets on the CYBERCOM teams. The Air Force and Navy have traditionally placed greater emphasis on the technical skill of their personnel, in part because of the demands of complex systems embedded in combat aircraft and naval vessels. These differences in personnel priorities can lead to interservice asymmetries in terms of standardizing professional military development of cyber operations personnel.

Complimenting this recruitment problem is the challenge of retaining trained personnel. As cyber operations personnel acquire skills and expertise through their military service, it increases their value on the private sector job market. For example, active duty officers commissioned through Reserve Officers' Training Corps (ROTC) programs involving scholarships commit to four to five years of active duty service. After advanced training in defensive and offensive cyber operations, however, an officer has few years to gain operational experience before this mandatory active duty service period expires. Despite this relative lack of operational experience, these individuals are highly valued by the private sector. From conventional military operations, there are fewer immediate parallels to civilian jobs and so the risk of losing trained and talented personnel to the private sector is a less pressing challenge. One way to account for this could be modeled on how the military deals with highly trained fixed wing and rotary-pilots who are generally locked into extended service commitments in order to protect their substantial training investment from poaching by civilian airlines and aviation services.

The majority of military cyber operations take place remotely, with an extended development and intelligence-gathering pipeline far away from the battlefield. This emphasis on largely remote operations differs from purely conventional warfighting and presents a critical opportunity for the armed forces to recruit and retain a nontraditional type of warfighter, emphasizing, evaluating, and rewarding technical competencies over extensive physical fitness training, marksmanship, and small unit tactical acumen. It is incumbent on leaders to understand the mission-based cultural differences involved in different branches of the armed forces and make efforts to properly incentivize, promote, and compensate these cyber operations personnel to ensure long-term sustainability and retention.

Shaping an Effective Legal Regime to Govern Operations

The legal and regulatory environment surrounding rapidly changing technology can hamper the decision-making process for cyber-enabled warfare. Uncertainty and ambiguity creates challenges for operational commanders who prize clarity in their authority and the ability to respond quickly to developing events. At present, the permissions and authority required to conduct military cyber operations are substantially more restrictive than those for traditional kinetic operations.[16] There is a higher level of authority required to conduct an offensive cyber-attack against an adversary's computer network than for a fighter pilot to drop munitions on an enemy target. There are substantial authority differences between executing defensive cyberspace operations (DCO) and offensive cyberspace operations (OCO). The DCO activities are often preplanned and well defined, and thus the authorities needed for their execution have been worked out in advance.[17] OCO, on the other hand, requires authority to be given at a very high level of the chain of command, potentially directly from the White House. Because offensive operations are often executed at a rapid pace, joint force commanders with a mix of kinetic and cyber-enabled alternatives to achieve a specific outcome might deemphasize OCO because the approval process is too rigid and time consuming.

Informing Legislators

Legislators and their staffs often lack sufficient technical expertise, military experience, or time to evaluate the relative merits of competing programs when considering appropriations for military cyber operations or other cybersecurity topics. In 1995, Congress eliminated the in-house Office of Technology Assessment, which provided unbiased technical assessment on regulatory and budgetary legislation to members.[18] In 2012 Congress voted against its reestablishment, citing budgetary pressures.[19] As a result of the failure to holistically understand investments in military cyber operations, a diverse set of committees hold sway over U.S. cybersecurity funding without a great deal of coordination to identify redundancies and gaps. Committee and subcommittee mission statements reveal that many have overlapping cybersecurity authority.[20] This decentralized approach and shortfall in comprehensive understanding has led to generalized difficulty in developing useful legislation, with potentially harmful implications for U.S. national security.

Offensive Challenges

Offensive missions entail a shared use of network technology between the military and the intelligence Community (IC). One of the most critical issues to address is finding a balance between the strategic need to safeguard the sources and methods of U.S. intelligence with the military's need to achieve combat-oriented objectives. The military and the IC possess fundamentally different approaches and attitudes toward intelligence gathering. Where the military is both a producer and consumer of intelligence, the IC is focused on collection and analysis. The military tends to be more concerned with the implications of cyber-enabled warfare for immediate operational objectives so intelligence is a means to an end: capture/kill missions, seizing tactical objectives, enabling freedom to maneuver, etc. The IC by contrast has a primarily analytic outlook and is focused on safeguarding the technical means of collection, exploring new avenues for exploitation, and publishing reports based on operational and strategic analysis to inform policymakers. This is the core competency of the IC and is crucial for the survivability and long-term health of the United States. The shared, and often competing, dynamic between the military and the IC requires a delicate working relationship with regular information exchange and a shared system of goals and objectives between the two.

At present this sharing of resources creates an environment where combatant commanders know that the information they seek exists, but that due to the sensitivity of the collection method or source, they cannot gain access to it. This can breed hostility and frustration, degrading the working relationship between combatant commands and the IC. The combat commander must understand that in order to continue to obtain this crucial information and data, the sources cannot be compromised, while the IC must understand that timely, accurate, and relevant information allows commanders to engage and destroy the enemy. It is the symbiosis of these two disparate intentions that will create an effective fighting force.

Defensive Challenges

Existing doctrine on defensive operations for kinetic environments is well established, a culmination of lessons learned, trial and error, and military thought that has been codified and well socialized throughout all levels of leadership. That these plans can be detailed at a granular level and maintain their relevance from engagement to engagement is due in part to the fact that conventional warfare evolves more slowly than cyber-enabled warfare. Being both relatively new and undefined, cyber-enabled warfare does not possess well-developed defensive doctrine and often labors under uncertainty over the potential utility and consequences of different capabilities. This has led to two principle defensive challenges: anonymity and the long time horizon of engagements.

Conventional warfare is less impacted by anonymous behavior than cyber-enabled warfare as there are a plethora of detection methods at a nation's disposal to determine the origin of an attack. Technology makes it possible to determine the precise launch point of a missile and to track it in flight, satellites allow for observation of troop movements, and soldiers can observe the source and direction of enemy gunfire. These methods provide concrete, evidence-based knowledge of not only the means of attack, but its origin as well. Across cyberspace, competent threat actors are able to obfuscate their attacks to create uncertainty about their true location and make it difficult, or at times impossible, for U.S. assets to authenticate the source. While advances have been made in the technical ability to attribute cyber-attacks, the most advanced and dangerous adversaries work tirelessly to ensure some degree of anonymity. Traditional military doctrine falls short in addressing how to respond to an attack of unverifiable origin.

Military cyber operations must also maintain substantially higher degrees of stealth than their conventional counterparts because their success depends on remaining undetected on a target system. Due to the clandestine nature of the mission, these attacks are often not detected in real time and may remain hidden for years.[21] For example, Stuxnet was suspected to have initially infected Iranian nuclear enrichment equipment several years prior to discovery, evolving through multiple versions of the weapon. Traditional military doctrine does not provide guidance on how to respond to an attack that occurred months or years in the past. Additionally, even if it is possible to identify the attacker and to discover the attack while it is ongoing, the bounds of a reasonable response have not been defined. There are many questions related to cyber-enabled warfare remain to be answered so that the joint cyber force operates from a definitive and shared set of applicable military doctrine and cybersecurity policy.

RECOMMENDATIONS FOR BUILDING THE JOINT CYBER FORCE

Grappling with the offensive and defensive challenges facing the joint cyber force will require rethinking many of the military's traditional recruitment, training, and operational planning processes. These changes are best conducted proactively rather than in response to a crisis. The following are several recommendations to drive the expansion and sustainment of a strong cyber defense in the United States.

Clarify Congressional Responsibilities

Congress should consolidate responsibility and oversight for military cyber operations, including defensive missions, into fewer committees. Centralizing consideration of military cyber operations appropriations and oversight under one body would help to build the familiarity and expertise of legislators and their staff with key procurement, operational, and strategic issues over time. As an example—the House Armed Services Committee is currently organized into subcommittees, each with a discrete substantive focus like Seapower, Strategic Forces, and Emerging Threats. Bills that originate in House Armed Services may require input and attention from Science, Space, and Technology, which oversees NIST, as well as review by the Foreign Relations committee. A single authoritative committee for military cyber operations, in the House and Senate each, could help to build the administrative and topical expertise required to imbue the joint cyber force with key resources and compliment them with effective oversight. As commanding officer of CYBERCOM and director of the NSA, Admiral Michael Rogers, noted in recent testimony, "the global movement of threat activity in and through cyberspace blurs the U.S. government's traditional understanding of how to address domestic and foreign military, criminal and intelligence activities."[22]

Promote New Models for Defensive Cyber Operations Participation

Training and retaining highly capable cyber operations personnel is one of the primary challenges facing the military services. In tandem with leadership in the National Guard, the DoD Office of the Under Secretary for Personnel and Readiness should put forth recommendations to develop a permanent investment in a new commission model for trained cybersecurity officers.

There are two compelling alternatives. One model, advocated by Stanford professor Steve Blank, amounts to the creation of a Cyber-ROTC program at universities around the country. Such a program would invite computer science students and those with other relevant skills to enter the military's cybersecurity ranks directly as a commissioned officer upon graduation in exchange for a four-year scholarship. The program could involve rethinking mandated physical and active duty commitments for participants, an activity critical to resolving the interoperability, staffing, and retention challenges currently facing CYBERCOM. Extending active duty commitments but limiting deployment requirements or streamlining training through integrating cyber missions with ROTC curriculum could serve to extend the length of effective service delivered by each newly trained cyber-operations officer.

A second model amounts to a cyber operations militia. Pioneered by Estonia in 2010 in response to a cyber-attack by Russia, this "Kuberkaitseliit" allows civilians with relevant experience to volunteer for public defense activities, including penetration testing or "red team" activities.[23] While the United States lacks a comparable program at the federal level, certain states are pioneering joint civilian-military partnerships. Louisiana recently initiated the Cyber Defense Incident Response Team (C-DIRT), which organizes and trains volunteers from the National Guard with cybersecurity expertise, regardless of their existing assignments.[24] Michigan is pioneering a Cyber Civilian Corps (MiC3) in partnership with both National Guard and State Police units that welcomes civilian volunteers from the private sector.[25] Both programs present intriguing innovations that seek to mobilize a wealth of U.S. talent against critical cyber threats.

Involve the National Guard

To address issues pertaining to technology interoperability, DoD should activate portions of the National Guard under Title 10, which covers conventional military operations by active duty forces or Title 32, which deals directly with the National Guard, authorities to leverage the expertise resident within the Army and Air Force National Guard components. By consolidating cyber capabilities development for the services within National Guard, the larger joint cyber force will be able to enjoy the cost savings benefits associated with a unified and singular technology development pipeline. The joint cyber force would also benefit from the technical expertise of the National Guard, many of whose cyber operations billets are filled with individuals who serve in cybersecurity positions in the civilian world. The National Guard could thus serve as a sort of testing ground for development of the latest cyber operations capabilities and strategies.

In tandem with a renewed approach to officer recruitment, the military should promote further integration of National Guard units into the active force for military cyber operations. Expanded National Guard funding and capabilities for cyber operations could enable the U.S. military to better retain and utilize experienced personnel as they leave active duty units. This entails bolstering National Guard unit budgets and billeting so they can capture the interest of service members transitioning out of the active force and offer advantageous training exercises to those working in cybersecurity in the private sector after leaving their full-time roles. In this way, the United States military can cultivate a depth of personnel with relevant skillsets that are constantly bolstered with experience and cutting-edge innovations through work in the private sector. Additional resources could help states prioritize cybersecurity by emulating programs like Louisiana's C-DIRT and Michigan's MiC3 in conjunction with the National Guard.

CONCLUSION

The United States' joint cyber force will have a variety of internal and externally imposed challenges to grapple with in the coming decades. Less than twenty years into the twenty-first century, the world has become exposed to the potential power of cyberspace within the national security realm. The use of Stuxnet against Iran and a data breach of the United States' Office of Personnel Management (OPM) are just two of the most notable cyber incursions from this young century. The world's strongest military and national security organizations will likely continue to develop and integrate their respective cyber equities, and the United States should not stand idly by. The joint cyber force, through CYBERCOM, faces substantive challenges interacting with a coherent Congressional authority, overcoming issues of technological interoperability and coherent training curricula between services, recruiting and retaining talent, and sharing network operations infrastructure with the

IC. To appropriately engage these challenges, U.S. policymakers should leverage the resident expertise and infrastructure present with the National Guard, clarify cyber-related legislative issues by streamlining the organization of Congressional oversight, and promote recruitment and retention by offering new commissioning models and opportunities for service members leaving the active force. By implementing these recommendations, the U.S. policy community can ensure that CYBERCOM is a flexible, quicker moving, and generally more adaptive organization, leaving the joint cyber force well positioned for future operational demands.

CHAPTER HIGHLIGHTS

U.S. Cyber Command (CYBERCOM). Founded in 2009, CYBERCOM was formed under the existing Strategic Command (STRATCOM) and tasked with a broad mandate. CYBERCOM is the umbrella organization over the joint cyber force with primary responsibility to execute cyber operations in defense of U.S. national security interests. The term "joint cyber force" should be understood as a collection of units from two or more Department of Defense (DoD) military services.

CYBERCOM Divisions. CYBERCOM executes its mission across three sets of teams: National Mission Teams (NMTs)—tasked with "defending the nation's critical infrastructure and key resources"; Cyber Protection Teams (CPTs)—perform defensive measures including penetration testing and hunting attackers within U.S. military networks; and Combat Mission Teams (CMTs)—provide "cyber support to military operational and contingency plans." Personnel openings are filled by the four branches and each team is assigned one of the three distinct missions.

Joint Cyber Force Challenges. (1) Redundant cyber tool acquisition has led to reduced interoperability; (2) differentiation in conventional mission sets between the services has resulted in varied standards for training and technology; (3) finding and retaining qualified personnel is difficult and training requirements for military cyber operations differ from strictly kinetic roles; (4) the legal and regulatory environment can hamper the decision-making process for cyber-enabled warfare (challenge for operational commanders to respond quickly); and (5) legislators and their staff often lack sufficient technical and military experience and time to evaluate the relative merits of competing cyber-related programs when considering appropriations.

Managing Competing Interests. The military is concerned with cyber-enabled warfare implications for immediate operational objectives; the intelligence community (IC) is focused on safeguarding the technical means of collection, exploring new avenues for exploitation, and informing policymakers. Combat commanders need to understand sources must not be compromised, and the IC must understand that timely, accurate, and relevant information allows commanders to engage and destroy the enemy.

Recommendations. Challenges facing the joint cyber force will require rethinking many of the military's traditional recruitment, training, and operational planning processes. Options include increasing the role of the National Guard, creating a primary Committee in the House and Senate to handle military cyber issues, and developing new models for cross-training service members across the active force and implementing new programs to strengthen retention.

NOTES

1. **Disclaimer**: All views and concepts expressed in this chapter originate solely with the authors and do not represent the official positions or opinions of the U.S. Government, the U.S. Department of Defense, the U.S. Intelligence Community, the U.S. National Guard, or Deloitte & Touche LLP.

2. Jennifer Valentino-Devries and Danny Yardon, "Cataloging the World's Cyberforces," *Wallstreet Journal* (October 11, 2015), accessed March 28, 2016, http://www.wsj.com/articles/cataloging-the-worlds-cyberforces-1444610710.

3. Tom Shanker, "New Military Command for Cyberspace," *New York Times*, (June 29, 2009), Factiva.

4. "U.S. Cyber Command," *US STRATCOM,* last modified March 2015, https://www.stratcom.mil/factsheets/2/Cyber_Command/.

5. "Use of Army and Air Force as Posse Comitatus," *18 U.S.C. 1385,* January 3, 2012, https://www.gpo.gov/fdsys/granule/USCODE-2011-title18/USCODE-2011-title18-partI-chap67-sec1385.

6. The Tenth Amendment to the U.S. Constitution reserves protection and regulation of property rights to the states, and courts have traditionally not abrogated that right to the federal government except in cases of Constitutional violations. See Gary Pecquet, "Private Property and Government Under the Constitution," *Foundation for Economic Education*, January 1, 1995, accessed March 31, 2016, http://fee.org/articles/private-property-and-government-under-the-constitution/.

7. State Active Duty Status enables governors to mobilize the state National Guard in response to man-made and natural disasters, including those resulting from cyber-attacks. Also see Title 32 Duty, pursuant to Article 1, Section 8 of the U.S. Constitution and Title 32 USC 901–908, which authorizes use of the Guard under

continuing state control but at federal expense when approved by the Secretary of Defense or designee.

8. Louisiana Army National Guard Lt. Col. Henry T. Capello (Chief Communications Plans Officer, Cyber Defense Incident Response Team), personal interview, March 12, 2016.

9. U.S. Joint Chiefs of Staff, *Joint Publication 1* (Washington, DC: U.S. Joint Chiefs of Staff, 2013), accessed March 31, 2016, http://www.dtic.mil/doctrine/new_pubs/jp1.pdf.

10. Except in the case of MARFORCYBER, which is commanded by a two-star general

11. U.S. Cyber Command Combined Action Group, comp, "Beyond the Build: How the Component Commands Support the U.S. Cyber Command Vision," *Joint Force Quarterly,* no. 80 (2016): 86–93, accessed March 31, 2016, http://ndupress.ndu. edu/Media/News/NewsArticleView/tabid/7849/Article/643106/beyond-the-build-how-the-component-command-support-the-us-cyber-command-vision.aspx.

12. William Welsh, "Cyber Warriors: The Next Generation," *Defense Systems,* January 23, 2014, accessed March 31, 2016, https://defensesystems.com/articles/2014/01/23/next-generation-cyber-warriors.aspx.

13. U.S. Joint Chiefs of Staff. *Joint Publication 3-12(R), Cyberspace Operations* (Washington, DC: U.S. Joint Chiefs of Staff, 2013), accessed March 31, 2016, http://www.dtic.mil/doctrine/new_pubs/jp3_12R.pdf.

14. "Mission Analysis for Cyber Operations of Department of Defense," *USA Department of Defense,* August 21, 2014, accessed March 28, 2016, https://info.publicintelligence.net/DoD-CyberMissionAnalysis.pdf.

15. Aliva Sternstein, "Why the Pentagon's Cybersecurity Dollars Don't Add Up," *Defense One,* March 31, 2015, accessed March 31, 2016, http://www.defenseone.com/technology/2015/03/why-pentagons-cybersecurity-dollars-dont-add/108895/.

16. Anne I. Harrington and Catherine A. Theohary, "Cyber Operations in DoD Policy and Plans: Issues for Congress," *Congressional Research Service,* January 5, 2015, accessed March 31, 2016, https://fas.org/sgp/crs/natsec/R43848.pdf.

17. An exception to this is CND-RA, which does then require additional authority.

18. Kim Zetter, "Of Course Congress Is Clueless About Tech—It Killed Its Tutor," *WIRED,* April 21, 2016, https://www.wired.com/2016/04/office-technology-assessment-congress-clueless-tech-killed-tutor/.

19. Timothy Lee, "Congress is clueless on technology—and just voted to keep it that way," *Vox,* May 2, 2014, accessed March 31, 2016, http://www.vox.com/2014/5/2/5674934/congress-votes-to-stay-clueless-about-technology-issues.

20. "Committees of the U.S. Congress," *Congress.gov,* accessed March 31, 2016, https://www.congress.gov/committees.

21. Brian Krebs, "Catching Up on the OPM Breach," *Krebs On Security,* June 15, 2015, accessed March 31, 2016, https://krebsonsecurity.com/2015/06/catching-up-on-the-opm-breach/.

22. Cheryl Pellerin, "Cybercom Chief: Cyber Threats Blur Roles, Relationships," *U.S. Department of Defense,* March 6, 2015, accessed March 31, 2016, http://www.defense.gov/News-Article-View/Article/604225.

23. P.W. Singer, and Allan Friedman, *Cybersecurity and Cyberwar* (New York: Oxford University Press, 2014), 238.

24. Garrett L. Dipuma, "Louisiana National Guard cyber team trains to defend Web," www.army.mil, November 23, 2015, accessed March 31, 2016, http://www.army.mil/article/159030/Louisiana_National_Guard_cyber_team_trains_to_defend_Web/.

25. "About MiC3," *Michigan Cyber Civilian Corps*, 2016, accessed March 31, 2016, http://www.micybercorps.org/.

Chapter 19

The Practical Impact of Classification Regarding Offensive Cyber Operations

Herbert S. Lin and Taylor Grossman

Cyberspace has become an increasingly important part of global affairs, compelling the U.S. government to sound a loud alarm about the dangers that America must be prepared to face and the importance of defending its systems and networks. At the same time, until recently, the U.S. government has been virtually silent on what it is prepared to do regarding the conduct of offensive operations in cyberspace. If recent trends toward greater openness on this front do not continue (and they may well not), the U.S. government's long-standing inclination to classify virtually all information about its offensive cyber capabilities and its thinking about how these capabilities should be used will have serious negative consequences for U.S. cyber strategy, tactics, and operations.[1]

Defensive and Offensive Operations in Cyberspace

In recent years, the U.S. government—and even the Department of Defense—has published a variety of official documents related to cybersecurity.[2] Much has been written about the possibility that terrorists or hostile nations could mount damaging attacks against the United States or its interests. Such concerns arise from the fact that the U.S. economy and critical infrastructure depend on reliably functioning, secure computer systems and networks.

Not surprisingly, most of these documents address the defensive side of cybersecurity. Consistent with the public emphasis on cyber defense and common usage of the term, the Oxford English Dictionary defines cybersecurity as "the state of being protected against the criminal or unauthorized use of electronic data, or the measures taken to achieve this," so even a phrase such as "the defensive side of cybersecurity" is arguably redundant.

There are far fewer documents in the public domain that address the U.S. ability to conduct offensive cyber operations. But, of course, nothing precludes the United States from going on the offensive in cyberspace, that is, from conducting offensive operations by using various cyber capabilities. Indeed, the reality that adversaries may be able to harm U.S. information systems or physical infrastructure through actions conducted in cyberspace, is evidence enough that the United States could take similar action against adversaries and conduct offensive cyber operations against its adversaries.

In very broad strokes, the cyber operations that concern the United States—attacks against U.S. critical infrastructure and military systems, espionage against government and private sector targets to generate information that could be used against U.S. interests—are cyber operations that the United States could carry out against its own adversaries.[3]

Secrecy and Classification Regarding Offensive Operations in Cyberspace

Unclassified U.S. government discussion of America's offensive cyber capabilities has been quite limited for many years. Why is this the case? It cannot be because knowledge of offensive cyber operations must be kept secret—the U.S. government has discussed extensively in the press how such operations might be used against American interests. It is also unlikely to be because the techniques and technologies of cyber offense themselves are secret—the broad strokes are largely known to the technical cybersecurity community, and some cases are discussed in great detail in the public domain.

Given the implausibility of these two reasons, one could easily draw the conclusion that what is sensitive and must be classified is the fact of U.S. government interest about such matters, rather than those matters themselves. Indeed, for a long time, the U.S. government did not want to advertise to the world that the nation even had an interest in carrying out offensive cyber operations, and U.S. policy regarding the classification of this interest reached absurd extremes. Michael Hayden, former director of both the NSA and CIA, has noted that as recently as the early 2000s, even the phrase "offensive cyber operations" was classified. Not what it might mean, or what the targets would be, or what technologies would be involved—merely the phrase itself.[4]

Starting around 2010, evidence of U.S. interest in offensive operations in cyberspace began to emerge. For example, Stuxnet—what was eventually identified as a cyber-attack on Iranian uranium-enrichment centrifuges—first surfaced in the fall of 2010 when malware began to appear in industrial control systems involving Siemens equipment.[5] Over the next few years, various sources pointed to the United States and/or Israel as being responsible, and most analysts have concluded that the United States played a major role in the development and deployment of Stuxnet, even though the United States has never formally acknowledged its involvement.

Then, in May 2011, the Obama administration said that "the United States will respond to hostile acts in cyberspace as we would to any other threat to our country. . . . We reserve the right to use all necessary means—diplomatic, informational, military, and economic— . . . in order to defend our Nation, our allies, our partners, and our interests."[6] This statement does not explicitly acknowledge that the United States would conduct offensive cyber activities to defend its interests, but in context, the statement is certainly suggestive. Later, in July 2011, Vice Chair of the Joint Chiefs of Staff James Cartwright complained about the inadequacies of a "purely defensive" approach to cybersecurity, again suggesting that an offensive dimension to cybersecurity might be valuable.[7]

Despite several pieces of indirect evidence suggesting U.S. interest in offensive aspects of cybersecurity over the years, relevant strategy and doctrine has remained highly classified. However, in April 2015, Secretary of Defense Ashton Carter took a remarkable step—he spoke authoritatively about the use of offensive cyber operations as he unveiled the new Department of Defense (DoD) cyber strategy.[8] His speech explicitly noted that one of the DoD missions in the cyber domain is to "provide offensive cyber options that, if directed by the President, can augment our other military systems."[9] The new strategy document instantly became the most open publically available DoD or U.S. government publication regarding the role of offensive options in cyberspace.[10]

Why Excessive Secrecy About Offensive Cyber Operations Harms U.S. Interests[11]

Whether this new openness will continue remains to be seen. To provide additional rationale for continuation and expansion of this kind of increased transparency, this paper focuses primarily on how overclassification regarding the offensive cyber capabilities of the United States has a negative impact on strategy, operations, and tactics in cyberspace.

Executive Order 13526 establishes the framework for classification of national security information.[12] Such information is classified when "the unauthorized disclosure of the information reasonably could be expected to result in damage to the national security, which includes defense against transnational terrorism, and . . . [it is possible] to identify or describe the damage."[13] Classification is graduated along a sliding scale of importance from Top Secret to Confidential. Materials are classified at the highest level, Top Secret, if they meet the criterion that, if improperly released they "could reasonably be expected to cause *exceptionally grave damage* [emphasis added] to the national security."[14] The definitions for "secret" and "confidential" substitute the words "serious damage" and "damage," respectively.

There are, of course, many valid reasons for classifying information. For example, making public what the United States knows about the capabilities and intentions in cyberspace of specific named adversaries may compromise sources and methods of gathering intelligence. Exposing a particular operational program that takes advantage of specific vulnerabilities in adversary systems alerts adversaries to remediate those vulnerabilities—which is one reason the Snowden revelations were so damaging to U.S. security interests. Yet, classification of U.S. thinking about offensive cyber operations goes far beyond such understandable reasons. Classification of essentially all aspects of U.S. interests in offensive cyber operations has become the norm, not the exception, and has hindered important collaboration and discussion within the national security establishment to the detriment of both strategy and tactics.

Impact of Overclassification on Strategy and Policy Formulation

New types of weapons often demand new strategies and doctrine for their use, and cyber weapons are no exception. As the National Research Council noted in 2009,

> [t]oday's state of affairs regarding public discourse on cyber-attack is analogous to the nuclear debate of 50 years ago. At that time, nuclear policy issues were veiled in secrecy, and there was little public debate about them. Herman Kahn's books (On Thermonuclear War, Thinking the Unthinkable) were the first that addressed in the open literature what it might mean to fight a nuclear war. These seminal pieces did much to raise the public profile of these issues and stimulated an enormous amount of subsequent work outside government that has had a real impact on nuclear policy.[15]

In short, the cyber-equivalent of Herman Kahn has not yet emerged. Although the destructive potential of cyber weapons has been known in the "geek" world for decades, only in recent years have the military services come to grips with the implications of using such weapons. However, secrecy about these weapons, and how they might be used in offensive cyber operations, has a negative impact on the development of strategy and policy. Michael Hayden wrote:

> [d]eveloping policy for cyberops is hampered by excessive secrecy (even for an intelligence veteran). I can think of no other family of weapons so anchored in the espionage services for their development (except perhaps armed drones). And the habitual secrecy of the intelligence services bled over into cyberops in a way that has retarded the development—or at least the policy integration—of

digital combat power. It is difficult to develop consensus views on things that
are largely unknown or only rarely discussed by a select few.[16]

The most insidious effect of secrecy about offensive cyber capabilities is
that would-be strategists have only a limited (and in many cases an incorrect) understanding of what can and cannot be done through military or
intelligence cyber operations. It is an unfortunate reality that to many policymakers, computers and communications technologies are quite foreign. And
yet, government policymakers and academic political scientists alike often
preface their remarks about cyber strategy or doctrine by saying "I'm not a
technical person, but. . . ."[17] Because cyber operations are still relatively new,
most people within government don't have significant experience with cyber
capabilities. They don't know what effects are possible, or what intelligence
requirements exist for considering a cyber operation. For the most part, they
simply don't understand what a realistic "cyber option" truly entails.

Secrecy and classification potentially reduce the coherence of cyber strategy. Because of the restrictions imposed by a "need to know" environment,
individuals in the National Security Agency may be unaware of developments in doctrine occurring in the Office of the Secretary of Defense, and
so forth. Key debates surrounding the use of offensive cyber operations for
national security purposes may happen in intellectual silos. Without cross-
pollination and engagement across agencies, the resulting strategy could easily be inconsistent and possibly deficient.

Overclassification inhibits possible collaboration between the government
and independent nongovernment researchers, such as university faculty members. Most scholars work almost exclusively with unclassified sources. While
some have ventured into the realm of strategy and doctrine around offensive
cyber operations without access to classified materials, the vast majority has
found it easier to stay away from the subject matter entirely.[18] The result is
a deep loss for strategic thought. Academics aren't necessarily even coming
to the *wrong* conclusions about the development and use of offensive cyber
capabilities—as a class, they simply aren't coming to any conclusions at all.
In this regard, the study of strategy regarding offensive cyber capabilities
is quite unlike that of the 1950s and 1960s, during which nongovernment
researchers such as Bernard Brodie, Herman Kahn, and Thomas Schelling
played key roles in developing nuclear strategy.[19]

Secrecy and classification also make it difficult to engage in unclassified
discussions. Guidelines for the protection of classified information force
cleared individuals to be certain that cyber-related information they discuss
publicly is indeed unclassified—otherwise, they are obligated to treat any
material received in classified settings as classified even if the material
in question is in fact unclassified. Out of an abundance of caution, many

cleared individuals are thus reluctant—even fearful—of discussing any topics remotely related to what has been marked secret. Hypothetical situations are suddenly off limits, even if purely fabricated, because they may bump up against elements of existing cyber capabilities that have been strictly classified. Cyber specialists are often wary of entering a conversation that involves only unclassified information because they're afraid of what they may let slip.[20]

Overclassification regarding policy relevant to offensive cyber operations inhibits public exposure and thus increases the likelihood that policy will be formulated with short-term interests foremost in mind. Greater public exposure—or at least discussion within the broader national security community—would shed more light both on the promise and the pitfalls and difficulties of such operations.

As an example that has received considerable public attention, consider the Snowden revelations, starting in 2013, about various classified surveillance programs of the National Security Agency. In large part responding to public concerns about these programs, President Obama said in January 2014,[21]

> Intelligence agencies cannot function without secrecy, which makes their work less subject to public debate. Yet there is an inevitable bias not only within the intelligence community, but among all who are responsible for national security, to collect more information about the world, not less. So in the absence of institutional requirements for regular debate—and oversight that is public, as well as private—the danger of government overreach becomes more acute.

Intelligence gathering and surveillance using cyber means are types of offensive cyber operations, even if they are used by the intelligence community rather than by the Department of Defense. The programs revealed by Snowden were formulated in secret after the 9/11 attacks as part of a large-scale government effort to prevent such attacks from ever happening again. A major irony, of course, is that if the Bush administration had explicitly and openly asked Congress for the authority for these programs in the immediate wake of the attack, it would have been granted that authority, and perhaps the uproar over the Snowden programs and "warrantless surveillance" would have been diminished.

Impact on Operations

As for the operational impact, it is of course true that many details are fragile and sensitive—adversary knowledge of such details could compromise a planned or ongoing operation. The particulars of an ongoing or imminent cyber operation are kept secret for the same reason that troop movements or specific weapons to be used in an engagement are concealed until just before an attack—the more an enemy knows, the better their defense will be.

But secrecy and classification about strategy, doctrine and the general shape and scope of offensive operations also have negative tactical consequences. For example, secrecy and classification mean that in most cases, those responsible for offensive cyber operations can't talk openly to peers who work in other fields. There is no opportunity for information exchange or professional development when these individuals can't compare the trade-offs of using offensive cyber capabilities versus using kinetic arms with an artillery officer, or discuss contingency operations with an aviator. Shop talk has been rendered all but impossible. If you are a cyber specialist, your group of relevant professional colleagues has shrunk to those who also work directly in your field.

Overclassification can make it challenging for individuals placed into responsible positions to get up to speed quickly if they do not already have the basic and fundamental background knowledge needed. Because cyber operations are so new, those placed in relevant staff positions or command billets have built their operational experience in other fields. Some aspects of that experience carry over to cyber operations—but others do not. Without routine access to information about offensive cyber operations, these individuals have no reasonable opportunity for exposure to the basic operational issues (because they have no "need to know" in their current duty assignments). Yet, they are expected to be in a position to make sound policy judgments when they fill their cyber operations billets.

On the flip side, those who do not specialize in cyber operations need a general familiarity with them so they can understand and assess what the operational issues associated with the use of offensive cyber capabilities means for the responsibilities of their current positions. Otherwise, service members of other military occupational specialties will be unable to reasonably consider such capabilities in planning an operation when other options—an air campaign, deploying small infantry forces, mobilizing artillery—are much more broadly and deeply understood. Perhaps even more important, should a non-cyber specialist encounter a cyber-attack by an enemy, he or she will have a much narrower understanding of how to respond. If under fire, a young Marine lieutenant understands how to call in artillery or close air support. Yet, that person likely has no idea what support would entail in the event of a cyber-attack.

Concerns about how front-line personnel should respond to a tactical cyber incident are accentuated because kinetic conflict is likely to be preceded by the use of cyber weapons. Offensive cyber operations may well be the first indication that kinetic conflict is imminent, a point highlighted in the recent DoD cyber strategy.[22] If this is true, the response to a cyber incident—or the appropriate first use of offensive cyber operations—may be the last opportunity to take action to avert the outbreak of wider (possibly kinetic) conflict, a fact that places an even higher premium on taking actions that are well reasoned and fully informed.

These comments are not to suggest that bottom-up ignorance of cyber capabilities are the only source of instability. Indeed, other instabilities arise from the possibility (indeed, under many circumstances, the high probability) that those at the top of the chain of command are not fully informed of activities being conducted at lower levels in the command hierarchy. The operational footprint left by offensive cyber operations is small, a fact that may tend to render such operations less visible to senior decision-makers. Thus, there is a risk that operations that would normally be regarded as routine could lead to misperceptions on the part of the adversary that lead to inadvertent escalation.[23] But such risks do not arise from the overclassification of information related to offensive operations in cyberspace.

Moving Forward

When asked about the rationale for the high degrees of classification regarding offensive cyber operations (see table 19.1), many insiders with clearances point to the fact that such operations—in an espionage or intelligence-gathering context—have been part of the National Security Agency's stock in trade for many years. The NSA, as an organization, has long cultivated a culture of intense silence on matters of data collection, infiltration, and most other operational policies. Because within the NSA resides the vast bulk of U.S. government expertise regarding penetration of adversary computer systems, NSA is of necessity the "go-to" agency within the federal government when such expertise is needed for offensive cyber operations conducted in a military context—and these insiders believe that the culture of secrecy has carried over to discussions of such operations.

A related argument is that official silence about matters related to U.S. offensive cyber operations allegedly reduces the attention that other nations pay to that particular topic, and thus increases the likelihood that adversaries will be lulled into a false sense of security. Thus, they will fail to take actions that might thwart U.S. cyber operations in the future.[24]

Others have also speculated that against the backdrop of U.S. calls for a free, open, and more secure internet worldwide, public acknowledgment by the U.S. government of its offensive cyber activities, which include cyber-enabled surveillance and intelligence gathering, would lay bare a hypocritical policy on this topic and undercut U.S. influence on the former objective.[25] This line of argument further suggests that American activities legitimize comparable activities by other nations, thus increasing the level of cyber insecurity for all.[26]

Table 19.1 Classification of Offensive Cyber Operations Comparison

Classification Advantages	*Classification Disadvantages*
• Publicly acknowledging how much the United States understands adversarial intentions could compromise sources and methods of intelligence gathering • Adversary knowledge of sensitive details on how the United States conducts cyber operations could have serious operational impact by compromising a planned or ongoing operation • Official silence about matters related to U.S. offensive cyber operations allegedly reduces the attention that other nations pay to that particular topic, and thus increases the likelihood that adversaries will be lulled into a false sense of security	• Hinders important collaboration and discussion within the national security establishment to the detriment of both strategy and tactics • Would-be strategists have only a limited (and in many cases an incorrect) understanding of what can and cannot be done through military or intelligence cyber operations • Secrecy and classification potentially reduce the coherence of cyber strategy • Inhibits possible collaboration between the government and independent nongovernment researchers • Inhibits public exposure and thus increases the likelihood that policy will be formulated with short-term interests foremost in mind • Makes it challenging for individuals placed into responsible positions to get up to speed quickly if they do not already have the background knowledge needed

But the United States has long acknowledged and discussed its capabilities, intentions, strategy, objectives, and doctrine when other instruments of military power are concerned. And given how much the United States *is* willing to discuss offensive cyber operations of various kinds conducted against itself and its own interests (see, for example, those described in endnote 2), one can hardly say that the United States is actively trying to keep the topic of offense in cyberspace quiet. What it *does* appear to be doing is trying to keep quiet the topic of U.S. offense in cyberspace, and in light of what the Snowden revelations have shown, that seems to be a fool's errand in the current environment.

Today, policy—and indeed knowledge—regarding U.S. capabilities for and conduct of offensive cyber operations have become so deeply obscured behind classification levels that even within the national security establishment, the level of discourse has been severely hampered. Narrowing the field of people who can draw informed conclusions about offensive cyber operations is virtually certain to result in the slower development of poorer strategy, and by reducing the number of people who can play, the government has placed limits on creative thinking and collaboration.

This point has been emphasized by Lt. General Edward Cardon, the head of Army Cyber Command, who said in 2014 that "solutions to difficult problems do not always surface through the chain of command. . . . [T]alent exists at all levels in our organizations, and our soldiers and civilians of all ranks have never failed to amaze me with their ability to innovate and devise incredible solutions to our most difficult problems. . . . [This is] the foundation upon which I have approached my position here at Army Cyber Command."[27]

The arguments in favor of greater openness and less classification regarding the offensive side of cyber policy and security are not intended as an indictment of all such classification. Some degree of classification is entirely necessary, especially with regard to specific operations or knowledge related to adversary capabilities and intentions. But a better balance needs to be struck between openness and classification.

How would we know a better balance when we see it? One possible standard to assess this balance is the proposition that policymakers—both in the military and their civilian overseers—need enough knowledge and insight to be able to ask the right questions, even if they don't know all of the answers. They need to know in general terms what cyber operations can and cannot do, what is needed to prepare for such operations, and how the outcomes of offensive cyber operations, both successful and unsuccessful, might implicate other interests and equities, such as inadvertent conflict escalation. As an illustration of a useful work with this end in mind, the National Academies produced a volume in 2009 that described U.S. policy and technology regarding offensive operations in cyberspace. This volume was based on what could be learned from unclassified sources, derived from first principles of technology, and inferred from existing military thinking about conflict in noncyber domains.[28]

A second standard is based on the fact that cyberspace has been declared a domain in official DoD doctrine. That declaration suggests that all members of the armed forces—regardless of military specialization (and their civilian policy counterparts)—should know as much about cyber operations as they do other forms of combat: air-to-air, submarine warfare, artillery, armor, and so on. Uniformed service members need a thorough knowledge of their military specialties, but a broad-based knowledge enables them to see how their specialties fit into the larger picture of combat operations. Obtaining that broad base of knowledge is a key element of professional military education (PME), but most PME is derived from unclassified sources, and public domain journals and other widely available materials play a central role in these PME curricula. Thus, PME will fail to provide adequate exposure to cyber operations if relevant materials continue to be excessively classified.

A third standard is open discussion about offense in cyberspace that helps the defensive efforts. An example of such openness is the presentation by Rob Joyce at the January 2016 Usenix Enigma Conference, whose theme is emerging threats and novel attacks. Joyce was (and at the time of this writing is) the head of the NSA's Tailored Access Operations unit, which is responsible for gaining access to a variety of surveillance targets deemed interesting by the NSA. In a talk entitled "Disrupting Nation State Hackers," Joyce said "[I am here] to tell you as a nation state exploiter what can you do to defend yourself to make my life hard. . . . Not many people will stand on the stage and have the perspective of an organization that does exploitation and be able to talk to those elements that really would disrupt the nation-state hackers."[29]

As offensive cyber operations become more important to the Department of Defense and its subsidiary components and start to play a more central role in national security strategy, it is not at all clear that the secrecy that characterized offensive cyber operations for intelligence is desirable for offensive cyber operations in a military context. We can only hope that the trend toward greater openness about such matters will continue.

CHAPTER HIGHLIGHTS

Overclassification of Offensive Cyber Operations. Unclassified U.S. government discussion of America's offensive cyber capabilities has been quite limited for many years. For a long time, the U.S. government did not want to advertise to the world that the nation even had an interest in carrying out offensive cyber operations, and U.S. policy regarding the classification of this interest reached absurd extremes.

Rationale for Classification. Exposing a particular operational offensive cyber program that takes advantage of specific vulnerabilities in adversary systems alerts adversaries to remediate those vulnerabilities.

Keeping Coherent Cyber Strategy. Secrecy and classification potentially reduce the coherence of cyber strategy. Because of the restrictions imposed by a "need to know" environment, individuals in the National Security Agency may be unaware of developments in doctrine occurring in the Office of the Secretary of Defense, and so forth. Without cross-pollination and engagement across agencies, the resulting strategy could easily be inconsistent and possibly deficient.

Adoption Across the Services. Military service members who do not specialize in cyber operations need a general familiarity with them so they can understand and assess what the operational use of offensive cyber capabilities means for the responsibilities of their current positions as well as future billets. Otherwise, service members of other military occupational specialties will be unable to reasonably consider such capabilities in planning an operation. Concerns about how front-line personnel should respond to a tactical cyber incident are accentuated because kinetic conflict is likely to be preceded by the use of cyber weapons.

Enabling Discourse. Policymakers (both military and civilian) need to know in general terms what cyber operations can and cannot do, what is needed to prepare for such operations, and how the outcomes of offensive cyber operations, both successful and unsuccessful, might implicate other interests and equities, such as inadvertent conflict escalation.

NOTES

1. Selected portions of this text are drawn from William A. Owens, Kenneth W. Dam, and Herbert S. Lin, eds., *Technology, Policy, Law, and Ethics Regarding U.S. Acquisition and Use of Cyberattack Capabilities* (Washington, DC: National Academies Press, 2009), http://www.nap.edu/catalog/12651.

2. For a sampling of such reports (and perspectives on the topic), see https://www.dhs.gov/cybersecurity-publications; http://www.gsa.gov/portal/content/104639; https://www.hsdl.org/ (search for the term "cybersecurity"); and http://www.gao.gov/key_issues/cybersecurity/issue_summary.

3. The one exception to this point is that for many years, the United States has abided by a stated policy of not conducting "industrial" espionage—that is, espionage conducted for the purpose of economically benefiting particular private sector companies.

4. Of course, as a broad statement, it is widely accepted that overclassification of all kinds of government national security information is a problem. The 1994 report Redefining Security found that "the classification system . . . has grown out of control." (Joint Security Commission, Redefining Security, 1994, available at http://oai.dtic.mil/oai/oai?verb=getRecord&metadataPrefix=html&identifier=ADA390669.) The 9/11 Commission found that overclassification was a threat to national security (National Commission on Terrorist Attacks Upon the U.S., The 9/11 Commission Report: Final report of the National Commission on Terrorist Attacks Upon the United States [2004]). The Public Interest Declassification Board found in 2012 that "present practices for classification and declassification of national security information are outmoded, unsustainable and keep too much information from the public." (Public Interest Declassification Board, Transforming the Security Classification System 1 [2012], available at http://www.archives.gov/declassification/pidb/recommendations/transforming-classification.pdf.) Nevertheless, overclassification of information about the offensive side of cybersecurity is particularly egregious. An

interesting parallel from nuclear history is the fact in the early 1950s, a high-level Q clearance (that granted access to data related to atomic energy) was associated with the term "intercontinental ballistic missile." See Fred Kaplan, *The Wizards of Armageddon*, Stanford University Press, Stanford, CA, 1991.

5. Riva Richmond, "Malware Hits Computerized Industrial Equipment," *New York Times*, September 24, 2010, http://bits.blogs.nytimes.com/2010/09/24/malware-hits-computerized-industrial-equipment.

6. "International Strategy for Cyberspace," *White House*, 2011, available at https://www.whitehouse.gov/sites/default/files/rss_viewer/international_strategy_for_cyberspace.pdf. The strategy was released in May 2011 (see https://www.whitehouse.gov/blog/2011/05/16/launching-us-international-strategy-cyberspace).

7. Kevin Baron, "U.S. cyber defenses 'way too predictable' says Cartwright," *Stars and Stripes* (blog), July 14, 2011, http://www.stripes.com/blogs/stripes-central/stripes-central-1.8040/u-s-cyber-defenses-way-too-predictable-says-cartwright-1.149174.

8. "The DoD Cyber Strategy," U.S. Department of Defense, April 2015, http://www.defense.gov/Portals/1/features/2015/0415_cyber-strategy/Final_2015_DoD_CYBER_STRATEGY_for_web.pdf.

9. Defense Secretary Ash Carter (Remarks by Secretary Carter at the Drell Lecture Cemex Auditorium, Stanford Graduate School of Business, Stanford, California, April 23, 2015), http://www.defense.gov/News/News-Transcripts/Transcript-View/Article/607043.

10. Herbert Lin, "Reflections on the New DoD Cyber Strategy: What Is New, What Is Still Missing," in preparation as of March 2016.

11. This section draws in part from a National Research Council report, William A. Owens, Kenneth W. Dam, and Herbert S. Lin, eds., *Technology, Policy, Law, and Ethics Regarding U.S. Acquisition and Use of Cyberattack Capabilities* (Washington, DC: National Academies Press, 2009), http://www.nap.edu/catalog/12651.

12. The full process and authorities associated with the classification of national security information is complex. Of particular significance is that to date, the Congress has deferred to the executive branch the determination of policy with respect to the classification of national security information. An overview of processes and authorities can be found in Kevin R. Kosar, "Classified Information Policy and Executive Order 13526," *Congressional Research Service*, 2010. Available at https://www.fas.org/sgp/crs/secrecy/R41528.pdf.

13. Executive Order 13526, 3 C.F.R. 298 (2009), available at https://www.whitehouse.gov/the-press-office/executive-order-classified-national-security-information.

14. Executive Order 12356-Classified National Security Information (2009), available at https://www.whitehouse.gov/the-press-office/executive-order-classified-national-security-information.

15. William A. Owens, Kenneth W. Dam, and Herbert S. Lin, eds., *Technology, Policy, Law, and Ethics Regarding U.S. Acquisition and Use of Cyberattack Capabilities*.

16. Michael V. Hayden, "The making of America's cyberweapons," *Christian Science Monitor*, February 24, 2016, available at http://www.csmonitor.com/World/Passcode/Passcode-Voices/2016/0224/The-making-of-America-s-cyberweapons.

17. An interesting debate that periodically flares between those who come to cyber policy and security from the technical side and those who come to it from the policy side is the extent and nature of the technical knowledge that is needed to formulate and execute cyber policy effectively. The former assert that a substantial degree of technical knowledge is needed, and the latter disagree. For example, Michael Daniel, special assistant to the president and cybersecurity coordinator, said in 2014 that "Being too down in the weeds at the technical level could actually be a little bit of a distraction." (See http://www.govinfosecurity.com/interviews/michael-daniels-path-to-white-house-i-2422.) The comment was interpreted widely by technically inclined experts as "bragging about his lack of technical knowledge." (See, for example, https://twitter.com/EdFelten/status/502519622437179392 and http://www.vox.com/2014/8/21/6053819/white-house-cybersecurity-czar-brags-about-his-lack-of-technical.) Others with more background on the policy side disagreed. (See http://www.govinfosecurity.com/blogs/in-defense-michael-daniel-p-1725/op-1.)

18. For example, Reardon and Choucri published a survey of the literature on the role of cyberspace and information technology that covered eight major policy journals, twelve scholarly IR journals, and six general political science journals between the years 2001–2010. They found a total of forty-nine articles, of which by their count only nineteen addressed the relationship between cyberspace and international security, most of which were concentrated in the policy journals surveyed. By this author's own estimate of the articles found, at most eight were found in the non-policy journals. Of these, only five focused on cyber conflict and international security. See Robert Reardon and Nazli Choucri, "The Role of Cyberspace in International Relations: A View of the Literature," paper prepared for the 2012 ISA Annual Convention, San Diego, CA, April 1, 2012, available at http://ecir.mit.edu/index.php/research/working-papers/461-the-role-of-cyberspace-in-international-relations-a-view-of-the-literature.

19. For accounts of the key roles played by non-government researchers in the development of nuclear strategy, see Fred Kaplan, *The Wizards of Armageddon* (Stanford: Stanford University Press, 1991); Tami Davis Biddle, "Shield and Sword: U.S. Strategic Forces and Doctrine Since 1945," in *Long War: A New History of U.S. National Security Policy Since World War II*, ed. Andrew Bacevich (New York: Columbia University Press, 2009); and David Hounshell, "The Cold War, RAND, and the Generation of Knowledge, 1946–1962" (Santa Monica: RAND, 1998), available at http://www.rand.org/content/dam/rand/pubs/reprints/2008/RP729.pdf.

20. The inanity of government regulations regarding leaked classified documents compounds this problem. Cleared individuals are not even allowed to read such documents in insecure environments, even if the uncleared person next to him or her in the Wi-Fi enabled coffee shop is doing exactly that.

21. "Transcript of President Obama's Jan. 17 speech on NSA reforms," *Washington Post,* https://www.washingtonpost.com/politics/full-text-of-president-obamas-jan-17-speech-on-nsa-reforms/2014/01/17/fa33590a-7f8c-11e3-9556-4a4bf7bcbd84_story.html.

22. "The DoD Cyber Strategy," U.S. Department of Defense, April 2015.

23. William A. Owens, Kenneth W. Dam, and Herbert S. Lin, eds., *Technology, Policy, Law, and Ethics Regarding U.S. Acquisition and Use of Cyberattack Capabilities.*

24. See, for example, the statement by James Clapper, Director of National Intelligence, that "disclosing information about the specific methods the government uses to collect communications can obviously give *our enemies a "playbook" of how to avoid detection." DNI Statement on the Collection of Intelligence Pursuant to Section 702 of the Foreign Intelligence Surveillance Act, June 8, 2013, available at http://www.dni.gov/index.php/newsroom/press-releases/191-press-releases-2013/872-dni-statement-on-the-collection-of-intelligence-pursuant-to-section-702-of-the-foreign-intelligence-surveillance-act.

25. For example, Richard Fontaine has noted the worldwide condemnation of the United States that followed after the Snowden revelations of secret surveillance programs as contrasted with various pronouncements supporting the Internet freedom agenda. See Richard Fontaine, "Bringing Liberty Online: Reenergizing the Internet Freedom Agenda in a Post-Snowden Era," Center for a New American Security, September 2014, available at http://www.cnas.org/sites/default/files/publications-pdf/CNAS_BringingLibertyOnline_Fontaine.pdf.

26. See, for example, Zachary Keck, "Has Snowden Killed Internet Freedom?" *The Diplomat*, July 13, 2013, available at http://thediplomat.com/2013/07/has-snowden-killed-internet-freedom/, and Ron Diebert, "The Geopolitics of Cyberspace After Snowden," *Current History* 114, no.768(2015):9-15, available at http://www.currenthistory.com/Deibert_CurrentHistory.pdf.

27. "Q&A: Lt. Gen. Edward C. Cardon," www.kmimediagroup.com, March 28, 2014, available at http://www.kmimediagroup.com/articles2/430-articles-mit/q-a-lt-gen-edward-c-cardon/5590-q-a-lt-gen-edward-c-cardon.

28. William A. Owens, Kenneth W. Dam, and Herbert S. Lin, eds., *Technology, Policy, Law, and Ethics Regarding U.S. Acquisition and Use of Cyberattack Capabilities.*

29. Kim Zetter, "NSA Hacker Chief Explains How To Keep Him Out Of Your System," *Wired*, January 28, 2016, at http://www.wired.com/2016/01/nsa-hacker-chief-explains-how-to-keep-him-out-of-your-system/. The actual video can be found at https://www.youtube.com/watch?v=bDJb8WOJYdA.

Chapter 20

Creating Influence
through Information

Kat Dransfield, Abraham Wagner,
and Rand Waltzman

The United States is struggling to develop coherent national policies and the legal freedom of maneuver necessary to create influence through information. The ongoing crisis in Syria demonstrates consistent failure on the part of defense and intelligence organizations to create favorable security outcomes across the risk spectrum. More specifically, it demonstrates a failure on the part of the security apparatus to understand networked, information-centric organizations and how they exert influence. From transnational groups such as ISIS, to sovereign nations like Russia, to single terrorist actors in Norway, adversaries have outpaced the U.S. security complex in terms of its understanding of, and investment in, the information space.

The U.S. government should establish information as a strategic imperative vital to national security and invest accordingly. Furthermore, our information strategy must be part of a larger integrated national strategy that acknowledges not just the technical but also the political, economic, and psychosocial dimensions of the information environment (IE). In order to do so, several policy changes are needed: (1) revise intelligence oversight and protocols to give government the same rights to analyze public data as nongovernmental organizations and adversaries; (2) establish a cabinet-level information branch within the government to coordinate information efforts beyond the Department of Defense (DoD); (3) create an international legal framework to establish globally recognized operating norms and enforcement tools within the information space; and (4) create risk transfer mechanisms that allow for informational risk transfer with and between the public and private sector.

BACKGROUND

The DoD defines the IE as "the aggregate of individuals, organizations, and systems that collect, process, disseminate, or act on information."[1] Furthermore, the DoD defines "cyberspace" as "a global domain consisting of the interdependent networks of information technology infrastructures and resident data, including the internet, telecommunications networks, computer systems, and embedded processors and controllers."[2] However, the DoD tends to focus on technical specifications and components when describing the information realm without regard for the new sociocultural, political, and economic phenomena they enable.[3] The inability to holistically analyze the threat landscape perpetuates an outdated information strategy focused on incremental implementation of expensive fences and features that centralize control, all of which come at the expense of agility, mobility, and flexibility.[4] Analog strategies based on consolidating and safeguarding authority and infrastructure have proven futile, particularly against networked, information-centric threats such as ISIS who are willing to accept greater risk in how they operate.

The Weaponization of the Information Environment

Rand Waltzman[5]

Both as individuals and collectively, we make decisions and behave in a way that reflects our perception of the world and our interpretation of the information available to us. The creation of the Internet and Social Media (ISM) has resulted in massive changes of scale in time, space and cost of information flows. The diffusion of information is now practically instantaneous across the entire globe. This has resulted in a qualitatively new landscape of influence and persuasion.

ISM provides new ways of constructing realities for actors, audiences and media. It fundamentally challenges the traditional news media's function as gatekeepers and agenda-setters. The ability to influence is now effectively "democratized," since any individual or group has the potential to communicate and influence large numbers of others online in a way that would have been prohibitively expensive in the pre-internet era. This landscape is also significantly more quantifiable. Data from ISM can be used to measure the response of individuals as well as crowds to influence efforts, and the impact of those operations on the structure of the social graph. Influence has also become far more concealable. Users may be influenced by information provided to them by anonymous strangers, or even in the simple design of an interface.

The nature of interaction within the information environment (IE) is rapidly evolving and old models are becoming irrelevant faster than we can develop new ones. The resulting uncertainty leaves us exposed to dangerous influences without proper defenses. The IE can be broadly characterized along both technical and psychosocial dimensions. IE security today (often referred to as cybersecurity) is primarily concerned with defense of its purely technical features—for example, defense against denial of service attacks, botnets, massive thefts of IP and other attacks that typically take advantage of security vulnerabilities.

This view alone is too narrow, however. For example, little attention has been paid to defending against incidents like the April 2013 Associated Press Twitter hack, in which a group used ("hijacked") the news agency's Twitter account to put out a message reading "Two explosions in the White House and Barack Obama is injured."[6] The result of this message, with the weight of the Associated Press behind it, was a drop and recovery of roughly $136 billion in equity market value over a period of about 5 minutes. This attack exploited both the technical (hijacking the account) and psychosocial (understanding how the markets would react) features of the IE.

This is an example of *cognitive hacking*. Key to the successes of these cognitive hacks were the unprecedented speed and the extent to which the essential disinformation could be distributed. Another core element of the success of this effort was their authors' correct assessment of a *cognitive vulnerability* of the intended audience—a premise that the audience is already predisposed to accept without too much critical thinking, because it makes a fundamental emotional appeal to existing fears or anxieties. And while the execution of this strategy relies on fundamentally new features of the IE, some of the underlying principles have been known throughout recorded history. Today, the manipulation of our perception of the world is taking place on scales of time, space and intentionality that were previously unimaginable. It is all shaped by the information we receive. And that, precisely, is the source of one of the greatest vulnerabilities we as individuals and as a society must learn to deal with. ❖

Networks

Unlike hierarchical organizations, networks are built around functions rather than authorities and value outcomes over process. The precise configuration and mobilization of individuals, resources, or information within the network may be irrelevant as long as they produce outputs within parameters of acceptable risk. For example, the beliefs of a disenfranchised youth in Paris are unimportant so long as he or she detonates a dirty bomb in a metro anywhere in the world. Networked threats achieve their objectives and maintain their "brands" through a spectrum of acceptable transactions, not by centralizing control or information flows. Similarly, a piece of malicious software launched by a criminal group in China is impervious to traditional forms of political, economic, or military coercion. The malware itself is essentially an ambivalent piece of code with one goal: to infect as many "hosts" or "nodes" as it possibly can. Malware has the capacity to destroy financial markets, and perhaps even fundamentally disrupt national and international systems of government.

The unique qualities of networks and how they are leveraged to construct novel threats requires radically different risk models and investment priorities. Both state and nonstate actors outside of the United States understand this reality and have adopted multidimensional information strategies designed to penetrate existing networks and construct new ones. These information strategies emphasize the nonlinearity of information transfer, the importance of virality, the power of human augmentation, and include significant resource commitments in funding new tools and techniques.

Shortfalls in the U.S. Information Paradigm

By contrast, the U.S. government and DoD's information ecosystem evolved with no strategic vision in mind. The information ecosystem was built around industrial age principles, most notably the premise that systematically reducing vulnerabilities increases security. In practical terms, this translates into continued application of legacy approaches to networked threats consisting of: reactive broadcast messaging efforts internally and externally, direct targeting of military or militarized adversary assets, and the fortification of cyber fences to achieve security objectives. A system or network is only as valuable as the information contained within. Ponderous broadcast messaging and targeting particular individuals for kinetic elimination is less effective in a network where relationships are peer-to-peer rather than hierarchical. These careful refinements of industrial age warfare and media have difficulty delivering influencing effects which can compete with networked organizations where culture, ideology, infrastructure, and information are experienced proximately. In many cases, the elimination of individual nodes may be imperceptible even to first degree connections. The hacker group "Anonymous" makes this point clear.

Simply building higher digital walls is a futile exercise in spending that overlooks the quantity, diversity, and mutability of threats and leaves investment in information catastrophe response extremely underfunded. The current U.S. funding profile reflects a disproportionate investment in stopping informational threats rather than acknowledging that information vulnerabilities are a quotidian problem requiring management, not prevention. The speed of change outpaces our recognition of problems and adoption of safeguards to respond to them. There is no such thing as a zero-risk environment, so the governing philosophy must be optimized for detection, speed of evolution, and response rather than vulnerability reduction.

However, US government information principles are currently organized and funded around systems and hardware without regard to the data contained within. The DoD builds and uses some of the most advanced sensor technology available, yet they are treated and employed only as extensions of outdated, analog warfighting tactics rather than as key components of warfighting and business strategies. Evidence of this is provided by the fact that we see artificial intelligence applications occurring only at the edges of our organization, such as in underwater and airborne surveillance. Meanwhile, the fact that the Pentagon—the center of the military's business operation—struggles to automate basic information sharing and apply statistical modeling techniques makes the information crisis apparent. Fear of information compromise combined with a lack of analytic talent and tools leads to the underutilization of data, while the reservoir of data available to adversaries and private sector competitors continues to increase in scope and complexity.

How then should the U.S. government look to apply information against networked adversaries with highly sophisticated information strategies? Most notably, our policy must convey a more inclusive definition of the IE that recognizes the interconnectedness of the data ecosystem. This requires acknowledging that informational threats cannot be segregated along governmental and nongovernmental lines, as the manipulation of information in increasingly networked communities rarely affects a single aspect of social, political, economic, or virtual life.

Integrated Strategies

Russia and China have applied resources on a massive scale to developing and executing a cohesive information strategy. For example, Chinese investment in Silicon Valley companies is an effort to capture emergent technologies. Matched with domestic regional incubator cities (with Beijing focusing on internet services, Shanghai on internet and makerspaces, Shenzhen on electronic hardware, and Chengdu on software, games and culture), and the ability to do agile, iterative production, the Chinese information technology business methodology is both globally pervasive and aligned with its national political agenda and military strategy.

Leaders within the Chinese military proposed a concept of "unrestricted warfare," a campaign that begins long before any armed conflict is apparent. This "warfare" seeks to disrupt potential enemies using the vulnerabilities of their (real or potential) information systems, without regard for international norms or laws. In addition, "the formulation of comprehensive strategies has enabled linking and consolidation of the modern tools available to the Russian leadership, such as information technologies, modern military forces, and other levers of influence."[14] In the case of Crimea, "the 'battlefield' was carefully prepared with the use of political, economic and informational tools."[15] Finally, "The ISIS media network today is always 'on.' whether from the organization itself or through its network of supporters. ISIS media has a dynamic strategy, and the general technical quality of production is constantly improving."[16]

8th-Century Ideology and 21st-Century Technology

Abraham R. Wagner

The rising tide of violence from radical extremists, including ISIS and other Islamist groups, presents a new set of challenges to U.S. policymakers. Unlike traditional threats from state actors, ISIS is operating on an increasing number of fronts in the Middle East and continues to make ever greater use of social media to support its operations. Social media has evolved rapidly, bringing a host of benefits as well as new challenges to national security. It is certainly true that this issue area has not escaped the attention of the media, responsible government agencies or the broader research community. Rather, the operative question is *why* so little has been done to date, and what are the impediments to doing a better job?

For one thing, the research base in this increasingly critical area is relatively limited, both within the U.S. government as well as the scholarly community. For decades, the Intelligence Community (IC) has failed to adequately support what was known as "open source" research, which was traditionally limited to analysis of broadcast and print media. Social media, however, has radically changed this analytical landscape, as new media sources have now become central to the operations of violent extremists. ISIS in particular has worked to employ social media for education and training, including an online guide for mothers on how to raise extremist children. The impact of ISIS use of social media has been enormous especially for the recruitment of fighters and other operatives for ISIS, including through YouTube videos, photos and hashtags as well as dedicated web sites and specialized applications. The organization is now producing "quality horror," with a measurable impact on the rate of recruitment among foreign fighters as a result.

Looking at the current state of what the U.S. government now calls "countering violent extremism" (CVE) the picture is not encouraging. The Department of Homeland Security now has a "CVE Coordinator" but no serious programs. The State Department has an operational program, but also only very limited funds. Elements of the IC and Defense Department are also involved, and they tend to treat the problem as a "boutique item" with little in terms of actual programs. By all accounts, the United States is losing the battle, and losing it badly. Stopping ISIS use of social media is largely impossible and could be counterproductive. Tracking ISIS use of social media is important, but requires better programs with adequate funding. The United States should focus on several critical areas including automated analysis of the vast amount of information available via social media. Current efforts here are not coordinated, and it would be impossible to recruit, train and pay the number of human analysts required. As well, the method by which ISIS attracts and inspires adherents is still not widely understood, and there are important tools from neuroscience and related fields that could be applied here.

It would be possible to match ISIS in scope, scale and quality, but current efforts simply don't exist or are grossly inadequate. Adequate funding would help this problem, along with greatly expanding the State Department's Center for Strategic Counterterrorism Communication. The conflicts in Iraq, Syria and Yemen will continue regardless of what transpires in social media, and the United States cannot seriously impact their outcomes via that medium. At the same time, other threats to the U.S. and Western nations remain uncertain. There are many posts and Tweets in social media promising horrific and deadly attacks, but it is often hard to match real intent and actual capabilities. Critical here is the recruitment and radicalization process, with social media at the heart of the problem. ❖

Adapting to a New Model

State and nonstate actors in other parts of the world clearly view information as a high-value currency that can be created, disseminated, manipulated, hidden, and destroyed in order to achieve long-reaching effects in multiple domains. The Chinese example demonstrates how intellectual property transfer can create tremendous economic influence, while the Russian example demonstrates how disinformation in other domains (financial market data, mass media, etc.) can be used to seize geographic territory. Despite its lack of ethical sophistication, the ISIS organization operates one of the best designed communication networks, complete with media studios that have dwarfed countermessaging efforts by the world's best-funded State and Defense departments. [19]

By contrast, the United States continues to invest almost exclusively in a monolithic security apparatus focused on "hard" power. Unfortunately, the current resourcing mechanisms and political process disincentivize investment in and diversification of nonlethal options, to include information manipulation. The desire to preserve the status-quo military-industrial base currently stifles efforts to think more broadly about the construction of information-based influence beyond conventional military and state tools, whereas other state and nonstate actors have been able to establish information as a strategic priority within larger hybridized, public-private strategies. Evidence of this is provided by the regional Shanghai Cooperation Organization, who define "information war" as: "confrontation between two or more states in the information space aimed at damaging information systems, processes and resources, critical and other structures, undermining political, economic and social systems, mass psychologic[al] brainwashing to destabilize society and state, as well as to force the state to taking decisions in the interest of an opposing party."[20] Given that this is the position of our adversaries, the

United States should look to adopt a similar definition or risk continued mismatch in the application of its national resources.

Self-Mining as a Key Component of Information Strategy

Improving the efficacy of the U.S. government within the information realm requires one difficult admission: "at this point, all of our adversaries possess a significant asymmetric advantage over us as a result of policy, legal, and organizational constraints that we are subject to and they are not."[21] Most notably, the U.S. government is "subject to suffocating constraints on access to data."[22] Five exabytes of data were created globally before 2003. In 2013, five exabytes of data were being created each day, and Acxiom, the country's biggest customer data company, was already aggregating data on more than a billion monetary transactions daily over ten years ago.[23] Yet the current legal construct and security protocols prevent our government from accessing and leveraging it. Meanwhile, our adversaries as well as domestic private sector competitors maintain full access to the wealth of data about American citizens and interests.

The government void in the data mining space can be traced to a trust gap not shared with the private sector. Studies have shown that users are incredibly willing to hand over their data to private companies.[24] However, this trust among users is not replicated in the public sector. High-profile controversies like the disclosures of Edward Snowden and the Patriot Act have challenged whether government can be entrusted with translating its data practices into positive national security outcomes. Rather than attacking the problem of transparency, efficacy, and data stewardship head-on, the government has responded by enforcing increasingly conservative interpretations of its own policies and laws with respect to exploiting public data.

The disadvantage of the current legal constraints and risk aversion are twofold. The inability to execute data analytics on even a fraction of this ecosystem prevents the government from understanding its own vulnerabilities. In order to plan for informational threats, we must first have a way of mining our data legally to understand what information exists. At present, companies such as Google and Amazon, not to mention adversaries, squelch the government's knowledge of the American "data footprint."[25] It is alarming but telling that only after the War on Terror began, the DoD became interested in the collection and analysis techniques of the world's largest customer data company.[26] It illustrates that while the private sector has seen opportunity in data exploitation, the government continues to see only risk.

Building an information strategy absent of informational self-knowledge is the equivalent of formulating a city's tornado response plan without knowing which of its public buildings have basements. To provide an example, federal authorities report that China acquired personally identifying data on 22.1 million U.S. government employees during the OPM hack, and this number grows to a much larger fraction of American citizens when one considers the amount of relational data compromised during the breach.[27] This event not only signals a "new normal" in terms of catastrophic data loss, but the inability of data blind governments to execute critical public services and security functions in the twenty-first century. Particularly in the information space, predicting when the next crisis will be or what form it will take is virtually impossible. A key part of serving the public good moving forward will be a robust self-mining program, with both technical and regulatory constraints to preserve constitutional rights while preparing the government to respond.

Establish a Cabinet-Level Information Branch

The United States should consider creating a cabinet-level position to oversee the United States' information strategy, provide coordination across agencies, and partner with private sector financial industries and tech companies. There is a historical precedent for independent information arms of government dating back as far as the papacy in 1622, with Pope Gregory XV's establishment of the Office for the Propagation of Faith. Today, countries such as Russia have appointed information czars endowed with the authority and funding to execute national-level information campaigns.[28] Alternatively, groups such as ISIS maintain regional information Twitter hubs around which untraceable, ethereal accounts orbit. These Twitter hubs help cohere the global ISIS network by connecting people to resources and information and coordinating major efforts.[29] The United States has no similar mechanism that allows it to deliberately yet flexibly exert influence in the information space.

This stands in contrast to the oodles of ink spilled over cybersecurity. The OPM breach highlights the meaninglessness of the distinction between cyber and informational threats. More than being unhelpful, this distinction can actually be harmful, as it informs organizational structures and the distribution of statutory responsibilities. According to the Congressional Research Service, "authorities for U.S. military operations in cyberspace are not currently organized according to the nature of the perceived threat, whether espionage, crime, or war. Instead, authorities are organized according to the domain (.mil, .gov, .com, etc.) in which the activity is taking place, as opposed to its motivations or effects."[30]

However, typologizing attempts by adversaries to exert informational influence based on domain is a bit like organizing colors by shape. The domain is a descriptive term, and not necessarily a good predictor of effects, as most informational threats have social, political, and economic consequences in addition to first-order technical or structural repercussions. A lack of shared responsibility and coordination in responding to informational threats ignores the "transcendental properties" of digital information and its ability to inflict multiple forms of damage simultaneously and sometimes over an extended period of time.

Create Unified, Internationally Recognized Legal Frameworks and Enforcement Mechanisms

The laws and norms surrounding the movement of economic goods across geopolitical boundaries are well formed and tested. Unlike other domains, the information space is created, maintained, owned and operated collectively by public and private stakeholders across the globe, and not subject to geopolitical or natural boundaries.[31] Simultaneously, the potential harm proposed by massive scale information-based influence is obvious. The ability to generate and manipulate information at little to no cost has become ubiquitous; however, robust legal frameworks governing how state actors, individuals, and institutions interact with the information ecosystem do not yet exist.

The difficulty of assigning attribution to damages created by informational means ensures that the rule of law will be a substantial struggle to impose. This is compounded by the challenge of deriving intent and chains of causation that allow for liability to be fairly and credibly established. For example, a hacker could build malicious software based on knowledge of the present information ecosystem with the goal of achieving a certain outcome. However, the evolving nature of the information ecosystem combined with the ability of others to modify that piece of malware make predicting its effects almost impossible, even for the originating source. This is the "Office Space problem," where the effects of an activity in the information space are radically altered in scope or nature due to unanticipated design repercussions or changes to the environment. Just like an unforeseen glitch in the protagonist's plot in the movie Office Space created undesirable outcomes, so too can behaviors in the information space yield unexpected consequences.

To provide another example, research utilizing advanced statistical modeling techniques highlights the challenges of correlating virality with social media message and user traits, even in "simple" networked communities. Anticipating diffusion is difficult, as well as differentiating factors affecting virality from factors affecting influence.[32] The multidimensionality of networked communities and complexity of the network's layers—from the techno-semantic to the psychosocial—ensures that predicting behavioral effects in the information space is a bit like launching a missile without a guidance system—we understand the forces such as gravity that allow us to make general statements about the missile's trajectory, but will likely rule out low-probability events such as the missile being redirected toward a hospital after striking a bird. The difficulty of equating intent with outcome in the information realm is a problem for the Western legal framework and its Kantian epistemics. An ISIS twitter message intended to have only local or regional impact could conceivably be propagated by third parties (potentially even ISIS's enemies), making it difficult to determine what consequences for which ISIS would be legally liable.

Even if all of the conditions for prosecution and sentencing could be satisfied, the pluralism of rights frameworks across the globe renders law enforcement almost impossible. For example, while Western European rights frameworks are designed to protect consumers, U.S. law tends to create more favorable outcomes for producers. This applies to the digital space, where the law requires little in terms of transparency by companies such as Facebook that both mine and sell our personal data in order to create advertising revenues. The burden is on consumers to prove excessive harm in how their data was leveraged against them.

We have seen the difficulty American-based companies have had in retrofitting their business activities to meet legal norms in other parts of the world. The ruling on the ability of EU citizens to redact damaging personal information from the web sent huge ripples through news organizations, government regulatory bodies, and American-based technology providers alike.[33] The decision models, professional maxims, and equities of each party were in direct conflict with one another. Bits themselves are both ambivalent and infinitely replicable, and it is not until the semantic and network layers that our data is anthropically incorporated. The same sequence of information can be used by two users or information managers in fundamentally incompatible legal, political, and cultural systems. More recently, the repeal of the "Safe Harbor" agreement illustrates the difficulty in defining jurisdictions and lack of a universally recognized "public good."[34] However, the lack of a unified legal framework between the United States and EU understates the scope of the problem; other parts of the world have radically different rights structures that must be incorporated or at least acknowledged in international law surrounding the use of information.

To address the current legal construct, material damages and loss of life are explicitly and thoroughly covered by the Geneva Conventions; it is less clear what, if any, of these standards for international behavior can be generalized to the information space. Article 2(4) of the UN Charter states that "[a]ll Members [of the United Nations] shall refrain in their international relations from the threat or use of force against the territorial integrity or political independence of any state, or in any other manner inconsistent with the Purposes of the United Nations."[35] Even in the seemingly straightforward case of Edward Snowden where the information compromised on a massive scale was property of the U.S. security apparatus, we have seen much international consternation about the way forward. In addition, Russia's use of propaganda, blackmail and disinformation in the annexation of Crimea arguably constitute a crime, but have been largely unaddressed by the larger international community. The Snowden case and Russian example make it clear that interpreting "the spirit of international law" without making the laws surrounding information transactions more explicit is insufficient.

We will continue to see divergence in acceptable practices and increased harm potential until the U.S. government can help create a global imperative for a unified legal framework. Forcing state and nonstate actors to behave ethically in the information space is the by-product of instrumental and normative legitimation, and for both to occur there must be an internationally recognized legal antecedent. The difficulty in developing such a legal code cannot be understated, as it is not dissimilar from the world climate negotiations, which spanned the better part of twenty years. World climate negotiations were hindered not just by incongruous legal and market paradigms, but by radically different economies and valuations of the environment.[36] Conceivably, any attempts to establish an international informational rule of law will be problematized by the multiplicity of information economies in various stages of development across the world. The development of an international order is absolutely vital but a long-term strategic endeavor.

Creating Informational Risk Transfer Mechanisms Between the Public and Private Sector

The September 11, 2001, attacks were an illustration of how a networked, decentralized terrorist organization could inflict tremendous damage on American markets and morale. It demonstrated how an amorphous network could damage the world's largest economy at virtually no cost. The attacks on New York and Washington, DC, sent the U.S. terrorism insurance market into peril, it was a difficult to forecast low-probability, high-consequence event that lead to huge losses and an insurance pricing crisis. In order to stabilize the market, President George W. Bush signed into law the Terrorism Risk Insurance Act, which made the U.S. government the catastrophic backstop for the insurance market in the event of crisis.[37] Shared ownership in the event of catastrophe provided the government and private sector with a common language and protocol for dealing with losses due to terrorism. By providing reinsurance coverage, the government catalyzed a more sophisticated system of managing and spreading terrorism risk.

Information risk and terrorism risk are both unpredictable events that can have devastating and long-lasting consequences at little cost to perpetrators. In both cases, the infraction is likely to be nonattributable or at least nonpunishable. Like terrorism, rules in the information space are largely unenforceable, requiring a much greater focus on management and response rather than prevention and punishment. And like terrorism, "because IT dependency and concomitant insecurities have come so quickly, the United States lacks a shared understanding of acceptable and unacceptable risk and of the proper roles of the federal government and the private sector."[38] Developing ways to commodify and trade informational risk is already underway in the private sector.[39] Further, techniques for pricing informational risk will likely include allowing the "crowd of hackers" to exploit applications and systems, thereby exposing vulnerabilities.[40] System and information managers will pay a premium for having their weaknesses exposed, which then allow their risk to be traded within an insurance structure.

The commodification of information and cyber risk through an insurance structure in which the U.S. government provided a catastrophic backstop would provide the quantitative framework for governmental and nongovernmental entities to trade and diversify risk. Other countries such as China have recognized the state's role in fostering an innovation economy,[41] realizing that it cannot achieve influence in the twenty-first century without successful, mutually beneficial public-private partnerships. [42] The US government would be well-advised to follow suit, and it must be prepared to offer its own information companies something in return. Establishing risk transfer criteria could be the first step in healing the relationship between government and critical information players, particularly in Silicon Valley.

CONCLUSION

Currently, the U.S. government's approach to information remains perilous compared to its competitors, who have much more flexible, innovative, and decentralized approaches to using information to achieve influence. Both state and nonstate actors have made a strategic decision to incorporate information into their organizational strategies and have resourced them accordingly. As a result, these actors are setting the norms for behavior within the information space, and we are likely to see more, rather than less, instability as more users come online. Between 1995 and 2010, the number of internet-connected people leaped from an estimated 16 million to more than 1.7 billion.[43] Simultaneously, the digital connective tissue between individuals continues to grow. Facebook recently announced higher levels of degree centrality between users, trumping established thought about the connectedness of the world population.[44] A new set of political, economic, sociocultural, and cognitive dynamics based on digital rather than geographic proximity has been enabled, creating new vulnerabilities as well as new opportunities. If the United States wants to achieve influence, rethinking its approach to information is not optional. From a policy perspective, this could be most effectively addressed by removing barriers to understanding public data, created a dedicated cabinet-level position to manage information, prioritizing the codification of legal behavior in the information space alongside the international community, and creating public-private risk transfer mechanisms. Together, these policies will help ensure the United States has the tools necessary to promote global stability and solve the complex problems of the next information age.

CHAPTER HIGHLIGHTS

Influencing Through Information. Information must be an explicit part of a larger integrated national strategy that acknowledges not just the technical but also the political, economic, and psychosocial dimensions of the information environment.

Overcoming a Legacy Vision. The U.S. government and Department of Defense's information ecosystem evolved around industrial age principles, most notably the premise that systematically reducing vulnerabilities increases security.

Leveraging Technology. The ability to influence is now democratized, in that any individual or group has the potential to communicate and influence large numbers of others online in a way that would have been prohibitively expensive in the pre-internet era.

Adversarial Advantage. Most of our adversaries possess an enormous asymmetric advantage over us as a result of policy, legal, and organizational constraints regarding data utilization that we are subject to and they are not.

Strategic Social Media. The United States should focus on several critical areas to counter ISIS, including large-scale collection of social media, analytical tool development, understanding the radicalization process, and creating a countervailing social media message.

Forming a National Information Strategy. To create a national information strategy, the following policy changes should be implemented: (1) revise intelligence oversight and protocols to give government the same rights to analyze public data as nongovernmental organizations and adversaries; (2) establish a Cabinet-level information branch within the government to coordinate information efforts beyond the Department of Defense; (3) create an international legal framework to establish globally recognized operating norms and enforcement tools within the information space; and (4) create risk transfer mechanisms that allow for informational risk transfer with and between the public and private sector.

NOTES

1. A. Wagner, R. Waltzman, & A. Fernandez, "The War Against ISIS Through Social Media," *American Foreign Policy Council* 12 (2015), http://www.afpc.org/publication_listings/viewPolicyPaper/2907.

2. A.I. Harrington & C.A. Theohary, "Cyber Operations in DoD Policy and Plans: Issues for Congress," *Congressional Research Service* (2015), https://fas.org/sgp/crs/natsec/R43848.pdf.

3. A. Wagner, R. Waltzman, & A. Fernandez, "The War Against ISIS Through Social Media," *American Foreign Policy Council* 12 (2015), http://www.afpc.org/publication_listings/viewPolicyPaper/2907.

4. R.J. Danzig, "Surviving on a Diet of Poisoned Fruit Reducing the National Security Risks of America's Cyber Dependencies" (2014), *Center for New American Security,* http://www.cnas.org/sites/default/files/publications-pdf/CNAS_Poisoned-Fruit_Danzig_0.pdf.

5. Since May 2015, Dr. Rand Waltzman is the associate director of research of the Software Engineering Institute of Carnegie Mellon University. For five years prior to that he was a program manager at DARPA managing the SMISC program in foundations of social media and the ADAMS program in big data anomaly detection.

6. Max Fisher, "Syrian Hackers Claim AP Hack that Tipped Stock Market by $136 Billion. Is it Terrorism?" *Washington Post*, April 23, 2013, https://www.washingtonpost.com/news/worldviews/wp/2013/04/23/syrian-hackers-claim-ap-hack-that-tipped-stock-market-by-136-billion-is-it-terrorism/.

7. K. Dransfield & M. Sullivan, "The Fallacy of Information Dominance," *United States Naval Institute Blog,* September 1, 2015, http://blog.usni.org/2015/09/01/the-fallacy-of-information-dominance.

8. B. Schneider & J. Wolff, "The Threats and Tradeoffs of Big Data" (2008). *Berkman Radio.* Podcast, https://soundcloud.com/radioberkman/the-threats-and-tradeoffs-of-big-data.

9. R.J. Danzig, "Surviving on a Diet of Poisoned Fruit Reducing the National Security Risks of America's Cyber Dependencies," http://www.cnas.org/sites/default/files/publications-pdf/CNAS_PoisonedFruit_Danzig_0.pdf.

10. Ibid.

11. M. McCuaig-Johnston & M. Zhang, "China's Innovation Incubators: Platforms for Partnerships," *Asia Pacific Foundation of Canada* (2015), https://www.asiapacific.ca/sites/default/files/filefield/apfc_report_incubators-pd05.pdf.

12. Qiao Lang & Wang Xiangsui, *Unrestricted Warfare* (Beijing: PLA Literature and Arts Publishing House, 1999), http://www.cryptome.org/cuw.htm.

13. P. Dombrowski & C.C. Demchak, "Cyber war, cybered conflict, and the maritime domain," *Naval War College Review* 67, no. 2, (2014), 71+, http://go.galegroup.com/ps/i.do?id=GALE%7CA366344681&v=2.1&u=palo_alto&it=r&p=AONE&sw=w&asid=a4e0397390262cc268f31b85c9d12b0e.

14. Ven. K. Bruusgaard, "Crimea and Russia's strategic overhaul," *Parameters* 44, no. 3 (2014), 81, http://go.galegroup.com/ps/i.do?id=GALE%7CA397579205&v=2.1&u=palo_alto&it=r&p=AONE&sw=w&asid=9d3c8e323263deb626b6d789f8f1710d.

15. Ibid.

16. A. Wagner, R. Waltzman, & A. Fernandez, "The War Against ISIS Through Social Media," *American Foreign Policy Council* 12 (2015), http://www.afpc.org/publication_listings/viewPolicyPaper/2907.

17. Abraham Wagner is currently a lecturer in law at Columbia Law School and senior fellow at the Center for Advanced Studies on Terrorism (CAST). Previously he served in several positions in the U.S. government for over thirty years in the national security and intelligence areas.

18. State Department Memo from Undersecretary Stengel (June 9, 2015) to Secretary Kerry.

19. A. Wagner, R. Waltzman, & A. Fernandez, "The War Against ISIS Through Social Media," *American Foreign Policy Council* 12 (2015), http://www.afpc.org/publication_listings/viewPolicyPaper/2907.

20. N. Melzer, "Cyberwarfare and International Law," *UNIDIR Resources*, 2011, http://unidir.org/files/publications/pdfs/cyberwarfare-and-international-law-382.pdf.

21. A. Wagner, R. Waltzman, & A. Fernandez, "The War Against ISIS Through Social Media," *American Foreign Policy Council* 12 (2015), http://www.afpc.org/publication_listings/viewPolicyPaper/2907.

22. Ibid.

23. S. Gunelius, "The Data Explosion in 2014 Minute by Minute—Infographic," *ACI Information Group*, 2014, http://aci.info/2014/07/12/the-data-explosion-in-2014-minute-by-minute-infographic/; H. Abelson, K. Ledeen, & H. Lewis, "Blown to Bits: Your Life, Liberty, and Happiness After the Digital Explosion," *Nieman Journalism Lab*, 2008, http://www.niemanlab.org/pdfs/blowntobits.pdf.

24. N.S. Kim & D.A.J. Telman, "Internet giants as quasi-governmental actors and the limits of contractual consent," *Missouri Law Review* 80, no. 3 (2015), 723+, http://go.galegroup.com/ps/i.do?id=GALE%7CA436797291&v=2.1&u=palo_alto&it=r&p=AONE&sw=w&asid=25b56c50fcc8f5c99e5e209b12ab4f65.

25. Ibid.

26. H. Abelson, K. Ledeen, & H. Lewis, "Blown to Bits: Your Life, Liberty, and Happiness After the Digital Explosion," *Nieman Journalism Lab*, 2008 http://www.niemanlab.org/pdfs/blowntobits.pdf.

27. E. Nakashima, "Hacks of OPM databases compromised 22.1 million people, federal authorities say," *The Washington Post*, July 9, 2015, https://www.washingtonpost.com/news/federal-eye/wp/2015/07/09/hack-of-security-clearance-system-affected-21-5-million-people-federal-authorities-say/.

28. A. Wagner, R. Waltzman, & A. Fernandez, "The War Against ISIS Through Social Media," *American Foreign Policy Council* 12 (2015), http://www.afpc.org/publication_listings/viewPolicyPaper/2907.

29. G. Freeman & R. Schroeder, "Social Media Exploitation: An Assessment," *Naval Postgraduate School,* Monterey, CA, U.S. (2014).

30. A.I. Harrington & C.A. Theohary, "Cyber Operations in DoD Policy and Plans: Issues for Congress," *Congressional Research Service,* 2015, https://fas.org/sgp/crs/natsec/R43848.pdf.

31. N. Melzer, "Cyberwarfare and International Law," *UNIDIR Resources,* 2011, http://unidir.org/files/publications/pdfs/cyberwarfare-and-international-law-382.pdf.

32. T.A. Hoang & E.P. Lim, "Virality and Susceptibility in Information Diffusions," in *ICWSM,* 2012, http://www.aaai.org/ocs/index.php/ICWSM/ICWSM12/paper/view/4584/4977.

33. Arthur Charles, "Explaining the 'right to be forgotten'—the newest cultural shibboleth," *The Guardian,* May 14, 2014, http://www.theguardian.com/technology/2014/may/14/explainer-right-to-be-forgotten-the-newest-cultural-shibboleth.

34. N. Drozdiak & S. Schechnerr, "EU Court Says Data-Transfer Pact With U.S. Violates Privacy: Decision will affect about 4,500 companies that move, store personal data," *The Wall Street Journal,* 2015, http://www.wsj.com/articles/eu-court-strikes-down-trans-atlantic-safe-harbor-data-transfer-pact-144412136.

35. N. Melzer, "Cyberwarfare and International Law," *UNIDIR Resources,* 2011, http://unidir.org/files/publications/pdfs/cyberwarfare-and-international-law-382.pdf.

36. C. Figueres, "Trends and challenges of climate change negotiations: Interview with Christiana Figueres, the United Nations climate chief (Executive Secretary of the UNFCCC)," *Pricewaterhouse Coopers, LLP,* 2011, http://christianafigueres.com/publications/pwc%20climatechange-cfigueres.pdf.

37. Terrorism Risk and Insurance (2015), *Insurance Information Institute,* http://www.iii.org/issue-update/terrorism-risk-and-insurance.

38. R.J. Danzig, "Surviving on a Diet of Poisoned Fruit Reducing the National Security Risks of America's Cyber Dependencies," http://www.cnas.org/sites/default/files/publications-pdf/CNAS_PoisonedFruit_Danzig_0.pdf.

39. Cybersecurity, *Center for Insurance Policy and Research,* 2015, http://www.naic.org/cipr_topics/topic_cyber_risk.htm.

40. It Takes a Crowd to Beat a Crowd (2015), *Bug Crowd,* https://bugcrowd.com/what-we-do.

41. M. McCuaig-Johnston & M. Zhang, "China's Innovation Incubators: Platforms for Partnerships," *Asia Pacific Foundation of Canada,* 2015, https://www.asiapacific.ca/sites/default/files/filefield/apfc_report_incubators-pd05.pdf.

42. Ibid.

43. N. Melzer, "Cyberwarfare and International Law," *UNIDIR Resources,* 2011, http://unidir.org/files/publications/pdfs/cyberwarfare-and-international-law-382.pdf.

44. Jonah Bromwich, "Six Degrees of Separation? Facebook Finds a Smaller Number," *New York Times,* February 4, 2016, http://www.nytimes.com/2016/02/05/technology/six-degrees-of-separation-facebook-finds-a-smaller-number.html?_r=0.

Concluding Remarks

Trey Herr and Richard M. Harrison

Cybersecurity policy presents an array of both human and technical challenges. The goal of this book has been to present a broad selection of those issues which are, or will soon be, part of the national conversation. We advance no partisan agenda, nor do we advocate for a particular ideological stance in our approach to these topics. Each chapter contained here is limited in its recommendations solely to the subject matter that it covers. Nevertheless, there are common themes stretching across these pages—themes which provide an abstract roadmap of sorts that can help guide public policy among the issue areas of cybersecurity.

These are Public/Private Problems

The federal government has a burgeoning and legitimate interest in the status of information assurance standards and internet security governance, among other policy issues relating to cyberspace. But the majority of connected devices and the preponderance of internet infrastructure rests in private hands. That the principal environment for contemporary military cyber operations in many cases is privately held networks and spectrum represents a similar hurdle. It is equally true, however, that much of the private sector is not able or willing to take on these security challenges, either because of costs or legal restrictions.

A balance needs to be struck between public and private interests, between various actors and stakeholders, and among the many solutions that these actors present to pressing cybersecurity policy challenges. While that balance may well shift, depending on government activity and the role of the private sector in a particular scenario, there must be a shared responsibility between legislators, regulators, justices, and bureaucrats on the one hand, and business leaders, shop owners, and individuals on the other.

Beware Holding a Hammer and Seeing Only Nails

We have a tendency to militarize language in our discussions of cybersecurity. Incidents become attacks, tools become weapons, criminals become attackers, and so forth. One problem with this approach is that it can raise the importance of largely pedestrian events to the level of national security crises, skewing the distribution of resources and attention. The breaches at Target and Home Depot were undertaken by small groups with the intent to steal information and generate financial gain. These sorts of incidents tend to be the norm, rather than the exception. Stuxnet, for all of its innovation and geopolitical impact, was part of a minute minority of the infections, compromises, and security incidents that are reported daily. These incidents, and hundreds of similar ones that occur every year, involve nonstate actors stealing information from or disrupting the business activities of private actors across the country and around the world. These groups and their tools are pursued by law enforcement agencies and, when possible, prosecuted.

By contrast, actions, whether by state or nonstate actors, that attempt to destroy digital information or physical hardware fall into the realm of military cyber operations and can be treated as a national security issue. Breaking things with code is difficult, and requires a great deal of substantive expertise about the target. Writing software to steal keystrokes or credit card information is comparatively easy, which is why it happens far more frequently.

These distinctions are important. How we understand and talk about the world shapes our potential responses to it. There are issues of national security and challenges for law enforcement at play under the broad umbrella of cybersecurity. Accurately describing the adversaries, problems, and practical solutions within each of these disparate camps, and resisting the temptations of alarmism in favor of nuance should be the core underpinnings of our ongoing dialogue.

Education and Transparency

The marketplace is a highly imperfect but tremendously powerful tool for driving the behavior of firms and organizations. A common theme among many of the chapters in this book is the importance of opening up marketplaces, for products or ideas, and allowing their power to shape new strategies and more secure behavior.

Critical to enabling this market power is education and transparency, which are necessary to make consumers in these markets into well-informed decision-makers in their own right. Such education can happen in myriad ways, from labels describing the cyber safety design practices of automakers that allow individuals to compare high- and low-performing companies to breach notifications (which assist consumers in pressuring underperforming firms and create incentives to encourage improvements). Making consumers aware of good security practices and, within each of these markets, creating channels of transparency to ensure that performance information is clearly communicated, is key to success.

Managing the Vulnerability Economy

Across all sectors, irrespective of the domain or industry, connected computing devices are susceptible to exploitation because of flaws and inherent vulnerabilities. The software in our cellphones, cars, and thermostats are all susceptible to compromise, owing to some combination of design error, adversary innovation, and human fallibility. As several of the chapters outline, managing the "vulnerability economy" is an increasingly pervasive challenge—one addressed today in various ways, from the government acquisition and use of zero-days to attempts to curtail the market for malicious software.

The participants in this economy can be either friendly or malicious. Google, the National Security Agency (NSA), and eastern European criminal groups all have interests of one sort of another, and no single proposal will "solve" the vulnerability problem. Our challenge is not to fix vulnerabilities, but to manage how they impact our security against attackers of all types. There are key trade-offs in this management problem; how should we reward researchers who find and disclose bugs to vendors rather than keeping them secret for greater profit? And how should we preserve the capability of national intelligence programs while improving security for citizens and individuals? The stakes, moreover, are set to grow bigger still. Cars are now computers, automakers are software vendors, and, in coming years, if a device can be made to talk over a network, it will undoubtedly do so. The task facing policymakers, then, is to expand corporate policies and government regulations to properly account for and accommodate a growing ecosystem of vulnerabilities and threats.

Long-Term Reform: Embrace Innovation

That the internet has embedded itself into society, into our commerce and our politics, into the devices we depend on. With this increased connectivity comes a need to encourage innovation. Novel ideas about the devices we own, as well as the means by which to secure them, are essential to both economic growth and security. The rationale for increased interconnectedness, despite heightened vulnerability, is productivity and efficiency. Cars with internet connected, "always-on" infotainment system are a convenience and a luxury. They are also increasingly ubiquitous. The fact that they are susceptible to compromise shouldn't be a call to ban them, but an impetus to secure them. The policy recommendations of these chapters generally encourage new ways to foster security innovation, rather than cripple usability or economic activity.

That is a view supported by history. The story of security in computing and connected devices is one of continual innovation; as defenders improve their techniques and technology, adversaries respond. The goal should be to enhance this cycle in favor of the defense, encouraging new companies and new ideas to come to market, discouraging onerous and static regulatory requirements, and creating a permissive structure for testing and mitigation. To manage the problems of today and tomorrow, it will take a significant research effort, as well as communication and collaboration across an array of disciplines. Academia will play an invaluable role in providing research opportunities, developing new skill sets, and training professionals for the labor market. The private sector will play a significant part as well, encouraging new techniques and innovative methods to address evolving threats. These dynamics, together with better-informed consumers and a more effective workforce, will be crucial for managing and upgrading systems in both the private and public sectors.

Considerations

The issues addressed in this book set the stage for a discussion of how the myriad issues under the umbrella of cybersecurity policy can and should be addressed. Public policy is not a standalone solution for the issues listed here, but it is an essential part of the puzzle nonetheless. This book offers a framework for considering broad reforms across information assurance and cyber safety, cyber crime, internet security governance, and military cyber operations. It prompts us to think about and address key policy challenges as part of an ecosystem of ideas. The issues addressed in these pages will greatly affect the way citizens communicate, as well as the ability of the United States to conduct espionage, trade, and defend critical infrastructure.

How we treat the cybersecurity challenges of today will shape how we experience the future. Perfect security is impossible, but better security is not only feasible; it could be soon within our grasp. Our task is to continue to foster innovation and acknowledge the limitations of both public and private approaches in isolation. For the policymaking community, the watchword must be to "do no harm." Far too often in the past several decades has public policy imposed new limitations and challenges to security research and innovation. If we simply accept cyber insecurity and labor under the misconception that the natural state of connectivity is vulnerability and exposure, we will reduce the quality of our human experience.

Better policy is needed. But in order to enhance their approaches, policymakers must gain a better understanding of the issues dominating the cyber landscape today: the need to adequately protect data, devices, and networks; the necessity of combatting cyber criminals; proper procedures for governing the security of the internet; and better comprehension of military cyber operations and their role in and national security.

The path forward will not be easy. As we embark on the next information age, this work is not intended to be a solution to the incredibly complex challenge that an ever-interconnected society poses. But it is our attempt to help mitigate some of the threats endemic to this new domain, so that we can better manage our cyber *insecurity*.

Glossary

AECA: The Arms Export Control Act, passed in 1976 established the International Traffic in Arms Regulations (ITAR) and the United States Munitions List (USML) administered by the Department of State.

As-a-Service: Software platform or service delivered over the internet rather than hosted locally on a user's machine.

Availability: Ensuring that authorized parties are able to access information on a computer system when needed.

Black Hat: Malicious actors working with the intent of gaining unauthorized access into and manipulating computer systems and networks.

Border Gateway Protocol (BGP): BGP is the typical means of communicating information about how to navigate in and between so many different networks over the internet; BGP acts as a sort of travel guide to different networks using a distributed database of IP locations, essentially maps of the internet and subsidiary networks.

Botmaster: An individual responsible for the care and feeding of the flock of zombie machines, which make up a botnet.

Botnet: A collection of internet-connected computers under the control or manipulated by a third party, generally used to distribute malware or spam e-mail; can serve as a propagation method.

Breach Notification: Formal notice from a company or other entity to a consumer of the loss of confidentiality of their personal information.

Budapest Convention: This convention on cyber crime is the first international agreement to address internet and computer crime by bringing domestic laws closer into coordination, providing enhanced investigative authorities for international efforts, and building foundation for policy coordination and cooperation between states.

Bug Bounty Program: See VRP.

Certificate Authority (CA): One actor that acts as a key in a chain of trust that includes browsers, operating systems or servers, end users, and observers.

Certificate Revocation Lists (CRL): The public audit trails that CAs periodically publish, and organizations consult, to track invalid certificates.

Confidentiality: The property that information is not made available or disclosed to unauthorized individuals, entities, or processes.

Coordinating Committee for Multilateral Export Controls (CoCom): The export of encryption technology to the Soviet bloc or general public was strictly controlled by this committee.

Combat Mission Team (CMT): CMTs cover offensive cyber operations to include providing, "cyber support to military operational and contingency plans" that may be included in broader military campaigns.

Commercial Off the Shelf (COTS): Soft- or hardware systems purchased directly from a commercial vendor; often used in a military or government procurement context to differentiate from customized solutions or products requiring further research and development.

Communications Assistance for Law Enforcement Act (CALEA): Pub. L. No. 103-414, 108 Stat. 4279, codified at 47 USC 1001-1010); a U.S. wiretapping law passed in 1994 that requires firms who manufacture or purchase telecommunications equipment to establish either a hardware or software backdoor in their devices that allows for law enforcement to conduct surveillance into communications.

Computer Fraud and Abuse Act (CFAA): In 1984, the U.S. Congress enacted the CFAA, defining a set of federal crimes directed at computer hacking and other forms of unauthorized access on computers and computer networks; amended nine times since then, today the CFAA is an essential tool used by law enforcement for the investigation, prosecution, and deterrence of computer crime.

Content Delivery Network (CDN): Collections of servers distributed across the world to store large quantities of content close to areas of high demand.

Critical Infrastructure: One of sixteen sectors in the United States whose assets, systems, and networks, whether physical or virtual, are considered so vital to the United States that their incapacitation or destruction would have a debilitating effect on security, national economic security, national public health or safety, or any combination thereof; defined in PPD-21: Critical Infrastructure Security and Resilience.

Critical Infrastructure Protection (CIP): Covers security standard setting and security control design efforts focused on high-risk commercial facilities or government assets with substantial national security value.

CYBERCOM (U.S. Cyber Command): Organization with operational control of military cyber forces for offensive and defensive cyber operations in defense of U.S. national security interests.

Cyber Crime: Covers both law enforcement and government activity to target adversary groups and criminals as well as regulatory and legislative efforts to incentivize better security practices and reporting by victims; does not address physically destructive incidents.

Cyber Insurance: The provision of insurance coverage for a range of information assurance failures and adversarial events like data breaches; shifts financial liability for the event from a customer to an insurance firm.

Cyber Operational Preparation Environment (Cyber OPE): An offensive cyber operation that focuses on gaining access to, and information about, a target system.

Cyber Protection Team (CPT): CPTs perform a broad range of defensive measures, including penetration testing and hunting attackers within U.S. military networks.

Cyberspace: The DoD defines "cyberspace" as "a global domain consisting of the interdependent networks of information technology infrastructures and resident data, including the internet, telecommunications networks, computer systems, and embedded processors and controllers."

CVSS (Common Vulnerability Scoring System): Used to "code" vulnerabilities according to their severity and potential for exploitation by a third party.

Data Breach: A security incident where personally identifying or otherwise sensitive information is made available to unauthorized third parties, copied, or stolen.

Deep Packet Inspection: Malicious software designed to extract or modify data and system processes.

Defensive Cyber Operations (DCO): DCO are intended to defend Department of Defense (DoD) or other friendly cyberspace; they are passive and active cyberspace defense operations to preserve the ability to utilize friendly cyberspace capabilities and protect data, networks, net-centric capabilities, and other designated systems.

Department of Defense Information Network (DoDIN): The DoDIN handles routine information assurance. It acts to translate the URL in a browser bar into an IP address.

Digital Encryption Standard (DES): A federal standard encryption algorithm based on the symmetric Lucifer cipher.

Distributed Denial of Service (DDoS): An overwhelming amount of digital traffic pointed at a single device; intended to disrupt or disable a connected device and knock it offline, a DDoS can take place over a number of network protocols including IP.

Domain Name System (DNS): The DNS serves as the internet's address book, translating plain language URLs (www.google.com) into internet protocol (IP) addresses (74.125.151.254).

Domain Name Service Security Extensions (DNSSEC): This process authenticates individual DNS server records first by a central server called the DNS root zone, and then through a chain of trust to pass an authenticated record from the root to child zones and on down to the recipient; DNSSEC can provide authentication of the origin of DNS data and assurance that the content of the DNS transaction has not been manipulated in transit.

Domain Name System Authentication for Named Entities (DANE): A new internet protocol that would perform authentication and fix some of the flaws with CAs; with DANE, the owner of a domain name could securely bind part of a TLS certificate to a DNS name using the DNSSEC to sign the record and prevent forgery, all without consulting a CA.

Dropper: A malicious payload intended to infect a target machine and then retrieve additional malware from a command-and-control server elsewhere on the internet.

Encryption: Encryption is a process used to establish trust and secure data across networks of every stripe and purpose.

End User License Agreement (EULA): A legal agreement between a software vendor and customer, establishing the latter's rights for use of the product.

Executive Order 13636: Many federal agencies were tasked with helping to improve the information assurance posture of the nation's critical infrastructure.

Executive Order 13691: Promotes public-private cooperation on cybersecurity information sharing by calling on the DHS to encourage the establishment of so-called Information Sharing and Analysis Organizations (ISAO).

Exploit: A piece of code, which takes advantage of a flaw or feature in software (a vulnerability) to support the operation of a malicious payload or propagation method.

Exploit kit: Combination of a propagation method, often a compromised web server, and a set of exploits rented as a package or service to distribute malicious payloads.

The Federal Information Security Management Act (FISMA): Passed in 2002, the act establishes a system of basic security controls and impact assessment measures for federal information systems.

Hacking Back: Also known as Active Defense; when an information insurance professional charged with defending a corporate or government agency pursues an unauthorized intruder back to a source computer, perhaps deploying offensive hacking tools and techniques to retrieve stolen data or disable the attack.

Honey Nets: Using systems that appear genuine, this strategy is based upon trying to hide real network traffic and computers among fake versions.

Internet Corporation for Assigned Names and Numbers (ICANN): An international organization responsible for technical maintenance of the Domain Name System's core servers as well as administration of generic top level domains (GTLD).

Industrial Control Systems (ICS): Systems that control physical devices; this can include critical infrastructure like hydroelectric dams, power grids, manufacturing facilities, oil and gas pipelines, oil drilling rigs and more.

Information Assurance: Protection of an information system's confidentiality, integrity, and availability.

Information Environment: Defined by the Department of Defense as "the aggregate of individuals, organizations, and systems that collect, process, disseminate, or act on information."

Information Operations (IO): IO focus on attacking an adversary's human or automated decision-making, as well as on bolstering that of friendly forces; these focus on diverse areas such as military deception, operations security, public affairs, and often include elements of cyber operations but can be broader, encompassing messaging and persuasive efforts governed by separate doctrine and employing a different set of personnel.

Information Sharing and Analysis Center (ISAC): Nonprofit or government entities which aggregate information about threat actors and security incidents that is then shared with participating members.

Information Sharing and Analysis Organization (ISAO): ISAOs are intended to serve as venues for collaboration on threat intelligence and incident response established by a mutually engaged group of willing members; ISAOs are organized along a common affinity or community of interests based on individuals, industry, geography, or even a particular event.

Integrity: The property of an information system which refers to protecting information from being modified by unauthorized parties.

International Traffic in Arms Regulations (ITAR): The International Traffic in Arms Regulations, established by the Arms Export Control Act (AECA), controls the United States Munitions List and implements relevant regulations in the control for sale or disclosure of sensitive military items.

Internet Exchange Point (IXP): These are the physical infrastructure that carry content from Internet Service Providers (ISPs) and Content Delivery Networks (CDNs) and determine where that content is routed between networks. IXPs are variously joined by radio, copper cable, and fiber-optic links.

Internet Engineering Task Force (IETF): The IETF is a nonprofit group composed of hundreds of technical experts and computer scientists which acts to debate and set standards for internet routing, content delivery, design, and more.

Internet Security Governance: All forms of international collaboration over security issues, including how to maintain a secure and functional internet and cross-national challenges like export controls for malicious software and arrest of foreign nationals.

Internet Service Provider (ISP): An ISP is a company that provides internet service, be that to individual homes or whole continents; chains of ISPs form the routing layer for data to move across the web.

Keylogger: A malicious payload designed to record all inputs from a keyboard as users type passwords and other potentially sensitive information.

Malware: Malicious software, the combination of a propagation method, exploits, and a payload.

Malware Market: A series of online forums and social networks where actors buy, trade, and sell malicious software components and services; includes both offensive and defensive markets.

Military Cyber Operations (MCO): The organizations, policy, and law related to deploying destructive digital or physical effects on target computer systems or defending against such. Covers both defensive and offensive cyber effects operations.

Military Information Support Operations: Actions taken to convince enemy, neutral, and friendly nations and forces to take actions favorable to the United States and its allies.

Mutual Legal Assistance Treaty: MLATs are a mechanism for countries to share information related to ongoing investigations in circumstances where foreign assistance is necessary for a domestic prosecution; they provide a legal basis for international law enforcement activity like extradition and the seizure of assets.

N-Day: A vulnerability or exploit, which has been publicly or partially disclosed sufficient to initiate the patching process; N refers to the number of days since the vulnerability was disclosed.

National Cybersecurity and Communications Integration Cell (NCCIC): The NCCIC acts as the primary interface for sharing information with the federal government.

National Institute of Standards and Technology (NIST): The National Institute of Standards, housed within the Department of Commerce, is responsible for developing standards for technology and measurement including security controls and risk assessment programs for federal information systems; successor to the National Bureau of Standards (NBS).

National Mission Teams (NMT): NMTs are tasked with "defending the nation's critical infrastructure and key resources," including identifying enemy forces, tracking them, and disrupting their activities against U.S. targets.

National Strategy for Trusted Identities (NSTIC): The NSTIC began through a public-private partnership focused on developing interoperable standards for identity and is a related trust-focused issue that has implications for the internet; NSTIC outcomes include defining core principles for an Identity Ecosystem, issuing grants for companies working on innovative, pilot identity solutions, and building a foundation framework for companies to adopt and self-certify through displaying a trust icon.

National Telecommunications and Information Administration (NTIA): NTIA is an executive branch agency under the Department of Commerce. It is responsible for advising the president on telecommunications and information policy issues.

Offensive Cyber Operations (OCO): OCO cyberspace operations intended to project power by the application of force in or through cyberspace.

Online Certificate Status Protocol: OCSP is an alternative or complement to Certificate Revocation Lists, allowing a client to consult an OCSP server to determine in real time whether a specific certificate is valid; OCSP needs less bandwidth in order to report on certificate status that certificate revocation lists (CRL) and is a more efficient way of checking certificate status though some OCSP servers also rely on CRL lists

Packet: A specifically formatted unit of data that is carried over a series of networks.

Patch: A software "fix" or workaround developed by (or in some cases supplied by security researchers to) a vendor to correct a software vulnerability; often required for full payout when submitting vulnerabilities at bug bounty competitions.

Patching: The process of developing and issuing a workaround or fix for a vulnerability.

Payload: The component of malware with purpose, designed to achieve some discrete outcome like log keystrokes or create a backdoor; specific types may involve more complex functions like ransomware which will encrypt some or all of a user's files and demand a financial ransom in exchange for the key.

Penetration Testing: Adversarial security testing; conducting mock attacks and evaluations on organization's security systems in order to identify and remediate weak points and vulnerabilities in software, hardware, or human processes.

Presidential Policy Directive 21 (PPD-21): PPD-21 identifies sixteen critical infrastructure sectors including chemical manufacturing, the financial services industry, and electricity generation. Each of these has been highlighted as "essential services that underpin American society."

Propagation Method: A software tool intended to transport malware from one place to another; can range from physical media like USB keys to the purely digital forms like e-mail.

Public-Key Infrastructure (PKI): Public-Key Infrastructure covers the hardware, software, people, and policies necessary to manage a public-key cryptosystem including key management and revocation.

Pwn2Own: A competition held in Canada where researchers were given set amounts of time to find vulnerabilities in major commercial software and prove their effectiveness with a rudimentary exploit.

Reverse Engineering (RE): Analyzing a code sample in order to reconstruct the software's full functionality and logical structure.

Risk Management Framework (RMF): The Risk Management Framework is a collection of standard controls and risk assessment practices along with the associated implementation and management guidelines for information security in Department of Defense (DoD) and Intelligence Community organizations produced by NIST and the DoD.

Secure Sockets Layer (SSL): Secure Sockets Layer/Transport Layer Security are application layer protocols to create cryptographically secure links between computers over the web.

Supervisory Control and Data Acquisition (SCADA): A type of industrial control system (ICS); according to the Department of Homeland Security "SCADA systems are highly distributed systems used to control geographically dispersed assets, often scattered over thousands of square kilometers, where centralized data acquisition and control are critical to system operation. They are used in distribution systems such as water distribution and wastewater collection systems, oil and gas pipelines, electrical power grids, and railway transportation systems."

Transport Layer Security (TLS): TLS is an evolution of Secure Sockets Layer and works to secure data in motion between a webserver and a device, creating an encrypted tunnel between the two.

Transmission Control Protocol/Internet Protocol (TCP/IP): The TCP/IP is the backbone of the internet; it defines the standard construction and transmission of packets over the internet.

United States Computer Emergency Readiness Team (US-CERT): US-CERT provides cybersecurity to federal civilian executive branch issues and develops cybersecurity information for other branches and agencies.

USML: The United States Munition List, administered by the State Department, governs the items designated as military articles and restricted under the International Traffic in Arms Regulations (ITAR).

Vendor: A company that makes or sells software or software libraries included in other products; can include nonprofit organizations tasked with maintaining open source libraries like OpenSSL.

Vulnerability: A feature or flaw in a piece of software, which allows for unintended operations to be performed by a third party.

Vulnerability Disclosure: Communicating information about a vulnerability to a software vendor or some other party either privately or in public ("full disclosure").

Vulnerability Contributor Program (VCP): The VCP purchases vulnerability and exploit information with the intent of disclosing it to vendors after a delay, sometimes substantial, in which subscribers have exclusive access.

Vulnerability Purchase Program (VPP): A vulnerability purchase program is any form of organized purchase of vulnerability information and exploit techniques as through competitions or bug bounties.

Vulnerability Rewards Program (VRP): Firms such as Google and Amazon have designed these programs to encourage researchers to disclose vulnerabilities directly in return for prestige and a cash reward.

Wassenaar Arrangement: A multilateral voluntary export harmonization regime created in 1996 for member states to coordinate their respective domestic export policies.

White Hat: Security researchers wearing the "white hat" and working to defend users and improve information security.

Zero-Day: A vulnerability or exploit that has not been publicly or partially disclosed and so remains unknown to the vendor.

Index

235–36; national conflicting with personal, 278; policy challenges with, xv, 347–51; public and private interests in, 347–48; sliding scale of, 33–40, 42, 44n12; technical knowledge for policy in, 326n17; terminology of, xv; trust and, xiii; zero-day vulnerabilities disclosure for, 278.

See also sliding scale, of cybersecurity

Cybersecurity Act of 2015, 20–22, 25

Cybersecurity Framework, of NIST, 36, 116, 137–38, 235–36

Cybersecurity Information Sharing Act (CISA), 16n27, 20

cybersecurity insurance. *See* cyber insurance

cybersecurity policy. *See* policy

cyberspace, 355; components of, xvi; DoD definition of, 330; International Strategy for Cyberspace, 228.

See also defensive cyberspace operations; Internet; Military Cyber Operations; offensive cyberspace operations

Cyber Underwriters Lab (UL), 116

cyber war, MCO compared to, 261

DANE. *See* DNS Authentication for Named Entities

Daniel, Michael, 283–84, 326n17

Darkode, 114

DARPA. *See* Defense Advanced Research Project Agency

data at rest, 176

data breaches, 355; consumer action after, 138–39; cost of, 138; definition of, 137; disclosure laws for, 95–96, *96*; harm from, 147; Home Depot network breach, xviii, 348; incentives to invest in security for, 137–38, 144, 152n29; individual harms

stemming from, 89; Office of Personnel Management data breach of 2015, xiv, 147–48; reputation damage from, 140; stages of, 138, *139*; Target network breach, xvii, xviii, 3, 138, 348.

See also cyber crime

data breach notification laws. *See* breach notification laws

data in motion, 176

data mining, US challenges with, 336–37

Data Security and Breach Notification Act of 2015, 145

DCO. *See* defensive cyberspace operations

DDoS attacks. *See* distributed denial of service (DDoS) attacks

DEA. *See* Drug Enforcement Agency

DEC. *See* Digital Equipment Corporation

decentralization, of Internet, 226

deception, 4

Deep Packet Inspection (DPI), 194, 355

Defense Advanced Research Project Agency (DARPA), 41

defense-in-depth, 4

Defense Industrial Base Cyber Security and Information Assurance, 7

Defense-specific Information Assurance Certification and Accreditation Process (DIACAP), 7–8

defensive cyberspace operations (DCO), *262*, 355–56; definition of, 261, 300; inadequacies of, 315; OCO authority compared to, 303–4; public writing on, 313; scope of, 300–301

DeNardis, Laura, 229

Department of Commerce, 228

Department of Defense (DoD), xiii, 7–8, 282; certifications of, 11; cyberspace definition of, 330; "Hack the Pentagon" program of,

Contributors

Richard M. Harrison is the director of operations and defense technology programs at the American Foreign Policy Council (AFPC). He currently serves as the managing editor of AFPC's *Defense Dossier* e-journal and as the editor of the *Defense Technology Monitor* e-bulletin. He also directs a briefing series on Capitol Hill to educate Congressional Staff on defense technology issues affecting U.S. national security. Previously, he worked at Lockheed Martin where he functioned as a systems engineer. He completed his MA in security studies from Georgetown University's School of Foreign Service and earned a BS in aerospace engineering from Pennsylvania State University.

Trey Herr, PhD, is a fellow with the Belfer Center's Cyber Security Project at the Harvard Kennedy School. His work focuses on trends in state-developed malicious software, information security risk, and the structure of criminal markets for malware. Trey is also a nonresident fellow with New America's Cybersecurity Initiative and previously worked with the Department of Defense to develop a risk assessment methodology for information security threats. He holds a PhD and MA in political science from George Washington University and a BS in theater and political science from Northwestern University.

CONTRIBUTOR BIOGRAPHIES

Adrienne Allen is cybersecurity consultant with Slalom Consulting in San Francisco, where she focuses on risk management and cyber incident response planning in critical infrastructure and innovation-space technology organizations. Formerly a lead associate with Booz Allen Hamilton in Washington, DC, she worked closely with the Department of Homeland Security (DHS) and graduated from the University of Virginia and Johns Hopkins University, where she concentrated on internet governance and security policy.

Dr. Aaron Brantly is an assistant professor in the Department of Social Sciences, the Army Cyber Institute, and the Combating Terrorism Center at the United States Military Academy. He has ten years of experience working in international development with a focus on information communications technologies (ICT) innovation and security and holds a PhD in political science with a focus on international relations and comparative politics from the School of Public and International Affairs at the University of Georgia.

Jane Chong is a graduate of Yale Law School. She previously researched national security issues at the Brookings Institution as a Ford Foundation Law School Fellow.

Joshua Corman is a founder of "I am The Cavalry" (iamthecavalry.org) and a director of the Cyber Statecraft Initiative for the Atlantic Council. Corman previously served as a CTO for Sonatype and as a director of security intelligence for Akamai, and played senior research and strategy roles for The 451 Group and IBM Internet Security Systems. He cofounded @RuggedSoftware and @IamTheCavalry to encourage new security approaches in response to the world's increasing dependence on digital infrastructure. Josh's unique approach to security in the context of human factors, adversary motivations, and social impact has helped position him as one of the most trusted names in security. He is also serving as an adjunct faculty for Carnegie Mellon's Heinz College and is on the 2016 HHS Cybersecurity Task Force.

Dr. Ryan Ellis is an assistant professor of communication studies at Northeastern. His research and teaching focus on topics related to communication law and policy, infrastructure politics, and cybersecurity. Prior to joining Northeastern, Ryan held fellowships at the Harvard Kennedy School's Belfer Center for Science and International Affairs and at Stanford University's Center for International Security and Cooperation (CISAC). He received a PhD in communication from the University of California, San Diego.

Kat Dransfield holds a BS in English from the U.S. Naval Academy and an MSc in social science of the internet from the University of Oxford. She is FitzGerald Scholar and previously worked as an analyst with the Department of the Navy's Office of Strategy and Innovation. She has also served as an assistant task officer for the Chief of Naval Operations Executive Panel and as an editorial team leader and contributor to the U.S. Naval Institute Blog.

Mailyn Fidler is a Fellow at the Berkman Klein Center for Internet & Society at Harvard Law School. She has an MPhil in international relations from Oxford University, where she was a Marshall Scholar, and a joint degree from Stanford University in computer science and political science. She has worked with a variety of organizations on tech policy issues. Her academic work on tech policy issues, including software vulnerabilities, has been drawn on by the European Parliament and nongovernmental organizations.

Dr. Allan Friedman is the director of cybersecurity initiatives in the Office of Policy Analysis and Development at the National Telecommunications and Information Administration (NTIA), U.S. Department of Commerce. Prior to joining the federal government, Friedman was a noted cybersecurity and technology policy researcher, with positions at George Washington University, the Brookings Institution, and Harvard University. He has a degree in computer science from Swarthmore College, and a PhD in public policy from Harvard University, and is the coauthor of *Cybersecurity and Cyberwar: What Everyone Needs to Know* (Oxford University Press, 2014).

Taylor Grossman is a technology analyst at Clark Street Associates, a consulting firm in Palo Alto that works with emerging technology companies. Previously, she was a cyber research associate at the Hoover Institution, Stanford University, where she conducted research in cyber policy and cybersecurity. She has also served on the staff of the Office of the Assistant Secretary of Defense for Public Affairs. Taylor has a BA in political science with distinction and honors in international security studies from Stanford University. Her senior thesis on homeland security warning systems won the Firestone Medal for excellence in undergraduate research.

Lauren Boas Hayes is a cyber threat intelligence professional at Deloitte & Touche LLP who lives in Oakland, California, by way of Washington, DC. She works at the nexus of the public and private sectors to develop cyber threat intelligence programs. She has worked in, and studied, the foreign policy community and seeks to shape U.S. engagement in cyberspace.

Drew Herrick is a political science PhD candidate specializing in international relations and research methods at George Washington University. He is also a non-resident national cybersecurity fellow in the International Security Program at New America. His research primarily focuses on the intersection of international security and technology, especially counter-norm activity, offensive social media operations, and the military value of cyber capabilities (drewherrick.com).

Jonah Force Hill is an internet policy specialist in the Office of International Affairs at the National Telecommunications and Information Administration (NTIA), U.S. Department of Commerce. He works on a range of Internet policy issues, including global data flows, Internet "fragmentation," and cybersecurity policy. Previously, he served at a San Francisco-based national security consultancy where he advised corporate and public-sector clients on cybersecurity policy and strategy at the U.S. Department of State, and at the Office of the Cybersecurity Coordinator at the White House. He holds an MPP from the Harvard Kennedy School of Government, an MTS from Harvard Divinity School, and a BA from the University of California, Los Angeles.

Robert M. Lee is the CEO of the critical infrastructure cybersecurity company Dragos Security LLC, a SANS Institute course author and researcher, and a PhD candidate at Kings College London. He gained his start in cybersecurity as an Air Force Cyber Warfare Operations Officer in the U.S. Intelligence Community. He may be found on Twitter @RobertMLee.

Dr. Herbert S. Lin is a senior research scholar for cyber policy and security at the Center for International Security and Cooperation and Research Fellow at the Hoover Institution, both at Stanford University. He is one of twelve commissioners selected by the White House and Congressional leadership for the President's Commission on Enhancing National Cybersecurity. He is also the chief scientist emeritus for the Computer Science and Telecommunications Board, National Research Council (NRC) of the National Academies, and an adjunct senior research scholar and senior fellow in cybersecurity (not in residence) at the Saltzman Institute for War and Peace Studies in the School for International and Public Affairs at Columbia University. Prior to his NRC service, he was a professional staff member and staff scientist for the House Armed Services Committee (1986–1990). He received his doctorate in physics from MIT.

Anastasia Mark is a China specialist at Deloitte & Touche LLP, with a focus on cybersecurity and other issues of national defense. She graduated from Dartmouth College in 2011 with a Bachelor's degree in political science and government and will graduate from Georgetown University in 2016 with a Master of Arts degree in East Asian Studies.

Robert Morgus is a policy analyst with New America's Cybersecurity Initiative where his research focuses on policy and other interventions to lessen the number and impact of cybersecurity incidents. His past research has focused on the intersection of cybersecurity and international affairs around incident response, risk management, and international norm development. Morgus has spoken about cybersecurity at a number of international forums, including NATO's CyCon, the Global Conference on Cyberspace at The Hague, and Cy Fy 2015 in New Delhi, India. His research has been published by the *New York Times*, Slate, the IEEE, peer-reviewed academic journals, and numerous other national and international media outlets.

Professor Paul Ohm is a professor of law at the Georgetown University Law Center where he specializes in information privacy, computer crime law, intellectual property, and criminal procedure and serves as a faculty director for the Center on Privacy and Technology at Georgetown. Before becoming a professor, he served as an honors program trial attorney in the U.S. Department of Justice's Computer Crime and Intellectual Property Section, during which time he advised federal law enforcement agents and prosecutors in the enforcement of the Computer Fraud and Abuse Act.

Eric Ormes is a cybersecurity specialist currently working in the private sector. He was previously employed by the U.S. government including service as a United States Air Force Communications and Information Officer.

Jason Rivera is a professionally internationally experienced intelligence, cyber operations, and investigations expert who possesses over nine years innovating at the intersection of security operations and technology. He is a manager at Deloitte & Touche LLP where he specializes in the development of cyber threat intelligence, investigations, and security operations programs for both commercial and federal clients. Prior to Deloitte, Jason served for approximately seven years in the United States Army as an intelligence officer where he attained the rank of Captain and played a variety of roles to include assignments at the National Security Agency and the United States Cyber Command, as well as having served in combat tours overseas.

Sasha Romanosky, PhD, researches topics concerning the economics of security and privacy, national security, applied microeconomics, and law and economics. He is a policy researcher at the RAND Corporation. Sasha holds a PhD in public policy and management from Carnegie Mellon University and a BS in electrical engineering from the University of Calgary, Canada. He was a Microsoft research fellow in the Information Law Institute at New York University and was a security professional for over ten years within the financial and e-commerce industries at companies such as Morgan

Stanley and eBay. Sasha is also a coauthor of the Common Vulnerability Scoring System (CVSS), an international standard for scoring computer vulnerabilities.

Paul Rosenzweig is the founder of Red Branch Consulting PLLC, a homeland security consulting company, and a senior advisor to The Chertoff Group. Mr. Rosenzweig formerly served as the deputy assistant secretary for policy in the Department of Homeland Security and is a distinguished visiting fellow at the Homeland Security Studies and Analysis Institute and a professorial lecturer in Law at George Washington University.

Matthew Russell is an experienced cyber intelligence consultant at Deloitte & Touche LLP and a veteran special operations intelligence operator and instructor, specializing in low-visibility, high-risk intelligence collection operations. He is an internationally seasoned expert who specializes in developing programmatic solutions to difficult business and cybersecurity issues. Matt effectively operates in both the federal and commercial lines of business by incorporating and optimizing intelligence collection and analytic activities across diverse client environments.

Nathaniel Tisa is a researcher at Deloitte & Touche LLP and policy advocate focused on the intersection of law, technology, and civil liberties and its implications for national security. He graduated from Georgetown University in 2014 and will enter law school as a JD candidate in Fall 2016.

Dr. Abraham Wagner is a lecturer in law at Columbia Law School and a senior fellow at the Center for Advanced Study on Terrorism. Dr. Wagner holds both PhD and JD degrees and served for over thirty years in various U.S. government posts at the National Security Council, the Intelligence Community, and Department of Defense, including the Defense Advanced Research Projects Agency (DARPA) at the time of the transition to the internet. He has also served on the Defense Science Board and the scientific advisory boards of NSA and CIA. For two years he served as the co-chair of an advisory panel for the Director of Central Intelligence focused on the evolution of cyberspace (Global Information Infrastructure) and requirements for the Intelligence Community.

Dr. Rand Waltzman joined the Software Engineering Institute of Carnegie Mellon University as an associate director of research in May 2015 after a five-year tour as a program manager in the Information Innovation Office of Defense Advanced Research Projects Agency (DARPA). At DARPA, he created and managed the Social Media in Strategic Communications program as well as the Anomaly Detection at Multiple Scales insider threat detection program. Previously, he worked at Lockheed Martin Advanced Technology Laboratories (LM-ATL), the Royal Institute of Technology in Stockholm, University of Maryland, Teknowledge Corporation, and the Applied Physics Laboratory of the University of Washington.

David Weinstein is the Chief Technology Officer (CTO) for the State of New Jersey. He previously served as the state's first cybersecurity advisor. Prior to returning to his native state of New Jersey, Dave served at the United States Cyber Command at Fort Meade, where his portfolio spanned cyber operations, policy, and planning. In 2014, Dave was recognized by Forbes as a "top cyber policy expert," and his analysis and commentary has been featured in numerous media and academic publications. Dave is a cybersecurity fellow with New America and an "Influencer" with the Christian Science Monitor's Security and Privacy project. In 2016, the New Jersey Tech Council awarded Dave the Non-Profit CISO of the Year. Dave holds degrees from Johns Hopkins University Georgetown University's School of Foreign Service.

Heather West leads public policy for the Americas at Mozilla, the maker of the Firefox browser. She is part policy-to-tech translator, part product consultant, and part long-term Internet strategist. She was recognized as one of the 2014 Forbes 30 Under 30 in law and policy and is a Christian Science Monitor Passcode Influencer. She helped found the public policy team at CloudFlare, a website performance and security company, served as a global and federal privacy and security issue expert on Google's public policy team, and started her career working on privacy and identity management at the public interest group Center for Democracy and Technology. She holds a dual B.A. in computer science and cognitive science from Wellesley College and is a certified information privacy professional (CIPP/US).

Beau Woods is the deputy director of the Cyber Statecraft Initiative in the Brent Scowcroft on International Security and an active participant in the "I Am The Cavalry" initiative. These activities focus on ensuring the connected technology that can impact life and safety worthy of our trust. Prior to that, Beau spent over a decade in information security, providing strategy, guidance, and advisory. Over the past several years, he has consulted with the private sector, NGOs, U.S. agencies, and legislative staff, and the White House. Beau graduated from the Georgia Institute of Technology with a BS in psychology.